ENGLISH

COMMUNICATION SKILLS IN THE NEW MILLENNIUM

GRADE 6

LANGUAGE HANDBOOK

J.A. Senn
Carol Ann Skinner

PERFECTION LEARNING® CORPORATION

CRITICAL READERS

Lisa Adkins
Pflugerville ISD,
Pflugerville, Texas

Jan Graham
Cobb Middle School,
Tallahassee, Florida

Lisa Joyner
McDougal Middle
School
Chapel Hill, North
Carolina

Eddie Martinez
Bailey Middle School,
Austin, Texas

Jeri Putnam
Pflugerville Middle
School, Pflugerville,
Texas

PROJECT MANAGER
Sandra Stucker Blevins

EDITORIAL DIRECTOR
Sandra Mangurian

EDITORIAL STAFF
Marianne Murphy
Marlene Greil
Donna Laughlin
Susan Sandoval
Vicki Tyler
Catherine Foy
Michelle Quijano
Elizabeth Wenning
Cheryl Duksta
Margaret Rickard

PRODUCTION DIRECTORS
Gene Allen, Pun Nio

PHOTO RESEARCH AND
PERMISSIONS
Laurie O'Meara

ART AND DESIGN
Pun Nio
Leslie Kell
Rhonda Warwick

PRODUCTION
Bethany Powell
Isabel Garza
Rhonda Warwick

COVER
Leslie Kell Designs
Pun Nio
Images © Photodiscs, Inc.

EDITORIAL AND PRODUCTION
SERVICES
Book Builders, Inc.
Gryphon Graphics
Inkwell Publishing
  Solutions, Inc.
NETS

Printed in the United States of America.

For information, contact Perfection Learning®
1000 North Second Avenue, P.O. Box 500
Logan, Iowa 51546-0500.
Phone: 1-800-831-4190 • Fax: 1-800-543-2745
perfectionlearning.com

ISBN-13: 978-1-58079-396-4   3 4 5 6 7 8 RRD 18 17 16 15 14
ISBN-10: 1-58079-396-7

SENIOR CONSULTANTS

Tommy Boley, Ph.D.
Director of English Education
The University of Texas at El Paso
El Paso, Texas

Deborah Cooper, M.Ed.
Coordinating Director of PK-12
    Curriculum
Charlotte-Mecklenburg Public Schools
Charlotte, North Carolina

Susan Marie Harrington, Ph.D.
Associate Professor of English,
    Director of Writing, Director of
    Placement and Assessment, and
    Adjunct Assistant Professor
    of Women's Studies
Indiana University-Purdue University,
    Indianapolis
Indianapolis, Indiana

Carol Pope, Ed.D.
Associate Professor of Curriculum
    and Instruction
North Carolina State University
Raleigh, North Carolina

Rebecca Rickly, Ph.D.
Department of English
Texas Tech University
Lubbock, Texas

John Simmons, Ph.D.
Professor of English Education
    and Reading
Florida State University
Tallahassee, Florida

John Trimble, Ph.D.
University Distinguished Teaching
    Professor of English
The University of Texas
Austin, Texas

CONTRIBUTING WRITERS

Jeannie Ball

Grace Bultman

Richard Cohen

Elizabeth Egan-Rivera

Laurie Hopkins Etzel

Bobbi Fagone

Lesli Favor

Nancy-Jo Hereford

Susan Maxey

Linda Mazumdar

Elizabeth McGuire

Shannon Murphy

Carole Osterink

Michael Raymond

Duncan Searl

Jocelyn Sigue

Lorraine Sintetos

James Strickler

Diane Zahler

Kathy Zahler

LANGUAGE

Grammar

CHAPTER 1 The Sentence

CHAPTER 2 Nouns and Pronouns

CHAPTER 3   Verbs and Complements

CHAPTER 4   Adjectives and Adverbs

CHAPTER 5 Other Parts of Speech and Review

CHAPTER 6 Phrases

CHAPTER 7 Sentence Structure

Usage

CHAPTER 8 Using Verbs

CHAPTER 9 Using Pronouns

CHAPTER 10 **Subject and Verb Agreement**

CHAPTER 13   End Marks and Commas

CHAPTER 14   Italics and Quotation Marks

CHAPTER 15 — Other Punctuation

Spelling

CHAPTER 16 — Spelling Correctly

Study and Test-Taking Skills Resource

LANGUAGE

e firs
nd almo
oped for so
hless. The ho
miraculo
o fe

CHAPTER 1

The Sentence

Directions
Write the letter of the term that correctly identifies the underlined word or words in each sentence.

EXAMPLE **1.** <u>White squirrels</u> live in Olney, Illinois.

    1 A simple subject
      B complete subject
      C simple predicate
      D complete predicate

ANSWER **1 B**

1. The people of this town first <u>saw</u> the squirrels eighty years ago.
2. The squirrels <u>have white fur and pink eyes</u>.
3. <u>In most cases squirrels gray, reddish brown, or brown fur</u>.
4. <u>A law in Illinois</u> protects these rare animals from careless drivers.
5. <u>The town government posted squirrel signs on the highway</u>.
6. <u>Is there a fine for hitting a squirrel?</u>
7. In 1963, <u>Amos Peters</u> and a work <u>crew</u> built the world's narrowest bridge in Olney.
8. This unusual bridge <u>was made</u> for the squirrels.
9. <u>Nutty Narrows Bridge</u> crosses Olympia Way, the main street in town.
10. The townspeople <u>put</u> peanuts on the bridge and <u>tempted</u> the squirrels across the first time.

1 **A** simple subject
   B complete subject
   C simple predicate
   D complete predicate

2 **A** complete subject
   B complete predicate
   C compound subject
   D compound verb

3 **A** sentence fragment
   B inverted order
   C verb phrase
   D complete predicate

4 **A** compound subject
   B compound verb
   C complete subject
   D complete predicate

5 **A** interjection
   B exclamatory sentence
   C interrogative sentence
   D declarative sentence

6 **A** sentence fragment
   B inverted order
   C verb phrase
   D complete predicate

7 **A** complete subject
   B complete predicate
   C compound subject
   D compound verb

8 **A** verb phrase
   B inverted order
   C sentence fragment
   D complete predicate

9 **A** compound subject
   B compound verb
   C simple subject
   D simple predicate

10 **A** complete subject
   B complete predicate
   C compound subject
   D compound verb

Jacob Lawrence. *"In a free government, the security of civil rights must be the same as that for religious rights. It consists in the one case in the multiplicity of interest, and in the other, in the multiplicity of sects."* (the words of James Madison), 1976. Opaque watercolor and pencil on paper, mounted on fiberboard, 30 by 22 ⅛ inches. National Museum of American Art, Smithsonian Institution, Washington, D.C.

Describe What are the most striking colors in the painting and where are they repeated?

Analyze How does the artist use white to create movement? How does the artist use color to direct your focus? What do the lines of movement in the painting draw your eye toward?

Interpret How does the title relate to what you see in the painting?

Judge Imagine expressing the mood of this painting in writing. Do you think it would be best expressed in a poem, a story, a newspaper article, or a composition? Why?

At the end of this chapter, you will use the artwork to stimulate ideas for writing.

A Sentence

Why do you speak or write? You have information or ideas you want other people to know. This information is so important you want to make sure people understand what you are saying or writing. To do this, you must be able to recognize complete thoughts and use them.

A **sentence** is a group of words that expresses a complete thought.

A group of words that does not express a complete thought is called a **fragment**. Notice in the following examples that fragments leave unanswered questions. More information must be added to make the fragments into sentences.

FRAGMENT	Writes for the local newspaper. *(Who writes?)*
SENTENCE	My Uncle Juan writes for the local newspaper.
FRAGMENT	His news article. *(What did it do?)*
SENTENCE	His news article appeared on the front page today.

You can learn more about fragments on pages L35–L37.

CONNECT TO SPEAKING AND WRITING

When talking to someone, you often use fragments to express ideas. In informal speech this works well because you are using facial expressions and body language to help convey meaning. When you write, however, the reader depends on your words alone for meaning. That's why it is important that you write in complete sentences.

PRACTICE YOUR SKILLS

● Check Your Understanding

Recognizing Sentences

Contemporary Life **Label each group of words *S* for *sentence* or *F* for *fragment*.**

1. A visit to the newspaper office.

2. Black ink spilled on the floor.

3. Heard the loud noise of the printing press.

4. The phone rang often.

5. Men and women at desks.

6. The reporter spoke to our class.

7. The tall man in the first office.

8. The secretary near the computer smiled.

9. Uncle Juan writes about government.

10. Wrote a story about the election.

11. He writes very well.

12. His articles awards.

13. There are two trophies on his desk.

14. The newspaper staff welcomed us.

15. They a newspaper to each student.

● Connect to the Writing Process: Revising

Writing Complete Sentences from Fragments

16.–22. **Add information to turn each of the sentence fragments from the preceding exercise into a sentence. Remember to begin each sentence with a capital letter and to end it with a period or other punctuation mark.**

Kinds of Sentences

All sentences are complete thoughts, but different sentences can have different purposes. Most sentences make a statement. Others ask a question or give a command, and a few sentences express strong feeling. To decide what punctuation mark should go at the end of a sentence, think about the purpose of that sentence.

A **declarative sentence** makes a statement or expresses an opinion. It ends with a period.

> We spent five hours at the zoo. (statement)
>
> Tigers are the most beautiful animals of all. (opinion)

An **interrogative sentence** asks a question. It ends with a question mark.

> Have you ever seen a Siberian tiger?

An **imperative sentence** makes a request or gives a command. It ends with either a period or an exclamation point.

> Hand me that book about wild cats.
> (This imperative sentence ends with a period because it is a mild request.)
> Don't spill your drink on it!
> (This imperative sentence ends with an exclamation point because it is a strong command.)

An **exclamatory sentence** expresses strong feeling. It ends with an exclamation point.

> A tiger escaped from the zoo!
> (This exclamatory sentence expresses excitement.)

PRACTICE YOUR SKILLS

● Check Your Understanding
Classifying Sentences

Science Topic **Label each of the following sentences *declarative*, *imperative*, *interrogative*, or *exclamatory*.**

1. Do you know where Bengal tigers live?

2. Most Bengal tigers live in India.

3. Look for India on the map.

4. The male Bengal tiger is about 10 feet long and weighs up to 575 pounds.

5. That is an enormous animal!

6. This tiger does not live in prides like the lion.

7. Did you know that it is a solitary creature?

8. What do tigers eat?

9. They eat other animals, fish, and even crocodiles.

10. Listen to another fact about Bengal tigers.

11. The pattern of black stripes is different on each tiger.

12. The white tiger is extremely rare!

13. Did you know that a black tiger with tawny stripes was once found?

14. These beautiful animals have almost no enemies.

15. Look up information about tigers on the Internet.

● Connect to the Writing Process: Editing
Adding End Marks to Sentences

Write each sentence, using the correct end mark. Then label each sentence *declarative*, *imperative*, *interrogative*, or *exclamatory*.

16. Ts'ai Lun of China first reported making paper in A.D. 105

17. How did he first make his paper

18. He beat old rags and fishing nets into a soft pulp

19. How can someone make paper from plants

20. Boil the plants and beat them into a soft pulp

21. Spread the pulp on a stretching frame

22. Flatten the dried tissue with weights

Communicate Your Ideas

APPLY TO WRITING
Postcard: *Sentence Variety*

You are on vacation in your favorite place. Write a postcard to your best friend telling him or her about where you are and what you are doing. As you write, use at least one of each kind of sentence. After you finish, label each of your sentences *declarative, interrogative, imperative,* or *exclamatory.*

Subjects and Predicates

A sentence expresses a complete thought because it always has two parts. The first part of the sentence is the complete subject. The **subject** names the person, place, thing, or idea the sentence is about. The second part of the sentence is the complete predicate. The **predicate** tells what the subject is or does.

A **complete subject** includes all the words used to identify the person, place, thing, or idea that the sentence is about.

complete subject

The human body needs nutritious food.

(*The human body* names what the sentence is about.)

complete subject

That athlete on television is very healthy.

(*That athlete on television* names whom the sentence is about.)

A **complete predicate** includes all the words that tell what the subject is doing or that tell something about the subject.

complete predicate

The human body **needs nutritious food**.

(*Needs nutritious food* tells what the complete subject does.)

complete predicate

That athlete on television **is very healthy**.

(*Is very healthy* tells what the subject is.)

COMPLETE SUBJECT	COMPLETE PREDICATE
(Names the person, place, thing, or idea the sentence is about.)	(Tells what the subject is or does.)
PERSON Humans of any age	require plenty of rest.
PLACE The United States	has many health clubs.
THING A high, constant fever	is dangerous for humans.
IDEA A person's self-image	affects his or her health.

PRACTICE YOUR SKILLS

● Check Your Understanding

Finding Complete Subjects and Predicates

Science Topic **Write each sentence. Then draw one line under each complete subject and two lines under each complete predicate.**

1. The white cells in your blood fight disease.

2. A baby's skull is soft at birth.

3. Most people over twenty-one have thirty-two permanent teeth.

4. Your liver stores extra vitamins and minerals.

5. Hair on your head grows a half inch each month.

6. A person's normal body temperature is 98.6°F.

7. Every cell in your body needs protein.

8. Your stomach stretches like a balloon.

9. People's voices get deeper around the age of fourteen.

10. Your rib cage protects your lungs.

Combining Complete Subjects and Predicates

Match each subject in the first column with a predicate in the second column. Then combine them to write five sentences that make sense. Be sure to begin each sentence with a capital letter and end each one with an appropriate end mark.

11. the girl's team	**a.** leaks after a heavy rain
12. the coach	**b.** called a foul
13. the sweaty players	**c.** won the championship
14. the referee	**d.** jumped to their feet
15. our team's uniforms	**e.** supports the team
16. the screaming fans	**f.** praised the girls' team
17. my oldest sister	**g.** are green and yellow
18. the gym roof	**h.** left the basketball court
19. our whole school	**i.** plays on the team
20. basketball	**j.** is my favorite sport

▶ Simple Subjects

Most complete subjects include more than one word. Some complete subjects are quite long. Others are quite short. Within each complete subject, however, there is one main word that tells what the sentence is about. This main word is called the simple subject.

A **simple subject** is the main word in the complete subject.

To find the simple subject, ask yourself *Who or what is doing something?* or *About whom or what is the statement being made?* In the examples on the following page, the simple subject is underlined once.

Many signs of the ancient Inca remain in South America.

(What word answers the question *Who or what is doing something? Signs* is the simple subject.)

The Andes Mountains were home to the Incas.

(What word answers the question *About whom or what is the statement being made?* The simple subject is *Andes Mountains*. In this case, the simple subject is two words because both words are the name of one place.)

A complete and a simple subject can be the same.

Francisco Pizarro led the conquistadors against the Incas in 1530.

(*Francisco Pizarro* is the simple subject as well as the complete subject. Both words are the name of one person.)

Riches filled the Inca empire.

Throughout the rest of this book, the simple subject will be called the subject.

PRACTICE YOUR SKILLS

● Check Your Understanding
Finding Complete and Simple Subjects

 History Topic **Write each complete subject. Then underline each simple subject.**

1. The Incas built a great empire in South America in the fifteenth century.

2. This mighty empire stretched two thousand miles.

3. Many great roads connected the capital with other parts of the empire.

4. Runners for the government carried messages six hundred miles in just five days on these roads.

5. The capital of the empire was in present-day Peru.

6. Some buildings were covered in gold.

7. Six million Indians lived in the empire.

8. The people of this civilization were very smart.

9. Workers built irrigation systems and terraced farms.

10. Central governments in cities planned these projects.

● Check Your Understanding
Finding Subjects

History Topic **Write each simple subject.**

11. Native Americans lived throughout the Western Hemisphere before European settlement.

12. They hunted deer, buffalo, and other game.

13. Some groups of expert farmers grew potatoes, tobacco, tomatoes, and other plants.

14. The Plains Indians lived on the vast plains of the central United States.

15. The large, furry buffalo of the plains provided these people with food and materials for shelter.

16. Buffalo hides provided excellent protection against cold winds.

17. Native Americans of the Southwest built large dwellings of adobe, wood, and stone.

18. Spanish settlers called these structures pueblos.

APPLY TO WRITING
Description: *Subjects*

The Kachinas are important spirits in the religion of the Pueblo peoples of North America. There are many different kinds. Men of the tribe dress up like Kachinas and visit Pueblo villages. They bring gifts to the children. They also dance and sing. Kachina dolls, like the Hopi one pictured here, are given to the children of the tribe so they can learn about their culture.

Write a brief description of this Kachina doll. What does it look like? What is it made of? How would its different textures feel? After writing your description, read it again and correct any errors you find. Also, underline the subjects in five of your sentences.

● Simple Predicates, or Verbs

Like complete subjects, most complete predicates contain more than one word. Within each complete predicate, however, there is one main word or phrase that tells what the subject is or does. This main word or phrase is called the simple predicate, or verb.

A **simple predicate,** or **verb,** is the main word or phrase in the complete predicate.

Certain verbs can be found by asking *What is the subject doing?* or *What did the subject do?* These verbs show action. In the following examples, the verbs are underlined twice.

The astronauts **prepared carefully for a space walk.**

(What word answers the question *What did the subject do? Prepared* is the simple predicate, or verb.)

The planets in our solar system **revolve around the sun.**

(What word answers the question *What did the subject do? Revolve* is the simple predicate, or verb.)

Some verbs do not show action. Verbs of this kind tell something about the subject. The following is a list of verb forms that are used to make a statement about a subject.

COMMON VERBS THAT MAKE STATEMENTS				
am	are	is	was	were

Mars **is the fourth planet from the sun.**
The space shuttle **was a blur of red, white, and blue.**
The astronauts **were in space for six days.**

A complete predicate and a simple predicate can be the same, as in the following examples.

The rocket **landed**.
Crowds of onlookers **cheered**.
The happy astronauts **waved**.

CONNECT TO SPEAKING AND WRITING

When you speak to people or when they read your work, your words are creating pictures or images in their minds. Verbs can help you make that picture more interesting. Using vivid verbs can draw sharp images in the minds of your listeners or readers. Read the following four sentences, and compare the pictures they bring to your mind.

The astronaut walked across the moon's surface.

The astronaut bounded across the moon's surface.

The astronaut stumbled across the moon's surface.

The astronaut waltzed across the moon's surface.

You can learn about subject and verb agreement in Chapter 10.

PRACTICE YOUR SKILLS

● Check Your Understanding
Finding Complete Predicates and Verbs

Science Topic **Write each complete predicate. Then underline each verb.**

1. Astronomers looked closely at Mars for the first time in 1965.

2. *Mariner 4* flew by the planet.

3. Scientists learned many things about the "Red Planet" from this trip.

4. The red color of Mars is from rust.

5. Pictures of Mars show a solid surface.

6. The surface has many craters, volcanoes, canyons, and empty river beds.

7. The soil on Mars differs from Earth's soil.

8. The temperatures on Mars are very low.

9. Dust storms block the sun's radiation.

10. Ice caps cover both of the poles on Mars.

Check Your Understanding
Finding Verbs

General Interest **Write each verb.**

11. A statue in Peru dates back to pre-Incan times.

12. A small figure of the statue is a surfer.

13. Polynesian surfers performed for Captain Cook in 1777.

14. These surfers used wooden canoes and oars up to eighteen feet long.

15. People in California watched the first surfer in the United States in 1910.

16. Many early surfboards weighed over one hundred pounds.

17. Tom Blake invented a lighter surfboard in the 1920s.

18. He added a keel under the surfboard in 1935.

19. A keel gives a surfer more control of the direction of the surfboard.

20. Surfing gained wide popularity in the United States in the 1960s.

Completing Sentences

Add predicates to the complete subjects to create complete sentences. Remember to use vivid verbs to make your sentences interesting.

21. Some sports ▪.

22. Runners, swimmers, and cyclists ▪.

23. Joggers in the park ▪.

24. The trail on the mountainside ▪.

25. Most athletes ▪.

26. Proper shoes for exercise ▪.

27. A strong heart ▪.

28. Most people in America ▪.

29. Other people around the world ▪.

30. Many young children in school ▪.

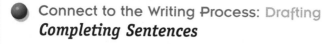

Communicate Your Ideas

APPLY TO WRITING

Persuasive Letter: *Verbs*

Your friends in the neighborhood want to form a sports team. The problem is that you and your friends cannot agree on what sport you should play. Write a letter to your friends in which you tell them what sport you think would be the best to play. List at least three good reasons to choose this sport. When you have finished writing, read your letter, correcting any errors you find. Also, underline the verbs in five of your sentences.

Verb Phrases

Sometimes a verb needs other words to help it make a statement or to tell what action is taking place. Such words are called **helping verbs,** or **auxiliary verbs**. The main verb plus any helping verbs makes up a verb phrase. The following is a list of common helping verbs.

COMMON HELPING VERBS	
be	am, is, are, was, were, be, being, been
have	has, have, had
do	do, does, did
OTHERS	may, might, must, can, could, shall, should, will, would

The verb phrases in the following examples are underlined twice, and the helping verbs are in bold type.

The cars **were** racing around the track.

The champion **had been** leading the pack all day.

Some of the common helping verbs in the box above can be main verbs. They are only helping verbs when they are part of a verb phrase.

MAIN VERB He **is** the car's owner.
HELPING VERB He **is** driving the car.

MAIN VERB The race car **had** a flat tire.
HELPING VERB The race car **had** stopped quickly.

Throughout the rest of this book, a verb phrase will be called a verb. *You can learn about agreement of subjects and verbs in Chapter 10.*

● Check Your Understanding
Finding Verb Phrases

General Interest **Write each verb phrase.**

1. Race cars can travel at high speeds.
2. The engines of these cars are designed for top performance.
3. These cars must be in excellent condition.
4. Race car drivers are trained for this kind of competition.
5. Schools for drivers can be found in many places in the United States.
6. Many young racers must have financial help.
7. Some corporations will sponsor young drivers.
8. Car races may be postponed due to poor weather conditions.
9. The winners of the big races may earn huge amounts of money.
10. This exciting sport can be very dangerous.

Interrupted Verb Phrases

Sometimes one or more words separate the parts of a verb phrase. The verb phrases in the following examples are in **bold** type.

My sister **has** nearly **missed** the bus twice this week.

Did she **miss** the bus yesterday?

(She *did miss* the bus yesterday.)

Mom **has** not **driven** us to school for years.

(*Not* and its contraction *n't* are never part of a verb phase.)

PRACTICE YOUR SKILLS

● Check Your Understanding
Finding Verb Phrases

Contemporary Life   **Write each verb phrase.**

1. My sister Hannah is not riding the bus with us today.

2. She did not set her alarm last night.

3. My mom did not wake Hannah this morning at the usual time.

4. Hannah has always been a late sleeper.

5. My sister is constantly making a fuss in the morning.

6. She doesn't like alarm clocks.

7. Did she awaken yet?

8. She still has not stirred from sleep.

9. My mom has finally awakened her.

10. Mom will probably drive her to school this morning.

● Connect to the Writing Process: Drafting
Writing Sentences with Verb Phrases

11.–20. Write ten sentences about school. Underline the verb or verb phrase in each sentence.

APPLY TO WRITING

The Writer's Craft: *Analyzing the Use of Verbs and Verb Phrases*

Authors use a combination of verbs and verb phrases when they write. Read the following passage from *Freckle Juice* by Judy Blume and follow the directions.

> Andrew Marcus wanted freckles. Nicky Lane had freckles. He had a million of them. They covered his face, his ears and the back of his neck. Andrew didn't have any freckles. He had two warts on his finger. But they didn't do him any good at all.
>
> —*Judy Blume,* Freckle Juice

- Write each verb or verb phrase in each sentence.
- What verb is repeated most often? Is it used alone or in a verb phrase?
- Can you think of any other verbs the writer could have used instead of the ones she did?

QuickCheck Mixed Practice

General Interest **Write the subject and the verb in each sentence.**

1. One famous TV cat was Morris.
2. Bob Martwick was looking for a special cat in 1966.
3. Hundreds of pictures of cats flooded Martwick's office.
4. The cats were of every size, shape, and color.

5. This trainer of animals didn't see the right cat in any of the pictures.

6. He was looking for an animal star.

7. The original Morris was living in an animal shelter in Chicago at the time.

8. This fifteen-pound tomcat eventually caught the eye of Martwick.

9. Stardom was his after only one audition.

10. An organization for animals gave Morris a Patsy Award in 1973.

11. This trophy is like an Oscar for animal actors.

12. All kinds of Morris products were for sale.

13. Fans of this cat could buy Morris bowls, T-shirts, and calendars.

14. Stores across the country were selling thousands of copies of his biography.

15. The book was called *Morris: An Intimate Biography*.

16. Morris's life was not always easy.

17. Round-the-clock guards were always with him.

18. Catnappers often followed him.

19. This famous cat died of heart failure in 1978.

20. The advertising campaign continued with a replacement for Morris.

Different Positions of Subjects

In most sentences the subject comes before the verb. When the subject comes before the verb, a sentence is in its

natural order. In the following examples, each subject is underlined once, and each verb is underlined twice.

> Those storm clouds are getting darker.
>
> The forecaster on television predicted rain today.

Sometimes, a sentence is not written in its natural order. When the verb comes before the subject, the sentence is in **inverted order**. To find the subject in a sentence in inverted order, turn the sentence around to its natural order.

> INVERTED ORDER   Across the sky gathered the dark clouds.
>
> NATURAL ORDER   The dark clouds gathered across the sky.
>
> INVERTED ORDER   Into their homes ran the children.
>
> NATURAL ORDER   The children ran into their homes.

Questions

Interrogative sentences are usually written in inverted order. In these sentences part of the verb phrase usually comes before the subject. To find the subject in an interrogative sentence, change the question into a statement.

> QUESTION   Are you prepared for bad weather this season?
>
> STATEMENT   You are prepared for bad weather this season.
>
> QUESTION   Hasn't the rain begun?
>
> STATEMENT   The rain hasn't begun.

Understood Subjects

The subject of an imperative sentence is not stated in the sentence, but it is understood to be there. *You,* the person or persons receiving the command or request, is always the **understood subject**.

> COMMAND OR REQUEST   (you) <u>Bring</u> the cat inside.
>
> (you) Please <u>close</u> the windows.

CONNECT TO WRITER'S CRAFT

Poets often choose to put the subjects of their sentences in different positions. This can add to the effect of the poem. In "April Rain Song," Langston Hughes chose to begin his poem with three imperative sentences. Notice how this adds rhythm to Hughes's words.

Let the rain kiss you.
Let the rain beat upon your head with silver
    liquid drops.
Let the rain sing you a lullaby.

—*Langston Hughes, "April Rain Song"*

PRACTICE YOUR SKILLS

● Check Your Understanding
Finding Subjects and Verbs

Contemporary Life   **Write the subject and verb in each sentence. If the subject is an understood *you,* write *you* in parentheses.**

1. Did I just hear thunder?

2. Please turn on the radio.

3. On the radio was a storm warning for our area.

4. Have you closed the windows?

5. Listen for raindrops.

6. Has Dad taken my umbrella again?

7. Will he be home soon?

8. Be careful on the wet streets.

9. From every corner and eave of our roof ran water.

10. Has the rain finally stopped?

11. Have you checked the vegetable garden lately?

12. Don't open the umbrella in the house!

13. From the roof came a strange noise.

14. Check the roof for water damage.

15. Did you see that bizarre lightning flash?

● Connect to the Writing Process: Drafting
Using Different Positions of Subjects

Write the kind of sentences indicated. Draw one line under the subject and two lines under the verb. If the subject is an understood *you*, write *you* in parentheses. Remember to begin your sentences with capital letters and end them with appropriate end marks.

16. an interrogative sentence

17. a declarative sentence in natural order

18. a declarative sentence in inverted order

19. an imperative sentence

20. an interrogative sentence

APPLY TO WRITING

The Writer's Craft: *Analyzing the Use of Inverted Order*

Poets often choose to put sentences in inverted order. Read these lines from a poem about a boy named Augustus and then follow the directions.

> Augustus was a chubby lad;
> Fat ruddy cheeks Augustus had:
> And everybody saw with joy
> The plump and hearty, healthy boy.
>
> —*Heinrich Hoffman,*
> **"The Story of Augustus Who Would Not Have Any Soup"**

- Write the line that is in inverted order. Then rewrite the line in natural order.

- Read the excerpt again with your new line in place. Which do you like better, the new version or the original?

- Give two reasons why Hoffman may have chosen to write this line in inverted order.

QuickCheck Mixed Practice

Contemporary Life — **Write the subject and verb in each sentence. If the subject is an understood *you*, write *you* in parentheses.**

1. Have you been to Europe?

2. Bring me that map.

3. I will show you our vacation route.

4. We traveled to England and France.

5. My family did not visit Italy.

6. Over the Atlantic Ocean flew our airplane.

7. Did the flight last a long time?

8. It seemed like days!

9. One highlight of the trip was the Tower of London.

10. Listen to this!

11. We saw Shakespeare's home in Stratford.

12. My brother wouldn't go to the top of the Eiffel Tower in Paris.

13. He is afraid of heights.

14. High in the tower climbed the rest of us.

15. Are you planning another trip soon?

Compound Subjects

Sometimes a sentence is about more than one person or thing. For that reason a sentence can have more than one subject. Two or more subjects that share the same verb are called a compound subject. The parts of a compound subject are usually joined by the conjunction *and, but,* or *or.*

> A **compound subject** is two or more subjects in one sentence that have the same verb and are joined by a conjunction.

In the following examples, each subject is underlined once and each verb is underlined twice. Notice that each subject shares the same verb—*make.*

ONE SUBJECT	Dogs make good pets.
COMPOUND SUBJECT	Dogs and cats make good pets.

COMPOUND SUBJECT	Dogs, cats, and fish make good pets.

You can learn more about compound subjects on pages L336–L337.

PRACTICE YOUR SKILLS

● Check Your Understanding
Finding Compound Subjects

Contemporary Life **Write each compound subject.**

1. My best friend, her family, and I went to the animal shelter.

2. She and her sister were adopting a pet from the shelter.

3. The meows of cats and the barks of dogs could be heard from the parking lot.

4. The men and women at the shelter were very helpful.

5. One poodle and a miniature collie were very playful.

6. A calico kitten and a Siamese cat were batting around a rubber ball.

7. My friend and her sister decided on a small white dog.

8. The woman at the adoption desk and her assistant asked my friend's mom lots of questions.

9. My friend's mom and dad paid the adoption fee.

10. My friend, her sister, and the little white dog played happily in the back seat all the way home.

Compound Verbs

Sometimes the subject is doing more than one thing, or more than one statement is being made about the subject. For these reasons, a sentence can have more than one verb. In a sentence where two or more verbs share the same subject, the sentence has a compound verb. The parts of a compound verb, like the parts of a compound subject, are usually joined by the conjunctions *and* or *or*.

A **compound verb** is two or more verbs that have the same subject and are joined by a conjunction.

Notice that each verb in the following examples shares the same subject—*vultures*.

ONE VERB	Vultures sleep on the island.
COMPOUND VERB	Vultures sleep and hunt on the island.
COMPOUND VERB	Vultures sleep, hunt, and eat on the island.

PRACTICE YOUR SKILLS

● Check Your Understanding
Finding Compound Verbs

Geography Topic **Write each compound verb.**

1. Have you ever read or studied about islands?
2. Read and learn more about them.
3. A long time ago, volcanoes exploded and poured lava out of their tops.
4. Smoke filled the air and choked animals and people.

5. Later the hot lava cooled and changed into islands.

6. Other islands were created or formed from erosion.

7. Water constantly washed away some of the land and created mounds.

8. The wind loosened the soil and blew it away.

9. In other places the earth dried and sank.

10. Water from the ocean then filled the low places and made new islands.

● Check Your Understanding
Finding Compound Subjects and Compound Verbs

Science Topic **Write each compound subject or compound verb. Label the words S for subject or V for verb.**

11. Helium and hydrogen make up Mercury's atmosphere.

12. Unmanned spacecraft photograph the surface of distant planets and collect soil samples.

13. A spacecraft landed on Venus and sent pictures of the planet back to Earth.

14. *Mariner 4* and other spacecraft have visited Mars.

15. *Voyager 2* flew past Jupiter and Saturn and found no solid surface for landing.

16. Telescopes and satellites have learned much about Jupiter and Saturn.

17. In 1610, Galileo looked through his telescope and discovered four of Jupiter's moons.

18. Ganymede and Europa are two of the moons of Jupiter.

19. The great winds on Saturn blow constantly and form colorful bands of clouds.

20. Venus, Mars, Mercury, Saturn, and Jupiter are visible from Earth without a telescope.

Adding Compound Subjects or Verbs

Rewrite each sentence, adding either a compound subject or a compound verb. The word in parentheses tells you what to add.

21. Josh studied the craters of the moon. (subject)

22. All my friends came over. (verb)

23. The moon shone in the night sky. (subject)

24. Those planets look close. (verb)

25. Stars sparkle. (verb)

26. Astronauts go into space. (verb)

27. I watched a recent movie about astronauts. (subject)

28. My grandfather gave me a book about the *Apollo* missions. (subject)

29. All books about astronomy interest me. (verb)

30. My class visited the space museum last fall. (verb)

Communicate Your Ideas

APPLY TO WRITING

Friendly Letter: *Compound Subjects and Verbs*

You have been chosen to be a part of the first manned mission to Jupiter. You are told that you can bring along only five personal items on the mission. Write a letter to the mission commander telling her what you have decided to bring and why you have chosen to bring these things. As you write, include at least two sentences with compound subjects and two sentences with compound verbs. Underline these sentences.

Science Topic **Write the subject and verb in each sentence. If the subject is an understood *you*, write *you* in parentheses.**

1. The Greeks were building gymnasiums over 2,500 years ago.

2. Boys and young men in Greece trained very hard for the Olympics.

3. Healthy bodies were important to the early Greeks.

4. Teenagers would spend many hours in a gymnasium every day.

5. Around the track ran the eager athletes many times.

6. These athletes also lifted weights and climbed ropes.

7. The Olympics was the goal of each boy.

8. Greek girls could not go inside the gymnasiums.

9. Do you agree with this rule?

10. Roman troops eventually entered Greece and conquered it.

11. One person in the Roman government canceled the Olympics.

12. The gymnasiums throughout Greece were officially closed in A.D. 392.

13. Would the Olympics ever begin again?

14. A man in Germany finally launched the Olympics again in the 1800s.

15. Watch the gymnastics during the next Olympics and remember the ancient Greeks.

Sentence Fragments

At the beginning of this chapter, you learned that an incomplete sentence is called a fragment.

> A **sentence fragment** is a group of words that does not express a complete thought.

To express a complete thought, a sentence must have a subject and a verb. If either part is missing, the group of words is a fragment. In the following examples, each subject is underlined once, and each verb is underlined twice.

No Subject	Towered above the valley.
	(*What* towered above the valley?)
Sentence	The mountains towered above the valley.
No Verb	A climber on a rope.
	(What did the climber *do?*)
Sentence	A climber on a rope dangled from a high cliff.
No Subject or Verb	Down the alpine slope. (*Who or what* was on the alpine slope? What *happened* there?)
Sentence	The group of mountain climbers made their way down the alpine slope.

Ways to Correct Sentence Fragments

When you finish writing, always read your work aloud. Listen and look for fragments. If you find any, correct them.

You can correct sentence fragments in one of two ways. One is to attach a fragment to a nearby sentence. The other is to turn the fragment into a sentence by adding words that make it a complete thought.

SENTENCE	Tim climbed the highest peak.
FRAGMENT	With a group of experienced hikers.
ATTACHED	Tim climbed the highest peak with a group of experienced hikers.
SEPARATE SENTENCES	Tim climbed the highest peak. He went with a group of experienced hikers.

CONNECT TO WRITER'S CRAFT

Poetry does not always follow the rules of conventional English. While most novelists, short story writers, and journalists usually write in complete sentences, poets often use fragments to convey their ideas. Read the following passage from "Slack's Garage" by Christine E. Hemp. Notice how the author mixes fragments with complete thoughts. How does her use of fragments affect the poem?

Why he comes here
every morning like clockwork
I don't know.
All bent up—
overalls hang on him
like some old oil rag.
Waits out front to pump

in the business he used to have.
De Sotos and slick red Buicks.

Look at those rows
of jacks, winches, and chains.
Even smells in here. Old
hoses, old gauges, old grease.
—*Christine E. Hemp, "Slack's Garage"*

PRACTICE YOUR SKILLS

● Check Your Understanding
Recognizing Sentence Fragments

Contemporary Life **Label each group of words either *S* for sentence or *F* for fragment.**

1. Reached for the rope.
2. The hook on her safety harness snapped.
3. The leader of the expedition followed the group.
4. Hikers all along the trail.
5. Their boots crunched on the new snow.
6. Beside the trail on the side of the mountain.
7. Was reaching for a handhold.
8. On the peak of the mountain.
9. They returned at eight o'clock sharp.
10. The mountain was a challenge.

● Connect to the Writing Process: Revising
Correcting Sentence Fragments

11.–15. Correct each fragment from the preceding exercise by writing one complete thought with a subject and predicate.

Rewrite the following paragraphs, correcting each sentence fragment. Begin each sentence with a capital letter and end each sentence with a period.

One day Frank and Ellen Hensel dug a one-acre pond. Near their Vermont home. Then, just for fun, they inflated a plastic toy dolphin. And floated it on the new pond. This blue-and-white beach toy had large eyes, long eyelashes, and a big broad smile. It bobbed in the breeze. And looked very much alive.

A large gray-and-black Canada goose. Suddenly appeared on the pond one day. A breeze caught the dolphin, and it drifted across the pond. The goose quickly paddled. After the plastic mammal.

Several days passed. The Hensels watched the goose. And worried about it. All the other geese were migrating to the South. Every day flocks of geese in V formations. Flew over their house.

One morning the Hensels heard the honking of the goose. And looked outside. A strong wind was blowing, and the dolphin was swirling in all directions. The goose was paddling as quickly as it could. But couldn't keep up.

The Hensels looked out the window. On the following morning. A branch had poked a hole. In the dolphin's side. It lay on its side, half under the water. Then the dolphin let out some bubbles. And sank to the bottom.

The goose was confused. It swam around its lost friend. In huge circles. It honked and flapped its wings. For two days the big bird watched over the blue and white form. At the bottom of the pond. Then finally, with a downward glance, the bird flapped its wings. And flew into the bright October sky.

Communicate Your Ideas

APPLY TO WRITING
Narrative: *Fragments and Complete Sentences*

In the last exercise, you read about a couple who witnessed a very strange incident. Have you ever seen anything like that? Maybe you've seen a cat swim or a cat and a dog that are best friends. Write about a time you saw something so unusual or interesting that you could hardly believe it. As you write, use the following groups of words in your narrative. Expand these fragments into complete sentences and then underline your new sentences.

- Right in front of me.
- The most amazing thing I've ever seen.
- To my surprise.
- Watched the action.

Sentence Diagraming

Throughout this chapter and the next six chapters of this book, you will read and *hear* how words are used in sentences. Now you have a chance to *see* how they are used. Diagrams are pictures of sentences. Diagrams can help you easily find and identify all the parts of a sentence.

Subjects and Verbs in Declarative Sentences Draw a straight baseline. Write the subject and the verb on this line. Then draw another line to separate the subject from the verb. Include capital letters but do not include punctuation.

Rain fell.

Rain	fell

Clouds are gathering.

Clouds	are gathering

Subjects and Verbs in Interrogative Sentences Turn a question into a statement and diagram it like a declarative sentence.

Is rain falling? (Rain is falling.) Has Sam gone? (Sam has gone.)

rain	Is falling

Sam	Has gone

Subject and Verbs in Imperative Sentences Write the understood *you* in parentheses in the subject position on the diagram.

Stop!

(you)	Stop

Compound Subjects and Verbs Write the parts of a compound subject or a compound verb on parallel lines. Write the word that joins them on a broken line between them.

Girls and boys were hurrying.

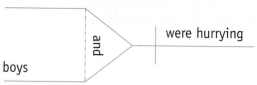

Justin runs and slips.   Stop and listen.

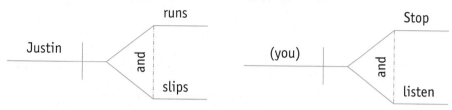

PRACTICE YOUR SKILLS

Diagraming Subjects and Verbs

Diagram the following sentences or copy them. If you copy them, draw one line under each subject and two lines under each verb. If the subject is an understood *you*, write *you* in parentheses.

   1. Birds leave.
   2. Leaves are falling.
   3. Are windows closing?
   4. Listen!
   5. Furnaces are starting.
   6. Plants freeze and die.
   7. Jerry and Martin are shivering.
   8. Is water freezing?
   9. Wait.
   10. Sun and warmth will return.

Finding Subjects and Verbs

Write the simple subjects and verbs in the following sentences. If a sentence has an understood subject, write *you* in parentheses.

1. Birds do not have teeth.
2. A tropical parrot can repeat human words.
3. Most birds build nests and lay eggs in them.
4. Does your family ever feed the birds in your yard?
5. Don't ever give birds anything salty.

Finding Subjects and Verbs

Write the subjects and verbs in the following sentences. If a sentence has an understood subject, write *you* in parentheses.

1. The Chinese grew roses and bred new kinds about five thousand years ago.
2. The ancient Romans strewed their halls with rose petals and put rosewater in their baths.
3. Empress Josephine cultivated a famous rose garden.
4. Europeans and Americans have created more than twenty thousand varieties of roses.
5. One dedicated grower is patiently working on a black rose.
6. Professional rose breeders are growing more fragrant roses nowadays.
7. Does the rose's fragrance draw bees to it?
8. Violet and apple are two of the seven basic rose scents.
9. Have you ever heard of a rose called American Beauty?
10. Watch for thorns on long-stemmed roses.

Understanding Kinds of Sentences

Write each sentence, adding a correct end mark. Then label each sentence using the following abbreviations.

declarative = *d.*   imperative = *imp.*
interrogative = *int.*   exclamatory = *ex.*

1. Did you know that you have a biological clock inside you
2. That's amazing
3. It controls when you feel like sleeping
4. Isn't it interesting that this clock is reset as you get older
5. Pay attention to when you feel sleepy

Using Subjects and Verbs

Write ten sentences that follow the directions below. (The sentences may come in any order.) Write about one of the following topics or a topic of your choice: what you like best about your school, how you would improve your school, or an interesting experience you have had at your school.

1. Write a declarative sentence.
2. Write an interrogative sentence.
3. Write an imperative sentence.
4. Write an exclamatory sentence.
5. Write a sentence with a verb phrase.
6. Write a sentence with an interrupted verb phrase.
7. Write a sentence with a compound subject.
8. Write a sentence with a compound verb.
9. Write a sentence with a compound subject and a compound verb.
10. Write any kind of sentence.

When you have finished, underline each subject once and each verb twice. Then check for capital letters and end punctuation.

Language and *Self-Expression*

Jacob Lawrence's picture makes a statement about being African American. The members of the young family have much to offer their country. What does America risk losing if some Americans are not allowed to be all they are capable of being?

What are your dreams for the future? How do you think your community will benefit if your dreams come true? Write a letter to yourself, describing your hopes and dreams. Write sentences that express your ideas clearly. Vary your writing by using compound subjects and verbs.

Prewriting Making a two-column chart can help you organize your thoughts. Note details about your dreams in one column. Write ideas about the possible effects of your actions in the other column.

Drafting Use your chart to help you recall your ideas. Your first paragraph should give a general idea of what you hope to do. Then focus on one kind of detail in each paragraph. Conclude by summarizing the contributions you hope to make.

Revising Read your opening paragraph to a classmate. Find out whether you have made the point of your letter clear. Each of your sentences should express a complete thought.

Editing Check your letter for errors in spelling and punctuation. Be sure that you have used the correct punctuation to end each sentence.

Publishing Make a final copy of your letter. Then seal it in an envelope addressed to yourself. On the envelope, write the date on which you plan to open the letter.

Another Look

A **sentence** is a group of words that expresses a complete thought.

Kinds of Sentences

A **declarative sentence** makes a statement or expresses an opinion. It ends with a period. *(page L7)*

An **interrogative sentence** asks a question. It ends with a question mark. *(page L7)*

An **imperative sentence** makes a request or gives a command. It ends with either a period or an exclamation point. *(page L7)*

An **exclamatory sentence** expresses strong feeling. It ends with an exclamation point. *(page L7)*

Subjects and Predicates

A **complete subject** includes all the words used to identify the person, place, thing, or idea that the sentence is about. *(pages L10–L11)*

A **complete predicate** includes all the words that tell what the subject is doing or that tell something about the subject. *(pages L10–L11)*

A **simple subject** is the main word in the complete subject. *(pages L12–L13)*

A **simple predicate**, or **verb,** is the main word or phrase in the complete predicate. *(pages L16–L17)*

A **compound subject** is two or more subjects in one sentence that have the same verb and are joined by a conjunction. *(pages L29–L30)*

A **compound verb** is two or more verbs that have the same subject and are joined by a conjunction. *(page L31)*

Other Information About the Sentence

Avoiding sentence fragments *(pages L35–L36)*

Using correct punctuation with sentences *(page L7)*

Recognizing verb phrases *(page L20)*

Recognizing interrupted verb phrases *(pages L21–L22)*

Recognizing natural order in sentences *(pages L24–L25)*

Recognizing inverted order in sentences *(page L25)*

Recognizing understood *you* as the subject *(page L26)*

Diagraming subjects and verbs *(pages L40–L41)*

 **Posttest**

Write the letter of the term that correctly identifies the underlined word or words in each sentence.

EXAMPLE **1.** Raccoons <u>look cute but have bad tempers.</u>
  1 A simple subject
      B complete subject
      C simple predicate
      D complete predicate

ANSWER **1 D**

1. <u>John</u> and <u>Marsha</u> came home from the movies.

2. A small, fat <u>raccoon</u> had broken into their very clean kitchen.

3. It <u>was</u> happily <u>going</u> through their cupboards.

4. <u>What a cute little creature it was!</u>

5. It <u>opened</u> a door and <u>pulled</u> out pots and pans.

6. <u>This curious and mischievous animal</u> was making a mess of the room.

7. <u>Now they wanted it out of the house immediately.</u>

8. They <u>opened</u> the back door and <u>banged</u> a broom near it.

9. <u>Clearly was not at all pleased with their lack of hospitality.</u>

10. The raccoon <u>knocked over all the flowerpots on their back porch.</u>

1 A simple subject
   B compound subject
   C sentence fragment
   D compound verb

2 A simple subject
   B complete subject
   C compound subject
   D simple predicate

3 A complete predicate
   B compound verb
   C verb phrase
   D sentence fragment

4 A imperative sentence
   B interrogative sentence
   C exclamatory sentence
   D declarative sentence

5 A complete predicate
   B compound verb
   C simple predicate
   D sentence fragment

6 A sentence fragment
   B compound subject
   C simple subject
   D complete subject

7 A declarative sentence
   B exclamatory sentence
   C sentence fragment
   D inverted order

8 A verb phrase
   B complete predicate
   C simple predicate
   D compound verb

9 A inverted order
   B sentence fragment
   C interrogative sentence
   D imperative sentence

10 A simple predicate
   B compound predicate
   C complete predicate
   D verb phrase

CHAPTER 2

Nouns and Pronouns

 **Pretest**

Directions
Read the passage and write the letter of the word or group of words that correctly completes each sentence.

EXAMPLE   In the 1800s, many __(1)__ headed west.
1 A them
   B pioneer
   C people
   D everyone

ANSWER   **1 C**

In the 1840s, __(1)__, a sixty-six-year-old widow, was enthusiastic about going west. __(2)__ was so determined to go that she lined up her ox team by __(3)__. With other members of __(4)__ family, she set out on the Oregon Trail. Unfortunately, __(5)__ told them to take the wrong path through the mountains. They continued on the __(6)__ until they realized it was not taking them in the right direction. Somehow she and her sick brother-in-law found __(7)__ stranded alone in the wilderness. Her brother-in-law could barely walk, but she helped __(8)__ to keep moving until they were found. __(9)__ was amazing because she had a lame hip and broken arm. Her arm hurt, but she bandaged __(10)__ and did not complain.

1 **A** she
   B woman
   C tabitha Brown
   D Tabitha Brown

2 **A** They
   B She
   C Her
   D It

3 **A** her
   B them
   C herself
   D themselves

4 **A** herself
   B its
   C her
   D their

5 **A** someone
   B anyone
   C another
   D both

6 **A** mountains
   B oxen
   C trails
   D trail

7 **A** himself
   B themselves
   C her
   D them

8 **A** his
   B himself
   C he
   D him

9 **A** Some
   B These
   C This
   D He

10 **A** it
   B them
   C her
   D those

Attributed to Tamura Suio. *Ladies' Pastimes in Spring and Autumn,* eighteenth century.
One handscroll, ink and color on paper, 12³/₈ by 96¹/₁₆ inches. The New York Public Library.

Describe How would you describe the overall movement of the picture—as calming or exciting?

Analyze Where does the artist use repetition in the picture? What do you think the purpose of the repetition is? Why do you think the artist used watercolor and ink to draw this picture? What makes you think so?

Interpret What social class do you think these women belong to? Why? Do you think the artist is critical of the women's activities? Why or why not? What does this painting tell you about the lives of women of their class in eighteenth-century Japan?

Judge Think about how an artist in modern America would paint a scene of women's pastimes. How might it be different from this painting?

At the end of this chapter, you will use the artwork to stimulate ideas for writing.

Nouns

Like people, words have jobs. A job is what someone or something does. Each word in a sentence does a particular job. Each job is called a **part of speech.** In English there are eight different parts of speech, as shown in the following list.

THE EIGHT PARTS OF SPEECH	
noun (names)	**adverb** (describes, limits)
pronoun (replaces)	**preposition** (relates)
verb (states action or being)	**conjunction** (connects)
adjective (describes, limits)	**interjection** (expresses strong feeling)

Nouns are the most common of the parts of speech. Sometimes nouns are called naming words because they name people, places, things, and ideas.

A **noun** is a word that names a person, place, thing, or idea.

NOUNS	
PEOPLE	Sarah, Jake, doctor, boys, team, chefs, Mr. Harrison, Ms. Chen
PLACES	home, hospitals, forest, zoo, Philadelphia, Yellow River, Greece
CONCRETE THINGS	pen, whistles, blanket, animals, sky, earth, bells (These things can be seen, heard, or touched.)

ABSTRACT THINGS	memory, dreams, minutes, headache, life, heat, science, summer (These things cannot be seen, heard, or touched.)
IDEAS AND QUALITIES	friendship, honesty, kindness, freedom, hope, courage, ambition, love, independence, peace, respect

CONNECT TO SPEAKING AND WRITING

Your writing will be more lively and interesting if you substitute a specific noun like *boulder, pebble,* or *gem* for a general noun like *stone.* Read the following sentences and compare the images each brings to mind.

GENERAL   The **water** washed across the **rock.**
SPECIFIC   The **river** washed over the **boulder.**

GENERAL   The **bird** landed in the tall **tree.**
SPECIFIC   The **robin** landed in the tall **pine.**

PRACTICE YOUR SKILLS

● Check Your Understanding
Finding Nouns

Contemporary Life **Write each noun. (There are thirty nouns.)**

1. The class went on a trip to Colorado.
2. The students slept in a tent under the tall trees.
3. Early one morning a deer came near the tent.
4. The campers fished in the river.
5. Margo and Anna caught four trout and a turtle.

6. The girls put the turtle back in the water.

7. Mr. Campbell and Margo cleaned the fish.

8. Logan and Tiffany cooked dinner over the fire.

9. The fish, potatoes, and beans tasted great!

10. The students agreed that the trip was fun.

● Connect to the Writing Process: Revising
Writing with Specific Nouns

Write two specific nouns for each general noun in the list below. Then write ten sentences, using your specific nouns.

11. city   **16.** country

12. game   **17.** food

13. sport   **18.** place

14. toy   **19.** shoe

15. person   **20.** book

▶ Common and Proper Nouns

Some nouns are the general names of people, places, and things. Nouns of this kind are called **common nouns.** Other nouns are the names of particular people, places, and things. These nouns are called **proper nouns.** A proper noun always begins with a capital letter.

COMMON AND PROPER NOUNS	
COMMON NOUNS	girl, state, team, building, day, teacher, organization
PROPER NOUNS	Sophie, Tennessee, San Francisco Giants, Empire State Building, Saturday, Mr. Green, Girl Scouts of America

Some proper nouns like *Empire State Building, San Francisco Giants,* and *Mr. Green* include more than one word. *Empire State Building* is still only one noun because it is the name of *one* building. *San Francisco Giants* is one noun because it is the name of *one* team. *Mr. Green* is only one noun because it is the name of *one* person.

You can learn more about the capitalization of proper nouns on pages L407–L420.

PRACTICE YOUR SKILLS

● Check Your Understanding
Finding Common and Proper Nouns

General Interest | **Make two columns on your paper. Write the common nouns in one column and the proper nouns in the other column.**

The Statue of Liberty was a gift to the Americans from the citizens of France. The huge lady stands in New York Harbor. Many tourists from across the globe visit the statue each year. People climb up stairs inside the statue and reach the crown. Visitors look at New York City from the twenty-five windows there. The statue has become a symbol of freedom to Americans and other people around the world.

● Check Your Understanding
Supplying Nouns

Contemporary Life | **Write a common or proper noun for each blank.**

1. At the skating rink, I saw ▓ and ▓.

2. I always bring my own ▓ and ▓ to the rink.

3. The rink is located near ▓ and ▓.

4. At the concession stand, I bought ▓ and ▓ for my friends.

5. I like to skate on Wednesday nights with ▓ and ▓.

6. Jackson thinks the best days to skate are ▓ and ▓.

7. Two other hobbies I enjoy on weekends are ▓ and ▓.

8. Two friends with whom I like to do things are ▓ and ▓.

9. Qualities I admire about them are their ▓ and ▓.

10. Someday I would like to be a ▓ or a ▓.

● Connect to the Writing Process: Editing
Capitalizing Proper Nouns

Write the proper nouns from the following paragraphs, beginning each with a capital letter.

In 1929, martin luther king, jr. was born in atlanta, georgia. This great american became pastor of the dexter avenue baptist church in montgomery, alabama. In 1955, he and other African American leaders led the famous bus boycott in that city.

In 1963, dr. king delivered his most famous speech in washington, d.c. More than 250,000 people gathered to hear him speak from the steps of the lincoln memorial.

APPLY TO WRITING

Friendly Letter: *Nouns*

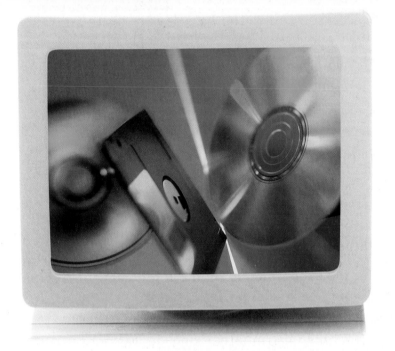

Your school is building a time capsule that will be buried for one hundred years. The students of the future will dig up the capsule to learn about the times before they were born. You have been asked to include two objects that symbolize the life of a young person today. You must also write a letter to the future students telling what the two items are and why you felt it was important to include them in a time capsule. After you finish your letter, read it and correct any errors. Then underline all the nouns you used in the letter.

Geography Topic

Make two columns on your paper. Write the proper nouns in one column and the common nouns in the other column.

Denmark is a small country on the North Sea. The country is on a peninsula called Jutland that sticks out into the sea. In addition to this area, the country also includes 2 large and 483 smaller islands.

Because of the country's location, many people work on the sea as fishers. There are many fishing villages in Denmark. The nation exports cod, herring, eel, and other fish to foreign countries.

Copenhagen is the capital of Denmark. It is the main center of industry. Aside from food products, the Danes also produce chemicals, metals, and machinery.

Tourism is also important to the Danish economy. Millions of tourists from Europe and around the world visit the country each year.

Denmark is considered a Scandinavian country. North of Denmark are two other Scandinavian countries, Norway and Sweden.

Pronouns

A **pronoun** is a word that takes the place of one or more nouns.

The second sentence in each pair of examples that follow is shorter and clearer because pronouns have been substituted for nouns.

> The quarterback injured **the quarterback's** knee when the **quarterback** was tackled.
>
> The quarterback injured **his** knee when **he** was tackled.
>
> At the concession stand, Felicia asked David if **David** would buy **Felicia** some popcorn.
>
> At the concession stand, Felicia asked David if **he** would buy **her** some popcorn.

Pronoun Antecedents

In the preceding example about Felicia and David, the pronoun *her* replaces *Felicia,* and the pronoun *he* replaces *David.* The word or group of words that a pronoun replaces, or refers to, is called its **antecedent.**

An antecedent often comes before the pronoun. It may be in the same sentence as a pronoun or in another sentence. In the following examples, arrows point from the pronouns to their antecedents.

> Felicia always supports **her** team.
>
> No one caught the football. **It** bounced into the end zone.

CONNECT TO SPEAKING AND WRITING

It's always important that your listeners and readers know to what or to whom your pronouns refer.

Unclear antecedents can cause a great deal of confusion. If the antecedent of a pronoun is unclear, it is best not to use the pronoun or to reword the sentence. This will make your meaning more easily understood.

UNCLEAR ANTECEDENT	Mike told Josh that his uniform was stained.
	(Whose uniform was stained, Mike's or Josh's?)
	Mom drove Kelli to the game, but she didn't go in.
	(Who did not go in to the game, Mom or Kelli?)
CLEAR	Mike told Josh that Josh's uniform was stained.
	Mom drove Kelli to the game, but Mom didn't go in.

You can learn more about pronouns and antecedents on pages L302–L305.

PRACTICE YOUR SKILLS

● Check Your Understanding
Finding Antecedents

 Write the antecedent or antecedents of each underlined pronoun.

Contemporary Life

1. The whole town turned out to support <u>its</u> football team.

2. A cheerleader roused the fans with <u>her</u> loud and spirited yell.

3. The referees blew <u>their</u> whistles when halftime began.

4. The teams ran toward <u>their</u> locker rooms.

5. The coach said, "Listen to <u>me</u>, players!"

6. The running back kept <u>his</u> eyes on the coach and listened carefully.

7. Meanwhile, on the field, the band members found <u>their</u> places.

8. One band member pounded <u>his</u> large bass drum.

9. The band leader called <u>her</u> group to attention.

10. The fans watched both bands perform <u>their</u> music.

Personal Pronouns

Personal pronouns are the kind of pronouns you use most often. Pronouns are divided into several groups, as shown in the following chart.

PERSONAL PRONOUNS	
FIRST PERSON	(speaker)
SINGULAR	I, me, my, mine
PLURAL	we, us, our, ours
SECOND PERSON	(person spoken to)
SINGULAR	you, your, yours
PLURAL	you, your, yours
THIRD PERSON	(person or thing spoken about)
SINGULAR	he, him, his, she, her, hers, it, its
PLURAL	they, them, their, theirs

Do not confuse *its* with *it's* or *your* with *you're*. *It's* is a contraction of the words *it is*. *You're* is a contraction of the words *you are*.

FIRST-PERSON PRONOUNS	**I** forgot to bring **my** water bottle with **me.**
	We were thirsty after **our** long bike ride yesterday.
SECOND-PERSON PRONOUNS	Did **you** remember to bring **your** water bottle?
	Yours is on the kitchen table.
THIRD-PERSON PRONOUNS	**He** told **her** about **his** bicycle accident.
	They haven't repaired **their** bicycles yet.

Reflexive Pronouns

The suffix *–self* or *–selves* can be added to some personal pronouns. The pronouns that are formed are called **reflexive pronouns.** These pronouns are used to refer to a noun or another pronoun.

REFLEXIVE PRONOUNS	
SINGULAR	myself, yourself, himself, herself, itself
PLURAL	ourselves, yourselves, themselves

Brooke helped **herself** to the tools in the garage.
(The reflexive pronoun *herself* refers to Brooke.)

We committed **ourselves** to finishing the project.
(The reflexive pronoun *ourselves* refers to *We.*)

Never use reflexive pronouns by themselves. They always must have an antecedent to refer to. Also, never use *hisself* or *theirselves.*

PRACTICE YOUR SKILLS

● Check Your Understanding
Finding Personal Pronouns

Contemporary Life   **Write each personal pronoun.**

1. Brooke told her mom that she was helping Jack.

2. Jack was fixing his bike.

3. Jack offered Brooke some of his mother's apple pie.

4. As she ate the pie, Brooke watched Jack work.

5. Jack told himself that he could fix the bike.

6. When Jack fell while riding his bike, some of the paint on it was damaged.

7. The pair knew that they could easily repaint Jack's bike.

8. Then Brooke and Jack worked on her bike.

9. Jack's bike with its new paint stood in the corner.

10. Brooke hoped her bike would look shiny too.

● Connect to the Writing Process: Revising
Using Personal Pronouns

Rewrite the following paragraph, replacing the underlined nouns with personal pronouns.

Alyssa and Alyssa's friends love to visit the zoo whenever the zoo is open. When Alyssa and Alyssa's friends go to the zoo, Alyssa and Alyssa's friends make Alyssa and Alyssa's friends' way to the reptile house.

APPLY TO WRITING

The Writer's Craft: *Analyzing the Use of Personal Pronouns*

Professional writers use personal pronouns, just as you do when you write. Read the following passage, and then follow the directions.

> In 1864 Caddie Woodlawn was eleven, and as wild a little tomboy as ever ran the woods of western Wisconsin. She was the despair of her mother and of her elder sister, Clara. But her father watched her with a little shine of pride in his eyes, and her brothers accepted her as one of themselves without a question. Indeed, Tom, who was two years older, and Warren, who was two years younger than Caddie, needed Caddie to link them together into an inseparable trio. Together they got in and out of more scrapes and adventures than any one of them could have imagined alone. And in those pioneer days, Wisconsin offered plenty of opportunities for adventure to three wide-eyed, red-headed youngsters.
>
> —*Carol Ryrie Brink*, Caddie Woodlawn

- Write the personal and reflexive pronouns in the passage. Next to the pronouns, write their antecedents. Circle the reflexive pronoun.

- Whom is this passage mostly about? How do you know that?

- How would this paragraph be different if Brink had used Caddie's name over and over?

 Indefinite Pronouns

Another group of pronouns is called **indefinite pronouns.** They are called indefinite pronouns because they usually do not have definite antecedents like personal pronouns do. Instead, indefinite pronouns usually refer to unnamed people or things.

COMMON INDEFINITE PRONOUNS			
all	both	few	nothing
another	each	many	one
any	either	most	several
anybody	everybody	neither	some
anyone	everyone	none	someone
anything	everything	no one	something

INDEFINITE PRONOUNS	**Many** of those dogs are gentle.
	My aunt has **several** of those dogs.
	Everyone at the picnic saw the dogs.

 Demonstrative Pronouns

Demonstrative pronouns are useful pronouns because they point out certain people or things.

DEMONSTRATIVE PRONOUNS			
this	that	these	those

DEMONSTRATIVE PRONOUNS	**That** is the cutest dog I've ever seen! Have you ever seen **this** before?

You can learn about demonstrative pronouns being used as adjectives on page L122.

PRACTICE YOUR SKILLS

 Check Your Understanding
Finding Indefinite and Demonstrative Pronouns

Contemporary Life **Write each indefinite and demonstrative pronoun. Label each one either *I* for indefinite or *D* for demonstrative.**

1. That is a good brand of dog food.

2. Most of these have plenty of nutrition for an active dog.

3. My dog will not eat any of the dry foods.

4. Rover always eats that brand of canned food.

5. Someone in our neighborhood owns a white German shepherd.

6. Everybody wonders how often the white dog gets fed.

7. What makes them wonder about that?

8. Both of my dogs could have beautiful coats.

9. One of my pets is a show dog.

10. Neither of them is purebred.

Connect to the Writing Process: Drafting
Writing Sentences with Indefinite and Demonstrative Pronouns

Write six sentences, using the following indefinite and demonstrative pronouns.

11. either	13. any	15. nothing
12. this	14. these	16. that

APPLY TO WRITING

E-mail Message: *Pronouns*

A friend in another city has written to you asking for advice. She wants to go on a class trip to Washington, D.C., but her parents have told her that she must raise part of the money herself. Write an E-mail message to your friend telling her good ways that people your age can earn extra money. As you write, use a variety of nouns and pronouns to make your writing more interesting and less repetitive. After you finish, underline the nouns and pronouns you used.

QuickCheck Mixed Practice

Contemporary Life **Write each personal pronoun and its antecedent.**

1. Mrs. Martinez told the class, "Today we will study the Middle Ages."

2. The teacher said that the Middle Ages was her favorite topic.

3. Ian asked Mrs. Martinez, "Do you know if children went to school back then?"

4. The teacher said that some children were educated, but that they were usually male and wealthy.

5. Mrs. Martinez told her students, "Many of you would not have been allowed an education back then."

6. Joni said, "That doesn't seem fair to me."

7. Mrs. Martinez asked the students if they would like to live in a castle.

8. Ian said that he would like to.

9. Mrs. Martinez explained, "A castle was damp and drafty. The temperature was often warmer outside than inside its walls."

10. The students agreed that they appreciated the warmth of a modern house.

 **QuickCheck** Mixed Practice

Contemporary Life

Make two columns on your paper. Write the nouns in one column and the pronouns in the other column.

1. On Sundays I read the comic strips in the newspaper.

2. My grandfather and I read them together.

3. My grandfather tells me about the comic books from his childhood.

4. Grandpa still has a huge collection of them.

5. He has the original book that featured Batman as a character.

6. His treasury of comics is worth thousands of dollars.

7. Sometimes Grandpa lets me and my friends look at his collection.

8. The comic books are stored in a dark closet.

9. They are wrapped in plastic bags for protection.

10. Everyone is excited to see the books.

Finding Nouns

Write each noun.

1. Most clams could fit in your hand.
2. The largest clams, however, weigh about five hundred pounds!
3. One such mollusk could provide a meal for several families.
4. Their shells are big enough to use for beds and bathtubs.
5. These giants are found in the Indian Ocean and in the Pacific Ocean near Australia.

Finding Pronouns and Their Antecedents

Write each personal pronoun and its antecedent.

1. The coaches gave their teams a pep talk before the game.
2. The team's uniforms were worn out. The school wasn't able to replace them.
3. Laura's shirt had a big mud stain on its back.
4. Max and I earned the money for new uniforms ourselves.
5. Has Timothy worn his new uniform yet?

Finding Pronouns

Label each pronoun, using the following abbreviations. There are 25 pronouns.

personal = *pers.*   reflexive = *ref.*
indefinite = *ind.*   demonstrative = *dem.*

1. Have you ever seen a shooting star?
2. Everyone saw Tommy and his friend at the mall.

3. Theirs is the car with all the luxury options.

4. Everything in our house is broken, and no one can fix anything.

5. Turtles carry their houses with them wherever they go.

6. My dad chose that himself!

7. Someone left this in the gym after practice.

8. Your car is blocking the Smiths' and ours, and neither of us can get out.

9. Those can't be the dishes we have to wash!

10. A beaver steers with its tail as it swims through water.

Using Nouns and Pronouns

Write ten sentences that follow the directions below. (The sentences may include other nouns and pronouns besides those listed, and the sentences may come in any order.) Write about one of the following topics or a topic of your own choice: why you like one season of the year best or why you dislike one season most.

Write a sentence that . . .

1. includes nouns that name a person, a place, and a thing.

2. includes a noun that names an idea or a quality.

3. includes a common noun that names a person.

4. includes a proper noun that names a person.

5. includes a common noun that names a place.

6. includes a proper noun that names a place.

7. includes several personal pronouns.

8. includes a reflexive pronoun.

9. includes one or two indefinite pronouns.

10. includes a demonstrative pronoun.

When you are finished, put an _N_ over each noun and a _P_ over each pronoun.

Language and *Self-Expression*

In Japan it was a sign of high birth for men and women to be accomplished in brush painting and writing poetry. The artist who painted this painting was showing what he felt were suitable pastimes for wealthy women. What activities does he approve of?

The members of your family may enjoy pastimes similar to the ones shown in the painting—and ones that are quite different. If your family went to live in a space station on the moon, what recreational items would they take to amuse themselves? Write a few paragraphs telling why you chose these things, using a variety of pronouns.

Prewriting Make a chart showing each family member and the activities he or she enjoys. Decide how you will group information—by family member, by kind of activity, or in another way.

Drafting Use your chart to help you make your list and write your explanatory paragraphs. Create an introductory sentence or sentences that explain why you have written these paragraphs.

Revising Read aloud or show what you have written to a classmate. Ask whether the information is organized in a way that makes sense. Check for sentences that are out of place. Be sure that you have chosen the appropriate pronouns.

Editing Check your paragraphs for errors in punctuation and spelling. If you use the proper trade names of games or other toys, be sure to capitalize them correctly.

Publishing Prepare a final copy and give each family member a copy to look at as you discuss your list.

A **noun** is a word that names a person, place, thing, or idea.

Kinds of Nouns

A **common noun** names any person, place, or thing. *(pages L53–L54)*

A **proper noun** names a particular person, place, or thing. *(pages L53–L54)*

A **compound noun** is made up of more than one word. *(page L54)*

A **pronoun** is a word that takes the place of one or more nouns.

An **antecedent** is the noun that a pronoun refers to or replaces.

Kinds of Pronouns

A **reflexive pronoun** refers to or emphasizes another noun or pronoun. *(page L61)*

An **indefinite pronoun** refers to unnamed people, places, things, or ideas. *(page L64)*

A **demonstrative pronoun** points out a specific person, place, thing, or idea. *(pages L64–L65)*

Other Information About Nouns and Pronouns

Recognizing the eight parts of speech *(page L51)*

Capitalizing proper nouns *(pages L53–L54)*

Using personal pronouns *(pages L60–L61)*

Posttest

Directions

Read the passage and write the letter of the word or group of words that correctly completes each sentence.

EXAMPLE
    _(1)_ saw a traditional hula dance on our visit to Hawaii.

    1 A They
       B Few
       C We
       D Ourselves

ANSWER
    1 C

Native Hawaiians keep _(1)_ heritage alive by telling ancient stories and performing the dances that go along with _(2)_ . In the past, an *apo* was _(3)_ who could chant a story two or three hours long after hearing _(4)_ only once. Short chants were always accompanied by music and dancing. Today's dancers do not all wear the grass skirts that _(5)_ see in pictures. A traditional female dancer usually dresses _(6)_ in a long, loose cotton dress. A male dancer is likely to wear clacking shells around _(7)_ ankle. _(8)_ have garlands of flowers around their necks. _(9)_ are called *leis*, and a dancer may put on _(10)_ at once.

1 **A** his
   B any
   C their
   D its

2 **A** them
   B it
   C both
   D themselves

3 **A** many
   B her
   C someone
   D those

4 **A** them
   B it
   C him
   D all

5 **A** we
   B they
   C anybody
   D he

6 **A** themselves
   B her
   C them
   D herself

7 **A** their
   B his
   C all
   D your

8 **A** He
   B Both
   C Anybody
   D No one

9 **A** That
   B It
   C These
   D Them

10 **A** theirs
   B their
   C each
   D several

CHAPTER 3

Verbs and Complements

 **Pretest**

Directions
Write the letter of the term that correctly identifies the underlined word or words in each sentence.

EXAMPLE **1.** Alison <u>was</u> the first one in the pool.
　　1 A action verb
　　　B helping verb
　　　C verb phrase
　　　D linking verb

ANSWER　　**1 D**

1. Dylan wore bright green swimming <u>trunks</u>.

2. Four girls <u>were playing</u> water polo.

3. Elena threw <u>Kayla</u> the ball.

4. Mariah <u>dove</u> into the pool.

5. Her dive was really a <u>belly-flop</u>.

6. She splashed <u>Dylan</u> and his <u>friend</u>.

7. They <u>sat</u> in the warm sun beside the pool.

8. They <u>were</u> too hot to mind.

9. Kayla invited <u>him</u> and <u>Brandon</u> for a game of water polo.

10. The boys were enthusiastic <u>players</u>.

1 **A** indirect object
  B direct object
  C predicate nominative
  D antecedent

2 **A** verb phrase
  B intransitive verb
  C helping verb
  D linking verb

3 **A** common noun
  B direct object
  C predicate nominative
  D indirect object

4 **A** intransitive verb
  B transitive verb
  C linking verb
  D helping verb

5 **A** direct object
  B predicate nominative
  C indirect object
  D action verb

6 **A** indirect object
  B direct object
  C compound indirect object
  D compound direct object

7 **A** helping verb
  B linking verb
  C action verb
  D transitive verb

8 **A** transitive verb
  B action verb
  C helping verb
  D linking verb

9 **A** compound direct object
  B compound indirect object
  C compound predicate nominative
  D antecedents

10 **A** direct object
  B predicate nominative
  C indirect object
  D action verb

Honoré Daumier. *Street Show*, ca. 1868.
Black chalk and watercolor on laid paper, 14⅜ by 10¹/₁₆ inches. The Metropolitan Museum of Art.

Describe   What do you see in this image? What kind of lines does the artist use?

Analyze   Why do you think the artist drew the image as he did? What colors stand out in contrast to the background color? How does the artist create motion?

Interpret   What are the people doing in this scene? What makes you think so?

Judge   The artist captures the energy of a street performance through his use of line. Do you think the artist sketched his drawing during the street show or later in the privacy of his own studio?

At the end of this chapter, you will use this artwork to stimulate ideas for writing.

Action Verbs

A group of words cannot be a sentence unless it includes a verb.

A verb is a word used to express an action or a state of being.

Some verbs are called action verbs because they most often show action or movement.

An **action verb** tells what action a subject is performing.

To find an action verb, first find the subject. Then ask yourself *What did the subject do?*

> The bat **flew** silently across the dark sky.
> (The subject is *bat*. What did the bat do? *Flew* is the action verb.)

Most action verbs show physical action, but some show mental action. A few verbs such as *have* and *own* show possession or ownership.

PHYSICAL ACTION	A bat **lives** in our barn.
	It **clings** to the rafters during the day.
MENTAL ACTION	Some people **believe** bats are dangerous.
	They **fear** the small mammals.
OWNERSHIP	Bats **have** poor vision during the day.
	They **possess** a unique type of vision.

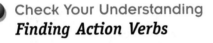
Have you ever listened to a radio announcer give a play-by-play description of a baseball game? Even though players are constantly *throwing* the ball, an announcer seldom uses the verb *throw*. Announcers know that overused verbs like *throw* do not create a clear picture in the minds of their listeners. As a result, announcers are constantly using colorful, action-packed substitutes such as *hurl, fire, propel,* and *thrust.*

When you speak and write, always look for these kinds of specific verbs. Stretch your mind and your vocabulary to find substitutes for overused verbs, or look in the dictionary or thesaurus.

You can learn about regular and irregular verbs on pages L233–L250.

PRACTICE YOUR SKILLS

● Check Your Understanding

Finding Action Verbs

Science Topic   **Write each action verb.**

1. Many people misunderstand bats.

2. Only the vampire bat drinks blood.

3. Most bats eat insects or fruit.

4. Bats see very well at night.

5. They also possess a special type of radar.

6. Bats have very strong wings.

7. They sleep upside down.

8. Their hind feet hold objects tightly.

9. Many farmers like bats.

10. Some bats devour harmful insects on a farm.

11. Bats live in many places.

12. The city of Austin, Texas, has a colony of bats under a bridge.

13. At sunset these Mexican freetail bats emerge.

14. They swirl out in a great cloud.

15. The bats stay only through the summer.

16. Most of the colony migrates south in the winter.

17. A few stay behind.

18. These few bats reside under the Congress Avenue Bridge year round.

19. The other bats return to Austin in the spring.

20. People in that city appreciate their bat colony.

● Check Your Understanding
Supplying Action Verbs

Contemporary Life **Write an action verb for each blank.**

21. All birds ▦ feathers.

22. The blue jay ▦ from tree to tree.

23. The robin ▦ the ground for seeds.

24. The chickadees ▦ their nests from bits of grass.

25. We ▦ birds through a good pair of binoculars.

● Connect to the Writing Process: Revising
Using Specific Verbs

Rewrite each sentence, replacing the underlined verb with a more colorful, action-packed verb.

26. Hawks <u>fly</u> overhead.

27. A kingfisher <u>dropped</u> toward the water's surface.

28. That eagle <u>got</u> a fish!

29. Rain <u>fell</u> on the happy ducks.

30. The whippoorwill <u>sounded</u> its mournful tune.

Communicate Your Ideas

APPLY TO WRITING
Description: *Action Verbs*

Do you enjoy reading comic books about superheroes? Imagine that you have just been hired by a comic book company. Your first assignment is to create a new superhero to appear in a future edition of the comic book. Write a description of your superhero. What does he or she look like? What special powers does he or she possess? In order to convince your boss to publish stories featuring your character, use specific, action-packed verbs in your description. Underline five verbs you used in your work.

Helping Verbs

The verb of a sentence is not always one word. The main verb can be written with **helping verbs**, or auxiliary verbs. The main verb plus any helping verbs is called a verb phrase.

A **verb phrase** is a main verb plus one or more helping verbs.

The following is a list of common helping verbs.

COMMON HELPING VERBS	
be	am, is, are, was, were, be, being, been
have	has, have, had
do	do, does, did
OTHERS	may, might, must, can, could, shall, should, will, would

In the following sentences, the verb phrases are in **bold** type.

My dad **has promised** us a parrot.
We **have been asking** for one for a long time.

Sometimes a verb phrase is interrupted by other words.

I **could**n't **sleep** last night.
We **are** really **getting** a parrot today!

To find a verb phrase in a question, make the question a statement.

QUESTION   Have you owned a parrot before?
STATEMENT   You **have owned** a parrot before.

Remember that even though it is more than one word, the verb phrase is called a verb.

PRACTICE YOUR SKILLS

● **Check Your Understanding**
Finding Verb Phrases

General
Interest **Write each verb phrase.**

1. Have you ever listened to a parrot?
2. Actually, parrots don't talk.
3. These beautiful birds can only imitate human sounds.
4. Many birds can mimic various sounds.
5. Some can even copy the songs of other birds.
6. Only the parrot, the raven, and the mynah bird can actually copy human speech.
7. People must train these birds very slowly.
8. New words must be repeated over and over again.
9. Eventually these birds will learn the new words.
10. They will never forget the words.

 **QuickCheck** Mixed Practice

Music
Topic **Write each verb or verb phrase.**

1. A guitar's sound is produced by the vibration of strings.
2. Guitars can be constructed from many different woods.
3. Different types of wood are used for the front, back, and neck of the instrument.
4. Guitars are related to the ancient lute.

5. Modern guitars usually have six strings.

6. Some are built with twelve strings.

7. The body of a guitar curves inward on the sides.

8. The strings of this instrument are usually made of metal or plastic.

9. The guitar appeared in Spain as early as the 1100s.

10. Music lovers know the quality of Spanish classical guitars.

11. In the United States, guitars are heard in many kinds of music.

12. Rock, folk, jazz, and classical musicians play the guitar.

13. This instrument can be plucked with the fingers or with picks.

14. Some guitarists strum a flat pick against the strings.

15. Other stringed instruments include the banjo, the mandolin, and the ukulele.

Direct Objects

The following groups of words each have a subject and a verb but do not make complete statements.

I want.   We took.

Another word, called a **complement**, is needed in each of the preceding examples. It will make the meaning of the words in the example complete.

I want **rice**.   We took a **bite**.

A direct object is one kind of complement. A direct object always follows an action verb.

A **direct object** is a noun or pronoun that answers the question *What?* or *Whom?* after an action verb.

To find a direct object in a sentence, first find the subject and the action verb. Then ask yourself *What?* or *Whom?* after the verb. In the following examples, subjects are underlined once, and verbs are underlined twice.

DIRECT OBJECTS

⌐d.o.⌐
We studied **Japan** in my geography class.

(We studied *what? Japan* is the direct object.)

⌐ d.o. ⌐
I really enjoyed that **chapter!**

(I enjoyed *what? Chapter* is the direct object.)

⌐ d.o. ⌐
The video showed Japanese **farmers** at work.

(The video showed *whom? Farmers* is the direct object.)

To find a direct object in a question, change the question into a statement.

QUESTION

Have you read that book about Japanese culture?

STATEMENT

⌐d.o.⌐
You have read that **book** about Japanese culture.

Two or more direct objects following the same verb are called a **compound direct object.**

People in Japan eat **fish** and **rice**.

┌d.o.┐   ┌d.o.┐

(People eat *what?* The compound direct object is *fish* and *rice*.)

PRACTICE YOUR SKILLS

● Check Your Understanding
Finding Direct Objects

Geography Topic

Write the direct object or compound direct object in each sentence.

1. Japan has very little land for farms.

2. Huge mountains cover the islands.

3. The Japanese use the available soil to the maximum.

4. They plant only the best seeds.

5. They spread fertilizers on the fields.

6. They use tractors and other helpful equipment.

7. Farmers grow rice and other crops.

8. Modern Japanese agriculture includes dairy farms.

9. The sea also provides the Japanese with another source of food.

10. The people of Japan raise fish in sea farms.

11. The Japanese eat much fish and other seafood.

12. Fish contains protein for healthy diets.

13. The Japanese also raise seaweed for food.

14. They wrap seaweed around rice and vegetables, fruit, or raw fish.

15. Japanese restaurants serve this special dish.

16.–20. Write five sentences about your favorite hobby. Be sure that each sentence contains a direct object. Underline the direct object.

● Indirect Objects

Many action verbs have direct objects. Some action verbs also have a second complement called an indirect object.

> An **indirect object** is a noun or pronoun that answers the question *To or for whom?* or *To or for what?* after an action verb.

To find an indirect object in a sentence, first find the direct object. Then ask yourself *To whom? For whom? To what?* or *For what?* about the direct object. Notice in the following examples that an indirect object always comes *before* a direct object.

INDIRECT
OBJECTS

$\overbrace{\quad}^{\text{i.o.}}$ $\overbrace{\quad}^{\text{d.o.}}$
We gave the new **student** a tour of the school.

(We gave a tour *to whom?* *Student* is the indirect object.)

$\overbrace{\quad}^{\text{i.o.}}$ $\overbrace{\quad}^{\text{d.o.}}$
Marissa bought **Fernando** a pencil.

(Marissa bought a pencil *for whom?* *Fernando* is the indirect object.)

To find an indirect object in a question, change the question into a statement.

QUESTION	Did Marissa show him the library?

STATEMENT   Marissa did show **him** the library.
$\overbrace{}^{\text{i.o.}}$ $\overbrace{}^{\text{d.o.}}$

(Marissa did show *to whom? Him* is the indirect object.)

QUESTION	Has the principal given him a student handbook?

STATEMENT   The principal has given **him** a student

handbook.

Two or more indirect objects following the same verb are called a **compound indirect object.**

Fernando told **Marissa** and **me** stories about Peru.

(He told stories *to whom? Marissa* and *me* are the compound indirect object.)

Remember that in order to have an indirect object, a sentence must also have a direct object.

PRACTICE YOUR SKILLS

● Check Your Understanding
Finding Indirect Objects

Contemporary Life **Write each indirect object or compound indirect object in each sentence.**

1. Our class gave Fernando a warm welcome.

2. The teacher read us an article about Fernando's country.

3. Fernando taught Joshua and Marissa some words in Spanish.

4. He told the class many interesting facts about Peru.

5. Fernando handed me a thick book with beautiful pictures of the Andes Mountains.

6. I read the class an interesting part about the Inca civilization.

7. Our whole class sent Fernando's friends some letters.

8. Fernando's friends in Peru wrote us a nice postcard.

9. They sent us a small piece of wool from an alpaca.

10. We showed the other sixth graders our Peruvian wool.

11. For centuries the alpaca has provided the South Americans beautiful wool for their clothes.

12. Fernando's mother brought each student a piece of colorful cloth.

13. She told us fascinating details about Peruvian textiles.

14. Fernando's mother supplied us with woolen thread for our loom.

15. We sent her a thank-you note.

● Connect to the Writing Process: Drafting
Writing Sentences with Direct Objects

16.–20. Write five sentences about birthdays. Be sure that each sentence has an indirect object. Underline the indirect object.

Communicate Your Ideas

APPLY TO WRITING

Letter to the Editor: *Direct Objects and Indirect Objects*

Your school has received a large donation of money from an unknown person. Because there are so many things that your school needs, the principal is not sure what to buy with the money. Think about what your school needs. Ask other students in your class. Then write a letter to the editor of the school newspaper suggesting three ways the principal could use the donation to improve your school. Be sure to list convincing reasons.

As you write, be sure that you include at least three sentences that have direct and indirect objects. After you have finished writing, read through your work, correcting any errors you find. Underline three sentences with direct and indirect objects and label these words in the sentences.

 QuickCheck Mixed Practice

Sports Topic

Write each complement. Label each one as either a *direct object* or an *indirect object*. (Some sentences do not have indirect objects.)

1. The pitcher wiped his hands.

2. He gave the catcher a wink.

3. The catcher punched his glove with his hand.

4. The batter gripped the bat tightly.

5. He gave the pitcher a long, hard stare.

6. Then, with the speed of lightning, the pitcher hurled the ball toward the batter.

7. The nervous batter swung his bat with all his strength.

8. He missed the ball completely.

9. The umpire called the third strike.

10. The pitch had completely fooled the batter!

⊙ Transitive and Intransitive Verbs

An action verb that has a direct object is called a **transitive verb**. You may recall that to find a direct object, you say the subject and the action verb. Then ask the question *What?* or *Whom?* The word that answers one of those questions is a direct object. A verb that does not have a direct object is called an **intransitive verb**.

TRANSITIVE VERBS	Adult birds **protect** their babies. (Birds protect *what? Babies* is the direct object. Therefore, *protect* is a transitive verb.)
	Robins **lay** beautiful blue eggs. (Robins lay *what? Eggs* is the direct object. Therefore, *lay* is a transitive verb.)
INTRANSITIVE VERBS	Geese **migrate** to the south in winter. (Geese migrate *what* or *whom?* Since there is no direct object, *migrate* is an intransitive verb.)
	They **will return** in summer. (They will return *what* or *whom?* There is no direct object, so *will return* is an intransitive verb.

Sometimes a verb can be transitive in one sentence and intransitive in another.

A hawk **circled** the open field.
(A hawk circled *what* or *whom? Field* is the direct object, so *circled* is a transitive verb in this sentence.)

A hawk **circled** in the open sky.
(A hawk circled *what* or *whom?* There is no direct object, so *circled* is an intransitive verb in this sentence.)

PRACTICE YOUR SKILLS

● Check Your Understanding
Understanding Transitive and Intransitive Verbs

 Contemporary Life **Write each action verb. Label each one as either *transitive* or *intransitive*. If a verb is transitive, write its direct object.**

1. We studied birds in my science class.
2. The teacher gave us a book about geese.
3. We studied owls and hawks, too.
4. We read some interesting facts about hummingbirds.
5. Our teacher hung a bird feeder outside the classroom window.
6. The feeder hung from a chain on the windowsill.
7. One day a squirrel ate from the bird feeder.
8. It leapt from a tree to the windowsill.
9. That squirrel feasted on birdseed.
10. The furry thief stole every bit of the birds' food!

Linking Verbs

Not all verbs show action. Verbs that do not show action are called **state-of-being verbs**. These verbs make a statement about a subject.

> My grandmother **was** here in December.

State-of-being verbs are often called linking verbs. These verbs link, or connect, the subject with another word in the sentence. In English the most common linking verb is *be*.

A **linking verb** links the subject with another word that renames or describes the subject.

> December **is** the last month of the year.
>
> (*Is* links *month* with *December*.)
>
> Last month **was** unusually cold.
>
> (*Was* links *month* with *cold*.)

The following is a list of common linking verbs.

COMMON FORMS OF *BE* USED AS LINKING VERBS			
be	was	could be	have been
is	were	should be	has been
am	shall be	may be	could have been
are	will be	might be	must have been

> Those red plants **are** poinsettias.
>
> They **were** a gift from my grandma.

Linking verbs can also have helping verbs.

> Poinsettias **have** always **been** my favorite plants.
>
> Those tropical plants **will be** too cold outside.
>
> The temperature **must have been** ten degrees.

PRACTICE YOUR SKILLS

● Check Your Understanding
Finding Linking Verbs

Science Topic **Write each linking verb.**

1. Poinsettias may be one of the most popular plants at Christmas time.

2. The poinsettia is a member of the spurge family of plants.

3. The red parts of the poinsettias are actually special kinds of leaves.

4. These petal-like leaves are bracts.

5. This beautiful plant has been a symbol of the Christmas season for many years.

6. A poinsettia will usually be colorful through December and January.

7. With proper care some plants could probably be beautiful even longer.

8. A poinsettia's pot should be the right size for the plant.

9. Florists must be careful with this very delicate Christmas flower.

10. Its stem might be fragile.

Additional Linking Verbs

In addition to forms of the *be* verb, other words can also be used as linking verbs. Remember, a linking verb links the subject with another word that renames or describes the subject.

ADDITIONAL LINKING VERBS					
appear	feel	look	seem	sound	taste
become	grow	remain	smell	stay	turn

My favorite fruit **remains** the apple.

(*Remains* links *apple* with *fruit*. *Apple* renames the subject.)

In winter, apple trees **appear** lifeless.

(*Appear* links *lifeless* and *trees*. *Lifeless* describes the subject.)

Sometimes the same word can be used as a linking verb in one sentence and as an action verb in another sentence. If the verb is linking two words, it is a linking verb. If it shows action, it is an action verb.

LINKING VERB   The apples **looked** ripe.

(*Looked* links *apples* and *ripe* because *ripe* describes *apples*.)

ACTION VERB   The farmer **looked** at the apples.

(*Looked* shows action. It tells what the farmer was doing.)

PRACTICE YOUR SKILLS

● Check Your Understanding
Finding Linking Verbs

Science Topic **Write each linking verb.**

1. Ripe apples usually taste sweet.
2. Some ripe apples turn red.
3. Others look green or golden.
4. All winter long, apple trees remain dormant.
5. They stay gray and leafless for months.
6. In spring the trees seem new again.
7. Their appearance grows healthier.
8. Leaves turn green.
9. The blossoms on the tree smell delicious.
10. Soon those blossoms become apples.

● Check Your Understanding
Finding Linking Verbs

General Interest **Write each linking verb.**

11. The Fourth of July is American Independence Day.
12. In 2076, America will be three hundred years old.
13. That could be a really big birthday party.
14. The bicentennial celebration in 1976 was spectacular.
15. That might have been the biggest celebration ever!
16. The sky on that evening grew dark.
17. The fireworks display above the Statue of Liberty was an incredible sight!

18. The dark sky turned light with the brilliance of the fireworks.

19. The celebration in 2076 might be even bigger.

20. Americans seem proud of their country.

● Connect to the Writing Process: Revising
Turning Questions into Statements

Turn each question into a statement. Underline the linking verb in each statement.

21. Is today Independence Day?

22. Has the sky grown dark?

23. Have you been calm today?

24. Will the fireworks display be ready?

25. Should the fireworks start at 9:00 P.M.?

Communicate Your Ideas

APPLY TO WRITING

The Writer's Craft: *Analyzing the Use of Linking Verbs*

Writers use both linking and action verbs when they write. Stories like fairy tales and fables often start with sentences that have linking verbs. Read the following passage and then follow the directions.

> In a far city there once lived a boy named Jan. His father was Anton the blacksmith. The family's home was a little house next door to the black-smith shop, in the shadow of a great church.
>
> Jan was small and quick and strong. He helped his father shoe the horses that were brought to the shop.
>
> —Clyde Robert Bulla, The Wish at the Top

- Write the verbs in the first four sentences. Are they action or linking verbs?
- Choose two sentences with linking verbs. Tell which words are being linked in the sentence.
- Could the author have reworded any of the sentences that have linking verbs? Try rewriting the second sentence, using an action verb instead of a linking verb. What happens?
- Why do you think authors of these kinds of stories use so many linking verbs in the beginning of a tale?

QuickCheck Mixed Practice

General Interest **Write each verb. Then label each one *action* or *linking*.**

1. For eight hundred years, no moose had lived in Sweden.
2. Then a female moose and two male moose swam to Sweden from a nearby country.
3. Their new lives seemed happy.
4. Then suddenly the female moose died.
5. The Swedish people were very upset about the loss of their only female moose.
6. Quickly they hunted for another female.
7. Eventually a man in Denmark offered them Hildy.
8. He had raised her on his farm.
9. She was a very gentle animal.
10. A forest in Sweden became Hildy's new home.
11. For a while, Hildy appeared content.

12. Then one day she marched into town.

13. All the people looked fearful.

14. A full-size moose can be very dangerous.

15. It can kill a person with one strike.

16. Poor Hildy felt very sad.

17. She was only looking for some new friends—human friends.

18. Some people were brave.

19. After all, this moose didn't look mean.

20. Hildy was happy!

21. Within a short period of time, she was friendly with all the people in town.

22. For the rest of her days, she lived at the zoo.

23. However, she could easily jump across a wide ditch around the zoo.

24. She would visit people in the town outside the zoo every day.

25. All the townspeople became Hildy's good friends.

Predicate Nominatives

The noun or pronoun that follows a linking verb and renames the subject is a complement called a predicate nominative.

A **predicate nominative** is a noun or a pronoun that follows a linking verb and identifies, renames, or explains the subject.

To find a predicate nominative in a sentence, first find the subject and the verb. Check to see whether the verb is a linking verb. Then look for a noun or a pronoun that follows the linking verb and renames the subject. One way to check for a predicate nominative is to put an equal sign between it and the subject.

PREDICATE
NOMINATIVES

The sixteenth president was
Abraham Lincoln.

(The predicate nominative is *Abraham Lincoln*. Abraham Lincoln = president)

He should be a **hero** to many Americans.

(The predicate nominative is *hero*. hero = he)

Two or more predicate nominatives following the same linking verb are called a **compound predicate nominative.**

Lincoln's vice presidents were **Hannibal Hamlin** and **Andrew Johnson.**

(Hannibal Hamlin, Andrew Johnson = vice presidents)

Another complement that sometimes follows a linking verb is a predicate adjective. You can learn about predicate adjectives on pages L125–L126.

PRACTICE YOUR SKILLS

● Check Your Understanding
Finding Predicate Nominatives

History Topic **Write each predicate nominative.**

1. Abraham Lincoln is probably the most famous president.

2. Many historians are experts on Lincoln's life.

3. Lincoln was the first Republican president.

4. As a child, Lincoln's best friends were books.

5. Mary Todd became his wife in 1842.

6. Lincoln became the nation's leader in 1861.

7. Lincoln had been a lawyer.

8. After his reelection in 1864, Lincoln remained president.

9. Andrew Johnson became president after John Wilkes Booth's assassination of Lincoln.

10. The Lincoln Memorial in Washington, D.C., is a monument to this great president.

● Check Your Understanding
Finding Predicate Nominatives

Geography
Topic
Write each predicate nominative. Then write the word that the predicate nominative renames.

11. Our national parks are America's treasures.

12. These natural places will be a legacy for future generations.

13. Yellowstone became the first national park in 1872.

14. The park's most popular site has always been Old Faithful.

15. To the park's early explorers, this geyser must have been an amazing sight!

16. Carlsbad Caverns National Park is a collection of more than eighty caves.

17. New Mexico is home to this incredible place.

18. The caves have been a national park since 1930.

19. Millions of years ago, the cavern was a long reef in an inland sea.

20. The Bat Cave of Carlsbad Cavern is a sanctuary for more than one million bats.

Supplying Predicate Nominatives

Write a predicate nominative for each blank.

21. A dog can be an excellent ■.

22. Two breeds of dog are ■ and ■.

23. My favorite dog has always been a ■.

24. My first pet was a ■.

Communicate Your Ideas

APPLY TO WRITING

Folk Story: *Predicate Nominatives*

Helen Cordero. *Storyteller,* 1965.
Slipped and painted earthenware, height 14 inches.
Museum of International Folk Art, Santa Fe, NM.

Pretend that you are the storyteller in this piece of art. What story are you telling these children? Write a tale that these children would enjoy. After you have written your tale, read over your work, correcting any errors you find. Identify any linking verbs and predicate nominatives you used.

Diagraming Verbs and Complements

Most complements are written on the baseline of a diagram along with the subject and the verb. An indirect object is the only exception. An indirect object is written on a line attached to the baseline below the verb.

Direct Objects Write a direct object on the baseline right after the verb. Then draw a short, straight line to separate the direct object from the verb. Write the parts of a compound direct object on parallel lines. Then write the word that joins the parts of the compound direct object on a broken line between them.

We ate watermelon.

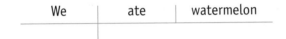

She likes peaches and plums.

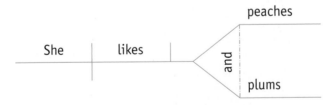

Indirect Objects Indirect objects are written on horizontal lines below the baseline. These horizontal lines are connected to the verb on the baseline by a slanted line. The parts of a compound indirect object are also written on parallel horizontal lines. The conjunction is placed on the broken line.

Gina gave us strawberries.

Give Mike and John apples.

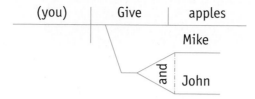

Predicate Nominatives   Write a predicate nominative on the baseline after the verb, and use a line slanted toward the verb to separate the predicate nominative from the verb. Write the parts of a compound predicate nominative on parallel lines.

Tomatoes are fruit.

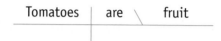

Women are gardeners and farmers.

PRACTICE YOUR SKILLS

Diagraming

Diagram the following sentences, or copy them. If you copy them, draw one line under each subject and two lines under each verb. Then label each complement using the following abbreviations:

direct object = *d.o.*   predicate nominative = *p.n.*
indirect object = *i.o.*

1. Parents are mothers and fathers.

2. Mom gives us encouragement.

3. Maria finds dogs and cats.

4. Pets become friends.

5. Uncle Louis teaches Dan and me Spanish.

Finding Action Verbs

Write each action verb. If the verb is part of a verb phrase, write the entire phrase.

1. On December 17, 1903, the Wright brothers made an announcement.
2. They had flown the first airplane at Kitty Hawk, North Carolina.
3. The newspaper reporters, however, didn't believe them.
4. For the next five years, the brothers gave demonstrations of their invention.
5. Editors still wouldn't send a single reporter.

Finding Linking Verbs

Write each linking verb. Then write the two words the verb links.

1. The use of some modern balloons seems unusual.
2. One helium-filled balloon is a great help to farmers.
3. The picture on the balloon looks familiar to people and to birds.
4. It is a hawk.
5. The black predator with its large wings appears real to other birds.

Identifying Complements

Write each underlined complement. Then label each one using the following abbreviations:

> direct object = *d.o.* predicate nominative = *p.n.*
> indirect object = *i.o.*

1. Colorado became a state in 1876.

2. We found some beautiful shells along the beach near Park Street.
3. Some sharks have no natural enemies.
4. The Adams family of Massachusetts gave their country two presidents.
5. The animal with the longest life is the giant tortoise.
6. Mr. Granger promised Maria extra help after school.
7. Have you ever thrown a boomerang?
8. During snowy winters, monkeys eat vines and tree bark.
9. Kim eagerly showed his mother his first report card of the school year.
10. Elephants are excellent swimmers in spite of their bulk.

Using Verbs

Write five sentences that follow the directions below. (The sentences may come in any order.) Write about the following topic or a topic of your own choice: a description of a relative or a good friend.

Write a sentence that...
1. includes an action verb.
2. includes an action verb with one or more helping verbs.
3. includes a linking verb.
4. includes an action verb with a direct object.
5. includes an action verb with a direct object and an indirect object.

When you are finished, underline each verb or verb phrase and label it *A* for action or *L* for linking.

Language and *Self-Expression*

Honoré Daumier's *Street Show* is a gesture drawing, a quick sketch of the subject, emphasizing action and motion, rather than detailed form. *Street Show* captures the excited gestures of the performer on the chair as he entertains the crowd and the steady beating of the drummer as he accompanies the performer.

You have probably seen performers singing, dancing, rapping, and acting. Perhaps you've seen someone shake and blush when he or she got up to sing in music class. Maybe you've stopped in the street to see a mime or a juggler. Think of one memorable performance you can use as the subject of a descriptive paragraph.

Prewriting Write the name of the performer at the top of a piece of paper. Then brainstorm words about the performance. List a variety of verbs such as *leaped, waved, shook,* and *shouted* to describe the action of the performance.

Drafting Using the words you have listed, write a descriptive paragraph. Begin by telling who was performing, where the performance took place, and what was performed. Then describe the actual event.

Revising Have a classmate read your paragraph to you. Does your paragraph clearly describe the performance? Revise the description as needed.

Editing Check your paragraph for errors in punctuation and spelling. Be sure that you used the past tense.

Publishing Work with your classmates to publish an entertainment magazine of your descriptions. If possible, print a copy for each student to take home.

Another Look

A **verb** is a word used to express an action or a state of being.

Kinds of Verbs

An **action verb** tells what action a subject is performing. *(page L77)*

A **helping verb,** or **auxiliary verb,** is a verb used with the main verb. *(page L81)*

A **verb phrase** is a main verb plus one or more helping verbs. *(page L81)*

A **transitive verb** is an action verb that has a direct object. *(pages L90–L91)*

An **intransitive verb** is an action verb that does not have a direct object. *(pages L90–L91)*

A **linking verb** links the subject with another word that renames or describes the subject. *(pages L92–L94)*

ADDITIONAL LINKING VERBS					
appear	feel	look	seem	sound	taste
become	grow	remain	smell	stay	turn

Complements

A **direct object** is a noun or a pronoun that answers the question *What?* or *Whom?* after an action verb. *(pages L83–L85)*

A **compound direct object** is two or more direct objects following the same verb. *(pages L84–L85)*

An **indirect object** is a noun or pronoun that answers the question *To or for whom?* or *To or for what?* after an action verb. *(pages L86–L87)*

A **compound indirect object** is two or more indirect objects following the same verb. *(page L87)*

A **predicate nominative** is a noun or pronoun that follows a linking verb and identifies, renames, or explains the subject. *(pages L98–L99)*

A **compound predicate nominative** is two or more predicate nominatives following the same verb. *(page L99)*

Directions
Write the letter of the term that correctly identifies the underlined word or words in each sentence.

EXAMPLE

1. Many scientists have studied bird <u>communication</u>.

1 **A** predicate nominative
B direct object
C indirect object
D action verb

ANSWER

1 B

1. All birdcalls <u>may</u> sound alike to you.

2. However, a bird knows its own mate's <u>cry</u>.

3. Baby birds <u>can</u> also recognize their parents' cries.

4. The babies <u>learn</u> these calls while still in the egg.

5. Birdcalls are usually simple, short <u>cries</u>.

6. They <u>are used</u> for many different functions.

7. Recognition is only <u>one</u> of those functions.

8. Alarm calls <u>warn</u> the flock of danger.

9. They give the <u>flock</u> a "flight" signal.

10. Then the birds <u>fly</u> into the air all at once.

1 A action verb
  B linking verb
  C transitive verb
  D helping verb

2 A indirect object
  B action verb
  C direct object
  D predicate nominative

3 A helping verb
  B linking verb
  C action verb
  D verb phrase

4 A intransitive verb
  B linking verb
  C transitive verb
  D helping verb

5 A action verb
  B indirect object
  C direct object
  D predicate nominative

6 A verb phrase
  B transitive verb
  C linking verb
  D helping verb

7 A indirect object
  B direct object
  C predicate nominative
  D subject

8 A intransitive verb
  B action verb
  C helping verb
  D linking verb

9 A direct object
  B indirect object
  C antecedent
  D predicate nominative

10 A helping verb
   B linking verb
   C transitive verb
   D intransitive verb

CHAPTER 4

Adjectives and Adverbs

Pretest

Directions
Write the letter of the term that correctly identifies the underlined word in each sentence.

EXAMPLE

1. Plant hunters lived <u>adventurous</u> lives.
   1 A adverb
   B adjective
   C predicate adjective
   D noun

ANSWER   **1 B**

1. Ernest Wilson was a <u>plant</u> hunter in the early 1800s.

2. He sent many <u>Chinese</u> plants back to the United States.

3. His <u>most</u> famous find was the regal lily.

4. <u>This</u> is now a very commonly grown lily.

5. Wilson <u>nearly</u> lost his leg looking for it.

6. He was looking for <u>this</u> lily in a remote area.

7. <u>Suddenly</u> an avalanche crashed down on him.

8. <u>A</u> rock broke his leg in two places.

9. His injury was extremely <u>painful</u>.

10. He <u>bravely</u> endured the three-day journey to the doctor.

1 **A** direct object
  B adjective
  C adverb
  D noun

2 **A** proper adjective
  B predicate adjective
  C common noun
  D proper noun

3 **A** article
  B adjective
  C adverb
  D pronoun

4 **A** pronoun
  B noun
  C adjective
  D adverb

5 **A** antecedent
  B adverb
  C adjective
  D article

6 **A** direct object
  B article
  C predicate adjective
  D adjective

7 **A** adverb
  B noun
  C article
  D adjective

8 **A** adverb
  B pronoun
  C article
  D direct object

9 **A** adverb
  B predicate nominative
  C predicate adjective
  D antecedent

10 **A** predicate adjective
  B adverb
  C antecedent
  D verb

Rosa Bonheur. *The Horse Fair,* 1853.
Oil on canvas, approximately 8 by 16 feet. The Metropolitan Museum of Art.

Describe   What three words or terms might you use to describe this painting to someone else?

Analyze   Where is the center of interest in this painting? Why is your attention drawn to this area?

Interpret   Do you think the artist wants you to feel that the men in the picture are having fun or working hard? What makes you think so? How does the appearance of the sky affect the mood of the picture?

Judge   Do you think this painting or a written description would more effectively capture the mood in this scene? Give reasons for your answer.

At the end of this chapter, you will use the artwork to stimulate ideas for writing.

Adjectives

KARINA: Please hand me the book on the shelf.
NATHAN: Which book?
KARINA: The **green** one.
NATHAN: There are two **green** books on the shelf.
KARINA: I want the **big green** book.
NATHAN: Oh, that one. Here you go!

Without the words *big* and *green,* Nathan never would have known which book Karina wanted. *Big* and *green* are adjectives. An *adjective* is an important part of speech. Adjectives add color and exactness to your writing.

An **adjective** is a word that modifies, or describes, a noun or a pronoun.

To find an adjective, look for each noun and pronoun. Then ask yourself the question *What kind? Which one? How many?* or *How much?* In the following examples, an arrow points to the word each adjective describes. Notice that an adjective usually comes before the word it describes. Also notice that more than one adjective can describe the same word.

WHAT KIND?	**fresh** water	**prickly** cactus
	hot, dry day	**thin, loose** clothing
	free food	**southern** state
	large blue sweater	**soft, fluffy** pillow
WHICH ONE?	**that** desert	**those** camels
HOW MANY?	**three** days	**many** nights
HOW MUCH?	**no** rain	**much** sunshine

PUNCTUATION WITH TWO ADJECTIVES

Sometimes you will write two adjectives together. If those two adjectives are not connected by *and* or *or,* you might need to put a comma between them. To decide whether a comma belongs or not, use the following test. Read the adjectives together with the word *and* between them.

- If the adjectives make sense, put a comma in to replace the *and.*
- If the adjectives do not make sense with the word *and* between them, do not add a comma.

COMMA NEEDED	The desert is a harsh, beautiful place. (*A harsh and beautiful place* reads well.)
COMMA NOT NEEDED	It was a hot summer day. (*A hot and summer day* does not read well.)

Usually no comma is needed after a number and after an adjective that refers to size, shape, or age. For example, no commas are used in the following sentences.

They rode **six tall camels.**
They slept in **a large white tent.**

CONNECT TO WRITER'S CRAFT

When you write, always choose fresh, specific adjectives that will create clear pictures in the minds of your readers. Adjectives can create a mood by making a room *dark* and *gloomy* or *bright* and *sunny.* They can also make a description exact. A *tasty, light* meal is very different from a *rich, heavy* meal. Use the dictionary or a thesaurus to look for colorful substitutes for dull, overused adjectives such as *good, nice, bad,* and *awful.*

Articles

The words *a, an,* and *the* form a special group of adjectives called **articles.** Use *a* before a word that begins with a consonant sound. Use *an* before a word that begins with a vowel sound.

ARTICLES			
a wildflower	**a** dune	**an** hour	**an** oasis

Since articles are used so often, you do not have to list them in the following exercises.

PRACTICE YOUR SKILLS

● Check Your Understanding
Finding Adjectives

Geography Topic **Write each adjective. Remember, do not list the articles *a, an,* and *the*.**

1. North Africa is a dry, harsh land.
2. In North Africa is the Sahara, the largest desert in the world.
3. It is about the same size as the United States.
4. Often hot, dry winds create sand dunes.
5. Dunes sometimes look like huge mountains of sand.
6. The Sahara has hot days and cold nights.
7. There is little water in the desert.
8. Years can pass with no rain.
9. Most water in the desert comes from underground streams.
10. In the desert, people wear long, loose robes as protection from the heat, cold, and sand storms.

Finding the Words Adjectives Describe

Music Topic **Write each adjective. Beside each one, write the word it describes.**

11. There are many interesting musical instruments in a band.

12. Most of them are wind instruments.

13. These instruments include different groups.

14. The large bassoon is one example of a reed instrument.

15. The brass instruments make noise by the vibration of the player's lips on a metal mouthpiece.

16. The flutes are a third group of instruments.

17. The tiny piccolo is a member of this family.

18. The organ is a different kind of wind instrument.

19. Musical sounds are produced by placing fingers on the keys.

20. The small keys send a burst of air to large pipes in the instrument.

● Connect to the Writing Process: Drafting
Using Specific Adjectives

Write two specific adjectives that could describe each noun. Then use one of your adjectives and the noun in a sentence.

21. person

22. storm

23. car

24. jungle

25. lake

26. tent

27. campfire

28. eclipse

29. tumbleweed

30. palm

APPLY TO WRITING

The Writer's Craft: *Analyzing the Use of Adjectives*

Authors use adjectives to make their work come alive. Read the following passage and then follow the directions.

> They took turns swinging across the gully on a rope. It was a glorious autumn day, and if you looked up as you swung, it gave you the feeling of floating. Jess leaned back and drank in the rich, clear color of the sky. He was drifting, drifting like a fat white lazy cloud back and forth across the blue.
>
> —*Katherine Paterson*, Bridge to Terabithia

- Write the adjectives in the passage. Beside them write the words they modify.

- Look at the places where Paterson put commas between her adjectives and the places where she did not. Do you agree that she punctuated these properly?

- Rewrite the passage without the adjectives. Read your new paragraph and compare it with Paterson's original. Which do you like better? Why?

- Paterson used more than one adjective to describe a noun. As a reader, do you find it effective or distracting? Explain your answer.

Proper Adjectives

America is a proper noun. It is the name of a particular place. *American* is a **proper adjective** because it is formed from the proper noun *America*. A proper adjective is used to describe a noun or a pronoun—*American flag*. A proper adjective always begins with a capital letter.

PROPER NOUNS AND ADJECTIVES	
PROPER NOUNS	Africa Mars Great Britain Hawaii Shakespeare
PROPER ADJECTIVES	**African** heritage **Martian** rocks **British** accent **Hawaiian** pineapples **Shakespearean** play

You can learn more about the capitalization of proper adjectives on page L425.

PRACTICE YOUR SKILLS

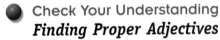 Check Your Understanding
Finding Proper Adjectives

Contemporary Life **Write each proper adjective. Beside each one, write the word it modifies.**

1. My family and I enjoyed a European vacation last summer.

2. My brother watched an Irish team play soccer.

3. My mother and sisters shopped for British crystal in England.

4. I enjoyed our peaceful stroll down the Parisian streets at daybreak.

5. The French cafés were crowded with hundreds of tourists.

6. Our Roman hotel had a great view of the Coliseum.

7. My sister enjoyed the spicy Italian food.

8. We saw an impressive collection of art at a Venetian museum.

9. My brother and I took a short tour of a Greek island.

10. We found that the Sicilian people were very friendly.

● Connect to the Writing Process: Editing

Capitalizing Proper Adjectives

Rewrite the following sentences, capitalizing each proper adjective.

11. During our vacation, we visited some german friends.

12. They took us skiing in the austrian mountains.

13. We also spent time visiting some scandinavian countries.

14. We saw the danish capital, which is Copenhagen.

15. Then we traveled east to the swedish coast.

16. As our european vacation continued, we visited Norway and Finland.

17. At a library, we heard a historian speak about norse mythology.

18. We saw many beautiful finnish lakes on our trip.

19. Though we had fun, we were glad to be back on american soil!

20. In our georgia home, we talk about our fantastic vacation.

APPLY TO WRITING
Postcard: *Adjectives*

You are on vacation in the place in the picture. Write
a postcard to your best friend. Tell him or her where
you are and what you are doing. Include a few details
that allow your friend to visualize your vacation spot.
As you write, use at least one proper adjective. Do not
forget to capitalize it. After you write, circle the
proper adjectives in your writing and underline all of
the other adjectives.

▶ Adjective or Noun?

A word's part of speech depends on how it is used in a
sentence. *Game* and *gym,* for example, can be either nouns
or adjectives. Each of these words is a noun when it is the
name of something, but an adjective when it describes a noun
or a pronoun.

NOUN	The **game** will start at two o'clock.
ADJECTIVE	The players were nervous on **game** day.
NOUN	The tournament was held in the **gym.**
ADJECTIVE	The boys scrambled across the **gym** floor.

PRACTICE YOUR SKILLS

● Check Your Understanding
Distinguishing Between Adjectives and Nouns

Contemporary Life **Write each underlined word and label it either *adjective* or *noun*.**

1. Did you go to the basketball game on Saturday?

2. That was a beautiful spring day.

3. The team was ready for the big tournament.

4. Before the game Jessie drank a big glass of water.

5. She certainly had a spring in her step that day!

6. Tracy dribbled the basketball down the court.

7. Her nerves were made of steel.

8. Her shot shattered the glass backboard.

9. Only the steel rim was left.

10. Now Tracy is the team captain.

● Connect to the Writing Process: Drafting
Writing Sentences with Adjectives and Nouns

Write two sentences for each of the following words. Use the word as a noun in the first sentence. Use the word as an adjective in the second sentence.

11. orange   **12.** car   **13.** television

14. computer   **15.** flower

Adjective or Pronoun?

This, that, these, and *those* can be used as adjectives. Words like these answer the adjective question *Which one?*

ADJECTIVES   I just read **that** book.
(*Which* book?)

She likes **those** authors best.
(*Which* authors?)

This, that, these, and *those* can also be demonstrative pronouns. These words are adjectives when they come before nouns and pronouns and describe the nouns or pronouns. They are pronouns when they stand alone and take the place of nouns.

PRONOUNS   I just read **that.**
(*That* takes the place of the noun *book.*)

She likes **those** best.
(*Those* takes the place of the noun *authors.*)

You can learn more about demonstrative pronouns on pages L64–L65.

PRACTICE YOUR SKILLS

● Check Your Understanding
Distinguishing Between Adjectives and Pronouns

Contemporary Life   **Write each underlined word and label it either** ***adjective* or *pronoun.***

1. Have your read <u>this</u> article?

2. I love <u>that</u> author.

3. Then you have seen <u>those.</u>

4. <u>That</u> is my favorite science fiction book.

5. <u>These</u> are good to read, too.

6. I enjoyed the short stories in <u>these</u> library books.

7. <u>This</u> is a good collection of magazines also.

8. <u>That</u> library is fun to visit.

9. <u>Those</u> librarians are very helpful.

10. Let's check out <u>these</u>.

Communicate Your Ideas

APPLY TO WRITING

E-mail Message: *Adjectives*

In *A String in the Harp,* Nancy Bond writes the following passage about fifteen-year-old Jen's first look at her new home, the town of Borth, Wales.

> The taxi stopped abruptly and they all climbed out. The wind hit them immediately, strong and boisterous. Jen wasn't prepared and she almost lost her balance. She looked about her and discovered they were at the top of a cliff; below and to the right were the lights of Borth proper where the station was. To the left were empty miles of sea as gray as the clouds overhead. The horizon was lost somewhere between. Nothing shielded them from the wind.
>
> —*Nancy Bond,* A String in the Harp

Imagine that this is your first look at your new home. Write an E-mail message to your best friend back home and tell him or her about this experience.

Describe what you see as you approach the house. Explain how the place made you feel and how you think you will like your new home. As you write, use specific adjectives to convey your feelings. Also, use the following words in your writing as the indicated part of speech. Underline these words.

- *taxi*—adjective
- *city*—adjective
- *this*—adjective
- *that*—pronoun
- *those*—adjective
- *these*—pronoun

QuickCheck   Mixed Practice

General Interest **Write each adjective. Beside each one write the word it describes. Do not include articles.**

1. Skateboards were invented in southern California.

2. In the 1960s, surfers wanted a way to surf when there were no waves.

3. These creative surfers nailed a skate to a plank of wood.

4. They called the sport "sidewalk surfing."

5. The new fad spread from that coast across the American states.

6. At first, people rode on city streets and sidewalks.

7. Later, enthusiastic skateboarders could ride in special places.

8. Protective gear should be worn during skateboarding.

9. You should always wear a good, strong helmet.

10. Wrist and knee pads provide additional protection.

● Predicate Adjectives

An adjective does not always appear in front of the word it describes. An adjective can also follow a linking verb and describe the subject of a sentence. Such an adjective is a complement called a predicate adjective.

A **predicate adjective** is an adjective that follows a linking verb and modifies, or describes, the subject.

COMMON LINKING VERBS				
FORMS OF THE *BE* VERB	be is am are	was were shall be will be	could be should be may be might be	have been has been could have been must have been
OTHERS	appear become feel	grow look remain	seem smell sound	stay taste turn

To find a predicate adjective, find the subject and the verb. Check to see whether the verb is a linking verb. Then find the adjective that follows the verb and describes the subject.

PREDICATE ADJECTIVES

That monkey seems **intelligent.**

(*Intelligent* describes the subject —*intelligent monkey.*)

Most gorillas are **huge.**

(*Huge* describes the subject —*huge gorillas.*)

Two or more predicate adjectives following the same linking verb are called a **compound predicate adjective.**

The spider monkey is **small** and **slender.**

(*Small* and *slender* both describe the subject—*small, slender monkey.*)

You can learn about other complements on pages L83–L87.

PRACTICE YOUR SKILLS

● Check Your Understanding
Finding Predicate Adjectives

General Interest **Write each predicate adjective.**

1. Monkeys usually look friendly.

2. They are often very noisy.

3. In trees, they seem safe from enemies.

4. The hair of some monkeys is red.

5. Their fur can be long or short.

6. Their fur, however, feels very coarse.

7. Of all the monkeys, the Red Howler is the largest.

8. The tail of this monkey is long and strong.

9. Most monkeys appear quite smart.

10. Some monkeys have even become popular as actors.

● Check Your Understanding
Supplying Predicate Adjectives

General Interest **Write a predicate adjective for each blank.**

11. The zoo can be ■.

12. At noon the tigers appear ■.

13. Penguins seem ■ in their cool habitat.

14. Sometimes elephants smell ■.

15. After our long walk through the zoo, we were ■.

16. The lion's growl is ■.

17. Most people at the zoo are ■.

18. The snake house could be ■.

19. In the past the wolves have been ■.

20. That day was ■!

● Connect to the Writing Process: Drafting
Writing Sentences with Predicate Adjectives

Write two sentences using the following adjectives. In the first sentence, place each adjective in its normal position before a noun. In the second sentence, use each adjective as a predicate adjective.

21. young   **22.** famous   **23.** warm

24. beautiful   **25.** cool

Communicate Your Ideas

APPLY TO WRITING

Descriptive Paragraph: *Adjectives*

Look very carefully at your right shoe. Describe it in five or six sentences for your classmates. For example, you might include the shoe's color, any marks on it, and the condition of the shoestrings. Your description should be so accurate that when your paragraph is read aloud by your teacher, anyone in the class can identify the shoe as yours. Be sure to use adjectives to make your description precise.

General Interest **Write each adjective. Do not list articles.**

1. Mel Fisher searched for eleven years and finally discovered the *Atocha* in the summer of 1985.

2. The *Atocha* is an old Spanish ship.

3. It sank during a terrible hurricane in 1622.

4. The search for the treasure was long and difficult.

5. Fisher first read old records in Seville, Spain.

6. The information was valuable.

7. Modern sonar also helped Fisher's search for the *Atocha*.

8. Fisher had found silver bars, gold coins, and jewelry.

9. The treasure site was guarded against thieves.

10. An American archaeologist worked with Fisher.

11. To him, this discovery is important.

12. From the wreckage, the archaeologist hoped to learn many things.

13. How were Spanish galleons built?

14. How did European sailors live and work 350 years ago?

15. These facts are valuable to researchers.

Adverbs

Like an adjective, an adverb is a **modifier.** An adverb modifies, or describes, another word in the sentence. Unlike an adjective, however, an adverb describes a verb, an adjective, or another adverb.

> An **adverb** is a word that modifies, or describes, a verb, an adjective, or an adverb.

Adverbs are important words because they make your writing more precise or exact. Notice, for example, how the second example is made more precise just by adding two adverbs.

> The lion stopped.
> **Then** the lion stopped **suddenly.**

You can easily recognize some adverbs because they end in *–ly.*

> **Silently** the lioness **slowly** stalked her prey.

The following list shows common adverbs that do not end in *–ly.*

COMMON ADVERBS			
again	far	never	soon
almost	fast	next	still
already	hard	not (n't)	then
also	here	now	there
always	just	often	too
down	late	quite	very
even	more	rather	well
ever	near	so	yet

Notice that *not* and its contraction *n't* are always adverbs.

This camera is**n't** working.
(This camera is **not** working.)

● Adverbs That Describe Verbs

Most adverbs describe verbs. To find these adverbs, ask yourself *How? When? Where?* or *To what extent?* about each verb. Notice that some of the following adverbs can come before the verb, while others come after the verb.

HOW?	The giraffe stepped **carefully.**
WHEN?	**Then** it reached for a leaf.
WHERE?	The zebra headed **north.**
TO WHAT EXTENT?	The reporter **almost** photographed the antelope.

More than one adverb can describe the same verb.

The male lion **always** growls **loudly.**

An adverb always describes the main verb plus any helping verbs. Notice in the second and third examples that an adverb sometimes interrupts a verb phrase.

The animals will drink **here** at sunset.

The scientist had **never** captured a hyena.

The hyenas would **always** hear his approach.

You can learn about using adjectives and adverbs to compare on pages L359–L364.

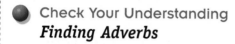
To make your writing more interesting, begin some of your sentences with adverbs. If all your sentences begin the same way, your writing can sound dull.

REGULAR ORDER   The tiger leaped **suddenly.**

VARIETY   **Suddenly** the tiger leaped.

PRACTICE YOUR SKILLS

● Check Your Understanding

Finding Adverbs

Science Topic   **Write each adverb and the word or words it modifies.**

1. In the past, scientists did not have much information about certain animals.

2. They never knew all the habits or homes of these animals.

3. With modern technology, that has already changed.

4. Now scientists can accurately track most animals through their daily activities.

5. However, they couldn't do their studies without the help of radio transmitters.

6. Often, these transmitters are securely attached to collars around animals' necks.

7. A scientist will quietly track a black bear, for example.

8. Dogs will bark loudly at a bear.

9. Immediately the bear will quickly climb a tree.

10. The bear is not interested in the scientist's work.

Distinguishing Between Adverbs and Adjectives

Science Topic **Write the correct adverb in parentheses. Then write the word or words the adverb modifies.**

11. Kangaroos move (quick, quickly) across the Australian plains.

12. Baby kangaroos sleep (cozy, cozily) in their mothers' pouches.

13. Great red kangaroos can (fast, sometimes) be seven feet tall.

14. They (often, immense) weigh more than two hundred pounds.

15. Their powerful legs and tail (usual, usually) help them.

16. They (easy, easily) avoid most of their enemies.

17. (Unfortunate, Unfortunately) they can't escape most human hunters.

18. This animal is (now, Australian) hunted for its beautiful pelt.

19. Kangaroos are (constant, constantly) foraging for food.

20. Kangaroos (starving, never) eat meat.

● Connect to the Writing Process: Revising
Using Adverbs to Add Interest

Rewrite the following sentences, adding an adverb or adverbs to make them more interesting. Underline your adverbs and draw an arrow from each one to the word or words it modifies.

21. The common house cat is attracted by the sound of a can opener.

22. These animals like a bowl of milk.

23. A cat will claw.

24. They may purr.

25. The cat will leap for any moving object.

26. Cats are abandoned in the city and in the countryside.

27. These cats must hunt for their food.

28. Some people will take a stray cat into their homes.

29. Many cats are rescued by hospitable farmers.

30. A good cat is an important creature on a farm.

31. They keep the mouse population to a minimum.

32. Scraps of food and milk are payment for them.

33. City cats wander around the streets.

34. Most cats find sympathetic humans.

35. Every animal deserves a good home.

Adverbs That Modify Adjectives and Other Adverbs

An adverb—such as *quite, rather, so, somewhat, too,* or *very*—can describe an adjective or another adverb. When it does, it usually comes before the word it describes.

DESCRIBING AN ADJECTIVE	The lake is **rather** choppy.
	(*Choppy* is a predicate adjective that describes *lake*. *Rather* is an adverb that tells how choppy the lake is.)
DESCRIBING AN ADVERB	The clouds moved **quite** rapidly.
	(*Rapidly* is an adverb that modifies *moved*. *Quite* is an adverb that tells how rapidly the clouds moved.)

PRACTICE YOUR SKILLS

● Check Your Understanding
Finding Adverbs

Contemporary Life **Write each underlined adverb and the word it modifies.**

1. The late summer storm in Kansas developed <u>quite</u> suddenly.
2. The thunder was <u>extremely</u> loud.
3. It seemed <u>too</u> early for sunset.
4. The <u>remarkably</u> fast rolling clouds had covered the afternoon sun.
5. <u>Very</u> soon the rain began.
6. The children seemed <u>very</u> afraid.
7. Their mothers' soothing words were <u>so</u> helpful.
8. The children became <u>somewhat</u> calmer.
9. The rain turned the temperature <u>rather</u> mild.
10. After the storm the children rushed to the yard <u>very</u> quickly.

● Connect to the Writing Process: Drafting
Writing Sentences with Adverbs

Using adverbs write sentences that follow each direction. Underline each adverb.

11. Include *too* to describe an adjective.
12. Include *very* to describe an adverb.
13. Include *not* to describe a verb.
14. Include *somewhat* to describe an adjective.
15. Include *quite* to describe an adverb.

APPLY TO WRITING
Narrative Paragraph: *Adverbs*

Luis Jiménez. *Vaquero,* 1980.
Fiberglass with acrylic urethane finish, height 16½ feet. National Museum of American Art, Washington, D.C.

Look carefully at this sculpture. Notice all the details. Imagine that you are the man on this horse. Write a narrative paragraph about this cowboy's adventure for your teacher. What has just happened? How did you get to this position? How are you feeling now? What are the thoughts in your mind? How does this end? As you write, use adverbs to make your work come alive. After you finish your narrative, read over your work and correct any errors. Underline the adverbs in your narrative.

Write each adverb.

1. Recently two California women amazingly survived an adventure of a lifetime.

2. These brave women were completely lost in the Indian Ocean.

3. They were extremely lucky.

4. They were having a very good time on vacation in Indonesia.

5. On a sixteen-foot boat, they excitedly headed to a nearby wildlife preserve.

6. They never made it.

7. Abruptly the boat's engine stopped in the middle of the ocean.

8. Soon their water supply was totally gone.

9. Then their boat crashed against a reef.

10. Luckily a helicopter crew rescued them rather quickly.

11. Such simple adventures can turn very dangerous without warning.

12. Many times, vacationers do not realize the risks in strange surroundings.

13. Often they are not trained properly for these adventurous excursions.

14. Boaters with little experience should never go on the water without a guide.

15. A competent guide can safely and quickly take you to your destination.

Sports Topic **Write each adjective and adverb. Beside each one, write the word it modifies. Do not include articles.**

1. An American athlete was born in 1940 in Tennessee.

2. This great runner was Wilma Rudolph.

3. As a small child, she suffered miserably with pneumonia and scarlet fever.

4. Rudolph was also infected with a terrible virus called polio.

5. Her left leg was paralyzed.

6. The doctors weren't hopeful about the chances for recovery.

7. They thought she would always wear a leg brace.

8. At thirteen, Rudolph bravely removed her brace.

9. Miraculously, she walked without it.

10. She became a member of the school track team.

11. Rudolph could run quickly.

12. At sixteen, she competed in the Olympic games in 1956.

13. She stunned the whole world.

14. Wilma Rudolph set a world record in two events.

15. Rudolph returned triumphantly to Tennessee.

Diagraming Adjectives and Adverbs

Adjectives and adverbs are both diagramed on slanted lines below the words they describe.

The orange tabby is prowling.

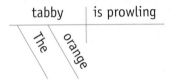

Most kittens sleep frequently.

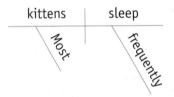

Adverbs that describe adjectives or other adverbs are connected to the words they describe.

That extremely fat cat loves tuna.

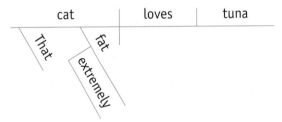

Smokey ran outside very quickly.

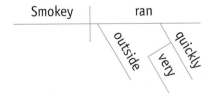

Very old dogs sometimes move quite slowly.

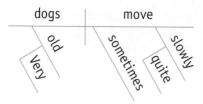

Predicate Adjectives   A predicate adjective is diagramed exactly like a predicate nominative.

That terrier is awfully small.

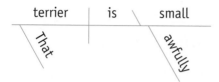

PRACTICE YOUR SKILLS

Diagraming

Diagram the following sentences or copy them. If you copy them, draw one line under each subject and two lines under each verb. Then label each modifier *adjective* or *adverb*. (Do not label the articles.)

1. Many violets are blooming.
2. Those daffodils look beautiful.
3. Several robins are chirping noisily.
4. The old dog is romping happily.
5. The children also seem happy.
6. Four large geese fly by.
7. Everyone has very big smiles.
8. Then dark clouds roll overhead.
9. The heavy rains have started.
10. They will last quite long.

CheckPoint

Finding Adjectives

Write each adjective. (Do not include articles.) Then write the word each adjective describes. There are 15 adjectives.

1. By 1972, twelve American astronauts had landed on the surface of the moon.
2. They returned with large samples of soil and rocks.
3. What have we learned from these explorations?
4. The surface of the moon is covered with a fine powdery dust.
5. Sometimes this dusty surface is deep.
6. Moon rocks are made of minerals and gases.
7. With no wind on the moon, these rocks hardly change.
8. The many footprints of the astronauts will probably never change either.
9. The astronauts left several instruments on the moon.
10. The information has been extremely valuable.

Finding Adverbs

Write each adverb. Then write the word or words each adverb describes. There are 15 adverbs.

1. Paula jumped high and easily cleared the pole.
2. The runners are coming out on the track.
3. The runners crouch down now.
4. Daniel always runs gracefully.
5. Does he practice regularly?
6. The unusually large crowd is wildly cheering.
7. Seldom do you see such a close race.

8. Jim is panting quite loudly.

9. He almost won the race.

10. Must we leave the stadium now?

Distinguishing Among Different Parts of Speech

Write each underlined word. Then label each one *noun*, *pronoun*, or *adjective*.

1. We have a <u>dog</u> named Max.

2. Everyone should know <u>that</u> information.

3. The <u>movie</u> reviews weren't very good.

4. Did anyone buy any of <u>these</u>?

5. That strange <u>telephone</u> is in the shape of a duck.

6. <u>That</u> is my correct address.

7. This canned <u>dog</u> food is on sale.

8. I saw a great <u>movie</u> last week at the Plaza Cinema.

9. I like <u>these</u> more than the red ones.

10. Did the <u>telephone</u> bill arrive yet?

Using Adjectives and Adverbs

Write five sentences that follow the directions below. (The sentences may come in any order.) Write about one of the following topics or a topic of your choice: the ugliest bug you have ever seen or the ugliest bug in your imagination.

Write a sentence that. . .

1. includes an adjective before a noun.

2. includes two adjectives before a noun.

3. includes a predicate adjective after a linking verb.

4. includes a proper adjective.

5. includes an adverb at the beginning of a sentence.

Language and *Self-Expression*

Rosa Bonheur was famous for her paintings of animals, especially horses. She spent many hours drawing living horses to get an understanding of their bodies and how they moved. She could not have been such a fine artist if she had not carefully observed even the smallest details.

Writers, too, write their best when they write about things they have witnessed firsthand. What details would you have noticed if you were standing next to Rosa Bonheur at this horse fair? Suppose that you are a fiction writer and want to use this setting for a story. Write a few paragraphs describing what you see. Use precise adjectives and adverbs to describe appearances and actions.

Prewriting Draw a cluster diagram, showing the elements of the picture you want to write about. Note the descriptive words and phrases you intend to use.

Drafting Use your diagram to draft an opening that gives an overall impression of the scene. Then add details that would be noticed on closer examination.

Revising Have a classmate read your paragraphs and offer feedback. Ask: *Do the first sentences give a clear overall view of the scene? Did I proceed by describing the things a viewer is likely to notice first? Does the sentence order make sense?*

Editing Check your paragraphs for errors in punctuation and spelling. If you have used an adjective or adverb more than once, try to substitute a different one.

Publishing Share your paragraphs with your class by reading them aloud or printing them and including them in a binder. Discuss how your impressions of the pictures varied.

Another Look

An **adjective** is a word that modifies, or describes, a noun or pronoun.

The words *a, an,* and *the* form a special group of adjectives called **articles**.

A **proper adjective** is an adjective formed from a proper noun.

PROPER NOUNS AND ADJECTIVES	
PROPER NOUNS	Africa Great Britain Hawaii Shakespeare
PROPER ADJECTIVES	**African** heritage **British** accent **Hawaiian** pineapples **Shakespearean** play

A **predicate adjective** is an adjective that follows a linking verb and modifies, or describes, the subject.

An **adverb** is a word that modifies, or describes, a verb, an adjective, or an adverb.

Other Information About Adjectives and Adverbs

Using punctuation with two adjectives *(page L114)*
Capitalizing proper adjectives *(pages L117–L118)*
Distinguishing between adjectives and nouns *(pages L120–L121)*
Distinguishing between adjectives and pronouns *(page L122)*
Recognizing adverbs that describe verbs *(page L130)*
Recognizing adverbs that describe adjectives and other adverbs *(page L133)*

Posttest

Directions
Write the letter of the term that correctly identifies the underlined word in each sentence.

EXAMPLE   **1.** The tribe camped <u>there</u> for several months.

      1 A pronoun
        B adjective
        C adverb
        D article

ANSWER   **1 C**

1. The people of the plains <u>most</u> often lived in tipis.

2. Twelve to twenty <u>buffalo</u> hides were used for one tipi.

3. The basic frame consisted of three or <u>four</u> heavy poles.

4. Smaller poles rested on <u>this</u> frame.

5. Tribes were <u>usually</u> known as three-pole people or four-pole people.

6. The <u>Comanche</u> tipis had four poles.

7. The chief's dwellings were <u>artistically</u> painted.

8. The paintings were quite <u>colorful</u>.

9. <u>The</u> chief's home had a streamer over its door.

10. <u>This</u> was made of buckskin, cloth, or fur.

1 **A** pronoun
   B antecedent
   C adjective
   D adverb

2 **A** adjective
   B noun
   C predicate nominative
   D antecedent

3 **A** article
   B adjective
   C noun
   D pronoun

4 **A** noun
   B article
   C pronoun
   D adjective

5 **A** adjective
   B noun
   C adverb
   D predicate adjective

6 **A** object
   B proper noun
   C proper adjective
   D antecedent

7 **A** adjective
   B adverb
   C predicate nominative
   D verb

8 **A** direct object
   B predicate nominative
   C predicate adjective
   D verb

9 **A** predicate adjective
   B article
   C noun
   D adverb

10 **A** adjective
    B noun
    C article
    D pronoun

CHAPTER 5

Other Parts of Speech and Review

 **Pretest**

Directions
Write the letter of the term that correctly identifies the underlined word or words in each sentence.

EXAMPLE

1. The police in Scotts Valley wanted an unusual <u>Website</u>.
   1 **A** adjective
   B noun
   C conjunction
   D pronoun

ANSWER   **1 B**

1. Sergeant John Weiss enjoyed training <u>new</u> police officers.
2. <u>He</u> often used his own cartoons during his lectures.
3. One of his co-workers <u>was designing</u> a Website.
4. Officer Loomis thought, "<u>Hey!</u> I have a great idea!"
5. He asked Sergeant Weiss to draw cartoons <u>for it</u>.
6. Weiss drew cartoons of <u>everyone</u> in the station.
7. They posted the cartoons <u>and</u> information about the officers.
8. They <u>also</u> offered an on-line tour of the police station.
9. Visitors could visit <u>either</u> the public rooms <u>or</u> the staff rooms.
10. This <u>California</u> Website became immediately popular.

1 **A** adjective
   B noun
   C proper noun
   D verb

2 **A** article
   B pronoun
   C noun
   D direct object

3 **A** preposition
   B noun
   C adverb
   D verb

4 **A** interjection
   B article
   C conjunction
   D pronoun

5 **A** verbal phrase
   B predicate nominative
   C direct object
   D prepositional phrase

6 **A** noun
   B pronoun
   C proper noun
   D preposition

7 **A** article
   B interjection
   C conjunction
   D preposition

8 **A** conjunction
   B preposition
   C adverb
   D interjection

9 **A** adverb
   B correlative
       conjunctions
   C adjective
   D interjection

10 **A** proper adjective
   B common noun
   C proper noun
   D verb

Doris Lee. *Thanksgiving,* 1935.
Oil on canvas, 28¹/₁₀ by 40 inches. The Art Institute of Chicago.

Describe   In what ways is this painting true to life? Are there any details in the painting that do not seem realistic? If so, what are they?

Analyze   How did the artist use the colors red and white to make the elements in the foreground seem connected to one another?

Interpret   What impressions of this holiday do you think the artist is trying to give you? Which elements make you think so?

Judge   If you could add something to Lee's painting, what would it be? Why?

At the end of this chapter, you will use the artwork to stimulate ideas for writing.

Prepositions

Pretend that someone has just asked you for directions to your school. A small word such as *before, at, across,* or *after* could make all the difference in whether or not that person finds the school based on your directions.

The building
before the intersection
at the intersection
across the intersection
after the intersection
} is the school.

The words *before, at, across,* and *after* show the relationship of the building to the intersection. These words are called prepositions.

A **preposition** is a word that shows the relationship between a noun or a pronoun and another word in the sentence.

The following is a list of the most common prepositions.

COMMON PREPOSITIONS			
about	behind	from	over
above	below	in	through
across	beneath	inside	to
after	beside	into	toward
against	between	near	under
along	beyond	of	until
among	by	off	up
around	down	on	with
at	during	out	within
before	for	outside	without

We spoke **during** my lessons.
The person **on** that horse is my instructor.
Don't ride **among** those tall trees.
Down the hill my instructor waited **for** me.

PRACTICE YOUR SKILLS

● Check Your Understanding
Supplying Prepositions

Contemporary Life | **Write a preposition for each blank. Do not use the same preposition more than once.**

1. The brown building ▨ the house is the stable.
2. Many beautiful horses live ▨ its roof.
3. I cannot wait ▨ the day of my riding lessons.
4. My horse's stall is ▨ the front.
5. His name is ▨ the door of his stall.
6. He can jump ▨ most ditches.
7. ▨ the stream he has lots of chances to jump.
8. I keep carrots for him ▨ my coat pocket.
9. I ride him ▨ the property.
10. ▨ you and me, my lessons are the best part of the week!

▶ Prepositional Phrases

A preposition is always the first word of a group of words called a prepositional phrase.

A **prepositional phrase** is a group of words made up of a preposition, its object, and any words that describe the object.

PREPOSITIONAL PHRASES	**During *lunch*** we visited the museum. (*Lunch* is the object of the preposition *during*.)
	They brought their lunch **with *them*.** (*Them* is the object of the preposition *with*.)
	We stayed **until the afternoon *lecture*.** (*Lecture* is the object of the preposition *until*.)

A prepositional phrase can have two or more objects. Such a phrase has a **compound object of the preposition.**

The lecture **about the *moon* and *stars*** was interesting.
(*Moon* and *stars* are objects of the preposition *about*.)

We will go **into the gift *shop* or the lunar *exhibit*.**
(*Shop* and *exhibit* are objects of the preposition *into*.)

A sentence can have more than one prepositional phrase, as shown by the following examples.

During the *lecture*, I took notes **on my *computer*.**

The distance **of the *moon* from the *earth*** is very great.

You can learn more about prepositional phrases on pages L177–L185.

CONNECT TO WRITER'S CRAFT

Normally, people write the way they talk. They usually begin a sentence with the subject. That is the normal order for a sentence. You can create variety in your writing by beginning some sentences with prepositional phrases.

| NORMAL ORDER | A shooting star drew an arc of light **across the night sky.** |
| VARIETY | **Across the night sky,** a shooting star drew an arc of light. |

PRACTICE YOUR SKILLS

● Check Your Understanding
Finding Prepositional Phrases

Contemporary
Life   **Write each prepositional phrase.**

1. A museum in Boston once had a wonderful idea.

2. It sold land on the surface of the moon.

3. The prices started at $25.

4. All of the lots had a good view of Earth.

5. All owners received "deeds" to their lunar property.

6. These unofficial deeds came with certain rights.

7. Property owners could walk, land, and settle on the moon.

8. For these rights owners made a promise.

9. They would respect any moon creatures within their property.

10. The museum used the money from these lunar sales for additional exhibits and programs.

● Check Your Understanding
Identifying Objects in Prepositional Phrases

History
Topic   **Write each prepositional phrase. Underline each preposition once and its object twice.**

11. The open-toed purple boots of Roman emperors were decorated with jewels and gold thread.

12. Some years later leather shoes from Africa arrived in Europe.

13. These shoes had long tips, and people often fell over them.

14. Eventually people fastened the tips of their shoes to their knees or waist.

15. These shoes, for all their problems, lasted through four centuries.

16. Then people wore wide shoes on their feet.

17. These shoes sometimes stretched beyond ten inches.

18. Inside them were wool, hair, or hay.

19. Because Louis XIV was not tall, he ordered high heels under his shoes.

20. These fancy shoes on the king's feet also had bows and flowers among their decorations.

● Connect to the Writing Process: Revising
Expanding Sentences with Prepositional Phrases

Write the following sentences, adding at least one prepositional phrase to each sentence.

21. We had a wonderful day.

22. We watched the people go by.

23. Someone waved at us.

24. People visited the lake.

25. We rented a canoe.

◉ Preposition or Adverb?

The same word can be a preposition in one sentence and an adverb in another sentence. How a word is used in a sentence determines what part of speech it is. A word such as *above* is a preposition only if it is part of a prepositional phrase. It is an adverb if it stands alone and answers the question *Where?*

PREPOSITION   A jet soared **above** the clouds.
(*Above the clouds* is a prepositional phrase.)

ADVERB	We heard a jet **above.** (*Above* is an adverb that tells *where* we heard the jet. It is not part of a prepositional phrase because there is no object of the preposition.)
PREPOSITION	The plane taxied ***down*** *the runway.*
ADVERB	The nose of the plane went **down.**

PRACTICE YOUR SKILLS

● Check Your Understanding

Distinguishing Between Adverbs and Prepositions

Contemporary Life

Label each underlined word as either an *adverb* or a *preposition*. If the word is a preposition, write the object of the preposition.

1. I spoke uneasily to the pilot <u>before</u> our afternoon flight.

2. I had never been on a plane <u>before</u>.

3. I sat <u>near</u> the window.

4. The clouds <u>outside</u> my bedroom window looked beautiful.

5. My sister saw snow-capped mountains <u>below</u> the plane.

6. The pilot pointed out a large lake <u>below</u>.

7. The pilot said our destination was <u>near</u>.

8. We headed <u>out</u> the door of the plane.

9. My sister stepped <u>out</u> first.

10. It was good to be <u>outside</u> again.

Writing Sentences Using Adverbs and Prepositions

Write two sentences for each of the following words. Use the word as an adverb in the first sentence. Use the word as a preposition in the second sentence.

11. up

12. around

13. above

14. through

15. inside

Communicate Your Ideas

APPLY TO WRITING

Writer's Craft: *Analyzing the Use of Prepositional Phrases*

Professional writers use a great deal of variety in their sentence structure. Poets, in particular, seek ways to make their work seem fresh and new. Read the following excerpt from Carl Sandburg's poem "Masses" and follow the directions below it.

> Among the mountains I wandered and saw blue
>   haze and red crag and was amazed:
> On the beach where the long push under the
>   endless tide maneuvers, I stood silent;
> Under the stars on the prairie watching the Dipper
>   slant over the horizon's grass, I was full of
>   thoughts.
>
> —*Carl Sandburg,* "Masses"

- Write all the prepositional phrases in this passage. Underline the preposition once and its object twice.

- Rewrite the first line of this poem, moving the prepositional phrase from the beginning of the line and placing it after the word *wandered*.

- Read your new line and compare it to Sandburg's original. Which do you like better? Why?
- What overall effect does Sandburg create by beginning each of these lines with a prepositional phrase?

QuickCheck Mixed Practice

Geography Topic **Write each prepositional phrase.**

1. By October the first snow falls in Yellowstone National Park.

2. Soon temperatures drop below zero.

3. Strong winds swirl the snow along the ground.

4. Winter at Yellowstone National Park will last for six long, cold months.

5. Around the park visitors will see some very unusual sights.

6. During the winter the geysers still erupt.

7. Underground steam explosions force hot water through a narrow opening.

8. Castle Geyser shoots water ninety feet into the air for nearly twenty minutes.

9. Old Faithful faithfully erupts on a fairly regular schedule.

10. After an eruption a geyser is quiet.

Conjunctions and Interjections

Conjunctions and interjections are parts of speech. Conjunctions connect words, and interjections show strong feeling.

A **conjunction** connects words or groups of words.

The following is a list of the most common coordinating conjunctions. These conjunctions connect single words and groups of words.

COORDINATING CONJUNCTIONS			
and	but	or	yet

CONNECTING WORDS	I want to be a *teacher* **or** a *singer*. (connects nouns)
	Those are jobs for *him* **and** *her*. (connects pronouns)
	Actors *rehearse* **and** *perform*. (connects verbs)
	Many careers are *interesting* **but** *dangerous*. (connects adjectives)
	Reporters must work *quickly* **yet** *accurately*. (connects adverbs)
CONNECTING GROUPS OF WORDS	I can work *in an office* **or** *at home*. (connects prepositional phrases)
	Firefighters *extinguish dangerous blazes* **and** *save people's lives*. (connects complete predicates)

Another kind of conjunction used in English is the correlative conjunction. **Correlative conjunctions** are pairs of conjunctions. Like coordinating conjunctions, these conjunctions connect words and groups of words.

CORRELATIVE CONJUNCTIONS		
both/and	either/or	neither/nor

CONNECTING WORDS	My uncle has served as **both** *a lawyer* **and** *a judge.*
	(connects nouns)
	A marine biologist's work seems **neither** *easy* **nor** *monotonous.*
	(connects adjectives)
CONNECTING GROUPS OF WORDS	After high school **either** *I will enroll in college courses,* **or** *I will attend the police academy.*
	(connects sentences)

CONNECT TO WRITER'S CRAFT

Conjunctions can be very useful words. You can avoid repetition by combining two sentences or their elements to make your writing clearer and more concise.

TWO SENTENCES	Mateo visited the newspaper office. His whole class went along.
COMBINED	Mateo **and** his whole class visited the newspaper office.
TWO SENTENCES	Cameron met Judge Chang. He did not interview the judge.
COMBINED	Cameron met Judge Chang **but** did not interview him.

An **interjection** is a word that expresses strong feeling.

COMMON INTERJECTIONS			
aha	oh	ugh	yes
goodness	oops	well	yikes
hooray	ouch	wow	yippee

An interjection at the beginning of a sentence is immediately followed by an exclamation point or a comma.

Goodness, that job seems difficult!

Yikes! I could never be an exterminator.

PRACTICE YOUR SKILLS

Check Your Understanding
Finding Conjunctions and Interjections

Contemporary Life **Write each conjunction and interjection. If the word is a conjunction, label it C. If it is an interjection, label it I.**

1. Yes, teachers must have a college degree.

2. Marcia would like to work with computers or in radio broadcasting.

3. Neither law nor medicine appeals to Stephen.

4. I will go to college and then get a good job.

5. Dana wants to work for the CIA but not the FBI.

6. Both Christopher and Josie are interested in corporate accounting.

7. Wow! I would love to be a pilot.

8. Choosing a career is difficult, but you have plenty of time to decide.

9. Next week a NASA scientist will visit either our class or theirs.

10. Well, that should be interesting.

● Connect to the Writing Process: Revising
Using Conjunctions to Combine Sentences

Combine each pair of sentences into one sentence, using a conjunction.

11. Reading is a great hobby. Reading is a good way to learn.

12. Libraries have huge collections of books. They also have magazines.

13. You should not be loud in the library. You should not run there.

14. Encyclopedias are in the reference section. Dictionaries are there also.

15. In a library you can read quietly. You can work on a computer.

16. You can search for a title on the computer. You can look for a title on the shelf.

17. The library sponsors informative nights. You can learn about interesting topics.

18. You can obtain a library card. You can borrow books.

● Connect to the Writing Process: Drafting
Writing Sentences with Interjections

Write a sentence for each of the following interjections.

19. Aha   **20.** Ouch   **21.** Yes   **22.** Ugh   **23.** Wow

APPLY TO WRITING

Journal: *Interjections and Conjunctions*

Carmen Lomas Garza. *Birthday Party,* 1989.
Oil on canvas, 36 by 48 inches. Collection of the artist.

Look carefully at this work of art, making mental
notes of details in the picture. Then imagine that this
birthday party has been thrown for you. Now, it is
late in the evening, and you sit down to write in your
journal. Describe your birthday party. Include lots of
action and tell how you felt. As you write, use at
least one coordinating conjunction, one pair of
correlative conjunctions, and one interjection.
Underline these parts of speech in your work.

Parts of Speech Review

This section reviews the eight parts of speech. Remember that a word does not become a part of speech until it is used in a sentence. The word *light,* for example, can be used as three parts of speech.

NOUN	The **light** of the moon brightened our path.
VERB	Please **light** the lantern.
ADJECTIVE	The telescope was small and **light.**

The following series of questions will help you determine a word's part of speech.

NOUN Is the word naming a person, place, thing, or idea?

Lane watches the **planets** through a **telescope.**

PRONOUN Is the word taking the place of a noun?

This is **his** telescope.

VERB Is the word showing action?

The stars **twinkled** in the night sky.

Does the word link the subject with another word in the sentence?

Astronomy **is** an interesting science.

ADJECTIVE Is the word describing a noun or a pronoun? Does it answer the question *What kind? How many? How much?* or *Which one?*

That **small red** planet is **beautiful.**

ADVERB	Is the word describing a verb, an adjective, or another adverb? Does it answer the question *How? When? Where?* or *To what extent?*

Usually the telescope works **quite well.**

PREPOSITION	Is the word showing a relationship between a noun or a pronoun and another word in the sentence? Is it part of a phrase?

After *dark* we'll take the telescope ***into*** the *backyard*.

CONJUNCTION	Is the word connecting words or groups of words?

Earth's neighbors are Mars **and** Venus. We can get a book about constellations **either** at the library **or** at a bookstore.

INTERJECTION	Is the word expressing strong feeling?

Wow! The sky is very clear tonight!

PRACTICE YOUR SKILLS

● Check Your Understanding
Identifying Parts of Speech

General Interest **Write each underlined word. Beside each one, write its part of speech, using these abbreviations:**

noun = *n.*   pronoun = *pro.*   conjunction = *con.*
adjective = *adj.*   adverb = *adv.*   preposition = *prep.*
verb = *v.*   interjection = *int.*

1. All the planets, except Earth, were named <u>for</u> <u>a</u> <u>god</u> or goddess in mythology.

2. <u>Mercury</u>, the planet closest <u>to</u> the sun, is named for the Roman god of travel.

3. Mercury <u>travels</u> around the sun in only <u>eighty-eight</u> days.

4. Venus is named for the goddess of love <u>and</u> <u>beauty</u>.

5. <u>She</u> was beautiful, and to people on Earth, Venus <u>is</u> the most beautiful planet.

6. It <u>shines</u> very <u>brightly</u> in the morning or evening.

7. <u>Sometimes</u> Venus looks like a beacon <u>or</u> the <u>taillight</u> of an airplane.

8. <u>Yes!</u> Jupiter is named for the <u>king</u> of the gods.

9. <u>It</u> is the <u>largest</u> planet.

10. The moons <u>around</u> Jupiter are <u>also</u> named after mythological characters.

● Check Your Understanding
Identifying Parts of Speech

History Topic **Write each underlined word. Beside each one, write its part of speech, using these abbreviations:**

noun = *n.*	pronoun = *pro.*	conjunction = *con.*
adjective = *adj.*	adverb = *adv.*	preposition = *prep.*
verb = *v.*	interjection = *int.*	

11. Hundreds of years ago, lotus plants were growing <u>in</u> a lake in <u>China</u>.

12. <u>Eventually</u> the <u>lake</u> dried up.

13. Many of the lotus <u>seeds</u> were preserved in the <u>hard</u> mud.

14. A <u>Japanese</u> scientist <u>carefully</u> dug some of the seeds out of the mud.

15. He put <u>them</u> into a box and forgot about them for <u>thirty</u> years.

16. In 1951, <u>he</u> gave two seeds to an <u>American</u> scientist.

17. Then <u>that</u> man returned to <u>America</u>.

18. He <u>put</u> the seeds on damp cotton under a <u>glass</u> cover.

19. <u>Surprise</u>! These seeds soon sprouted <u>and</u> grew into lotus plants.

20. <u>Now</u> the descendants of <u>those</u> seeds thrive in the Kenilworth Aquatic Gardens in Washington, D.C.

● Check Your Understanding
Identifying Parts of Speech

Science Topic **Write each underlined word. Beside each one, write its part of speech, using these abbreviations:**

noun = *n.*   pronoun = *pro.*   conjunction = *con.*
adjective = *adj.*   adverb = *adv.*   preposition = *prep.*
verb = *v.*   interjection = *int.*

21. Twice a year <u>many</u> animals make long <u>journeys</u>.

22. <u>They</u> migrate from place <u>to</u> place.

23. Swallows <u>are</u> great travelers.

24. Each spring these small birds leave Africa <u>and</u> fly to <u>Europe</u>.

25. <u>Faithfully</u>, many kinds of salmon migrate <u>from</u> rivers to the sea.

26. <u>Wow</u>! The <u>European</u> eel swims nearly three thousand miles.

27. <u>After</u> its long journey, <u>it</u> lays its eggs.

28. Reindeer live <u>near</u> the <u>North</u> Pole.

29. In <u>winter</u> their food supply grows <u>short</u> so they travel up to fifty miles per day.

30. The reindeer <u>travel</u> hundreds <u>of</u> miles to the south in search of food.

Identifying Parts of Speech

Science Topic **Write each underlined word. Beside each one, write its part of speech, using these abbreviations:**

noun = *n.*   pronoun = *pro.*   conjunction = *con.*
adjective = *adj.*   adverb = *adv.*   preposition = *prep.*
verb = *v.*   interjection = *int.*

31. A beehive is about the size of a small doghouse.

32. In summer it houses up to sixty thousand bees.

33. Wow! The queen bee has only one job.

34. She lays about fifteen hundred eggs each day.

35. Worker bees do all the household chores constantly.

36. The youngest bees always stay inside the hive.

37. They clean the cells or care for the eggs.

38. After three weeks they graduate to outside jobs.

39. Workers usually stay within two miles of the hive.

40. Goodness! In six weeks they wear out their wings and die.

Check Your Understanding
Completing Sentences with Different Parts of Speech

General Interest **Write each sentence completing it with the part of speech indicated in parentheses.**

41. Would ■ live in an underground house? (pronoun)

42. Baldasare Forestiere liked the ■ very much. (noun)

43. In 1906, he dug a ■ underground home. (adjective)

44. He carved it out of clay near Fresno, ■ . (noun)

45. He used only ■ tools such as a pick. (adjective)

46. ■ he scooped out only a kitchen and a bedroom, but then he dug more and more. (adverb)

47. ■ ! He eventually had sixty-five rooms. (interjection)

48. Most rooms had holes in the roof for light ■ air. (conjunction)

49. He ■ shrubs and tropical trees and added a fishpond and a fireplace for chilly nights. (verb)

50. Now this home is open ■ visitors. (preposition)

● Connect to the Writing Process: Drafting
Writing Sentences with Different Parts of Speech

Write five sentences that contain the indicated parts of speech. Underline and label each part of speech.

51. a verb and an interjection

52. an adjective and an adverb

53. a pronoun and a noun

54. a preposition and a conjunction

55. an adjective and a pronoun

Communicate Your Ideas

APPLY TO WRITING

Speech: *Parts of Speech*

Your school is having an election for class officers. You have decided to run for sixth-grade class president. Write a speech that you will deliver in front of all the sixth graders. Tell your classmates why you would be a good president and what you will do for them if you are elected. As you write, use each part of speech at least once. Underline one example of each part of speech and label it: *noun, verb, pronoun, adjective, adverb, preposition, conjunction,* or *interjection.*

CheckPoint

Finding Prepositions, Conjunctions, Interjections, and Prepositional Phrases

Write the following sentences. Label each preposition *(prep.)*, conjunction *(con.)*, and interjection *(int.)*. Then underline each prepositional phrase.

1. Does everyone in your home want a cat?
2. Wait! Do family members or friends get sick around cats?
3. A cat can live for eighteen years and will need your care and love during all those years.
4. Kittens shouldn't be taken from their mother before eight weeks.
5. Look for a kitten with bright eyes.
6. At your home you will need food for the new cat, but it should not be scraps from the table.
7. Make your cat a nice, warm bed inside a box.
8. Important! Never place a litter box near the cat's bed or food.
9. Yes! Excellent toys are pieces of string and small balls.
10. Shots will protect your cat against diseases.

Identifying Parts of Speech

Write each underlined word. Then write its part of speech beside each word, using the following abbreviations:

noun = *n.*   pronoun = *pro.*   adjective = *adj.*
adverb = *adv.*   conjunction = *con.*   verb = *v.*
interjection = *int.*   preposition = *prep.*

1. The <u>Italian</u> waiter was <u>extremely</u> polite.

2. <u>With</u> the main dish, you can have soup <u>or</u> a salad.
3. I have <u>never</u> tasted sun-dried <u>olives</u>.
4. <u>These</u> mushrooms are quite <u>tasty</u>.
5. <u>They</u> take great <u>pride</u> in their authentic Italian cooking.
6. This dish <u>came</u> from the region called <u>Siena</u>.
7. Slices <u>of</u> ham <u>and</u> cheese are wrapped around the chicken.
8. The chefs cover the chicken <u>with</u> <u>bread</u> crumbs.
9. They <u>toast</u> the cheese for a short <u>time</u>.
10. <u>Well</u>! I certainly don't like <u>these</u>!

Determining Parts of Speech

Write each underlined word. Then beside each word, label its part of speech: *noun, pronoun,* or *adjective.*

1. WDRC is my favorite <u>radio</u> station.
2. My sister just got a <u>diamond</u> engagement ring.
3. We should discuss <u>that</u> as soon as possible.
4. Listen to the special program on the <u>radio</u> tonight.
5. Is that a real <u>diamond</u>?
6. I baked <u>that</u> loaf of bread myself.

Using Parts of Speech

Write five sentences that follow the directions below. Then label the use of each word in the sentences.

1. Use *picture* as a noun and an adjective.
2. Use *up* as an adverb and a preposition.
3. Use *watch* as a noun, an adjective, and a verb.
4. Use *well* as a noun and an interjection.
5. Use *water* as a noun, an adjective, and a verb.

When you have finished, label each part of speech.

Language and *Self-Expression*

Thanksgiving Day means something different to each of us. Doris Lee chose to focus on the preparations in the kitchen rather than on the family sitting around a table. What do you think this says about her image of Thanksgiving?

Imagine that you are writing the script for a film about a family celebrating Thanksgiving. It could be the family in this picture, your own family, or an imaginary one. Writing in the present tense, describe what the camera sees and hears as you enter the room. What is the room like? What are the people in it doing and saying?

Prewriting Think geographically. Make a cluster diagram with notes on what is visible in each area of the room. Number your clusters in the order you will describe the areas. Make notes on possible dialogue.

Drafting Using the diagram, write your script. Your opening should give a general idea of the setting. Be very specific when you add details.

Revising Have a classmate read and give you feedback on your script. Ask whether there is anything that your partner is unable to see clearly. Make sure that your prepositional phrases are properly placed.

Editing Check your paragraphs for errors in punctuation and spelling. Be sure that you used commas and conjunctions correctly.

Publishing Read your script aloud to your classmates. Encourage them to close their eyes and visualize the scene as you read. Ask them to share their impressions.

Another Look

A **preposition** is a word that shows the relationship between a noun or a pronoun and another word in the sentence.

A **prepositional phrase** is a group of words made up of a preposition, its object, and any words that describe the object.

A **conjunction** connects words or groups of words.

COORDINATING CONJUNCTIONS			
and	but	or	yet

Correlative conjunctions are pairs of conjunctions that connect words and groups of words.

An **interjection** is a word that expresses strong feeling.

Other Parts of Speech

A **noun** is a word that names a person, place, thing, or idea. *(page L162)*
A **pronoun** is a word that takes the place of one or more nouns.
(page L162)
A **verb** is a word used to express an action or a state of being.
(page L162)
An **adjective** is a word that modifies, or describes, a noun or a pronoun.
(page L162)
An **adverb** is a word that modifies, or describes, a verb, an adjective, or an adverb. *(page L163)*

Other Information About Parts of Speech

Distinguishing between prepositions and adverbs *(pages L153–L154)*
Using coordinating conjunctions *(page L157)*
Using correlative conjunctions *(page L158)*
Reviewing parts of speech *(pages L162–L163)*

Directions
Write the letter of the term that correctly identifies the underlined word or words in each sentence.

EXAMPLE   **1.** Sugar <u>once</u> was very important in the South's economy.
    1 A adjective
    B noun
    C pronoun
    D adverb

ANSWER   **1 D**

1. Norbert Rillieux was born in Louisiana <u>in</u> 1806.

2. His mother may have been <u>either</u> a slave <u>or</u> a free woman.

3. Certainly he was free <u>himself</u>.

4. His father sent him <u>to</u> good schools in New Orleans.

5. He finished his education in a <u>French</u> college.

6. As an engineer he was interested in <u>steam</u> technology.

7. He <u>had</u> watched sugar refining on his father's plantation.

8. They used a slow <u>and</u> inefficient method.

9. "<u>Aha!</u>" Rillieux thought to himself. "There is a better way to do that!"

10. He invented a <u>much</u> better refining system, using steam power.

1 **A** article
   B preposition
   C conjunction
   D interjection

2 **A** article
   B preposition
   C correlative
          conjunctions
   D interjection

3 **A** noun
   B preposition
   C pronoun
   D adverb

4 **A** preposition
   B article
   C interjection
   D conjunction

5 **A** direct object
   B proper adjective
   C proper noun
   D adverb

6 **A** adverb
   B noun
   C verb
   D adjective

7 **A** helping verb
   B linking verb
   C main verb
   D verb phrase

8 **A** interjection
   B article
   C conjunction
   D preposition

9 **A** noun
   B adverb
   C adjective
   D interjection

10 **A** pronoun
    B adverb
    C adjective
    D article

Phrases

• •

Directions
Write the letter of the term that correctly identifies the underlined word or words in each sentence.

EXAMPLE
1. Some islands <u>in the Pacific Ocean</u> are live or dead volcanoes.

   1 A adverb phrase
     B proper noun
     C appositive phrase
     D adjective phrase

ANSWER
   1 D

1. Krakatoa, <u>a famous volcano</u>, is near Java.
2. Several volcanic cones once rose <u>from this uninhabited island</u>.
3. A series of eruptions began <u>in May, 1883</u>.
4. <u>By August</u>, the eruptions had become violent.
5. The first <u>of several huge explosions</u> took place on August 26.
6. People in Jakarta, <u>a city 100 miles away</u>, heard the blast.
7. <u>All the next morning</u>, eruptions shook the island.
8. The fourth blast, <u>the strongest one</u>, sent debris 50 miles into the air.
9. <u>After the eruptions</u>, only one third of the island remained.
10. Darkness fell over 300,000 square miles <u>around the volcano</u>.

1 A adverb phrase
  B adjective phrase
  C appositive phrase
  D predicate nominative

2 A adverb phrase
  B predicate nominative
  C adjective phrase
  D appositive phrase

3 A adverb phrase
  B adjective phrase
  C appositive phrase
  D none of the above

4 A direct object
  B adjective phrase
  C appositive phrase
  D adverb phrase

5 A adjective phrase
  B adverb phrase
  C complete subject
  D appositive phrase

6 A indirect object
  B adjective phrase
  C appositive phrase
  D adverb phrase

7 A adjective phrase
  B appositive phrase
  C adverb phrase
  D complete subject

8 A appositive phrase
  B adjective phrase
  C adverb phrase
  D none of the above

9 A appositive phrase
  B adverb phrase
  C adjective phrase
  D complete subject

10 A adjective phrase
  B complete predicate
  C adverb phrase
  D appositive phrase

Grant Wood. *American Gothic,*
1930.
Oil on beaver board, 29¾ by 25
inches. The Art Institute of Chicago.

Describe What shapes are repeated in the painting? Where are they repeated?

Analyze Who do you think the people in this picture are? What elements in the picture are clues to the kind of life they lead?

Interpret Europeon *Gothic* architecture was known for great solemn cathedrals with pointed arches and mythological sculptures. Why do you think Grant Wood called his painting *American Gothic?*

Judge This is one of the best known paintings by an American artist. Why do you think it became so famous?

At the end of this chapter, you will use the artwork to stimulate ideas for writing.

Prepositional Phrases

A **phrase** is a group of related words that acts like a single part of speech. You already know one kind of phrase—a prepositional phrase.

A prepositional phrase is a group of words that begins with a preposition, ends with a noun or a pronoun, and is used as an adjective or an adverb.

Since all prepositional phrases begin with a preposition, you should be familiar with the prepositions on the following list.

COMMON PREPOSITIONS			
about	beneath	into	to
above	beside	like	toward
across	between	near	under
after	beyond	of	underneath
against	by	off	until
along	down	on	up
among	during	out	upon
around	except	outside	with
at	for	over	within
because of	from	past	without
before	in	since	
behind	in front of	through	
below	inside	throughout	

PREPOSITIONAL PHRASES	Mountains tower **above the sea.**
	Many kinds **of animals** call Alaska home.

● Check Your Understanding
Finding Prepositional Phrases

| Geography Topic | **Write each prepositional phrase. Remember that a sentence can have more than one prepositional phrase.** |

1. Alaska is the largest state in the United States.

2. Native Americans hunted throughout this vast area for centuries.

3. With both volcanoes and ice floes, Alaska's landscape is varied.

4. Mount McKinley, near the middle of the state, is North America's highest peak.

5. Among Alaska's other features are the Malaspina Glacier and the Yukon River.

6. There are many open spaces throughout this large state.

7. Alaska juts far into the Arctic Circle.

8. A long pipeline stretches across the state.

9. The pipeline transports oil from Prudhoe Bay to Valdez.

10. During the summer Alaska experiences almost twenty-four hours of daylight every day.

● Adjective Phrases

You know that an adjective is a word that describes a noun or a pronoun. A whole prepositional phrase can act like a single adjective. It can also describe a noun or a pronoun. When it does, it is called an adjective phrase.

SINGLE ADJECTIVE   The **friendly** dog wagged its tail.

ADJECTIVE PHRASE   The dog **with the black spots**
                    caught the ball.

Notice that both the adjective *friendly* and the prepositional phrase *with the black spots* tell something about the *dog*. They both tell what kind of dog it is.

> An **adjective phrase** is a prepositional phrase that modifies, or describes, a noun or a pronoun.

An adjective phrase also answers the same questions that a single adjective answers: *Which one?* and *What kind?*

WHICH ONE?   That beagle **with the red collar** is
              my dog.

WHAT KIND?   I read a book **about dog breeds.**

Notice that in all of the preceding examples, an adjective phrase comes directly after the word it modifies. Of course, a sentence can have more than one adjective phrase.

One **of my friends** wrote a report **on Dalmatians.**

PRACTICE YOUR SKILLS

● Check Your Understanding
Finding Adjective Phrases

General
Interest   **Write each adjective phrase.**

1. Many people across the country keep pets.

2. There are many different breeds of dog.

3. Magazines about this animal are readily available.

4. Books from the library also have good information about dogs.

5. Millions of people adopt dogs from shelters each year.

6. Volunteers at animal shelters wash and feed dogs.

7. People with pets live longer lives.

8. Canines can be great companions to the elderly.

9. Dogs give a great deal of love.

10. The owners of dogs appreciate their loyalty.

● Check Your Understanding
Finding Adjective Phrases and the Words They Modify

General Interest **Write each adjective phrase. Beside each one, write the word it modifies.**

11. People keep pets of all kinds.

12. The animal shelter in your city probably houses many different animals.

13. Thousands of homeless cats live there.

14. Dogs of all sizes stay there too.

15. Many newspapers have columns about animals in the local shelter.

● Connect to the Writing Process: Revising
Adding Adjective Phrases

Rewrite the following sentences, adding at least one adjective phrase. Underline the noun or pronoun that each phrase modifies.

16. That dog is my best friend.

17. Hamsters make good pets.

18. My cousin has a pet turtle.

19. Obedience classes are a good idea.

20. The owners learn too.

APPLY TO WRITING

Personal Narrative: *Adjective Phrases*

Alma Gunter, *Dinner on the Grounds,* 1979–80.
Acrylic on canvas, 24 by 18 inches. African American Museum, Dallas, Texas.

Look closely at this painting. Imagine that you are the dog at the bottom left in this painting. For your teacher, write an account of your day at this picnic from the dog's point of view. Remember that a good narrative is told in time order, uses lots of description of setting and characters, and describes the feelings that the author experiences. As you write be sure to use at least four adjective phrases in your writing. When you have finished your narrative, underline the adjective phrases that you used.

Misplaced Adjective Phrases

Because adjective phrases tell something about the nouns or pronouns they describe, they should be placed as close to those words as they can. Sometimes, however, an adjective phrase will get too far from the word it describes. When it does, it is called a **misplaced modifier.** Sometimes a misplaced modifier confuses the meaning of a sentence, and sometimes it just makes the sentence sound very silly.

MISPLACED MODIFIERS

In the blue vase, Mom smelled the flowers. (Because the phrase is misplaced, the sentence seems to be saying that Mom is in the blue vase smelling the flowers.)

Mom gave a rose to a friend **without thorns.** (Because of the misplaced modifier, the sentence seems to be saying the friend without thorns received a rose from Mom.)

To correct a misplaced modifier, place the adjective phrase next to the word it actually describes.

CORRECT MODIFIERS

Mom smelled the flowers **in the blue vase.**

Mom gave a rose **without thorns** to a friend.

PRACTICE YOUR SKILLS

 Check Your Understanding
Identifying Misplaced Adjective Phrases

 Science Topic   **Read the following sentences. If the sentence contains a misplaced modifier, label it *I* for incorrect. If the adjective phrase in the sentence is placed correctly, write C.**

1. Most plants need sunlight with blooms.

2. Some of them like shady places.

3. Gardeners with minerals and vitamins should use fertilizers.

4. In containers many apartment dwellers raise tomatoes.

5. Insects will eat vegetable sprouts with hearty appetites.

6. Other insects promote the growth of healthy plants.

7. About gardens people can get hints.

8. Many sites on the Internet offer advice.

9. With questions plant experts can help people.

10. Growing a plant can be fun from a little seed.

● Connect to the Writing Process: Editing
Correcting Misplaced Modifiers

11.–17. Rewrite the incorrect sentences from the preceding exercise, placing the adjective phrase close to the noun it modifies.

● **Adverb Phrases**

Like a single adverb, a prepositional phrase can modify a verb. This kind of phrase is called an adverb phrase.

| SINGLE ADVERB | Sarah called **early.** |
| ADVERB PHRASE | Sarah called **before dawn.** |

In these examples both the adverb *early* and the prepositional phrase *before dawn* tell *when*.

An **adverb phrase** is a prepositional phrase that is used mainly to modify a verb.

Because adverb phrases do the same job as single adverbs, they also answer the same adverb questions: *Where? When?*

and *How?* Occasionally an adverb phrase will also answer the question *Why?*

WHERE?   We went **to an amusement park.**

                 Sarah ran **toward the bus.**

WHEN?   We left **at seven o'clock.**

                 Within an hour we arrived.

HOW?   Steve shouted **with excitement.**

                 With huge smiles we approached the ride.

WHY?   **Because of the long lines,** we waited.

                 People ride roller coasters **for thrills.**

As the preceding examples show, an adverb phrase can come anywhere in a sentence. In the following example, notice that the adverb phrase modifies the whole verb phrase.

I had been spending all my time **on the roller coaster.**

Also, just like adjective phrases, more than one adverb phrase can be in a sentence and modify the same verb.

For an hour we waited **in that line.**

PUNCTUATION WITH ADVERB PHRASES

If a short adverb phrase begins a sentence, usually no comma is needed. However, a comma should be placed after an introductory adverb phrase of four or more words, after two or more introductory phrases, or after a phrase that ends with a date.

No Comma	**During our trip** you should call home.
Comma	**During our class trip,** you should call home.
Comma	**During our class trip to the amusement park,** you should call home.
Comma	**During 1999,** I visited the amusement park.

Practice Your Skills

● Check Your Understanding
Finding Adverb Phrases

History Topic **Write each adverb phrase.**

1. During the 1700s, Russian fairs featured ice slides.

2. These rides were popular across the country.

3. The slides were built on a tall tower.

4. Riders sat on sleds.

5. Without fear people flew across the slick ice.

6. During the ride the sled required a skilled driver.

7. Poor drivers often crashed their sleds at the end.

8. Many people were hurt on the ice slides.

9. For safety reasons skilled drivers were hired.

10. This roller coaster-like ride spread across Europe.

● Check Your Understanding
Finding Adverb Phrases and the Words They Modify

History Topic **Write each adverb phrase. Beside each one, write the word it modifies.**

11. Many cultures have built pyramids across the world.

12. Before the pyramid tombs, the Egyptians buried their dead in sandpits.

13. They placed a rectangular structure over the burial place.

14. These mastabas held the sand in place.

15. Huge pyramids were built in Egypt.

16. Somehow the workers brought enormous stones to the site.

17. Before Columbus's arrival many American cultures had also built pyramids.

18. In Central and South America the people built pyramid-shaped temples.

19. An entire city was usually constructed around a pyramid.

20. The ancient priests worshipped there at all times.

● Connect to the Writing Process: Editing
Correcting Errors in Punctuation with Adverb Phrases

Read the following sentences. Add a comma to a sentence if one is needed. If a sentence is punctuated correctly, write C.

21. In Egypt at the base of the pyramids there is always activity.

22. After sunrise tourists arrive.

23. In the bazaars near the Sphinx salespeople attract tourists.

24. Through the crowds children sell souvenirs and trinkets.

25. Across the sand in the shadow of these ancient tombs tourists ride tall camels.

APPLY TO WRITING
Postcard: *Adverb Phrases*

Imagine that you are visiting Egypt. Write a postcard to a friend telling about your trip. Give your friend lots of details in a description that might make him or her want to visit this place. Before you begin writing, brainstorm ideas about the following:

- what you have seen
- what places you have visited
- how you got there
- what the weather is like
- how the place smells
- what sounds attract your attention

As you write, use at least two adverb phrases and underline them.

Write each prepositional phrase. Beside each one, write the word or words it modifies. Then label each prepositional phrase as an *adjective phrase* or *adverb phrase*.

1. The city of San Francisco has an interesting history.

2. In 1775, the first European explorers arrived in San Francisco Bay.

3. The Spanish explorers established forts and missions in the area.

4. The first name of this city was Yerba Buena.

5. The population had increased greatly by the mid 1800s.

6. Rich stores of gold had been discovered in California.

7. Seekers of wealth invaded the city.

8. Most of these prospectors never made their fortunes.

9. After the California gold rush, many people stayed in San Francisco.

10. The great earthquake of 1906 devastated the buildings of the city.

11. Huge cracks appeared in the streets and across buildings.

12. The shaking earth toppled lanterns and stoves in homes and buildings.

13. Fires burned the buildings of wood.

14. The spirit of the city was not devastated.

15. By 1909, most of San Francisco had been rebuilt.

Appositives and Appositive Phrases

When you are writing, sometimes it is necessary to explain or identify a noun or a pronoun. Often you can do this by adding another noun or pronoun called an appositive.

> Ms. Hunter teaches my favorite class, **history.**

> Ms. Hunter and Mr. Gonzales, **teachers,** plan lessons together.

An **appositive** is a noun or pronoun that identifies or explains another noun or pronoun in the sentence.

When an appositive has modifiers, it is called an **appositive phrase.**

> Today's lesson, **the one about first ladies,** was fascinating.

> Many first ladies, **wives of presidents,** have had interesting lives.

These examples show that a prepositional phrase can be part of an appositive phrase.

PUNCTUATION WITH APPOSITIVES AND APPOSITIVE PHRASES

If the information in an appositive is essential to the meaning of a sentence, no commas are needed. The information is essential if it identifies a person, place, or thing. However, a comma is needed before and after an appositive or an appositive phrase if the information is not essential to the meaning of the sentence.

You can usually tell if the information is essential or not by reading the sentence without the appositive. If it makes sense without the appositive, then the appositive is not essential.

ESSENTIAL	Former first lady **Nancy Davis Reagan** authored a book.
	(If Nancy Davis Reagan's name were dropped, the sentence would not make sense. Therefore, the appositive is essential and no commas are used.)
NOT ESSENTIAL	Nancy Davis Reagan, **a former first lady,** authored a book.
	(If the appositive phrase were dropped, the sentence would still make sense. Therefore, the appositive is not essential and needs a comma before and after it.)

You can learn more about using commas with appositives on page L462.

CONNECT TO WRITER'S CRAFT

When you write, you can use appositives to help make your writing clearer. When you place an appositive phrase next to a noun, you are adding information that helps make your writing more specific and easier to understand.

GENERAL	N. Scott Momaday wrote *The Way to Rainy Mountain.*
MORE SPECIFIC	N. Scott Momaday, **a Native American author,** wrote *The Way to Rainy Mountain.*
GENERAL	One of his books won the Pulitzer Prize.
MORE SPECIFIC	Momaday's book ***House Made of Dawn*** won the Pulitzer Prize.

PRACTICE YOUR SKILLS

● Check Your Understanding
Finding Appositives and Appositive Phrases

History Topic **Write each appositive or appositive phrase. Beside each one, write the word it renames.**

1. Martha Dandridge, a wealthy girl, was born on a Virginia plantation.

2. Her second husband, George Washington, became the first president.

3. Young Mary Todd, Abraham Lincoln's future wife, lost her mother at an early age.

4. In 1862, she was devastated by the loss of her son Willie.

5. Eleanor Roosevelt, wife of the thirty-second president, served as a United Nations delegate.

6. She wrote "My Day," a daily newspaper column.

7. Actress, Nancy Davis performed in eleven movies.

8. In Hollywood she met her husband, Ronald Reagan.

9. Hillary Rodham, a lawyer, married Bill Clinton.

10. *It Takes a Village,* Mrs. Clinton's book, was a bestseller.

● Connect to the Writing Process: Editing
Punctuating Appositives and Appositive Phrases

Rewrite the following sentences, underlining the appositive or appositive phrase in each. If an appositive or an appositive phrase is not essential to the meaning of a sentence, place a comma before and after it. If it is essential, write *E* after the sentence.

11. Lois Duncan an award-winning author has written many books for young people.

12. Her book *Summer of Fear* was made into a television movie.

13. In 1989, her teenage daughter Kaitlyn was killed.

14. *Who Killed My Daughter?* a nonfiction book by Lois Duncan is about the murder.

15. Mrs. Duncan a Florida native likes to get letters from her readers.

Communicate Your Ideas

APPLY TO WRITING

Description: *Appositives and Appositive Phrases*

Everyone should have someone to admire, such as Rosa Parks, pictured above. Write a description of someone you look up to. He or she can be someone you know or someone you've read about. Who is this person? What has he or she done to earn your respect? Why do you admire this person? As you write, use at least two appositives or appositive phrases in your work. Underline them.

General Interest **Write each phrase. Label each one as either adjective, adverb, or appositive.**

1. The president of the United States lives in the White House.

2. James Hoban, designer and builder of the White House, was an Irish immigrant.

3. John Adams and his wife became the first residents of the White House.

4. John, Jr., the son of President Kennedy, was its first baby resident.

5. Many pets have lived at the mansion.

6. Cats, dogs, and even a goat have been companions for presidents and their families.

7. President Carter's daughter Amy owned a cat.

8. The lawn of the White House is the site of the annual Easter Egg Roll.

9. Children roll hard-boiled eggs across the lawn.

10. Rutherford B. Hayes, the nineteenth president, officially opened the grounds for the Easter Egg Roll in 1878.

Diagraming Prepositional Phrases

A **prepositional phrase** is diagrammed underneath the word it describes.

Adjective Phrases   An adjective phrase is connected to the noun or pronoun it describes. The preposition is placed on a connecting slanted line. The object of the preposition is placed on a horizontal line that is attached to the slanted line. Any adjectives that describe the object of the preposition are attached on a slanted line under that noun or pronoun.

The team of eight horses was beautiful.

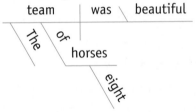

Adverb Phrases   An adverb phrase is connected to the word it modifies, which is usually the verb.

We walked along the river.

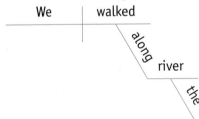

Appositives and Appositive Phrases An appositive is diagramed in parentheses next to the word it identifies or explains.

I like Mr. Weber, the coach of the soccer team.

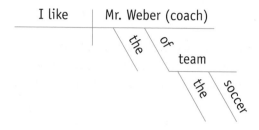

PRACTICE YOUR SKILLS

Diagraming

Diagram the following sentences or copy them. If you copy them, draw one line under each subject and two lines under each verb. Put parentheses around each phrase. Then label each one *adjective, adverb,* or *appositive.*

1. Many kids on my street rollerblade.
2. The good ones go to a rollerblade park.
3. My friend Paul collects comic books.
4. Comic books about superheroes are his favorite.
5. My grandparents travel to different countries.
6. They always send postcards during their trips.
7. Beth, my best friend, rides horses on weekends.
8. During the year I enjoy different sports.
9. I especially like a good game of baseball.
10. I always play first base, my best position.

Finding Prepositional Phrases

Write each prepositional phrase and each appositive phrase. Write the word or words each phrase describes. Then label each phrase *adj.* for adjective or *adv.* for adverb.

1. A grateful bee is a character in one Japanese folk tale.
2. A defeated warrior had hidden inside a cave.
3. Near him a bee struggled in the web of a spider.
4. The warrior freed the bee from the web.
5. During that night a man in brown appeared in his dreams.
6. He said, "Collect scores of old jars, and I will help you."
7. The hero of the story did this and then called his followers to him.
8. Bees from miles around hid themselves in the jars.
9. On the next day, the enemies of the small band attacked.
10. The bees swarmed on the enemy, and the enemy fled in terror from the forest.

Identifying Appositive Phrases

Write each appositive or appositive phrase. Then write the word the phrase identifies or renames.

1. The Bering Strait, a strip of water about 56 miles wide, separates Alaska from Siberia.
2. A year is only 88 days long on the planet Mercury.
3. We left San Juan, the capital, and headed southwest.
4. My friend Bert collects miniature flags.
5. The book *Kim* was written by Rudyard Kipling.

Understanding Phrases

Write the underlined phrase in each sentence. Then label each phrase *adjective*, *adverb*, or *appositive*.

1. Iceland is one <u>of the most active volcanic sites</u> in the world.
2. This country was nearly destroyed in 1783 <u>by lava eruptions</u>.
3. Laki, <u>the tallest mountain in the area</u>, had volcanic vents on either side of it.
4. Lava began pouring from these vents in June and flowed <u>for eight months</u>.
5. This was the earth's longest lava flow <u>in historical times</u>.
6. About 220 square miles were covered <u>with lava</u>.
7. A dark haze hung <u>over most of Europe</u>.
8. Poisonous fumes, <u>gases from the vents</u>, stunted crops.
9. Most <u>of Iceland's domestic animals</u> starved to death.
10. <u>In the following year</u>, one-fifth of Iceland's population died of famine.

Using Phrases

Write sentences that follow the directions below. (The sentences may come in any order.) Write about the following topic or a topic of your choice: your favorite television program.

Write a sentence that . . .

1. includes an adjective phrase.
2. includes an adverb phrase.
3. includes an introductory adverb phrase.
4. includes an appositive.
5. includes an appositive phrase.

When you have finished, underline and label each phrase. Then check for correct punctuation in each sentence.

Language and *Self-Expression*

Grant Wood intended this painting to show a farmer and his daughter. He often used family as models for his paintings. Wood's sister and his dentist posed for this picture. How do you think they felt about it?

There is more than one way to paint a portrait. Interview a special friend or family member about his or her interests and life history. Write the interview as a brief news article. Illustrate the final copy or print it on special paper. Then give it as a gift to the person you interviewed.

Prewriting Plan your questions before conducting the interview. During the interview, notice your subject's appearance. Create a sequence chart that shows how you will present information.

Drafting Use your chart to help you write the interview. Your first sentence should intrigue readers by mentioning something especially interesting about the subject.

Revising Read aloud your first sentence to a classmate. Ask whether it invites the reader to continue. Then have a classmate give you feedback on your news article. Make sure you have given enough information in phrases and appositives to make your meaning clear.

Editing Check your article for errors in punctuation and spelling. Be alert for punctuation errors with introductory adverb phrases and appositives.

Publishing Illustrate the final copy or print it on special paper. Read your article to your classmates before presenting it to the person you interviewed.

Another Look

A **prepositional phrase** is a group of words that begins with a preposition, ends with a noun or a pronoun, and is used as an adjective or an adverb.

An **adjective phrase** is a prepositional phrase that acts as an adjective and describes a noun or pronoun.

An **adverb phrase** is a prepositional phrase that acts as an adverb and modifies a verb.

Appositives and Appositive Phrases

An appositive is a noun or pronoun that identifies or explains another noun or pronoun in the sentence.

An **appositive phrase** is an appositive that has modifiers. *(pages L189–L190)*

Other Information About Phrases

A **misplaced modifier** is an adjective phrase that gets too far from the word it describes and confuses the meaning of a sentence. *(page L182)*
Punctuating with adverb phrases *(pages L184–L185)*
Punctuating with appositives and appositive phrases *(pages L189–L190)*
Diagraming prepositional phrases *(pages L194–L195)*

 **Posttest**

Directions

Write the letter of the term that correctly identifies the underlined word or words in each sentence.

EXAMPLE

1. Pitcairn Island, <u>a small volcanic crater</u>, lies southeast of Tahiti.

    1 **A** appositive phrase
       B predicate nominative
       C adverb phrase
       D adjective phrase

ANSWER   **1** **A**

1. In 1789, Captain Bligh was sailing <u>across the Pacific Ocean</u>.

2. His ship, <u>the *Bounty*</u>, carried a cargo of breadfruit.

3. Bligh, <u>a man with a terrible temper</u>, was disliked by his crew.

4. <u>In the Tonga Islands</u>, the crew mutinied.

5. They put Bligh and the men <u>on his side</u> into a small boat.

6. In an amazing feat <u>of navigation</u>, Bligh sailed 3,618 miles across the sea to safety.

7. The mutineers steered the *Bounty* <u>through the Polynesian Islands</u>.

8. Some <u>of them</u> left the ship and were captured later.

9. Eighteen men and women joined the crew of the *Bounty* <u>from Tahiti</u>.

10. They landed on the uninhabited Pitcairn Island <u>in 1790</u>.

1	**A**	appositive phrase	6	**A**	adverb phrase
	B	direct object		**B**	adjective phrase
	C	adjective phrase		**C**	appositive phrase
	D	adverb phrase		**D**	none of the above

2	**A**	appositive phrase	7	**A**	misplaced modifier
	B	adjective phrase		**B**	adjective phrase
	C	adverb phrase		**C**	adverb phrase
	D	misplaced modifier		**D**	appositive phrase

3	**A**	appositive phrase	8	**A**	appositive phrase
	B	adverb phrase		**B**	misplaced modifier
	C	adjective phrase		**C**	adverb phrase
	D	misplaced modifier		**D**	adjective phrase

4	**A**	misplaced modifier	9	**A**	proper noun
	B	adjective phrase		**B**	adverb phrase
	C	appositive phrase		**C**	misplaced modifier
	D	adverb phrase		**D**	appositive phrase

5	**A**	appositive phrase	10	**A**	adverb phrase
	B	adverb phrase		**B**	introductory adverb phrase
	C	adjective phrase		**C**	adjective phrase
	D	none of the above		**D**	appositive phrase

CHAPTER 7

Sentence Structure

 **Pretest**

Directions
Write the letter of the term that best identifies each sentence.

EXAMPLE **1.** The icy Bering Strait lies between Alaska and Russia.
   1 A simple sentence with compound verb
   B compound sentence
   C sentence fragment
   D simple sentence

ANSWER **1 D**

1. Big Diomede and Little Diomede are islands.
2. Little Diomede belongs to the United States, and Big Diomede belongs to Russia.
3. In 1987, a long-distance swimmer from California, Lynne Cox, swam from one island to the other.
4. No one had ever done this, she wanted to try.
5. The water was 39 degrees; she had never swum in such cold water.
6. In the Coast Guard's opinion, no one could survive for more than two hours in that cold sea.
7. She wore only a swimsuit and cap.
8. The distance between the two islands is 2.7 miles.
9. Cox was fighting the current and swam 4 to 6 miles.
10. She swam across in 2 hours and 12 minutes, a remarkable feat.

1. A compound sentence
   B simple sentence with compound subject
   C sentence fragment
   D simple sentence

2. A compound sentence
   B simple sentence with compound subject
   C simple sentence with compound verb
   D run-on sentence

3. A sentence fragment
   B run-on sentence
   C simple sentence with compound subject
   D simple sentence

4. A run-on sentence
   B sentence fragment
   C complex sentence
   D compound sentence

5. A sentence fragment
   B simple sentence with compound verb
   C compound sentence
   D run-on sentence

6. A compound sentence
   B simple sentence
   C simple sentence with compound subject
   D sentence fragment

7. A sentence fragment
   B simple sentence with compound verb
   C compound sentence
   D simple sentence

8. A simple sentence
   B simple sentence with compound subject
   C run-on sentence
   D sentence fragment

9. A sentence fragment
   B run-on sentence
   C simple sentence with compound verb
   D compound sentence

10. A sentence fragment
    B simple sentence with compound verb
    C simple sentence
    D run-on sentence

Christo and Jeanne-Claude. *Running Fence, Sonoma and Marin Counties, California,* 1972-1976.

Woven nylon fabric, stretched between steel poles, supported by steel cables, 18 feet by 24 ½ miles.

© 1976 Christo. Photograph by Jeanne-Claude.

Describe   You are looking at two works of art, not just one. What are these two? What makes each a work of art?

Analyze   The artists intended this work of art to change as the viewers looked at it. What are some ways in which the fence might change before your eyes?

Interpret   Do you think this artwork was intended to encourage people to appreciate nature? Why or why not?

Judge   What art forms does *Running Fence* remind you of? Why?

At the end of the chapter, you will use this artwork to stimulate ideas for writing.

Simple Sentences

There are different kinds of sentences. Including different kinds of sentences in your writing will give your writing more variety and make your writing more interesting. One kind of sentence is called a simple sentence.

> A **simple sentence** is a sentence that has one subject and one verb.

In the following examples, each subject is underlined once, and each verb is underlined twice.

ONE SUBJECT	A book can be a treasure.
ONE VERB	An encyclopedia contains information about many topics.

In a simple sentence, either the subject or the verb can be compound.

COMPOUND SUBJECT	Gary Paulsen and Katherine Paterson write novels for young adults. (Both subjects share the verb *write.*)
COMPOUND VERB	Some magazines seek and publish stories by young writers. (Both verbs share the subject *magazines.*)

CONNECT TO WRITER'S CRAFT

Writers often use sentences with compound subjects and verbs. They use compound elements in sentences to add rhythm and life to their work. Often they string together three subjects with one verb or three verbs with one subject for effect. Read the following examples aloud and listen to the rhythm created by the compound subjects and verbs.

COMPOUND SUBJECTS	The boy, his sister, and their dog entered the public library.
COMPOUND VERBS	Jonas walks, eats, and even sleeps with a book in his hand.

PRACTICE YOUR SKILLS

● Check Your Understanding
Understanding Simple Sentences

Literature Topic **Copy each simple sentence. Underline the subject once and the verb twice. Remember that some subjects and verbs may be compound.**

1. Adventure books fill the reader with suspense.

2. Gary Paulsen writes excellent adventures.

3. In *Hatchet*, thirteen-year-old Brian Robeson survives a plane crash and faces the Canadian wilderness alone.

4. Brian's father and mother are going through a divorce.

5. At the beginning of the book, Brian is flying to his father's house.

6. After the crash Brian finds food and builds a shelter.

7. A porcupine and a moose injure him.

8. Brian faces challenges, works hard, and overcomes many obstacles.

9. Throughout the book his future is uncertain.

10. *Hatchet* by Gary Paulsen contains a great deal of suspense and thrills for even the choosiest readers.

Communicate Your Ideas

APPLY TO WRITING

The Writer's Craft: *Analyzing the Use of Simple Sentences*

Using only simple sentences can make your writing seem less mature. However, sometimes writers use simple sentences in such a way that their writing seems mature and interesting. Read the passage and follow the directions.

> Cammy walked across the darkened room and turned on the light above the sink. She tiptoed to the bed, hopped up on the side rail and leaned close. Gram Tut's eyes were closed. Already the smell of the place, of old people, was up her nose. Cammy smacked a big kiss on her grandmother's cheek.
>
> —*Virginia Hamilton,* Cousins

- Copy the passage. Underline the subject of each sentence once and the verb twice.

- Rewrite the first sentence with a compound verb to make two separate sentences. Now read the passage with your new sentences in place of the old one. Do you prefer the sentence as Hamilton wrote it, or do you like your new version better? Explain your answer.

- What effect does the compound verb in the second sentence create?

- Why do you think Hamilton did not use compound subjects or verbs in the last three sentences?

Compound Sentences

Two or more simple sentences can be joined together to make another kind of sentence, a compound sentence.

A **compound sentence** is made up of two simple sentences, usually joined by a comma and the coordinating conjunction *and, but,* or *or.*

If the comma and the conjunction are dropped from a compound sentence, two simple sentences remain.

COMPOUND SENTENCE	Martina will play the flute in the concert, and Cody will record her music.
SIMPLE SENTENCES	Martina will play the flute in the concert. Cody will record her music.
COMPOUND SENTENCE	Vanessa is taking guitar lessons, but she can already play the violin.
SIMPLE SENTENCES	Vanessa is taking guitar lessons. She can already play the violin.
COMPOUND SENTENCE	Tonight our band will rehearse, or we will go to a concert.
SIMPLE SENTENCES	Tonight our band will rehearse. We will go to a concert.

As you can see in the preceding examples, the conjunction you choose adds to the overall meaning of the sentence. Use the conjunction *and* when the second part of a compound sentence adds more information. Use *but* when it shows contrast or gives a different point of view. Use *or* when it presents a choice. However, be careful not to confuse a compound sentence with a simple sentence that has a compound verb.

COMPOUND SENTENCE	Antonio practices his trumpet daily, and his hard work makes him a great musician.
	(The two subjects are *Antonio* and *work*.)
COMPOUND VERB	Antonio practices his trumpet daily and plays very well because of it.
	(There is only one subject, *Antonio*.)

PUNCTUATING COMPOUND SENTENCES

If the parts of a compound sentence are joined by a conjunction, add a comma. If the parts of a compound sentence are not joined by a conjunction, add a semicolon.

COMMA WITH A COMPOUND SENTENCE	The music was loud, but we did not turn it off.
SEMICOLON WITH A COMPOUND SENTENCE	The music was loud; our neighbor complained about the noise.

No comma comes between the parts of a compound verb.

NO COMMA WITH A COMPOUND VERB	We turned off the stereo and played our guitars.

Professional writers use many different kinds of sentences to make their writing interesting. You can combine simple sentences to add variety to your writing. Two sentences with the same subject can be combined into a simple sentence with a compound verb.

TWO SIMPLE SENTENCES	Rachel played the piano beautifully. She sang some great songs.
COMPOUND VERB	Rachel played the piano beautifully and sang some great songs.

Two closely related simple sentences with different subjects can be combined to form a compound sentence. Don't forget that you must use either a comma and a conjunction or a semicolon to join the sentences together.

TWO SIMPLE SENTENCES	Rachel played the piano beautifully. Gabriela listened with delight.
COMPOUND SENTENCE	Rachel played the piano beautifully, and Gabriela listened with delight.
	Rachel played the piano beautifully; Gabriela listened with delight.

PRACTICE YOUR SKILLS

● Check Your Understanding

Understanding Compound Sentences

Music Topic **Copy each compound sentence. Underline each subject once and each verb twice. Then circle each conjunction. Remember that some compound sentences do not contain conjunctions.**

1. Instruments with strings come in many varieties; they are among the most popular instruments.

2. No one knows the origin of the harp, but it is very ancient.

3. A harp may stand over six feet tall, and this instrument has many strings.

4. Egyptian tombs feature paintings of harps, and sculptors in ancient Greece made replicas of the instrument.

5. Ancient Greek musicians also played the lyre; the lyre is an instrument in the harp family.

6. The banjo came to America from Africa, and it is used in country and bluegrass music.

7. The sound can be very loud, or a player can pluck it softly.

8. The violin has four strings, but a guitar usually has six.

9. Guitar players pluck the strings with their fingers, or they can use a pick on the strings.

10. Violin players draw a bow across the strings, and the instrument responds loudly.

● Check Your Understanding

Distinguishing Between Simple and Compound Sentences

Science Topic **Label each sentence as either *simple* or *compound*. Remember that a simple sentence may have a compound subject or a compound predicate.**

11. A beam of light hits a diamond, and it splits.

12. Light strikes a needle; instantly a hole appears.

13. This light is a laser beam, and it is amazing.

14. Workers cut and weld metal with laser beams.

15. With laser beams scientists send signals into space and measure distances to other planets.

16. Laser beams read price codes on items in a grocery store and transfer the prices to the cash register.

17. Ordinary light is weak, but lasers are stronger.

18. Ordinary light spreads and fades in short distances.

19. Light from a laser moves in a straight line and travels long distances.

20. The power of a laser can be controlled, and scientists can adjust it for different jobs.

⬤ Connect to the Writing Process: Editing
Punctuating Compound Sentences

Write each compound sentence and punctuate it correctly. If a sentence does not need any punctuation, write *C* for correct.

21. An elephant is the largest land animal a blue whale is the largest sea animal.

22. An aardvark lives in Africa and eats termites.

23. A panda looks like a bear but the raccoon is its closest relative.

24. Male tigers always live and hunt alone.

25. Indian rhinoceroses have one horn African rhinoceroses have two horns.

26. Female lions care for their cubs and hunt for food.

27. A kangaroo measures 4 1/2 feet tall but its tail measures another 3 1/2 feet.

28. A female sheep is a ewe a male sheep is a ram.

29. A giraffe can be thirteen feet tall and weigh four thousand pounds.

30. Gorillas sleep fourteen hours a day but elephants sleep only two hours.

APPLY TO WRITING

E-mail Message: *Compound Sentences*

Your friend is looking for a good book to read. Write an E-mail to him or her recommending a book you have read recently. Tell your friend about the main characters and the plot. Remember, don't give away the ending!

After you have written your message, read it again and correct any errors. Underline three compound sentences you used in your work. If you did not use three compound sentences, perhaps you can combine some simple sentences to make a compound sentence. Be sure that all compound sentences are punctuated properly.

Science Topic **Label each sentence as either *simple* or *compound*.**

1. Shooting stars are not stars, and they do not shoot.

2. People see meteors and call them shooting stars.

3. A meteor shines brightly, but meteors are not stars.

4. Stars are suns far out in space, but meteors are bits of metal or rock.

5. Sometimes these bits of metal and rock streak through Earth's atmosphere and burn.

6. Meteors glow brightly, but we can see them for only a few seconds.

7. Most meteors burn up in Earth's atmosphere.

8. Others fall to Earth's surface; those meteors are called meteorites.

9. Scientists have collected and examined several thousand meteorites.

10. Most meteorites are very small, but some are large.

11. The American Museum of Natural History in New York has a meteorite on display; it weighs thirty-one tons.

12. It fell thousands of years ago in Greenland, and scientists brought it to the museum in 1906.

13. Only about 150 meteorites a year make it through the atmosphere and land on Earth.

14. In 1971, a meteorite went through the roof of a Connecticut home, but no one was hurt.

15. Eleven years later a meteorite hit another Connecticut house less than a mile away!

Run-on Sentences

When a compound sentence is written without a conjunction or proper punctuation, the result is a run-on sentence. Run-on sentences are confusing to read. One sentence runs into another. A reader is never sure where one idea ends and another begins.

> A **run-on sentence** is two or more sentences that are written as one sentence. They are separated by a comma or have no punctuation at all.

Some run-on sentences have only a comma and no conjunction. Other run-on sentences have neither a comma nor a conjunction.

RUN-ON SENTENCES	My bike has a flat, I don't have an air pump.
	(only a comma, no conjunction)
	A person can get thirsty on a bike cyclists carry water bottles on long rides.
	(no comma and no conjunction)

There are two ways to correct run-on sentences. You can write the two sentences as separate sentences.

SEPARATE SENTENCES	My bike has a flat. I don't have an air pump.
	A person can get thirsty on a bike. Cyclists carry water bottles on long rides.

You can also write the two sentences as a compound sentence with a comma and the conjunction *and, but,* or *or.*

COMPOUND SENTENCES	My bike has a flat, but I don't have an air pump.
	(The conjunction *but* was added.)
	A person can get thirsty on a bike, and cyclists carry water bottles on long rides.
	(The conjunction *and* and a comma were both added.)

You can combine closely related sentences from a run-on sentence into a compound sentence. If the sentences are not closely related, make them into separate sentences.

PRACTICE YOUR SKILLS

● Check Your Understanding

Identifying Run-on Sentences

General Interest **Label each run-on sentence *RO*. If a sentence is correct as written, write C.**

1. Bicycles became popular between 1890 and 1900 these years were "The Golden Age of the Bicycle."

2. The automobile arrived, and the bicycle craze ended.

3. Then around 1960, the bicycle staged a comeback cycling is now a popular hobby and sport.

4. Millions of people buy bicycles; every year more bikes than cars are sold.

5. Why do so many people ride bicycles there are many reasons.

6. Some people ride to school or work, others ride for pleasure.

7. Cycle races take place all across the world athletes love the challenge of this sport.

8. Some races take place on tracks, but the most challenging is the Tour de France.

9. Cycling is great exercise, and it is a great way to travel at the same time.

10. Bicycles have changed much over the past twenty years faster bikes are built every year.

● Connect to the Writing Process: Editing
Correcting Run-on Sentences

11.–16. Correct the run-on sentences from the preceding exercise.

● Connect to the Writing Process: Editing
Correcting Run-on Sentences

Rewrite the following paragraphs, correcting each run-on sentence. Remember to use capital letters, commas, conjunctions, and end marks carefully.

Second officer Harry Kindall first noticed the black and white terrier it was coming up the gangplank of the *Proud Lady*. Once on board the dog stood perfectly still and looked all around. The deck was loaded with lumber, the dog sniffed it carefully.

Then the dog returned to shore and boarded the next ship. Kindall watched the dog it repeated this same routine on each ship at the port. Soon Kindall got busy, at noon the *Proud Lady* left Canada for Japan.

Kindall found the dog early the next morning it was lying outside the captain's cabin. It had come aboard again and had stowed away. The sailors were friendly to the terrier, it seemed indifferent to them.

For eighteen days the *Proud Lady* plowed across the Pacific then the coast of Japan was sighted. The ship eventually reached the harbor and stopped between two other ships.

The terrier ran from one side of the ship to the other and looked at the other ships. Its tail switched back and forth, its nostrils quivered nervously. The nearest ship was a Dutch ship workers were unloading lumber from it.

Just then a rowboat with two men in it was lowered from the Dutch ship, the boat headed toward the shore. Suddenly the dog barked frantically, the rowboat stopped. The men looked up and saw the terrier.

One of the men in the rowboat jumped to his feet and called out excitedly to the dog. The rowboat turned back and headed toward the *Proud Lady*. The rowboat came alongside the ship, the dog leaped into the water. The man pulled the dog from the water and hugged it. The dog whined and licked his face the dog and its master were reunited. How had the dog picked the *Proud Lady* to find its master? No one knows— except, perhaps, the black and white terrier.

APPLY TO WRITING

Comparison-and-Contrast Article: *Run-on Sentences*

Pablo Picasso. *First Steps*, 1943.
Oil on canvas, 51¼ by 38¼ inches. Yale University Art Gallery, Gift of
Stephen C. Clark, B.A. 1903.

Look at this painting and the painting on the following page.

Vincent van Gogh. *First Steps, after Millet*, 1890.
Oil on canvas, 28 1/2 by 35 7/8 inches. The Metropolitan Museum of Art, New York. Gift of George N. and Helen M. Richard, 1964 (64.165.2) © 1982 by The Metropolitan Museum of Art, New York.

These paintings are being featured in an art exhibit at the local museum. Write an article for the newspaper in which you compare and contrast these two works by Picasso and Van Gogh. First tell what the paintings have in common. How are they similar? Then talk about how they are different. Finally, discuss which painting you prefer and tell why.

After writing the article, read it over. Did you find any run-on sentences? If so, prepare this article for publication by correcting the run-on sentences before you turn in your paper.

General Interest **Correct each run-on sentence. Add capital letters, commas, conjunctions, and end marks where needed. If a sentence is correct, write C.**

1. The first skyscrapers appeared in the late 1800s in Chicago they also appeared in New York City.

2. One famous skyscraper is the Empire State Building it is located in New York City.

3. This skyscraper has shops and restaurants, it also has banks.

4. The tallest buildings in the world are the Petronas Towers in Kuala Lumpur.

5. Most skyscrapers have two main sections these sections are the foundation (the section built underground) and the superstructure (the section built above the ground).

6. The foundation begins one or more stories below ground level.

7. Construction crews dig a large hole into this hole the crews begin placing steel beams, columns, and concrete which will serve as the building's support.

8. Once a foundation is complete, a skyscraper's above-ground floors and outside walls can be assembled the construction is supervised by a host of engineers and architects.

9. It can take three or more years to complete construction of a skyscraper.

10. The plumbing, air conditioning, and electrical systems in a skyscraper are very complicated specialists for each of these systems are consulted.

Diagraming Compound Sentences

A compound sentence is diagramed like two simple sentences with the subject and verb on the baseline. The direct object is also on the baseline as in the example below. The two diagrams are connected by a broken line. The broken line joins the two verbs. The conjunction that joins the two sentences is written on the broken line.

Chris caught three fish, and Dad cooked them.

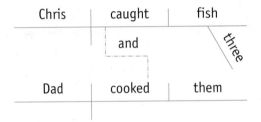

Chris will bake some potatoes, or Dad will fix some brown rice.

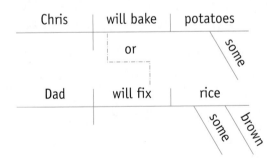

Dad and Chris like lemon on their fish, but neither likes tartar sauce.

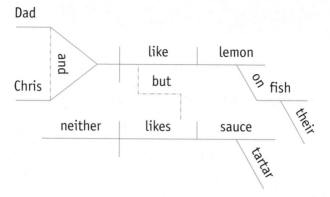

PRACTICE YOUR SKILLS

Diagraming

Diagram the following sentences or copy them. If you copy them, draw one line under each subject and two lines under each verb.

1. Rose read the poem, and we listened.
2. Mike made a home run, and the Warriors won.
3. You must row, or the boat will drift.
4. I like basketball, but Sarah prefers football.
5. Rachel lit the birthday candles, and everyone sang.
6. I opened a bank account, and now the money is earning interest.
7. We attended the dance, and the band played many old songs.
8. I rang the doorbell, but nobody answered it.
9. You can drive me, or I will take the bus.
10. The electricity went out, and we could not find any candles.

Recognizing Simple and Compound Sentences

Read each sentence and label it *simple* or *compound*.

1. Giants live on this earth, but they do not walk.
2. They live in California and are rooted in soil.
3. They are giant sequoia trees, and many tourists visit them each year.
4. Along with redwoods, the sequoias are the earth's largest living things.
5. Chief among these massive trees is the General Sherman, a 275-foot-tall sequoia.
6. The General Sherman is the thickest tree known, but it is by no means the tallest.
7. That title goes to the Howard Libby Redwood.
8. Its height is 362 feet, and it is more than 87 feet taller than the huge General Sherman.
9. The General Sherman's largest branch is seven feet thick, and a grown person could lie across it.
10. The sequoia's roots are shallow, but they cover three acres, the size of four football fields.

Correcting Run-on Sentences

Correct each run-on sentence by writing two simple sentences or a compound sentence.

1. Egyptians built the first nation, other nations conquered it many times.
2. I bought a sweater, it's too small for me.
3. My pen ran dry I don't have another one.

4. Some birds are building nests they look like sparrows.

5. The giant squid has huge eyes each one is as large as a basketball.

6. I studied for my social studies test for three hours it is tomorrow.

7. We might rent a movie, possibly Dad might take us bowling.

8. The earth is slowing down in 600,000,000 B.C., one day was only 21 hours.

9. I like comic movies, my older sister likes adventures.

10. In its early days, China was many small kingdoms the country was finally united in 221 B.C.

Understanding Sentence Structure

Write sentences that follow the directions below. (The sentences may come in any order.) Write about the following topic or a topic of your choice: something you find amazing in nature.

1. Write a simple sentence.

2. Write a simple sentence with a compound verb.

3. Write a simple sentence that is a question.

4. Write a compound sentence in which the two sentences are joined by *and*.

5. Write a compound sentence in which the two sentences are joined by *but*.

Remember to punctuate your sentences correctly.

Language and *Self-Expression*

Christo and Jeanne-Claude are famous for creating huge art forms that change the landscape. Thousands of people drove to see their *Running Fence* during the fourteen days it was on display.

What sight have you seen that is worth making a special effort to visit? What makes it intriguing? Create a brochure describing this place and encouraging people to visit it. Use both simple and compound sentences. Illustrate your brochure and share it with your classmates.

Prewriting Use a cluster diagram to identify the place's most interesting features. Number the clusters in the order in which you want to describe the features.

Drafting Use the notes on your diagram to draft your brochure. Your first sentence should capture your reader's attention, and your first paragraph should give an overall sketch of the place. Be sure to include at the end any information about visiting hours or admission fees.

Revising Have a classmate look over your work. Ask whether the information in each paragraph seems related and whether the organization makes sense. As you revise your brochure, make sure all your sentences are complete sentences.

Editing Check your brochure for errors in punctuation and spelling. Be especially careful to punctuate compound sentences correctly.

Publishing Illustrate your brochure and read it to your classmates before adding it to a travel and entertainment display in your classroom.

 **Another Look**

A **simple sentence** is a sentence that has one subject and one verb. It may have a compound subject or a compound verb.

A **compound sentence** is made up of two simple sentences, usually joined by a comma and the coordinating conjunction *and, but,* or *or.*

A **run-on sentence** is two or more sentences that are written as one sentence. They are separated by a comma or have no punctuation at all.

Other Information About Sentences

Choosing conjunctions in compound sentences *(page L209)*
Punctuating compound sentences *(page L209)*
Correcting run-on sentences *(pages L215–L216)*
Diagraming compound sentences *(pages L222–L223)*

Posttest

Directions

Write the letter of the group of words that best identifies each sentence.

EXAMPLE

1. In the 1850s, no train or pony express service could cross the Sierras in winter.
  1 **A** run-on sentence
    B compound sentence
    C simple sentence with compound subject
    D simple sentence

ANSWER   **1 C**

1. Snow piled up and cut off contact with the world.

2. Mail could not be sent from Nevada to California towns like Meadow Lake, Hangtown, and Poker Flat.

3. Sacramento advertised for someone to carry the mail through Carson Pass this was a distance of 90 miles.

4. Two men had tried to make the crossing on skis, known as "snowshoes," and had nearly died.

5. John Thomson's family were immigrants from Norway; in his childhood he had learned to ski there.

6. In 1851, he joined the Gold Rush but never was successful.

7. He signed up as postman, and he set out from Hangtown carrying one hundred pounds of letters on his back.

8. On his waxed skis, he could attain speeds of 90 mph.

9. It took him three days to reach Nevada, but he cut his time to two days on his return trip.

10. He had a real job after that, he carried mail for 13 years.

1 A run-on sentence
  B simple sentence
  C compound sentence
  D simple sentence with compound verb

2 A compound sentence
  B run-on sentence
  C simple sentence
  D sentence fragment

3 A compound sentence
  B run-on sentence
  C sentence fragment
  D simple sentence

4 A compound sentence
  B simple sentence with compound verb
  C simple sentence with compound subject
  D run-on sentence

5 A compound sentence
  B simple sentence with compound subject
  C simple sentence with compound verb
  D run-on sentence

6 A sentence fragment
  B run-on sentence
  C simple sentence
  D simple sentence with compound verb

7 A run-on sentence
  B compound sentence
  C simple sentence with compound subject
  D sentence fragment

8 A sentence fragment
  B run-on sentence
  C simple sentence
  D compound sentence

9 A run-on sentence
  B sentence fragment
  C simple sentence with compound verb
  D compound sentence

10 A run-on sentence
  B compound sentence
  C simple sentence with compound verb
  D simple sentence with compound subject

CHAPTER 8

Using Verbs

Pretest

Directions
Read the passage and choose the word that belongs in each underlined space. Write the letter of the correct answer.

EXAMPLE   The flu was __(1)__ around Dan's school.
          1 A go
              B gone
              C going
              D went

ANSWER   **1 C**

Dan has __(1)__ a terrible flu. His mother __(2)__ him to see the doctor. The doctor had already __(3)__ several of Dan's classmates. It was clear his mother should __(4)__ Dan stay home for a while. The doctor __(5)__ Dan's mother that he needed plenty of rest. Dan __(6)__ a long nap when he got home. His mother has __(7)__ him a lot of juice. Dan __(8)__ three glasses of it earlier this morning. His mother came into the room and __(9)__ him some chicken soup. A scientist __(10)__ that chicken soup really does make people feel better.

1	**A**	catch		**6**	**A**	takes
	B	caught			**B**	taken
	C	catching			**C**	took
	D	catches			**D**	taked
2	**A**	taking		**7**	**A**	gives
	B	takes			**B**	gave
	C	taken			**C**	giving
	D	took			**D**	given
3	**A**	saw		**8**	**A**	drunk
	B	seen			**B**	drinking
	C	see			**C**	drank
	D	seeing			**D**	drinks
4	**A**	leave		**9**	**A**	taken
	B	leaving			**B**	took
	C	let			**C**	brought
	D	lets			**D**	brung
5	**A**	told		**10**	**A**	find
	B	tells			**B**	finds
	C	telling			**C**	finding
	D	telled			**D**	found

Elizabeth Catlett. *Baile (Dance),* 1970.
Lino-cut, 16 by 30 inches. © 1996 Elizabeth Catlett/Licensed by VAGA, New York.

Describe   What method do you think the artist used to create this picture? Why do you think so?

Analyze   Where did the artist use diagonal lines in the artwork? What do you think the purpose of these lines is?

Interpret   Why do you think the artist made this scene very simple instead of using a lot of colors and details? When might a writer not use many details in a piece of writing?

Judge   Have you done any artwork that is similar to this? How was it similar?

At the end of the chapter, you will use this artwork to stimulate ideas for writing.

The Principal Parts of Verbs

As you know, a verb shows action or gives information about a subject. Another thing the verb does is tell when the action happens.

PRESENT ACTION	I **write** in my journal every day.
PAST ACTION	I **wrote** in my journal yesterday.
FUTURE ACTION	I **will write** in my journal tomorrow.

In order to show when the action happens, a verb changes its form. The different forms are made from the basic parts of the verb. These basic parts are called principal parts.

The principal parts of a verb are the present, the present participle, the past, and the past participle.

The following are the principal parts of the verb *work*. Notice that the present participle and the past participle must have a helping verb when they are used as verbs.

PRESENT	I often **work** after school.
PRESENT PARTICIPLE	I *am* **working** this afternoon.
PAST	I **worked** last Tuesday.
PAST PARTICIPLE	I *have* **worked** ten afternoons so far this month.

You can learn more about helping verbs on page L81.

Regular Verbs

Most verbs form their past and past participle the same way that the verb *work* does—by adding *–ed* or *–d* to the present. These verbs are called regular verbs.

A **regular verb** forms its past and past participle by adding –*ed* or –*d* to the present.

The principal parts of the verbs *stretch, lift, jog,* and *bury* follow. Notice that the present participle is formed by adding –*ing* to the present form. Also, as the rule says, the past is formed by adding –*ed* or –*d* to the present.

PRESENT	PRESENT PARTICIPLE	PAST	PAST PARTICIPLE
stretch	(is) stretching	stretched	(have) stretched
lift	(is) lifting	lifted	(have) lifted
jog	(is) jogging	jogged	(have) jogged
bury	(is) burying	buried	(have) buried

Sometimes when you add a word ending such as –*ing* or –*ed* to verbs such as *jog* and *bury,* the spelling changes. If you are unsure of the spelling of a verb form, look it up in the dictionary.

You can learn more about spelling changes on pages L564–L568.

PRACTICE YOUR SKILLS

● Check Your Understanding
Writing the Principal Parts of Regular Verbs

Make four columns and label them *Present, Present Participle, Past,* and *Past Participle.* Then write the four principal parts of each of the following regular verbs. Use the helping verb *is* when you write the present participle and the helping verb *have* when you write the past participle.

1. walk   **3.** drop

2. save   **4.** plan

5. carry	**8.** count
6. dream	**9.** remember
7. listen	**10.** hurry

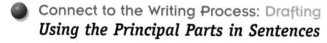

Connect to the Writing Process: Drafting
Using the Principal Parts in Sentences

Write four sentences for each of the following regular verbs. Write one sentence using the present, one sentence using the present participle, one sentence using the past, and one sentence using the past participle of each verb.

11. use

12. shop

13. talk

14. cook

15. try

Irregular Verbs

Some verbs do not form their past participle by adding –ed or –d. They are called irregular verbs.

An **irregular verb** does not form its past and past participle by adding –ed or –d to the present.

The following irregular verbs are grouped according to the way their past and past participles are formed. Remember, though, that the word *is* is not part of the present participle and the word *have* is not part of the past participle. Still, they have been added to the following lists of irregular verbs. They are there to remind you that all present participles and past participles must have a helping verb when they are used in a sentence.

Group 1 These irregular verbs have the same form for the present, the past, and the past participle.

PRESENT	PRESENT PARTICIPLE	PAST	PAST PARTICIPLE
burst	(is) bursting	burst	(have) burst
hit	(is) hitting	hit	(have) hit
put	(is) putting	put	(have) put

Group 2 These irregular verbs have the same form for the past and the past participle.

PRESENT	PRESENT PARTICIPLE	PAST	PAST PARTICIPLE
bring	(is) bringing	brought	(have) brought
catch	(is) catching	caught	(have) caught
hear	(is) hearing	heard	(have) heard
say	(is) saying	said	(have) said
tell	(is) telling	told	(have) told
think	(is) thinking	thought	(have) thought

PRACTICE YOUR SKILLS

● Check Your Understanding
Using the Correct Verb Form

Contemporary Life **Label each underlined verb form. Remember that *have*, *has*, or *had* is used with the past participle.**

1. Have you <u>heard</u> about our big win?
2. Brittany is <u>telling</u> me about it now.
3. Jesse <u>hit</u> the winning home run.
4. He <u>put</u> the ball in centerfield.
5. The shortstop almost <u>caught</u> it.
6. I have always <u>thought</u> highly of Jesse's batting ability.
7. After the game ended, his dad was <u>bursting</u> with pride.
8. The fans <u>said</u> Jesse's name over and over.
9. Jesse has <u>hit</u> many home runs this year.
10. This win has <u>put</u> our team in first place.

● Connect to the Writing Process: Revising
Correcting Verb Forms

Rewrite the following sentences, using the correct form of the verb.

11. Babe Ruth hitted 714 home runs in his career.
12. Some people sayed this record would never be broken.
13. They thinked it was impossible.
14. Have you heared about any of the more recent home run kings?
15. Have these players catched the fans' undivided attention?

Group 3   These irregular verbs form the past participle by adding −*n* to the past.

PRESENT	PRESENT PARTICIPLE	PAST	PAST PARTICIPLE
break	(is) breaking	broke	(have) broken
choose	(is) choosing	chose	(have) chosen
freeze	(is) freezing	froze	(have) frozen
speak	(is) speaking	spoke	(have) spoken
steal	(is) stealing	stole	(have) stolen

Group 4   These irregular verbs form the past participle by adding −*n* to the present.

PRESENT	PRESENT PARTICIPLE	PAST	PAST PARTICIPLE
blow	(is) blowing	blew	(have) blown
drive	(is) driving	drove	(have) driven
give	(is) giving	gave	(have) given
grow	(is) growing	grew	(have) grown
know	(is) knowing	knew	(have) known
see	(is) seeing	saw	(have) seen
take	(is) taking	took	(have) taken
throw	(is) throwing	threw	(have) thrown

PRACTICE YOUR SKILLS

● Check Your Understanding
Determining the Correct Verb Form

Contemporary Life — **Write the correct verb form for each sentence. Remember that *have, has,* or *had* is used with the past participle.**

1. Last winter the small lake in the middle of town (froze, frozen).

2. My dad (drove, driven) by that lake every day.

3. The wind had (blew, blown) for several days.

4. We had (knew, known) the winter would be harsh.

5. The ice on the lake (grew, grown) from the sides toward the middle.

6. We had never (saw, seen) it this cold before.

7. It (took, taken) a week for the surface to ice over.

8. However, the ice (broke, broken) very easily last year.

9. My dad had (give, given) me a hockey puck for my birthday.

10. My friends and I (threw, thrown) that puck across the ice toward each other.

● Check Your Understanding
Using the Correct Verb Form

Contemporary Life — **Decide whether each sentence needs the past or past participle form of the verb in parentheses. Then write the correct verb form. Remember that *have, has,* or *had* is used with the past participle.**

11. My grandmother has always (grow) beautiful roses.

12. She (speak) to our garden club at school last week.

13. Grandma told us why she has (choose) to plant only roses in her flower beds.

14. She (grow) up in a poor family in a village in Poland.

15. Across the village from her home, she had (see) a huge mansion with roses in the yard.

16. One day she (steal) a rose from the yard of the big house.

17. She felt ashamed that she had (take) the flower.

18. Grandma (know) it was wrong to steal.

19. She (break) down and cried.

20. On that day, she (grow) determined to raise her own beautiful roses.

● Connect to Speaking: Reading an Announcement
Correcting Verb Forms

Read the following announcement once silently. Then read the announcement aloud, correcting any misused verb forms.

Has anyone saw a stray white dog wandering near Fifth and Alexander Streets? This dog has broke out of the local animal shelter, and it may be dangerous to people. When a woman throwed a net over it, the dog growed aggressive toward her. City authorities have spoke with animal control about this dog. They ask that you call the animal shelter if you have saw this dog in your neighborhood.

Group 5 These irregular verbs form the past and the past participle by changing a vowel. The *i* in the present changes to an *a* in the past and a *u* in the past participle.

PRESENT	PRESENT PARTICIPLE	PAST	PAST PARTICIPLE
begin	(is) beginning	began	(have) begun
drink	(is) drinking	drank	(have) drunk
ring	(is) ringing	rang	(have) rung
sing	(is) singing	sang	(have) sung
swim	(is) swimming	swam	(have) swum

Group 6 These irregular verbs form the past and the past participle in various ways.

PRESENT	PRESENT PARTICIPLE	PAST	PAST PARTICIPLE
come	(is) coming	came	(have) come
do	(is) doing	did	(have) done
eat	(is) eating	ate	(have) eaten
fly	(is) flying	flew	(have) flown
go	(is) going	went	(have) gone
ride	(is) riding	rode	(have) ridden
run	(is) running	ran	(have) run
write	(is) writing	wrote	(have) written

When you write, you should always have a good dictionary handy. A dictionary can tell you much more about a word than just its definition. This handy reference book can also tell you how to pronounce a word, how to divide a word into syllables, what a word's history is, and how other forms of the word are spelled. If you are unsure of how a verb forms its principal parts, look it up in the dictionary. Its principal parts will be listed right after the entry word.

PRACTICE YOUR SKILLS

Check Your Understanding
Determining the Correct Verb Form

Contemporary Life
Write the correct verb form for each sentence. Remember that *have, has,* or *had* is used with the past participle.

1. The geese (flew, flown) south early last year.

2. The weather hadn't (began, begun) to change.

3. The summer birds still (sang, sung) in our pine trees.

4. They had already (ate, eaten) all the berries from our shrubs.

5. My cousins and I still (swam, swum) in the river.

6. We had (went, gone) to the river all summer.

7. Some days we (rode, ridden) our bikes to the water.

8. We had (ran, run) along the riverbank.

9. The birds had also (came, come) to the river.

10. They (drank, drunk) and bathed in the cool water.

General Interest **Decide whether each sentence needs the past or the past participle form of the verb in parentheses. Then write the correct form. Remember that *have, has,* or *had* is used with the past participle.**

11. Lately, the phones of personal trainers have (ring) more and more.

12. People in poor physical condition have (go) to them for advice.

13. Some people have (do) many kinds of exercise.

14. Across the country yesterday, many people (run) for their health.

15. Some (go) to their local YMCA or health club.

16. Many of them (swim) laps in a pool.

17. Cyclists have (ride) miles and miles for fitness.

18. Many athletes have (write) books about their fitness secrets.

19. Healthy people have always (drink) plenty of water.

20. They also have (eat) good, nutritious foods.

● Check Your Understanding
Finding Principal Parts in a Dictionary

Make four columns and label them *Present, Present Participle, Past,* and *Past Participle*. Then look up the following verbs in the dictionary and write their four principal parts. Remember to use *is* when you write the present participle and *have* when you write the past participle.

21. fall   **23.** sink

22. feel   **24.** buy

25. lose   **28.** lead

26. tear   **29.** cost

27. shrink   **30.** wear

● Connect to Speaking: Reading a Commercial
Correcting Verb Forms

Read the following commercial once silently. Then read the commercial aloud, correcting any misused verb forms.

You have drinked many different soft drinks. You have ate potato chips. Now try the latest product from Snack King: Chipsy Cola. Chipsy Cola satisfies your hunger and quenches your thirst—all at the same time! After you have ran, have swum, or have rode your bike, take a delicious break. Pop open a can of Chipsy Cola today. Yum!

Communicate Your Ideas

APPLY TO WRITING

Newspaper Article: *Using Irregular Verbs*

Write an article for the school newspaper that describes a recent sporting event you attended. In your article, use the past or past participle forms of at least five irregular verbs. The following are some irregular verbs you might use: *catch, go, run, break, steal, fly, throw, take, give, see, begin, say, tell, speak, think, choose, ride, know.*

Literature
Topic
Write the correct past or past participle form of each verb in parentheses.

1. Surely you have (hear) legendary stories about Pecos Bill.

2. People have (tell) tall tales about him for more than a hundred years.

3. Many writers have (write) about his enormous size and strength.

4. Over the years people have (know) him as a legendary cowboy.

5. People say that Pecos Bill (begin) life in an unusual way.

6. He (play) with bears and wildcats, instead of with other children.

7. He (live) and (eat) with coyotes.

8. As an adult, Pecos Bill once (catch) a ride on an Oklahoma cyclone across three whole states!

9. Eventually the cyclone (come) to a stop and (rain) on him instead.

10. Over the years, many cowboys have (speak) about that tremendous rainstorm.

11. Supposedly, the huge washout from that storm (create) the Grand Canyon.

12. Once an enormous mountain lion had (see) Pecos Bill in the canyon below.

13. The lion (wait) and (jump) him.

14. Soon fur (fly) in all directions.

15. The lion (beg) Pecos Bill for mercy.

16. Instead Bill (ride) the lion like a horse.

17. Bill (go) everywhere on his real horse.

18. He had (give) his horse dynamite as a colt.

19. A friend of Bill's (take) a ride on Bill's horse one day.

20. The horse (throw) the man into the air as high as Pike's Peak!

⊙ Six Problem Verbs

This section will cover six problem verbs. They are considered problems because people sometimes confuse their meanings.

bring and take

Bring indicates motion toward the speaker. *Take* indicates motion away from the speaker.

PRESENT	PRESENT PARTICIPLE	PAST	PAST PARTICIPLE
bring	(is) bringing	brought	(have) brought
take	(is) taking	took	(have) taken

BRING	He **brings** flowers to me every morning. He is **bringing** flowers to me now. He **brought** flowers to me yesterday. He **has brought** flowers to me for a month now.
TAKE	**Take** a rose to Aunt Sylvia. Mom **is taking** a daisy to her today.

My sister **took** an orchid to our neighbor yesterday.

I **have taken** a flower to my teacher every day this week.

PRACTICE YOUR SKILLS

● Check Your Understanding

Using the Verbs Bring and Take

Oral Expression **Read the following sentences aloud to practice saying the forms of *bring* and *take* and to hear these verbs used correctly.**

1. <u>Bring</u> me that book about flowers.
2. You can <u>take</u> the book to school with you.
3. My mom <u>brought</u> it home from the library.
4. She <u>is taking</u> our plants outside into the sunshine.
5. We <u>had brought</u> them into the house before the big freeze.

● Check Your Understanding

Using Bring and Take Correctly

Contemporary Life **Choose the correct verb in parentheses.**

6. Aunt Sylvia (brought, took) us to the botanical gardens at the park.
7. She (brought, took) us a camera to photograph the flowers.
8. My mother (brought, took) a picnic lunch to us.
9. While we looked at flowers, she (took, brought) our lunch across the gardens to a picnic table.
10. After lunch, Aunt Sylvia opened a bag she had (brought, taken) with her.

11. She had (brought, taken) us a strawberry pie.

12. After lunch, Aunt Sylvia (brought, took) us home.

13. We (brought, took) all of our stuff into the house.

14. Before Aunt Sylvia left, I (brought, took) her a surprise—a new guide to wildflowers.

15. She will (bring, take) us to the gardens again in the spring.

learn and *teach*

Learn means "to gain knowledge." *Teach* means "to instruct" or "to show how."

PRESENT	PRESENT PARTICIPLE	PAST	PAST PARTICIPLE
learn	(is) learning	learned	(have) learned
teach	(is) teaching	taught	(have) taught

LEARN
I **learn** foreign words easily.
I **am learning** some Spanish words now.
I **learned** some Greek words last week.
I **have learned** French and Italian words in the past.

TEACH
I **teach** some foreign words to my brother.
I **am teaching** my cousins some Spanish words.
I **taught** some Greek words to my father yesterday.
I **have taught** some Italian words to my neighbor.

PRACTICE YOUR SKILLS

● Check Your Understanding

Using the Verbs Learn and Teach

Oral Expression **Read the following sentences aloud to practice saying the forms of *learn* and *teach* and to hear these verbs used correctly.**

1. Teach me a song in Greek.

2. I have learned those words very quickly.

3. Mrs. Stephanopolous teaches our Greek lessons.

4. She has taught classes at our community center for two years.

5. Students learn about Greek language and culture from her.

● Check Your Understanding

Using Learn and Teach Correctly

Contemporary Life **Choose the correct verb in parentheses.**

6. Mr. Barnes (learns, teaches) math to us sixth-grade students.

7. He has (learned, taught) at our school for over thirty years.

8. My dad even (learned, taught) long division from Mr. Barnes.

9. Mr. Barnes (learned, taught) my mom also.

10. I have (learned, taught) so much from this excellent teacher.

11. Last week our class (learned, taught) about the metric system.

12. Mr. Barnes had already (learned, taught) us about standard measurement.

13. Tomorrow he will (learn, teach) us something new about measurment.

14. He (teaches, learns) math really well.

15. Mr. Barnes has (learned, taught) us many valuable new skills.

leave and *let*

Leave means "to depart" or "go away." *Let* means "to allow" or "to permit."

PRESENT	PRESENT PARTICIPLE	PAST	PAST PARTICIPLE
leave	(is) leaving	left	(have) left
let	(is) letting	let	(have) let

LEAVE   I **leave** for school at 8:00 a.m. every weekday morning.
I **am leaving** for school right now.
I **left** late for school last week.
I **have left** my house on time every day this week.

LET   I often **let** Jenna borrow my video games.
I **am letting** her keep one until Friday.
Once I **let** her keep one of my games for two weeks.
I **have let** other friends borrow my video games too.

You can learn about the problem verbs lie *and* lay *on pages L389–L390,* rise *and* raise *on pages L390–L391, and* sit *and* set *on page L391.*

PRACTICE YOUR SKILLS

● Check Your Understanding
Using the Verbs Leave *and* Let

Oral Expression **Read the following sentences aloud to practice saying the forms of *leave* and *let* and to hear these verbs used correctly.**

1. Let's leave because there's a stray dog in the yard.

2. You should not let your friend touch stray animals.

3. The dog has left our yard.

4. Don't let the dog get near our cat.

5. We left a message for animal control about the stray.

● Check Your Understanding
Using Leave *and* Let *Correctly*

Contemporary Life **Choose the correct verb in parentheses.**

6. We (let, left) our football at home.

7. Wade always (lets, leaves) Tim use his football.

8. Mom has (let, left) us stay and play football after school this week.

9. My brother Tim never (lets, leaves) me play with him and his friends.

10. Tim (let, left) his helmet at school.

11. Our neighbors (let, left) Tim and his friends play in their yards.

12. (Let, Leave) the younger boys play now.

13. Tim just (let, left) with his friends.

14. I sometimes (let, left) my little sister play with me and my friends.

15. Other times she (lets, leaves) my room when my friends come over.

Writing Sentences Using Problem Verbs

Write a sentence for each of the following verb forms.

16. let

17. bring

18. is leaving

19. learned

20. took

21. have taught

Communicate Your Ideas

APPLY TO WRITING
Short Story: *Using Problem Verbs*

Leo and Diane Dillon. Illustration from *Why Mosquitoes Buzz in People's Ears,* by Verna Aardema.
Watercolor, pastel, and ink.

Imagine that your class is writing stories for patients in the children's ward of a local hospital. Look at the work of art on the preceding page. Write a story using these animals as characters. Make the story fun and uplifting for the hospitalized children. As you write, correctly use at least one form of the following verbs in your story: *bring, take, learn, teach, let,* and *leave.* Underline these verbs in your story.

QuickCheck Mixed Practice

History
Topic
Correct each underlined verb form that is used incorrectly. If the verb form is correct, write C.

1. Many people have never <u>saw</u> the Colosseum in Rome.

2. Other tourists have <u>went</u> there many times.

3. Our social studies teacher <u>learned</u> us the history of this huge, ancient outdoor theater.

4. Ancient Romans entered and <u>left</u> the Colosseum easily because of its convenient seating arrangement.

5. Everyone in the city of Rome <u>comed</u> to events at the Colosseum.

6. The wealthy people of Rome even <u>let</u> their slaves attend.

7. Thousands of spectators <u>seen</u> animals and people fight to the death there.

8. They ate and <u>drunk</u> happily as they watched these spectacles.

9. Walkways originally <u>run</u> beneath the Colosseum.

10. The organizers of the shows <u>put</u> animal and human performers in these underground chambers.

Verb Tense

Every verb has six tenses: the present, past, future, present perfect, past perfect, and future perfect.

The time expressed by a verb is called the tense of a verb.

PRESENT	We **see** photos of wild animals.
	I **study** Africa at school.
PAST	We **saw** photos of wild animals yesterday.
	We **studied** Africa last week.
FUTURE	We **will see** photos of wild animals tomorrow.
	I **will study** Africa this summer.
PRESENT PERFECT	We **have seen** photos of animals all week.
	I **have studied** Africa several times.
PAST PERFECT	We **had seen** some photos of wild animals before we went to the zoo.
	After I **had studied** Africa for two weeks, I wrote a report about it.
FUTURE PERFECT	By Friday we **will have seen** over one hundred photos.
	By seventh grade I **will have studied** Africa for five years.

● Uses of the Tenses

The preceding examples of the regular verb *study* and the irregular verb *see* show that verbs in the English language have six basic tenses. All these tenses can be formed from the principal parts of a verb. Notice that some of the tenses also require a helping verb such as *have, has, had, will,* or *shall.*

Present tense is used to express an action that is going on now. To form the present tense, use the present form (the first principal part of the verb) or add *–s* or *–es* to the present form.

> PRESENT TENSE   A zebra **walks** to this watering hole.
> I **draw** pictures of wildlife.

Past tense expresses an action that has already taken place or that was completed in the past. To form the past tense of a regular verb, add *–ed* or *–d* to the present form. To form the past tense of an irregular verb, check a dictionary for the past form or look for it on pages L235–L241.

> PAST TENSE   A zebra **walked** to this watering hole yesterday.
>
> A moment ago, I **drew** a picture of the zebra.

Future tense is used to express an action that will take place in the future. To form the future tense, use the helping verb *shall* or *will* with the present form.

> FUTURE TENSE   A zebra **will walk** to this watering hole at sunset.
>
> Then I **shall draw** more pictures of the zebra.

You can learn about the proper use of shall *and* will *on page L391.*

Present perfect tense expresses an action that was completed at some indefinite time in the past. It also expresses an action that started in the past and is still going on. To form the present perfect tense, add *has* or *have* to the past participle.

PRESENT PERFECT TENSE	A zebra **has walked** to this watering hole for years.
	I **have drawn** pictures of the zebra before.

Past perfect tense expresses an action that took place before some other past action. To form the past perfect tense, add *had* to the past participle.

PAST PERFECT TENSE	The zebra **had walked** to the watering hole before I arrived.
	I **had drawn** my picture before I left the watering hole.

Future perfect tense expresses an action that will take place before another future action or time. To form the future perfect tense, add *shall have* or *will have* to the past participle.

FUTURE PERFECT TENSE	By the end of the week, that zebra **will have walked** to this watering hole seven times.
	I **shall have drawn** seven pictures by then.

CONNECT TO SPEAKING AND WRITING

Looking for errors in your use of verb tense should be part of the editing stage of your writing. One way to find verb errors is to read your work aloud. Hearing what you have written will often alert you to an incorrect verb tense. If you find errors, be sure to correct them.

PRACTICE YOUR SKILLS

● Check Your Understanding
Identifying Verb Tenses

Science Topic **Decide whether the tense of each underlined verb is *present, past, future, present perfect, past perfect,* or *future perfect.* Then write the name of the tense.**

1. Many different animals <u>live</u> in Africa.

2. Mountain gorillas once <u>roamed</u> across the continent's high places.

3. Today far fewer gorillas <u>exist</u> in the mountains.

4. Hopefully they <u>will</u> not <u>become</u> extinct.

5. Researcher Dian Fossey <u>devoted</u> eighteen years of her life to studying these animals.

6. Others <u>have studied</u> this magnificent ape also.

7. Before Fossey's work was published, many people <u>had believed</u> that gorillas were dangerous.

8. Because of her work, millions of people <u>have heard</u> about the problems of mountain gorillas.

9. New laws <u>have helped</u> endangered species such as the mountain gorillas.

10. By the end of the year, I <u>will have sent</u> fifty dollars to groups that protect endangered species.

● Check Your Understanding
Writing Different Tenses

History Topic **Write each underlined verb in the tense that is written in parentheses.**

11. Over 100,000 people <u>drive</u> across San Francisco's Golden Gate Bridge tomorrow. (future)

12. Millions of tourists <u>visit</u> the famous bridge over the years. (present perfect)

13. Most of them <u>take</u> pictures of the magnificent structure. (present perfect)

14. The construction of the bridge <u>begin</u> in 1933. (past)

15. The builders <u>take</u> many safety precautions. (past)

16. By the time the bridge was completed, however, a few workers <u>lose</u> their lives. (past perfect)

17. Builders <u>complete</u> the bridge in 1937. (past)

18. By the year 2037, the bridge <u>last</u> for a hundred years. (future perfect)

19. Today, this magnificent structure <u>remain</u> a symbol of San Francisco. (present)

20. I wish I <u>know</u> about the bridge before I planned my trip to San Francisco. (past perfect)

● Connect to the Writing Process: Drafting
Writing Sentences Using Verb Tenses

Write a sentence that follows each direction.

21. Use the verb *go* in the present tense.

22. Use the verb *do* in the past tense.

23. Use the verb *play* in the present perfect tense.

24. Use the verb *see* in the past perfect tense.

25. Use the verb *compete* in the future tense.

26. Use the verb *attend* in the future perfect tense.

● Shifts in Tense

Readers rely on verb tenses to understand when the actions of a story take place. When you write a story, be sure to keep your tenses consistent. For example, if you are telling a story that took place in the past, use the past tense of verbs. If you suddenly shift to the present, you will probably confuse your readers.

Avoid unnecessary shifts in tense within a sentence or within related sentences.

INCONSISTENT
> After I **placed** [past] my money on the counter, the clerk **gives** [present] me the baseball cards.

CONSISTENT
> After I **place** [present] my money on the counter, the clerk **gives** [present] me the baseball cards.

CONSISTENT
> After I **placed** [past] my money on the counter, the clerk **gave** [past] me the baseball cards.

INCONSISTENT
> Before I **leave** [present] for my baseball game, Mom **wished** [past] me luck.

CONSISTENT
> Before I **leave** [present] for my baseball game, Mom **wishes** [present] me luck.

CONSISTENT
> Before I **left** [past] for my baseball game, Mom **wished** [past] me luck.

PRACTICE YOUR SKILLS

● Check Your Understanding
Correcting Shifts in Tense

Sports Topic **Rewrite the underlined verbs so that they are in the correct tense.**

1. In 1927, Lou Gehrig becomes a hero when he hit his forty-seventh home run.

2. Lou Gehrig's teammates called him "The Iron Horse" because he <u>plays</u> so many consecutive games.

3. Until Gehrig <u>takes</u> his name off the Yankees lineup, he missed no games in fourteen years.

4. His record of playing 2,130 consecutive games <u>stands</u> until Cal Ripken, Jr., broke it in 1995.

5. Gehrig originally went to college on a football scholarship, but later he <u>decides</u> to play baseball.

6. He hit 534 career home runs before he <u>retires</u> in 1939.

7. He <u>plays</u> for the New York Yankees, the same team that included Babe Ruth.

8. Gehrig wore the number 4 on his jersey, and the Yankees <u>retire</u> that number.

9. Today, Gehrig is one of the most famous members of the Baseball Hall of Fame, and he <u>remained</u> a legend to many baseball fans.

10. Next summer I will visit the Baseball Hall of Fame, and I <u>looked</u> for souvenirs of this baseball legend.

● Connect to the Writing Process: Editing
Finding and Correcting Shifts in Tense

History Topic **Rewrite the following paragraph, correcting any unnecessary shifts in tense.**

In 1681, King Charles II of England granted William Penn a large portion of land in the New World. Penn established the colony of Pennsylvania. William Penn believes strongly in religious freedom. Many settlers to his colony were Quakers, a religious group to which William Penn himself belongs. Many people from

England settle in the new colony. People from other countries come to Pennsylvania also. German immigrants came and create successful farms in the middle of the colony.

APPLY TO WRITING
Friendly Letter: *Avoiding Shifts in Tense*

Red Grooms. *Subway* (detail from *Ruckus Manhattan*), 1976.
Mixed media, 9 by 18½ by 37 feet.

Look carefully at this piece of art by Red Grooms. Imagine that you are the man on the right in this work. Write a letter to your brother who is a farmer in Kansas. Describe a day in your life, beginning with your subway ride to work and ending with your subway ride home. Give your brother plenty of details, so that he will understand what it is like to live in a large city.

After you have written your letter, read it over carefully. Did you shift the tense of your verbs unnecessarily? If so, correct any errors before you turn in your work.

● Progressive Verb Forms

Each of the six tenses has a **progressive form.** These forms are used to express continuing or ongoing action. The progressive forms add special meaning to verbs that the regular tenses do not. Notice the differences in meaning in the following examples.

PRESENT	She drinks water.
	(*Drinks* shows that she can or does drink.)
PRESENT PROGRESSIVE	She is drinking water.
	(*Is drinking* shows that she is drinking right now.)

To form the progressive, add a form of the verb *be* to the present participle. Notice in the following examples that all of the progressive forms end in *–ing.*

PRESENT PROGRESSIVE	The young girl **is running.**
PAST PROGRESSIVE	The young girl **was running.**
FUTURE PROGRESSIVE	The young girl **will be running.**

PRESENT PERFECT PROGRESSIVE	The young girl **has been running.**
PAST PERFECT PROGRESSIVE	The young girl **had been running.**
FUTURE PERFECT PROGRESSIVE	The young girl **will have been running.**

PRACTICE YOUR SKILLS

● Check Your Understanding
Identifying Progressive Verb Forms

 **Write the progressive form verb phrase in the following sentences.**

1. In a short while, these cyclists will have been racing around the track for three hours.

2. After that, they will be pedaling for another three hours.

3. Most of these athletes have been training for this event for months.

4. Now last year's champion is pulling ahead of the pack.

5. Before November he had been considering retirement.

6. Many fans were regretting his decision.

7. Lately, though, he has been training very hard.

8. The champion has been hoping for a strong performance today.

9. He is riding much better than any of his opponents.

10. I predict that he will be standing in the winner's circle today.

Rewriting Verbs

Rewrite the following sentences, changing each verb to its progressive form.

11. I speak to you today from the U.S. Bicycle Challenge.

12. Over fifty of America's greatest athletes gather here.

13. They will compete against their toughest opponents.

14. They have practiced hard all year for this unique event.

15. The race begins now.

16. The judge gives the signal.

17. Cyclists race onto the track.

18. By the end of the day, they will have raced for six hours.

19. A newcomer has led the pack for several miles.

20. The excitement will continue all day.

Communicate Your Ideas

APPLY TO WRITING

TV Script: *Using Progressive Verb Forms*

For a TV cooking show or home repair show, write a short, humorous sketch in which everything goes wrong. Use at least four progressive verb forms in your script. For example, you might write the following: "I *am beating* these eggs while the chicken *is cooking*. Oh, no, smoke *is coming* out of the oven! Next, I *will be calling* the fire department!"

General Interest **Write the underlined verbs in the following sentences. Label the tense of each verb.**

1. Technological changes <u>continue</u> in our society.

2. In the past, people <u>struggled</u> to keep their food fresh.

3. By the 1970s, air conditioning <u>had changed</u> people's lives.

4. More and more people <u>moved</u> to the warmer climates.

5. Other innovations <u>have allowed</u> longer lives for people.

6. Researchers <u>will continue</u> the development of life-saving medicines.

7. At one time computers <u>took</u> up entire rooms.

8. Today engineers <u>have developed</u> palm-sized computers.

9. Manufacturers <u>will have improved</u> cars greatly within the next hundred years.

10. No one <u>knows</u> what changes the future <u>will bring</u>.

Using the Correct Verb Form

Write the past or past participle of each verb in parentheses.

1. I have (know) Michelle since first grade.
2. My father (drive) me to her house.
3. Heather and I (ring) her doorbell.
4. Her parents have (throw) a big party for her birthday.
5. We have (come) here for her party.
6. Her mother has (go) to pick up the birthday cake.
7. The baker (write) her name on the cake in pink letters.
8. Michelle has just (blow) out the candles.
9. She cut the cake after we had (sing) "Happy Birthday."
10. The afternoon (fly) by very fast.

Using the Correct Verb Form

Find and correct each verb form that is used incorrectly in the following sentences. If the verb form is correct, write C.

1. Two apple trees growed in Kyle's backyard.
2. Someone or something had stealed some of the apples.
3. The thief had chose the ripest ones on the low branches.
4. Who could have done this?
5. Kyle sat on the porch that afternoon.
6. He seen two deer under the tree.
7. Kyle speaked to them in a loud, angry voice.
8. The deer runned away at the sound of his voice.
9. He had drove the deer out of the yard.
10. He was not sure that they had went away for good.

Identifying Verb Tenses

Write each verb phrase. Then label its tense *present, past, future, present perfect, past perfect,* or *future perfect*.

1. The Machado family travels every summer.
2. They have just left on this summer's trip.
3. They will stay in Arizona for three weeks.
4. Mr. and Mrs. Machado had not planned a trip to Arizona originally.
5. They won a vacation to Arizona in a contest.
6. Sunland Travel Company will pay all their expenses.
7. Tony has already read a lot about Arizona's ancient cliff houses.
8. He had also learned about them in school.
9. The family plans to visit the Grand Canyon first.
10. They will have arrived by this time tomorrow.

Using Verbs Correctly

Write ten sentences that follow the directions below.

Write a sentence that . . .

1. includes the present tense of *read.*
2. includes the past tense of *choose.*
3. includes the future tense of *bring.*
4. includes the past perfect tense of *grow.*
5. includes the future perfect tense of *ride.*
6. includes any forms of the verbs *bring* and *take.*
7. includes any forms of the verbs *learn* and *teach.*
8. includes any forms of the verbs *leave* and *let.*
9. includes the progressive form *is hitting.*
10. includes the progressive form *was throwing.*

Language and *Self-Expression*

The artist captured a moment in time when three children were moved by the impulse to dance. What does her print suggest to you about the children? Do you think they are dancing for an audience?

Think of a performance you have watched. What impressed you most about it? Would you have encouraged someone else to go and see it? Write a review of the performance, as if you were writing it for a newspaper. Try to use past and past participle verb forms in your writing. Then publish your review in a class collection.

Prewriting Identify the different aspects of the performance in a cluster diagram. Make notes on its most striking features. Decide on the order in which you want to present the information. Put the most important details first.

Drafting Use your notes to write your review. Open with a paragraph that summarizes the performance and your thoughts about it. Your closing sentence or sentences should persuade your readers to see it.

Revising Have a classmate give you feedback on your review. Ask whether your first and last sentences relate to one another. Discuss whether you described the performance so that your reader can clearly visualize it.

Editing Check your review for errors in punctuation and spelling. Make sure you have no shifts in verb tense.

Publishing Prepare a clean copy of your review and read it aloud to a group of classmates. Then add it to a binder of performance reviews for everyone to read.

Another Look

Recognizing Sentences

The **principal parts** of a verb are the present, the present participle, the past, and the past participle.

A **regular verb** forms its past and past participle by adding *-ed* or *-d* to the present.

An **irregular verb** does not form its past and past participle by adding *-ed* or *-d* to the present.

The time expressed by a verb is called the **tense** of a verb.

Tenses of Verbs

Present tense is used to express an action that is going on now. *(page 255)*

Past tense expresses an action that already took place or was completed in the past. *(page 255)*

Future tense is used to express an action that will take place in the future. *(page 255)*

Present perfect tense expresses an action that was completed at some indefinite time in the past. *(page 256)*

Past perfect tense expresses an action that took place before some other past action. *(page 256)*

Future perfect tense expresses an action that will take place before another future action or time. *(page 256)*

Progressive forms of the six tenses are used to express continuing or ongoing action. *(pages 262–263)*

Avoid unnecessary shifts in tense within a sentence or within related sentences. *(pages 257–259)*

Other Information About Verbs

Spelling changes in verb forms *(pages 234–241)*
Using *bring* and *take* *(pages 246–247)*
Using *teach* and *learn* *(page 248)*
Using *leave* and *let* *(page 250)*

Posttest

Directions
Read the passage. Write the letter of the word that correctly completes each sentence.

EXAMPLE   Few people today have __(1)__ of John Symmes.

      1 A hear
        B heard
        C hears
        D hearing

ANSWER   **1 B**

In the early 1800s, Symmes had __(1)__ to the rank of U.S. Army captain. He __(2)__ interested in astronomy while he was in the army. He watched as some birds __(3)__ north at the winter's end. He thought about their migration and __(4)__ up with a reason for it. They were __(5)__ toward the sunlight coming from the North Pole! Symmes had __(6)__ the northern lights, and he believed they were reflected sunlight. The sun was __(7)__ out of a hole at the North Pole. He thought he __(8)__ for certain that the earth was hollow. He was sure another country would be __(9)__ under its crust. He __(10)__ to many people and told them about his idea.

1 **A** rose
   B rising
   C rises
   D risen

2 **A** grown
   B grew
   C grows
   D growing

3 **A** fly
   B flown
   C flew
   D flying

4 **A** come
   B came
   C comes
   D coming

5 **A** going
   B went
   C goes
   D gone

6 **A** sees
   B saw
   C seen
   D seeing

7 **A** rose
   B risen
   C rise
   D rising

8 **A** known
   B knew
   C knows
   D knowed

9 **A** found
   B find
   C finding
   D finds

10 **A** writing
    B written
    C wrote
    D writes

CHAPTER 9

Using Pronouns

Pretest

Directions
Read the passage and choose the pronoun that belongs in each underlined space. Write the letter of the correct answer.

EXAMPLE   When he turned 80, Mario Bauza celebrated __(1)__ birthday in a big way.

    1 A he
       B its
       C his
       D it's

ANSWER   **1 C**

New York Mayor David Dinkins said that __(1)__ was proclaiming a "Mario Bauza Day." __(2)__ is familiar with this name? I learned from __(3)__ mother that he was an outstanding musician. My mother knows about him, and __(4)__ said that he once played for the Havana Philharmonic Orchestra. In New York he became known for __(5)__ wonderful horn playing. The members of a band called Machito and His Afro-Cubans asked Bauza to be __(6)__ musical director. The band was revolutionary, and __(7)__ created Latin jazz single-handedly. Latin jazz stands out from other jazz because of __(8)__ unusual rhythm. At first some musicians made fun of Bauza's music because it was so different from __(9)__. Before long though, many came to him and asked him to teach __(10)__.

1	**A**	him	**6**	**A**	they	
	B	his		**B**	their	
	C	it		**C**	his	
	D	he		**D**	it's	
2	**A**	Whom	**7**	**A**	its	
	B	Who		**B**	it's	
	C	It		**C**	it	
	D	He		**D**	he	
3	**A**	her	**8**	**A**	its	
	B	mine		**B**	it's	
	C	my		**C**	it	
	D	me		**D**	his	
4	**A**	he	**9**	**A**	their	
	B	her		**B**	theirs	
	C	I		**C**	his	
	D	she		**D**	them	
5	**A**	his	**10**	**A**	him	
	B	her		**B**	it	
	C	its		**C**	they	
	D	he		**D**	them	

Lee N. Smith III.
*Intruder in the
Port,* 1993.
Oil and 3D
construction on panel,
78 by 96
by 7 inches.
Private collection.

Describe What are the children in the picture doing? What clues did the artist give to suggest what game they are playing?

Analyze The painting is divided into two parts. How did the artist use color to tie both parts together? What words would you use to describe the painter's style?

Interpret Do you think that the style of the painting suits its subject? Why or why not?

Judge Would you hang a copy of the picture in your own room at home? What are your reasons for responding as you did? Suppose the artist had written a poem to go with the painting. What would that poem be like?

At the end of the chapter, you will use this artwork to stimulate ideas for writing.

Kinds of Pronouns

Pronouns are words that take the place of nouns. Pronouns make it possible to avoid using the same nouns over and over again. *His* and *him* are personal pronouns. In the first example, these pronouns take the place of *Roberto*. In the second example, *she* and *her* are personal pronouns that take the place of *Ana*.

> Roberto carried **his** trumpet with **him** on the plane.
>
> Ana said **she** had left **her** guitar at the check-in counter.

Different personal pronouns can take the place of the same noun because there are different kinds of personal pronouns. In English there are three kinds of pronouns: subject pronouns, object pronouns, and possessive pronouns. Each one of these kinds of pronouns is used in a different way in a sentence.

	SUBJECT PRONOUNS	
	Singular	Plural
FIRST PERSON	I	we
SECOND PERSON	you	you
THIRD PERSON	he, she, it	they
	OBJECT PRONOUNS	
	Singular	Plural
FIRST PERSON	me	us
SECOND PERSON	you	you
THIRD PERSON	him, her, it	them

POSSESSIVE PRONOUNS		
	Singular	**Plural**
FIRST PERSON	my, mine	our, ours
SECOND PERSON	your, yours	your, yours
THIRD PERSON	his, her, hers, its	their, theirs

You can find out more about personal pronouns on pages L60–L61.

PRACTICE YOUR SKILLS

● Check Your Understanding
Identifying the Kinds of Personal Pronouns

Music Topic **Write the personal pronouns in each sentence. Then label them *subject, object,* or *possessive.* Some sentences have more than one pronoun.**

1. America can be proud of its musical history.

2. We should remember great musicians and honor them.

3. Many musicians first sang in their churches.

4. Mahalia Jackson sang gospel music, and she became world famous.

5. Her voice was unforgettable.

6. My grandmother told me about a musician named Duke Ellington.

7. His music still influences modern jazz players.

8. People flocked to see him.

9. He and his orchestra made an impression on millions of people.

10. Many other fabulous singers and musicians have entertained us.

▶ Subject Pronouns

The following list shows all the personal pronouns that are subject pronouns.

	SUBJECT PRONOUNS	
	Singular	Plural
FIRST PERSON	I	we
SECOND PERSON	you	you
THIRD PERSON	he, she, it	they

Subject pronouns are used two ways in a sentence.

Subject pronouns are used for subjects and predicate nominatives.

SUBJECT	**She** collects insects.
PREDICATE NOMINATIVE	The best collector is **she.**

Pronouns Used as Subjects

The subject of a sentence names the person, place, or thing the sentence is about. Subject pronouns are used as the subjects of sentences.

SUBJECTS	**He** studies spiders.
	Have **they** returned from the field trip?
	(Turn a question into a statement: *They have returned from the field trip.* Then it is easy to find the subject.)

Sometimes more than one word is the subject of a sentence. In such a sentence, the subject is called a **compound subject,** as in the following example.

COMPOUND SUBJECT	**Felicia** and **(he, him)** watch birds.

To decide which pronoun is correct, say each one separately. Say the sentence as if each pronoun were a simple subject.

CORRECT   **He** watches birds.
INCORRECT   **Him** watches birds.

When you separate the choices, it becomes easy to see and hear which pronoun is correct. In this sentence the subject pronoun *he* is the correct form to use.

CORRECT   Felicia and **he** watch birds.

You can learn more about finding subjects on pages L10–L13.

PRACTICE YOUR SKILLS

● Check Your Understanding
Using Subject Pronouns

Oral Expression   **Say each sentence aloud, trying each pronoun separately. Then say the sentence again, choosing the correct pronoun.**

1. My friends and (I, me) enjoy nature.

2. Samantha and (he, him) study insects.

3. Hannah and (her, she) focus more on plants.

4. Sondra and (them, they) especially like wildflowers.

5. My class and (I, me) took a field trip to a nearby natural area.

● Check Your Understanding
Using Subject Pronouns

Contemporary Life   **Write the correct personal pronoun in parentheses.**

6. Last week (us, we) went on a field trip to the forest.

7. Stephanie and (he, him) collected some leaves.

8. (Them, They) took samples of the soil in different parts of the forest.

9. The teachers and (us, we) brought lunches.

10. At lunch (us, we) discussed our observations.

11. Greg and (her, she) found the tracks of an animal.

12. The science teacher and (I, me) took a close look at the tracks.

13. Did you and (her, she) see the tracks?

14. The science teacher and (them, they) identified the source of the tracks.

15. My class and (I, me) had a great time.

Pronouns Used as Predicate Nominatives

A predicate nominative is a word that follows a linking verb—such as *is, was,* or *has been*—and identifies or renames the subject. Subject pronouns are used as predicate nominatives.

PREDICATE NOMINATIVES   My swim instructor is **he.**

Is that **they** in the boat?
(Turn the question into a statement: *That is they in the boat.* Then it is easy to see that *they* renames the subject.)

To find the correct pronoun in a compound predicate nominative, turn the sentence around. Make the predicate nominative the subject. Then say the sentence as if each pronoun were a simple subject.

PREDICATE NOMINATIVE   The other swimmers are **Jamie** and **(he, him).**

Jamie and **(he, him)** are the other swimmers.

CORRECT	**He** is the other swimmer.
INCORRECT	**Him** is the other swimmer.
CORRECT	The other swimmers are Jamie and **he.**

You can find a list of common linking verbs on page L92. You can learn more about predicate nominatives on pages L98–L99.

CONNECT TO WRITER'S CRAFT

Sentences with pronouns used as predicate nominatives may *sound* wrong to you, even though they are correct. When you write, you can simply avoid these awkward-sounding sentences by reversing them. Turn the predicate nominatives into subjects.

AWKWARD	My swim instructor is **he.**
BETTER	**He** is my swim instructor.
AWKWARD	The other swimmers are Jamie and **she.**
BETTER	Jamie and **she** are the other swimmers.

PRACTICE YOUR SKILLS

● Check Your Understanding
Using Pronouns as Predicate Nominatives

Oral Expression | **Turn each sentence around to make the predicate nominative the subject. Then say each pronoun separately to find out which one is correct. Repeat the sentence aloud with the correct pronoun.**

1. Two members of the swim team are Cindi and (he, him).

2. Our swimming teacher is (her, she).

3. The winners of the swim meet were Serena and (he, him).

4. The best swimmers are Tony and (them, they).

5. The newest members of the team are Lindsey and (us, we).

Using Pronouns as Predicate Nominatives

Contemporary Life **Write the correct personal pronoun in parentheses.**

6. The store's owners are that woman and (he, him).

7. Their best customer is (I, me).

8. Here are (us, we) in the picture behind the counter.

9. The clerk in the photograph is (he, him).

10. The customers here now are Jason and (I, me).

11. My favorite salespeople in this store are Christi and (her, she).

12. The last customers in the store were (them, they).

13. Is that (her, she) at the candy counter?

14. Their other loyal customers are Leisha and (them, they).

15. The ones in the magazine section are Liz and (us, we).

● Check Your Understanding
Supplying Subject Pronouns

Contemporary Life **Complete each sentence with a subject pronoun. (Do not use *you* or *it*.)**

16. ▨ helped build a house for that family.

17. Mark and ▨ cut the boards.

18. The roofers on the project were Mr. Washington and ▨.

19. The person in charge of all the workers was ▨.

20. Lena and ▨ helped install the carpet.

21. The designers of the home were Ms. Lopez and ▨.

22. ▓ was the hardest worker on the project.

23. Kristina and ▓ installed the doors and windows.

24. The handiest people were those girls and ▓.

25. ▓ felt great for helping with this important project.

● Connect to the Writing Process: Drafting
Writing Sentences Using Subject Pronouns

Write sentences that follow these directions.

26. Use *he* as a subject.

27. Use *Max and she* as a compound subject.

28. Use *my friends and I* as a compound subject.

29. Use *she* as a predicate nominative.

30. Use *Jack and I* as a compound predicate nominative.

● Connect to the Writing Process: Editing
Correcting Errors in the Use of Subject Pronouns

Rewrite the following sentences, correcting any errors in pronoun usage.

31. Fallon and him will write to Senator Jenkins in Washington.

32. The best writers in our class are Vanessa and her.

33. Kelly and them will ask the senator about a new law.

34. The two senators from our state are Melinda Jenkins and him.

35. The other senators and them know much about the new law.

APPLY TO WRITING

Postcard Message: *Using Subject Pronouns*

Claude Monet. *Beach at Trouville,* 1870.
Oil on canvas, 21¹⁵⁄₁₆ by 22⁵⁄₈ inches. Wadsworth Atheneum, Hartford.

Look carefully at this painting by Claude Monet.
Imagine that your family is vacationing at the
beautiful beach at Trouville. Write a postcard to your
grandmother, telling her about your trip. Describe the
sights, sounds, and smells around you. As you write,
use at least three subject pronouns. Make one of the
pronouns a predicate nominative. Underline these
pronouns in your message.

Contemporary
Life **Write the correct personal pronoun in the parentheses.**

1. Lori and (he, him) always tell the funniest elephant jokes.

2. (Them, They) make everyone laugh.

3. The winners of the local comedy contest were (them, they).

4. If you are wondering who the funniest girl is, Lori's sister is (her, she).

5. Our class and (her, she) watched a video of the competition.

6. Lori's sister and (us, we) laughed through the entire performance.

7. In my opinion, the funniest comedian was (her, she).

8. Now the biggest comedy fans at our middle school are (us, we).

9. Lori's best friends are Caroline and (I, me).

10. Lori and (us, we) will celebrate her victory at the ice cream parlor.

Object Pronouns

The following list shows the personal pronouns that are object pronouns.

OBJECT PRONOUNS		
	Singular	**Plural**
FIRST PERSON	me	us
SECOND PERSON	you	you
THIRD PERSON	him, her, it	them

Object pronouns are used in three ways in a sentence.

Object pronouns are used as direct objects, indirect objects, and objects of prepositions.

DIRECT OBJECT	I invited **them** to dinner.
INDIRECT OBJECT	Nick brought **her** some hot soup.
OBJECT OF A PREPOSITION	Emily brought the freshly baked bread to **us.**

Pronouns Used as Direct Objects

A direct object follows an action verb and answers the question *Whom?* or *What?*

DIRECT OBJECTS	I have known **them** for a long time. (I have known whom? *Them* is the direct object.)
	Did you meet **her** last summer? (Turn a question into a statement: *You did meet her last year.* You did meet whom? *Her* is the direct object.)

To find the correct pronoun in a compound direct object, say a sentence as if each pronoun were the only direct object.

DIRECT OBJECT	We met Wendi and (her, she) at camp.
INCORRECT	We met **she** at camp.
CORRECT	We met **her** at camp.
CORRECT	We met Wendi and **her** at camp.

You can learn more about direct objects on pages L83–L85.

PRACTICE YOUR SKILLS

● Check Your Understanding
Using Compound Direct Objects

Oral Expression **Say each sentence aloud, trying each pronoun separately. Then say the sentence again, choosing the correct pronoun.**

1. The Winstons called Sam and (I, me) for directions.

2. Mom helped Emily and (them, they) with dinner.

3. The Winstons had already met Nick and (he, him).

4. They told Nick and (us, we) about their recent trip.

5. The Winstons took Danny and (her, she) on a trip to Australia.

● Check Your Understanding
Using Object Pronouns as Direct Objects

Contemporary Life **Write the correct personal pronoun in parentheses.**

6. Mom called Emily and (I, me) in for dinner.

7. Nick joined the Winstons and (us, we).

8. The story of their trip to Australia fascinated Nick and (I, me).

9. A guide had told the girls and (them, they) about the Sydney Opera House.

10. The guide took Mr. Winston and (her, she) to the Australian outback.

11. After dinner Mom asked Emily and (I, me) for help with the dishes.

12. The Winstons thanked Mom and (us, we) for a great dinner.

13. We thanked (them, they) for their exciting stories.

14. The Winstons will invite (us, we) to their house next time.

15. I like Mrs. Winston and (he, him) very much.

Pronouns Used as Indirect Objects

An indirect object comes before a direct object and answers the questions *To or for whom?* or *To or for what?* To have an indirect object, you must also have a direct object.

INDIRECT OBJECTS	Chris gave **him** the directions.
	(Chris gave what? *Directions* is the direct object. Chris gave directions to whom? *Him. Him* is the indirect object.)
	David drew **them** a map.
	(David drew what? *Map* is the direct object. He drew the map for whom? *Them. Them* is the indirect object.)

To find the correct pronoun in a compound indirect object, say a sentence as if each pronoun were the only indirect object.

INDIRECT OBJECT	The principal gave the new students and (them, they) a warm welcome.

INCORRECT	The principal gave **they** a warm welcome.
CORRECT	The principal gave **them** a warm welcome.
CORRECT	The principal gave the new students and **them** a warm welcome.

You can learn more about indirect objects on pages L86–L87.

PRACTICE YOUR SKILLS

● Check Your Understanding
Using Compound Indirect Objects

Oral Expression **Say each sentence aloud, trying each pronoun separately. Then say the sentence again, choosing the correct pronoun.**

1. The library aide gave Becca and (he, him) a tour.

2. The librarian handed Dawn and (them, they) cards.

3. I showed Becca and (her, she) some good books.

4. They told the principal and (us, we) stories about their old school.

5. The new families wrote Tyler and (I, me) a thank-you note.

● Check Your Understanding
Using Object Pronouns as Indirect Objects

Contemporary Life **Write the correct personal pronoun in parentheses.**

6. The teacher read the new students and (we, us) a story about Theodore Roosevelt.

7. The library sent John and (I, me) some brochures about the American presidents.

8. I showed Hannah and (them, they) my brochures.

9. Take Jacob and (he, him) that book about Lincoln.

10. Our library has provided (us, we) with plenty of information for our research projects.

11. The teacher told Jacob and (us, we) the story of Lincoln's assassination.

12. She gave Anna and (them, they) some ideas for their projects.

13. The teacher asked John and (I, me) questions.

14. We told (her, she) our ideas.

15. We showed the principal and (her, she) our completed projects.

Pronouns Used as Objects of Prepositions

A prepositional phrase begins with a preposition—such as *to, for, near,* or *with.* A prepositional phrase ends with the object of a preposition. An object pronoun is used as an object of a preposition.

OBJECTS OF PREPOSITIONS	The phone call is for **her.**
	(*For her* is the prepositional phrase.)
	Keep the phone near **me.**
	(*Near me* is the prepositional phrase.)

To find the correct pronoun in a compound object of a preposition, say each pronoun separately as the only object.

OBJECT OF A PREPOSTION	The invitation was addressed to **Taylor** and **(I, me)**.
INCORRECT	The invitation was addressed to **I.**
CORRECT	The invitation was addressed to **me.**

| CORRECT | The invitation was addressed to Taylor and **me.** |

You can learn more about prepositional phrases on pages L177–L185.

PRACTICE YOUR SKILLS

● Check Your Understanding
Using Compound Objects of a Preposition

Oral Expression **Say each sentence aloud, trying each pronoun separately. Then say the sentence again, choosing the correct pronoun.**

1. Ryan and I brought birthday presents for Elizabeth and (he, him).

2. Elizabeth and Eric said thank you to Austin and (us, we).

3. We sang "Happy Birthday" to Eric and (her, she).

4. I had a great time with Ryan and (them, they).

5. At the party Elizabeth sat between Ty and (I, me).

● Check Your Understanding
Using Pronouns as Objects of Prepositions

Contemporary Life **Write the correct personal pronoun in parentheses.**

6. In the school elections, many students voted for Brandon and (he, him).

7. The most votes went to Toby and (her, she).

8. There was a tie between Erin and (he, him).

9. A few people voted for Marissa and (I, me).

10. I talked to Brett and (her, she) about our class leaders.

11. Between you and (I, me), I think Brett would have made a better president.

12. He will work with Brandon and (her, she) on the student council.

13. Next year I will run against Toby and (them, they).

14. Maybe more people will vote for Brett and (us, we) next time.

15. I hope there is not a tie between Brett and (I, me).

● Check Your Understanding
Supplying Object Pronouns

Contemporary Life **Complete each sentence with an object pronoun. Do not use *you* or *it*.**

16. The teacher gave Lianna and ▓ a sudden smile.

17. She told the class and ▓ about a great book.

18. My parents asked ▓ for a good reading list.

19. She gave my parents and ▓ a list of poems.

20. I read the poems with Dylan and ▓ after class.

21. My teacher looked everywhere for Tiffany and ▓.

22. We read some of the poems to my sister and ▓.

23. My teacher recited poems for my friends and ▓.

24. The school awarded Mr. Rodriguez and ▓ prizes.

25. I really admire Ms. Weaver and ▓.

● Connect to the Writing Process: Editing
Editing for Errors with Object Pronouns

Rewrite the following sentences, correcting the errors in pronoun usage.

26. Between you and I, this soup is too cold.

27. Mom ordered my sister and I another bowl.

28. The waiter brought a free dinner for Mom and we.

29. I thanked the hostess and he for such good service.

30. The band played a special song for my sister and I.

Writing Sentences with Object Pronouns

Write sentences that follow these directions.

31. Use *her* as the direct object.

32. Use *Jenny and him* as the compound direct object.

33. Use *us* as the indirect object.

34. Use *you and me* as the compound indirect object.

35. Use *Caitlin and her* as the compound object of the preposition *with*.

Communicate Your Ideas

APPLY TO WRITING

Thank-you Note: *Using Object Pronouns*

Hung Liu, *Feeding the Rabbit,* 1995.
Oil on canvas, 76 by 96 inches. Courtesy Bernice Steinbaum Gallery, Miami, FL.
Photograph by Adam Reich.

Look at *Feeding the Rabbit* by Hung Liu. Imagine that it is your birthday, and your aunt has given you this pet rabbit as a gift. Write a thank-you note to your aunt. Tell her how your friends reacted at your birthday party as they fed and played with your new pet. As you write the note, use at least three object pronouns in your writing. Make one a direct object, one an indirect object, and one an object of a preposition. Underline and label these object pronouns.

QuickCheck   Mixed Practice

Rewrite each sentence, correcting any errors in pronoun usage. If the sentence is correct, write C.

1. Without you and I, the party would have been dull.

2. We told Daniel and they funny stories about our cat.

3. During the party Will and I talked to Daniel's parents and sister.

4. The funniest person at the party was her.

5. Daniel and me ate two pieces of cake.

6. The winners of the game were Brady and she.

7. After the magic act, Megan and him clapped the most.

8. The magician invited Michelle and I onstage with he.

9. Were she and I good assistants?

10. At the end of the party, Daniel's parents thanked Brady and us for coming.

⏵ Possessive Pronouns

The following list shows the personal pronouns that are possessive pronouns.

POSSESSIVE PRONOUNS		
	Singular	Plural
FIRST PERSON	my, mine	our, ours
SECOND PERSON	your, yours	your, yours
THIRD PERSON	his, her, hers, its	their, theirs

Possessive pronouns are used to show ownership or possession.

The possessive pronouns in the box can be divided into two groups: (1) those that are used like adjectives to describe nouns and (2) those that are used alone.

USES OF POSSESSIVE PRONOUNS	
USED LIKE ADJECTIVES	my, your, his, her, its, our, your, their
USED ALONE	mine, yours, his, hers, its, ours, yours, theirs

My kite is flying high today, but **yours** has not caught the wind yet.

The red box kite is **mine,** and **his** kite is the bright green one.

Pronouns used as adjectives are sometimes called possessive adjectives.

Although apostrophes are used with possessive nouns, they are never used with the possessive forms of personal pronouns.

POSSESSIVE NOUN	Is this **Courtney's** kite?
POSSESSIVE PRONOUN	Is this kite **hers**? (not *her's*)

You can learn more about possessive nouns on pages L507–L509.

PRACTICE YOUR SKILLS

● Check Your Understanding
Using Possessive Pronouns

Oral Expression **Say each sentence aloud, trying each pronoun separately. Then say the sentence again, choosing the correct pronoun.**

1. This ball of string is Nicole's or (his's, his).

2. (Her, Hers) mom used lightweight tape to repair the kite.

3. (Ours, Our) kite-flying contest was very exciting.

4. Courtney watched (her, hers) kite soar into the air.

5. The judges voted (mine, my) the most beautiful kite in the contest.

● Check Your Understanding
Using Possessive Pronouns

General Interest **Write the correct personal pronoun in parentheses.**

6. The ancient Chinese were flying (their, theirs) kites thousands of years ago.

7. Today people from many nations around the world still fly (their's, theirs).

8. In America one of (our, ours) founding fathers flew a kite.

9. Benjamin Franklin tested (his's, his) theories about lightning and electricity with a kite.

10. Other inventors used kites in (their, theirs) experiments.

11. You should be careful when you fly (your, yours) kite.

12. Find an empty field or lot in (you, your) neighborhood.

13. Find a place like (my, mine), with few trees and no power lines.

14. It's the perfect place for (my, mine) little sister to fly (hers, her's).

15. To launch the kite, we stand with (our, our's) backs to the wind.

● Connect to the Writing Process: Editing
Correcting Errors with Possessive Pronouns

Rewrite the following sentences, correcting the errors in pronoun usage.

16. You can fly you kite in my yard.

17. I found his's kite.

18. Have you seen mine new ball of string?

19. That kite is their's.

20. Is that beautiful blue kite your's?

● Connect to the Writing Process: Drafting
Writing Sentences with Possessive Pronouns

Write sentences for each of these possessive pronouns.

21. hers   **22.** your   **23.** its   **24.** theirs   **25.** his

Possessive Pronoun or Contraction?

Because some contractions sound like some personal pronouns, they are easy to confuse.

POSSESSIVE PRONOUNS	its, your, their, theirs
CONTRACTIONS	it's (it is), you're (you are), they're (they are), there's (there is)

The best way to separate these words in your mind is to say the two words that a contraction stands for.

POSSESSIVE PRONOUN OR CONTRACTION?	**(You're, Your)** phone is ringing.
INCORRECT	**You are** phone is ringing.
CORRECT	**Your** phone is ringing.

PRACTICE YOUR SKILLS

● Check Your Understanding
Distinguishing Between Possessive Pronouns and Contractions

Oral Expression **Say each sentence aloud, trying each word separately. When you practice with the contraction, say the two words that the contraction stands for. Then say the sentence again, choosing the correct word.**

1. (They're, Their) calling you.

2. Please pick up (you're, your) phone.

3. This one is ours, and that one is (there's, theirs).

4. (It's, Its) easy to give clear directions.

5. (They're, Their) going to be late.

Distinguishing Between Pronouns and Contractions

Write the correct word in parentheses.

6. Is this (you're, your) home?

7. (There's, theirs) a beautiful dog in the yard.

8. (It's, Its) my brother's pet.

9. (They're, Their) such loyal animals.

10. That breed of dog is (you're, your) favorite.

Communicate Your Ideas

APPLY TO WRITING

The Writer's Craft: *Analyzing the Use of Personal Pronouns*

Writers use personal pronouns extensively in their writing. Otherwise, their work would become repetitive and uninteresting. In the following passage from *The Goats*, Brock Cole uses subject, object, and possessive pronouns to make his writing interesting. Read the passage and the directions on the following page.

The boy got out of the car slowly. "Hi, dog," he said, holding out the back of his hand so the dog could sniff at him. He could see it was confused. Its hackles were up, but it was wagging its tail.

Out of the corner of his eye he saw that the girl was out of the car and moving flat-footed toward the road.

"Don't run," he said. She had left the door open, so he took a step back and slammed it closed.

—Brock Cole, The Goats

- Write the personal pronouns in the passage. Label each one *subject pronoun*, *object pronoun*, or *possessive pronoun*.

- Why do you think the writer used so many pronouns in this short passage?

- The word *its* appears twice in the first paragraph. Is it a contraction or a possessive pronoun? How do you know?

- The word *it* appears in both the first and the last paragraph. Does *it* refer to the same thing each time? Explain your answer.

QuickCheck Mixed Practice

Contemporary Life **Rewrite each sentence, correcting any pronoun errors. If the sentence is correct, write C.**

1. Melinda carried the sandwiches to Larry and she.

2. Alicia joined the club with Raoul and I.

3. Diana and us have learned about hot-air balloons.

4. The coach drove the players and them to the game.

5. Their coming with us to the concert.

6. Each day, Ginny and her go for a long run.

7. The strongest competitors are Joe and him.

8. That was Betty and he at the back door.

9. The fire engine was flashing its red lights.

10. Your going to be late if you don't hurry.

11. Katie was looking at you and he on the balcony.

12. The rumbling noise alarmed Bryan and her.

Pronoun Problem: *Who* or *Whom?*

Some pronouns, called **interrogative pronouns,** are used to ask questions. Two interrogative pronouns are *who* and *whom*. *Who* is a subject pronoun, and *whom* is an object pronoun.

Who is used as a subject, just like the subject pronouns *I, he, she,* and *they*.

> SUBJECT **Who** will go to the movies with me?

Whom is used as a direct object and as an object of a preposition, just like the object pronouns *me, him, her,* and *them*.

> DIRECT OBJECT **Whom** did you see at the movies?
> (Turn a question into a statement: *You did see whom at the movie. Whom* is the direct object.)
>
> OBJECT OF A **For whom** did you buy that popcorn?
> PREPOSITION (*For whom* is a prepositional phrase.)

Whose can also be used as an interrogative pronoun. It will always show possession.

> **Whose** poster is this?

Do not confuse *whose* with the contraction *who's,* which means "who is."

 CONNECT TO WRITER'S CRAFT

To remember a principle of usage, a writer sometimes memorizes questions such as these:

Who is the subject?
To **whom** is the action directed?

PRACTICE YOUR SKILLS

● Check Your Understanding
Using Who and Whom

Contemporary Life **Write the correct pronoun from the parentheses.**

1. (Who, Whom) rode in the truck with you to the theater?
2. (Whose, Who's) popcorn is that?
3. With (who, whom) did you sit?
4. (Who, Whom) was the star of that award-winning film?
5. (Whose, Who's) candy is this?
6. (Who, Whom) will go to the movies with us next week?
7. By (who, whom) was the film directed?
8. (Whose, Who's) dad is buying the snacks?
9. (Who, Whom) among your friends have you told about the film?
10. From (who, whom) did you receive the free movie passes?

● Connect to the Writing Process: Drafting
Writing Sentences Using Interrogative Pronouns

Write sentences that follow the directions.

11. Use *who* as a subject.
12. Use *whom* as a direct object.
13. Use *whom* as the object of the preposition *to.*
14. Use *whose* in a question.
15. Use *who's* in a question.

Pronouns and Their Antecedents

The word that a pronoun refers to is called the pronoun's **antecedent.** The antecedent of a pronoun can be a noun or another pronoun. In the following examples, *Shauna* is the antecedent of *her,* and *they* is the antecedent of *their.*

| PRONOUNS AND ANTECEDENTS | **Shauna** and **her** band are playing. |
| | **They** always tune **their** guitars first. |

Because a pronoun and its antecedent refer to the same person, place, or thing, they must agree.

A pronoun must agree in gender and number with its antecedent.

Number indicates whether a noun or a pronoun is singular (one) or plural (more than one). A pronoun must be singular if its antecedent is singular. It must be plural if its antecedent is plural.

| SINGULAR | **Tim** enjoys **his** guitar lessons. |
| PLURAL | **Guitarists** get calluses on **their** fingers. |

A pronoun must also agree with its antecedent in gender. **Gender** indicates whether a noun or a pronoun is masculine, feminine, or neuter.

	GENDER		
MASCULINE	he	him	his
FEMININE	she	her	hers
NEUTER	it	its	

MASCULINE	**Kevin** tuned **his** guitar.
FEMININE	**Shauna** adjusted **her** microphone.
NEUTER	Lee put the **guitar** in **its** case.

Other personal pronouns—*I, me, mine, you, yours, they, theirs*—can refer to masculine, feminine, or neuter antecedents.

PRACTICE YOUR SKILLS

● Check Your Understanding
Making Pronouns and Their Antecedents Agree

Contemporary Life **Write the personal pronoun that correctly completes each sentence.**

1. The band members took ▪ places on the stage.
2. Kevin struck the first chord on ▪ guitar.
3. Shauna turned ▪ face to the audience.
4. The guitar was so loud we couldn't ignore ▪ sound.
5. The other band members clapped ▪ hands.
6. Maria kept a steady beat on ▪ drums.
7. The people in the audience jumped to ▪ feet.
8. Shauna finished ▪ last song.
9. Kevin gave the crowd ▪ thanks.
10. The auditorium was filled to ▪ limit.

● Connect to the Writing Process: Editing
Correcting Pronoun and Antecedent Agreement

Rewrite the following sentences, correcting any errors in pronoun and antecedent agreement.

11. Shauna snapped their fingers as she sang.
12. Before leaving the stage, Kevin waved to her mom.

13. Then he packed up its guitar.

14. Shauna put the microphone back in their place.

15. The fans clapped for its favorite band.

Indefinite Pronouns as Antecedents

Sometimes an indefinite pronoun will be the antecedent of a personal pronoun. The indefinite pronouns are listed in the following box. Notice that some of the indefinite pronouns are singular and some are plural.

INDEFINITE PRONOUNS	
SINGULAR	anybody, anyone, another, anything, each, either, everybody, everyone, everything, neither, nobody, nothing, no one, one, somebody, someone, something
PLURAL	both, few, many, several

A personal pronoun must be singular if its antecedent is one of the singular indefinite pronouns.

SINGULAR **One** of the boys lost **his** book.

Neither of the girls can find **her** homework.

When the gender of a singular indefinite pronoun is unknown, use *his or her* to refer to the indefinite pronoun.

Everyone should bring **his or her** notebook to the meeting.

Although the last sentence on the preceding page is correct, it may still sound awkward to you. You can sometimes eliminate a sentence like this one by rewriting it in the plural form.

PLURAL
All **students** should bring **their** notebooks to the meeting.

A personal pronoun must be plural if its antecedent is one of the plural indefinite pronouns.

Many of the students are reading **their** books.

Both of the girls enjoyed **their** stories.

You can find out more about indefinite pronouns on page L64.

CONNECT TO WRITER'S CRAFT

When you finish writing anything—from a letter to a science report—always edit your work. Check to see that you have used the correct form of each pronoun. Then make sure that each pronoun agrees with its antecedent in number and in gender. If you find any mistakes, take the time to correct them. A pronoun error can cause a reader to misunderstand what you are writing.

PRACTICE YOUR SKILLS

● Check Your Understanding
Making Pronouns Agree

Contemporary Life **Write the correct pronoun in parentheses.**

1. Many of the children in my family get books for (their, his or her) birthdays.

2. Everyone usually appreciates (their, his or her) gift.

3. Julie loved (her, its) book.

4. My cousins left (their, his or her) books at my house.

5. Did anybody finish reading (their, his or her) book?

6. Each of the books was signed by (their, its) author.

7. John says that Avi and Gary Paulsen are (his, their) favorite authors.

8. Both girls say that (their, her) favorite is Liz Harp.

9. Zack left (their, his) book on the bus.

10. One of the books was missing (its, their) cover.

● Connect to the Writing Process: Editing
Correcting Errors in Pronoun Agreement

Rewrite the sentences, correcting any errors in pronoun agreement.

11. Everyone should bring their favorite book.

12. All the boys remembered his notebooks.

13. Both of the girls forgot her pens.

14. Did the students bring his or her permission slips?

15. The book was put in their place on the shelf.

Communicate Your Ideas

APPLY TO WRITING

Editorial: *Making Pronouns and Antecedents Agree*

Write a brief editorial in which you try to persuade people to agree with your opinion on an important issue. In your editorial, include indefinite pronouns such as *everybody, nobody, anybody, either, neither, few, many,* and *some.* When you finish your editorial, check to be sure that each pronoun you used agrees in gender and number with its antecedent.

Contemporary Life

Read the following paragraphs, and look for errors in pronoun usage. Then rewrite the paragraphs correctly.

My friend Maria and me went to the library today. Maria found several books and showed it to the librarian and I. Them were all about elephants. Both of us are writing about elephants for her science reports.

A few of the books have some interesting facts in it. For example, at birth baby elephants are three feet tall and weigh two hundred pounds.

I called to Maria, and her and me read the next few sentences together. Whom would have thought that elephants walk on its toes? Much of the weight of an elephant is supported by pads on their feet. Elephants sometimes walk three hundred miles in search of food and water. Normally, them and they're calves walk at a speed of five miles an hour. For short distances, however, elephants can run as fast as twenty-four miles per hour.

Maria and I learned so much about elephants today. With who could we talk about what we'd learned? We decided to tell Josh about the elephants tomorrow at lunch. Josh and us will have a good time discussing these animals.

Using the Correct Kinds of Pronouns

Write the correct personal pronoun in parentheses.

1. (Who, Whom) did you see at the bowling alley?
2. Amber and (she, her) were bowling on one lane.
3. (We, Us) and our friends met at the alley.
4. I saw you and (they, them) coming in.
5. Melissa showed Andy and (I, me) a heavy ball.
6. I bowled right after Will and (she, her).
7. Those bowling shoes must be (your, yours).
8. The best bowlers are (he, him) and Will.
9. (Who, Whom) has the best score?
10. Justin and (he, him) are ahead right now.

Correcting Pronoun Errors

Write each sentence and correct any error. If a sentence is correct, write C.

1. Courtney and me are taking a photography class.
2. Who are you taking the class from?
3. Her and Mr. Yien take turns teaching the class.
4. Ms. King chose Jacob and I as models.
5. I took several photographs of Emily and him.
6. Sometimes us meet on weekends to take photos.
7. Megan, Jenny, and him have new cameras.
8. Whom are the best photographers?
9. The best photographers are Nick and she.
10. Are them and Kayla entering photos in the contest?

Making Pronouns and Their Antecedents Agree

Write the personal pronoun that correctly completes each sentence.

1. Lauren told Joshua about ▦ ballet rehearsal.
2. While Lauren was talking, ▦ and Joshua ran into some of their friends.
3. I am excited about ▦ part in the show.
4. We are going to put on ▦ performance in three weeks.
5. The lead dancers know their roles perfectly, and the rest of us are learning ▦.
6. David is a star pupil. The best dancers are Sarah and ▦.
7. Each girl in the production is being fitted for ▦ swan costume.
8. Most of them will wear white wings on ▦ backs.
9. David has the part of the hunter, and ▦ costume includes a bow and arrow.
10. The arrow looks sharp, but ▦ tip is just soft rubber.

Using Pronouns Correctly

Write ten sentences that follow the directions below.

Write a sentence that . . .

1. includes *Beth* and *I* as subjects.
2. includes *him* and *her* as direct objects.
3. includes the prepositional phrase *between you and me.*
4. includes the words *your* and *you're.*
5. includes the words *their* and *they're.*
6. includes *who.*
7. includes *whom.*
8. includes *nobody* as the subject.
9. includes *everyone* as the subject.
10. includes *many* as the subject.

Language and *Self-Expression*

Lee N. Smith says that many of his paintings show games that he played with friends in the open fields near his home.

Playing outdoors at night feels different from playing in bright daylight. Have you ever gone camping, star-gazed, or played tag outdoors at night? Describe the activity in a few paragraphs, as if you were setting the scene in a story. Tell what each person did. You can include dialogue. Use pronouns in place of names wherever they are appropriate. Then tape your description and share it with your friends.

Prewriting Make a chart that shows the sequence of events that you plan to describe. Beside each entry on the chart, give details about what people said and did and how everything looked.

Drafting Write the draft. Visualize each moment. Add more details. Your opening sentences should describe the setting, create the mood, and tell readers what is happening.

Revising Have a classmate read your draft and give you feedback. If your partner was confused by your description of any incident, ask what you can do to clarify it. Make sure all pronouns agree with their antecedents.

Editing Check your paragraphs for errors in punctuation and spelling. Be sure you did not use apostrophes in possessive pronouns.

Publishing Prepare a final copy and record it on audiotape or CD. You may want to make an illustration like Lee N. Smith's to accompany it. Make the recording and your artwork available to your classmates for listening and viewing.

Another Look

Subject pronouns are used for subjects and predicate nominatives.

Object pronouns are used as direct objects, indirect objects, and objects of prepositions.

Possessive pronouns are used to show ownership or possession.

Interrogative pronouns are used to ask questions. *(page L300)*
Indefinite pronouns refer to unnamed people, places, things, or ideas. *(pages L304–L305)*

Pronouns and Their Antecedents
The noun that a pronoun refers to or replaces is called its **antecedent**. *(page L302)*
A pronoun must agree in gender and number with its antecedent. *(pages L302–L303)*

Other Information About Pronouns
Using pronouns as direct objects *(pages L285–L286)*
Using pronouns as indirect objects *(pages L287–L288)*
Using pronouns as objects of prepositions *(pages L289–L290)*
Distinguishing between possessive pronouns and contractions *(page L297)*
Using indefinite pronouns as antecedents *(pages L304–L305)*

POSSESSIVE PRONOUNS		
	Singular	Plural
FIRST PERSON	my, mine	our, ours
SECOND PERSON	your, yours	your, yours
THIRD PERSON	his, her, hers, its	their, theirs

Directions
Read the passage and choose the word or group of words that belongs in each sentence. Write the letter of the correct answer.

EXAMPLE   The twins went for a balloon ride on __(1)__
              birthday.
              1 A our
                 B his
                 C their
                 D your

ANSWER   **1 C**

"May we visit __(1)__ uncle in Albuquerque?" asked Brittany and Brandon.

Their mother said, "I will telephone __(2)__ brother and ask him." Uncle Tom said that __(3)__ would be delighted to see them.

Albuquerque is famous for __(4)__ annual Hot Air Balloon Fiesta. Uncle Tom owns __(5)__ own balloon. About 500 balloonists came to the Fiesta with __(6)__ balloons. Many had designed __(7)__ balloons to resemble cartoon characters. Uncle Tom pointed to a balloon with a cat's face and said, "That one is __(8)__ ."

Brittany asked her uncle, "Will you photograph Brandon and __(9)__ next to the balloon?"

" __(10)__ wants to go for a balloon ride now?" asked Uncle Tom.

1 **A** our
   B my
   C their
   D her

2 **A** his
   B mine
   C my
   D their

3 **A** they
   B him
   C she
   D he

4 **A** it's
   B its
   C their
   D his

5 **A** its
   B him
   C his
   D it's

6 **A** their
   B they
   C his
   D its

7 **A** it
   B their
   C they
   D them

8 **A** its
   B our
   C my
   D mine

9 **A** them
   B him
   C me
   D I

10 **A** Neither
    B Both
    C Who
    D Whom

CHAPTER 10

Subject and Verb Agreement

Pretest

Directions

Read the passage and choose the word or group of words that belongs in each underlined space. Write the letter of the correct answer.

EXAMPLE ___(1)___ they ever eaten *tamales*?

      1 A Do
        B Have
        C Does
        D Has

ANSWER   **1 B**

    One of the most popular foods of the Rio Grande Basin ___(1)___ the tamale. This food always ___(2)___ been associated with Christmas celebrations. These delicious treats ___(3)___ easy to make. A wrapping of corn husks or banana leaves ___(4)___ around a tamale. First, a mixture of coarsely ground corn and fat ___(5)___ on the stove. Then the cooks ___(6)___ the mixture over the leaves or husks. Several spoonfuls of filling ___(7)___ put on top of that. Chicken, beef, or pork ___(8)___ a good meat filling. The cooks then ___(9)___ up the tamales. Each of them ___(10)___ steamed for about one hour.

1	**A**	were		6	**A**	take
	B	are			**B**	spread
	C	has			**C**	takes
	D	is			**D**	puts

2	**A**	has		7	**A**	is
	B	have			**B**	has
	C	are			**C**	are
	D	is			**D**	have

3	**A**	are not		8	**A**	make
	B	is not			**B**	has
	C	was			**C**	have
	D	has			**D**	makes

4	**A**	are		9	**A**	spread
	B	go			**B**	rolls
	C	were			**C**	roll
	D	goes			**D**	spreads

5	**A**	has		10	**A**	is
	B	simmers			**B**	have
	C	makes			**C**	are
	D	cook			**D**	were

Gerhard Marcks. *Cats* (from *Erste Mappe: Meister der Staatlichen Bauhauses*), 1921.
Woodcut, 9½ by 15¼ inches. Philadelphia Museum of Art: Print Club Permanent Collection.
Photograph by Laura Voight, 1996.

Describe How would you describe the subject and the style of this print to someone else?

Analyze How are the shapes of the cats distorted? Why do you think Gerhard Marcks chose to distort their shapes?

Interpret Does this print give you a sense of the personalities of the cats? What words do you think the artist would use to describe them? Why?

Judge If you were to make a print that showed two cats, how would it be similar to or different from Marcks's print? What words would you use to describe the cats you created?

At the end of this chapter, you will use the artwork to stimulate ideas for writing.

Agreement of Subjects and Verbs

If you have ever played dominoes, you know that you must match the number of dots on one of your tiles with a tile that has the same number of dots. A six goes with a six, and a two goes with a two. Subjects and verbs must match, just like the tiles in dominoes.

Subjects and verbs match when there is **agreement** between them. One basic rule applies to all subjects and verbs.

A verb must agree with its subject in number.

 Number

All nouns, pronouns, and verbs have number. **Number** is the term that is used to indicate whether a word is singular (one) or plural (more than one). In this chapter you will learn that the number of a verb must agree with the number of its subject, which will either be a noun or a pronoun.

The Number of Nouns and Pronouns

The plural of almost all nouns is formed by adding –*s* or –*es* to the singular form. A few nouns, however, form their plurals in other ways. These irregular plurals are always listed in the dictionary.

	NOUNS		
SINGULAR	spider	mosquito	mouse
PLURAL	spider**s**	mosquito**es**	**mice**

Since pronouns take the place of nouns, pronouns also have number. The pronoun *you* can be either singular or plural.

SUBJECT PRONOUNS	
SINGULAR	I, he, she, it
PLURAL	we, they

You can learn more about spelling plural nouns on pages L554–L561.

PRACTICE YOUR SKILLS

● Check Your Understanding
Determining the Number of Nouns and Pronouns

Label each word *singular* or *plural*.

1. candles
2. we
3. Maine
4. plate
5. tables
6. he
7. feet
8. flies
9. apple
10. they
11. women
12. cities
13. daisy
14. it
15. bricks
16. skateboard
17. Lee
18. desks
19. teeth
20. she

The Number of Verbs

In the present tense, most verbs add *–s* or *–es* to form the singular. Plural forms in the present tense drop the *–s* or *–es*.

	SINGULAR		PLURAL
The actor	sings. speaks. watches.	The actors	sing. speak. watch.

The verbs *be, have,* and *do* have special singular and plural forms in the present tense. *Be* also has special forms in the past tense.

FORMS OF *BE, HAVE,* AND *DO*		
	Singular	**Plural**
be	is (present)	are (present)
	was (past)	were (past)
have	has	have
do	does	do

In the examples throughout this chapter, each subject is underlined once, and each verb is underlined twice.

SINGULAR   He is the star of the school play.
Katie has a copy of the script.

PLURAL   They were at the auditorium.
The girls have their costumes.

PRACTICE YOUR SKILLS

● Check Your Understanding
Determining the Number of Verbs

Label each verb *singular* or *plural*.

1. Jason rehearses
2. she was
3. classes have
4. we were
5. theater opens
6. actors are
7. artist paints
8. it is
9. they do
10. Hollywood has

Singular and Plural Subjects

The number of a verb must agree with the number of its subject, whether the subject is a noun or a pronoun.

A singular subject takes a singular verb.

A plural subject takes a plural verb.

To make sure a verb agrees with its subject, ask yourself two questions: (1) *What is the subject?* and (2) *Is the subject singular or plural?* Then choose the correct verb form.

SINGULAR	Jan sings in the chorus.
PLURAL	They sing in the chorus.
SINGULAR	Tyler paints the scenery.
PLURAL	His brothers paint the scenery.

CONNECT TO SPEAKING AND WRITING

It is sometimes easier to *hear* errors in subject and verb agreement than it is to *see* them. When you are choosing which form of the verb to use with a certain subject, say aloud each form of the verb with the subject. Usually your ear will tell you which is correct.

PRACTICE YOUR SKILLS

● Check Your Understanding
Making Subjects and Verbs Agree

Oral Practice **Say the subject aloud followed by each of the verbs in parentheses. Then choose the correct verb and repeat the phrase.**

1. animals (roams, roam)

2. the coyote (howls, howl)

3. a rabbit (nibbles, nibble)

4. porcupines (sticks, stick)

5. frogs (leaps, leap)

● Check Your Understanding
Making Subjects and Verbs Agree

If the item is singular, write it in the plural form. If the item is plural, write it in the singular form.

6. day dawns

7. birds eat

8. they growl

9. he sniffs

10. stars flicker

11. trees grow

12. storm rages

13. she hunts

14. leaves hang

15. dog barks

● Check Your Understanding
Making Subjects and Verbs Agree

Science Topic **Write each subject and label it *singular* or *plural*. Then write the form of the verb in parentheses that agrees with the subject.**

16. A small lizard (darts, dart) through the woods.

17. It (looks, look) for insects for its dinner.

18. Suddenly two birds (attacks, attack) the lizard.

19. One bird (grabs, grab) the lizard by the tail.

20. Instantly the tail (falls, fall) off.

21. Then the tailless lizard (runs, run) to safety.

22. Within eight to twelve weeks, it (has, have) a new tail.

23. Some worms (grow, grows) new sections.

24. Some snails even (gets, get) new eyes.

25. The name of this process (is, are) *regeneration*.

Correcting Errors in Subject and Verb Agreement

Rewrite the verb in each sentence to correct errors in subject and verb agreement. If the sentence is correct, write C.

26. A salamander are an amphibian.

27. In Austin, Texas, a special kind of salamander live in the cold-water springs of Zilker Park.

28. They is the Barton Springs salamanders.

29. The Barton Springs salamanders are totally aquatic.

30. Unlike other salamanders, they has gills throughout their entire life span.

Communicate Your Ideas

APPLY TO WRITING

The Writer's Craft: *Analyzing Subject and Verb Agreement*

Writers always check the subjects and verbs in their writing to make sure they agree. Read this passage from *After the Rain*. Then follow the directions.

> The nurses give him pills for pain, take his temperature and his blood pressure, check the IV, talk to him coaxingly or sweetly or heartily. "How are you today, lovey? Come on now, aren't you going to say hello to me? And I thought you liked me.... Well, this isn't like you, Mr. S., I'm disappointed!"
>
> He answers nothing, remains mute, stubborn, enclosed in himself and his anger.
>
> —*Norma Fox Mazer,* After the Rain

- Look at the first sentence of the passage. What is the subject?

- The verb in this sentence is compound. There are four verbs. Write them. Do all the verbs agree with the subject? How do you know?

- The last sentence has two verbs. What are they? What subject do they agree with?

- Does Mazer use any conjunctions to join the verbs in either the first or last sentence? How does this affect the sentences?

- Why do you think Mazer chose to write these sentences in this way?

QuickCheck — Mixed Practice

Geography Topic — **Write each subject and label it *S* for singular or *P* for plural. Then write the form of the verb in parentheses that agrees with the subject.**

1. Many places (has, have) a structure as their symbol.

2. The Eiffel Tower (is, are) the symbol of Paris, France.

3. China's symbol (is, are) the Great Wall.

4. Rome's special structure (is, are) the Colosseum.

5. Big Ben (chimes, chime) over the city of London.

6. Moscow (remains, remain) home to Red Square.

7. America's presidents (lives, live) in the beautiful White House in Washington, D.C.

8. Egypt's national symbol (are, is) the Sphinx.

Common Agreement Problems

The agreement between subjects and verbs in some situations needs a little extra attention. Here are some of those situations.

▶ Verb Phrases

A **verb phrase** is a main verb plus one or more helping verbs. If a sentence includes a verb phrase, the subject must agree in number with the first helping verb.

In the following examples, the subjects are underlined once and the verbs are underlined twice. The first helping verb in each verb phrase is in bold type.

SINGULAR	George Washington **has** been known as "the father of our country" for centuries. (*George Washington* and the helping verb *has* agree because they are both singular.)
PLURAL	Our Presidents **are** elected by the American people. (*Presidents* and the helping verb *are* agree because they are both plural.)

The first helping verb in a verb phrase must agree in number with the subject.

The following box shows the singular and plural forms of common helping verbs.

COMMON HELPING VERBS	
SINGULAR	am, is, was, has, does
PLURAL	are, were, have, do

SINGULAR	Jim **is** writing a book about presidents.
PLURAL	My parents **are** reading about Grover Cleveland.
SINGULAR	No woman **has** been president of the United States.
PLURAL	Many men **have** served as president.
SINGULAR	John F. Kennedy **was** elected in 1960.
PLURAL	Americans **were** shocked by his assassination in 1963.

PRACTICE YOUR SKILLS

● Check Your Understanding
Making Subjects and Verbs Agree

General Interest **Write each subject. Then write the form of the helping verb in parentheses that agrees with the subject.**

1. Only two U.S. presidents (has, have) ever been impeached.

2. George Washington (was, were) not elected president by popular vote.

3. Abraham Lincoln (was, were) born in 1809.

4. He (is, are) remembered as "Honest Abe."

5. In 1865, the American people (was, were) devastated by his assassination.

6. Four U.S. presidents (has, have) been Whigs.

7. Today, the two major political parties (is, are) called the Democrats and the Republicans.

8. Americans (does, do) hold high standards for their national leaders.

9. Our political system (relies, rely) on the voters.

10. However, many people (does, do) not vote in elections.

● Connect to the Writing Process: Drafting
Writing Sentences with Verb Phrases

Write a sentence for each of the verb phrases below. Underline the subject once. Write an *S* above the subject if it is singular. Write a *P* above it if it is plural.

11. is speaking

12. have prepared

13. do make

14. has been thinking

15. are going

● Connect to the Writing Process: Editing
Correcting Errors in Subject and Verb Agreement

Rewrite the verb phrase to correct any errors in subject and verb agreement. If the sentence is correct, write C.

16. Right now, many telephones are ringing across this expansive country.

17. The telephone were invented by Alexander Graham Bell over a century ago.

18. It have changed greatly through the years.

19. Early telephones is displayed in museums.

20. The first telephone was not equipped with a dial or buttons.

21. Telephone operators was needed for all connections between callers.

22. Great changes in communication have evolved because of technological advances.

23. People today do communicate in many ways besides the telephone.

24. Computers have provided us with another tool for communication.

25. However, some people does not own a computer or a telephone.

● *Doesn't* or *Don't*

You already know that *does* is singular and *do* is plural. Sometimes, however, these words are used in contractions: *doesn't* (does not) and *don't* (do not). When a contraction is used, agreement with a subject can be confusing. There is an easy way to solve this problem. Always read a sentence aloud, saying the individual words of a contraction when you are checking for agreement.

The verb part of a contraction must agree in number with the subject.

INCORRECT	That singer **do**n't **know** the song.
CORRECT	That singer **does** not **know** the song.
CORRECT	That singer **does**n't **know** the song.
INCORRECT	The microphones **does**n't **have** enough volume.
CORRECT	The microphones **do** not **have** enough volume.
CORRECT	The microphones **don't** **have** enough volume.

Because the preceding rule applies to all contractions, you should remember which contractions are singular and which are plural.

CONTRACTIONS	
SINGULAR	isn't, wasn't, hasn't, doesn't
PLURAL	aren't, weren't, haven't, don't

PRACTICE YOUR SKILLS

● Check Your Understanding
Making Subject and Verbs Agree

Contemporary Life **Write each subject. Then write the contraction in parentheses that agrees with the subject.**

1. That guitar (doesn't, don't) work anymore.

2. It (isn't, aren't) mine.

3. My brother (hasn't, haven't) bought a new guitar.

4. That (wasn't, weren't) my favorite song.

5. These songs (isn't, aren't) popular anymore.

6. Those guitars (hasn't, haven't) ever sounded better.

7. Those musicians (isn't, aren't) playing very loudly.

8. They (wasn't, weren't) expecting a large audience.

● Connect to the Writing Process: Drafting
Writing Sentences with Contractions

Choose the correct verb form in each parentheses. Then write a complete sentence.

9. The music (doesn't, don't)

10. Those drums (isn't, aren't)

11. The saxophone (doesn't, don't)

12. The band director (doesn't, don't)

13. (Aren't, Isn't) the players

Correcting Errors in Subject and Verb Agreement

Rewrite the contractions as necessary to correct any errors in subject and verb agreement. If the sentence is correct, write C.

14. Those students doesn't ever practice their pieces.

15. The musicians weren't prepared for the concert.

16. The music teacher haven't told them the date of the next show.

17. He hasn't decided when to schedule it.

18. That student don't want it to be next Friday.

19. He aren't excited about an evening performance.

20. The girl aren't worried about her solo.

21. She doesn't mind playing alone.

22. The band members isn't sure about their roles in the show.

23. The band haven't played for large audiences yet.

Prepositional Phrases after Subjects

Often one or more prepositional phrases may come between a subject and a verb. These phrases can create an agreement problem. It is a common mistake to make the verb agree with the object of the preposition instead of the subject because the object of the preposition is closer to the verb.

The agreement of a verb with its subject is not changed by any interrupting words.

In the following examples, the subject and the verb in each sentence agree in number even though other words come between them. The best way to be sure subjects and verbs agree in these sentences is to take out any prepositional phrases. Once you have done this, it is easier to make sure the subject and verb agree.

SINGULAR   That girl on the parallel bars is my sister.
(*Is* agrees with the subject *girl,* not with the object of the preposition *bars*—even though *bars* is closer to the verb.)

PLURAL   Those boys in the competition are in my class.
(*Are* agrees with the subject *boys,* not with the object of the preposition *competition*—even though *competition* is closer to the verb.)

You can learn more about prepositional phrases on pages L177–L185.

PRACTICE YOUR SKILLS

● Check Your Understanding
Making Subjects and Verbs Agree

Sports Topic   **Write the subject of each sentence. Then choose the correct verb in parentheses.**

1. Olympic gymnasts from around the world (competes, compete) in the summer games.

2. The young women on the U.S. gymnastics team (devotes, devote) their lives to the sport.

3. Other events in the summer competition (includes, include) boxing, soccer, and track and field.

4. Long-distance runners on the track (keeps, keep) a steady pace at the start of the race.

5. Athletes in the race (uses, use) all their energy.

6. A boxer on the Olympic team (has, have) worked very hard.

7. All movements in boxing (requires, require) concentration.

8. The medal ceremony at the end of each event (brings, bring) tears to many eyes.

9. The national anthem of the gold medal winners (stirs, stir) their emotions.

10. The athletes in the Olympics (is, are) proud.

● Connect to the Writing Process: Editing
Correcting Subject and Verb Agreement

Rewrite the verbs in the following sentences to make them agree with their subjects. If the sentence is correct, write C.

11. Most athletes in a world competition have played their sport for a long time.

12. Many female skaters does begin their careers on the ice by age five.

13. The girls at that young age skates every day.

14. Sometimes the parents of these girls hire a private coach.

15. The coaches of gifted athletes do challenge them.

16. The leader of the rink teaches many skills.

17. The fans of young athletes provides them with much moral support.

18. Most athletes are very nervous before their first competition.

19. The support of their families are very important.

20. Only the best athletes in the world become Olympians.

Communicate Your Ideas

APPLY TO WRITING
Friendly Letter: *Subject and Verb Agreement*

Write a fan letter to your favorite athlete. Let the athlete know how long you have been watching his or her career and how he or she has inspired you. Write one sentence in which you use the contraction *doesn't* and another with *don't*. After you write your letter, check it for any errors in subject and verb agreement.

QuickCheck   Mixed Practice

General Interest   **Write the subject of each sentence. Then write the form of the verb in parentheses that agrees with the subject.**

1. The Ferris wheel (was, were) introduced at the 1893 World's Colombian Exposition in Chicago.

2. The builder of this new amusement ride (was, were) George W. Ferris.

3. The cars of a Ferris wheel usually (holds, hold) two or three people.

4. The original Ferris wheel (was, were) equipped with thirty-six wooden cars that held sixty people total!

5. Another popular ride at modern amusement parks (is, are) the roller coaster.

6. This ride (was, were) developed in Russia.

7. Early roller coasters (wasn't, weren't) much like the ones today.

8. Most carnivals (doesn't, don't) have one permanent home.

9. These popular attractions (moves, move) from town to town.

10. The circus, with its performers and animals, also (travel, travels) from place to place.

11. People in a small town or a large city (is, are) still excited by the arrival of the circus.

12. Most amusement parks in this country (has, have) permanent locations.

13. A family with children often (plans, plan) its entire vacation at an amusement park.

14. The children (isn't, aren't) often bored at these vacation spots.

15. A fun place for the children (isn't, aren't) too hard to find.

Other Agreement Problems

When you edit your writing, pay special attention to the following agreement problems as well.

▶ Subjects After Verbs

A sentence in **natural order** has the subject before the verb. Some sentences, however, have a verb or part of a verb phrase before the subject. Such a sentence has **inverted order.** A verb always agrees with its subject, whether the sentence is in natural or inverted order.

> The subject and the verb of a sentence in inverted order must agree in number.

NATURAL ORDER — My favorite books are on that shelf.

INVERTED ORDER — On that shelf are my favorite books.

When you are looking for the subject in a question, turn the question into a statement.

QUESTION — Have your friends read this book?

STATEMENT — Your friends have read this book.

CONNECT TO WRITER'S CRAFT

Sentences in inverted order have a rhythm that works well with poetry. The subjects in each line of this excerpt are underlined once and the verbs twice.

> Slung on his shoulder is a handle halfway across,
> Tied in a big knot on the scoop of cast iron
> Are the overalls faded from sun and rain . . . .
>
> —*Carl Sandburg,* "The Shovel Man"

PRACTICE YOUR SKILLS

● Check Your Understanding
Making Subjects and Verbs Agree

Contemporary Life **Write each subject. Then write the verb in parentheses that agrees with the subject.**

1. On that table (lies, lie) my favorite book.

2. (Has, Have) she read it?

3. On that author's every word (hangs, hang) my imagination.

4. In this book (is, are) many interesting plot twists.

5. For instance, at the bottom of an old trunk (lies, lie) a mask.

6. Whose mask (is, are) it?

7. The mask (gives, give) a clue to the unsolved mystery.

8. At the center of the novel (is, are) a brave girl.

9. Throughout the book (was, were) one unanswered question.

10. (Does, Do) this book sound interesting to you?

● Connect to the Writing Process: Drafting
Writing Sentences in Inverted Order

Add words to complete each sentence starter. Write the complete sentence. Underline the subject once and the verb twice.

11. On the beach was

12. In the sand were

13. Across the waves dove

14. Through the blue sky soars

15. Where was

Rewrite the following sentences, correcting any errors in subject and verb agreement. If the sentence is correct, write C.

16. In the newspaper were a report about an approaching hurricane.

17. Before a big storm comes high waves on the beach.

18. Against high winds struggles birds.

19. Across the windows of one house were protective wooden shutters.

20. In the stores was desperate people.

21. Was they buying enough supplies?

22. On the radio was warnings about the storm.

23. Across the sky gathers dark clouds.

24. In their houses sits nervous residents of the city.

25. Do a great clean-up effort occur after the storm?

● Compound Subjects

Some sentences have two subjects that share the same verb. You may recall that such a subject is called a **compound subject.** Usually the parts of a compound subject are joined by a single conjunction such as *and* or *or,* or by a pair of conjunctions such as *either/or* or *neither/nor.*

When the parts of a compound subject are joined by *and,* the verb is usually plural.

When a subject is more than one, it is plural. The verb, therefore, must also be plural to agree with the subject.

PLURAL VERBS	Katya **and** Tamara help the art teacher each day after school.
	This book **and** these magazines focus on the works of Pablo Picasso.

When the parts of a compound subject are joined by *or, either/or,* or *neither/nor,* agreement between the subject and the verb follows a different rule.

When the parts of a compound subject are joined by *or, either/or,* or *neither/nor,* the verb agrees with the subject closer to it.

SINGULAR VERB	Monday **or** Tuesday is the day of the art show.
	(The verb *is* is singular because *Tuesday,* the subject closer to it, is singular.)
PLURAL VERB	**Either** the encyclopedias **or** the other reference books are on the shelf.

This rule applies even when one subject is singular and the other subject is plural.

SINGULAR VERB	**Neither** the paintings **nor** the sketch was a popular attraction.
	(The verb is singular because *sketch,* the subject closer to it, is singular.)
PLURAL VERB	**Neither** the sketch **nor** the paintings were a popular attraction.
	(The verb is plural because *paintings,* the subject closer to it, is plural.)

● Check Your Understanding

Making Subjects and Verbs Agree

Art Topic **Write each compound subject. Then write the correct form of the verb in parentheses.**

1. Paintings and sculptures (is, are) found in museums around the world.

2. Murals or art (is, are) seen on the sides of buildings in many cities.

3. Sometimes neither the artist's name nor address (is, are) known.

4. Wood or other materials (is, are) used for sculpture.

5. Neither pastels nor charcoal (is, are) difficult to draw with.

6. Charcoal and pastels (is, are) messy.

7. A few lessons and a little practice (improves, improve) even the youngest artist.

8. Neither good paint nor any other art supplies (is, are) inexpensive.

9. Oil paints and brushes (costs, cost) a lot of money.

10. Watercolors or tempera paint (is, are) usually less expensive.

11. Neither oil paints nor colored ink (is, are) easy for beginners to use.

12. Black ink or charcoal (is, are) a better choice.

13. Some artists and printers (makes, make) etchings on a metal plate.

14. A needle (is, are) used on the plate.

15. Different papers (affects, affect) a piece of art.

Writing Sentences with Compound Subjects

Add words to complete each sentence starter. Write the complete sentence. Underline the compound subject once and the verb twice.

16. Either Paul or Sarah

17. The gallery and the museum

18. Watercolors and oil paints

19. The sketch pads or the paper

20. Neither the teacher nor the students

Connect to the Writing Process: Editing
Editing for Errors in Agreement

Rewrite the following sentences correcting any errors in subject and verb agreement. If the sentence is correct, write *C*.

21. Paige and Chris take art lessons.

22. Either she or he win the school's art contest.

23. Oil painting or watercolors is Paige's favorite tools.

24. Neither Chris's teacher nor his parents watches him at work on his art.

25. A quiet room or an outdoor setting inspires Chris.

26. Neither his sculpture nor his paintings has ever won first place.

27. His drawings and his pots has won grand prizes.

28. Either Paige's ceramics or her needlework catch people's attention.

29. Neither our principal nor the art teachers has volunteered to judge this year.

30. Either a savings bond or cash are usually the prize for first place.

APPLY TO WRITING

Poem: *Subject and Verb Agreement*

Mary Cassatt. *Little Girl in a Blue Armchair,* 1878.
Oil on canvas, 35¼ by 51⅛ inches. © 1996 Board of Trustees, National Gallery of Art, Washington, D.C. Collection of Mr. and Mrs. Paul Mellon.

Look carefully at this piece of art by Mary Cassatt. Notice the figures in the picture and the colors. Write a poem for your teacher about this work of art. Remember that not all poems have to rhyme. You, as the poet, can decide whether to use rhyme. Before you start writing, brainstorm some ideas using the following questions.

- What is the little girl thinking? How does she feel?

- What time of day is it?

- What might the girl have been doing during the day?

In at least two lines of your poem, use inverted sentence structure. In another line, use a compound subject. Be sure that your subjects and verbs agree.

Science Topic **Write each subject. Then write the form of the verb in parentheses that agrees with the subject.**

1. Neither the moon nor the stars (is, are) visible on cloudy nights.

2. In the clear sky at night (appears, appear) millions of points of light.

3. The points of light (is, are) stars or planets.

4. Across the sky (stretches, stretch) the vast Milky Way Galaxy.

5. In our solar system (is, are) nine planets.

6. Venus and Mars (is, are) Earth's neighbors.

7. Neither the surface temperature nor the atmosphere on Saturn (supports, support) human life.

8. The surfaces of some planets (is, are) not solid.

9. Jupiter and Saturn (is, are) gas planets.

10. Neither Mercury nor Venus (has, have) a moon.

11. Either a telescope or binoculars (helps, help) stargazers.

12. Neither quasars nor black holes (is, are) easy to understand.

13. Black holes in space (is, are) dense areas with a gravitational pull.

14. Either astronomy or other sciences (is, are) interesting to study.

15. Neither scientists nor other people (knows, know) everything about space.

Agreement Problems with Pronouns

When certain pronouns are used as subjects, they can present subject-verb agreement problems.

You and *I* as Subjects

The pronouns *you* and *I* are exceptions to the two rules for agreement between subject and verbs. *You* is always used with a plural verb.

PLURAL VERBS	Jamie, <u>you</u> <u>have</u> a great voice for stage musicals.
	Girls, <u>you</u> <u>sing</u> well enough together to form a group.
	Do <u>you</u> <u>like</u> the way they sing?

I usually takes a plural verb.

PLURAL VERBS	<u>I</u> <u>make</u> good grades in choir because <u>I</u> <u>enjoy</u> it so much.
	<u>I</u> <u>have</u> a concert tomorrow in the large auditorium.
	<u>I</u> <u>like</u> having an audience.

The singular verbs *am* and *was* are also used with *I*.

SINGULAR VERBS	<u>I</u> <u>am</u> in the school choir.
	<u>I</u> <u>was</u> at choir practice this afternoon until four o'clock.

PRACTICE YOUR SKILLS

● Check Your Understanding
Making Verbs Agree with **You** *and* **I**

Contemporary Life **Write the form of the verb in parentheses that agrees with the subject.**

1. I (has, have) two brothers in the high school choir.

2. You (is, are) a great singer.

3. Today you (sounds, sound) very tired.

4. I (has, have) some new sheet music.

5. You (needs, need) more help with that song.

6. I (am, are) taking voice lessons.

7. You (has, have) a lovely voice.

8. I (was, were) singing that song yesterday.

9. You (was, were) working on it too.

10. I (wants, want) a microphone for my birthday.

● Connect to the Writing Process: Editing
Correcting Errors in Subject-Verb Agreement

Rewrite the following sentences, correcting any errors in subject-verb agreement. If the sentence is correct, write C.

11. I is taking piano lessons.

12. You has some natural talent.

13. You are a good pianist.

14. I has a great music teacher.

15. Today you seems happy with your performance.

16. I has been practicing.

17. You has a beautiful piano.

18. You needs a good piano bench.

Agreement Problems with Pronouns **L343**

19. I like that brown bench.

20. I am storing my sheet music in it.

21. I wants a career in music.

22. You is talented enough to make it.

⏵ Indefinite Pronouns

Sometimes an indefinite pronoun is the subject of a sentence. To make a verb agree with a subject that is an indefinite pronoun, you need to know which indefinite pronouns are singular and which are plural.

A verb must agree in number with an indefinite pronoun used as a subject.

The following is a list of common singular and plural indefinite pronouns.

COMMON INDEFINITE PRONOUNS	
SINGULAR	anybody, anyone, each, either, everybody, everyone, neither, nobody, no one, one, somebody, someone
PLURAL	both, few, many, several

Singular indefinite pronouns used as subjects always take a singular verb. Plural indefinite pronouns used as subjects always take a plural verb. Any prepositional phrases that come between an indefinite pronoun subject and the verb do not change this agreement.

SINGULAR   No one <u>is</u> home.

(*Is* agrees with the singular indefinite pronoun *no one.*)

One of the boys <u>was</u> there.

(*Was* agrees with the singular indefinite pronoun *one*, not with the object of the preposition *boys*.)

PLURAL   <u>Both</u> <u>leave</u> the house at eight o'clock.

(*Leave* agrees with the plural indefinite pronoun *both*.)

<u>Many</u> in that house <u>keep</u> regular schedules.

(*Keep* agrees with the plural indefinite pronoun *many*, not the object of the preposition *house*.)

You can learn more about indefinite pronouns on page L64.

PRACTICE YOUR SKILLS

● Check Your Understanding
Making Verbs Agree with Indefinite Pronouns

Contemporary Life   **Write the form of the verb in parentheses that agrees with the subject.**

1. Both of those girls (is, are) always on time for school.

2. Neither (has, have) ever missed the bus.

3. One of their brothers (is, are) always late.

4. Each of the children in that family (is, are) expected to cook breakfast.

5. Few (goes, go) without their first meal of the day.

6. Everyone in the family (cooks, cook) well.

7. Many of their friends from school (comes, come) to their house before class.

8. No one ever (goes, go) away hungry.

9. Everybody in the neighborhood (likes, like) that family.

10. Several of the children (bakes, bake) cookies for their neighbors.

● Check Your Understanding
Making Verbs Agree with Indefinite Pronouns

Contemporary Life **Write the form of the verb in parentheses that agrees with the subject.**

11. Several of those stores (sell, sells) CDs.

12. Each of you (needs, need) a good CD player for your CDs.

13. Few of the stores (has, have) those products.

14. Anyone in the music store (knows, know) about those titles.

15. Somebody in the store (is, are) buying other music products.

16. Both of the CDs by that artist (is, are) sold out.

17. Either of those CDs (makes, make) a good present.

18. Nobody (wants, want) that group's old CD.

19. Somebody in the neighborhood (plays, play) that song too often.

20. Everyone (appreciates, appreciate) a great song.

● Connect to the Writing Process: Drafting
Writing Sentences with Indefinite Pronoun Subjects

Add words to complete each sentence starter. Write the complete sentence. Be sure that each verb agrees with its subject.

21. Each of the stores

22. Several of the customers

23. Everyone

24. Few of his friends at school

25. Someone in the back row

● Connect to the Writing Process: Editing
Correcting Errors in Subject-Verb Agreement

Rewrite the following sentences, correcting any errors in subject-verb agreement. If the sentence is correct, write C.

26. Everyone in my family recycle glass bottles and aluminum cans.

27. Both of these kinds of containers are very common.

28. Few finds recycling difficult at this point in time.

29. Many of the cities in America has a recycling facility or center.

30. Each of your recycled household items helps planet Earth.

31. Do anybody in your school recycle paper for extra money?

32. Everybody is responsible for the health and cleanliness of the planet.

33. Somebody do not know about the importance of recycling.

34. Several of us speaks about recycling to our local elementary school.

35. Neither of the students throws his or her aluminum cans in the garbage.

APPLY TO WRITING

A Story: *Subject-Verb Agreement*

Frontispiece for *The Baby's Own Aesop* by Walter Crane.
Frederick Warne and Co., Ltd.

Look carefully at this picture. Imagine what story this child could be reading to the animals. Using this idea, write a story for a first-grade class at the local elementary school. Use interesting characters and vivid description in your writing.

Write one sentence with *you* as the subject and one sentence with *I* as the subject. Use at least two indefinite pronouns as subjects. After you finish writing, edit your story for any errors in subject and verb agreement.

Literature Topic **Write each subject. Then write the form of the verb in parentheses that agrees with the subject.**

1. Everyone (has, have) heard of Frankenstein.

2. Many of us (hasn't, haven't) heard of Mary Shelley.

3. This author of the novel *Frankenstein* (was, were) born in 1797.

4. In the book (is, are) a monstrous creature.

5. However, Frankenstein in Shelley's novel (is, are) not the monster.

6. You (finds, find) that Victor Frankenstein is a doctor.

7. The book and the movies about Frankenstein (has, have) been very popular.

8. Most of the movies (doesn't, don't) really follow the book closely.

9. Now you (knows, know) some things about the unusual story.

10. The author of this book (was, were) married to the poet Percy Bysshe Shelley.

11. Both of her parents (was, were) famous.

12. About this novel (writes, write) many authors.

13. You (has, have) many ways to find out more about Mary Shelley.

14. Either an encyclopedia or books (has, have) information about Mary Shelley and *Frankenstein*.

15. Almost everyone (is, are) interested in this novel.

Making Subjects and Verbs Agree

Write the form of the verb in parentheses that agrees with each subject.

1. The boat's sails (was, were) billowing in the wind.
2. I (am, are) watching the boats come in.
3. You (has, have) to join us on the balcony.
4. (Does, Do) the boats stay out at sea in weather like this?
5. The winds from the northeast (has, have) been strong.
6. The blue and green boats (is, are) heading this way.
7. Only a few (is, are) still out to sea.
8. (Wasn't, Weren't) those waves high?
9. The foam on the waves (looks, look) like soap bubbles.
10. (Is, Are) that an otter family or just floating logs?

Finding Errors in Subject and Verb Agreement

Find and write each verb that does not agree with its subject. Then write each sentence correctly. If a sentence is correct, write C.

1. Was you asking about animal survival in the winter?
2. Hibernation or winter-sleep are the solution for some mammals.
3. Woodchucks and ground squirrels goes into hibernation.
4. Both becomes very cool and still.
5. The breathing rate of hibernating woodchucks are one breath every six minutes.
6. Does black bears hibernate like woodchucks?
7. This big mammal dozes during the cold months.

8. One of the bear's winter habits are waking and wandering for a while.

9. I was reading about animals in underground tunnels.

10. Deep drifts of snow acts like insulating blankets.

Editing for Subject and Verb Agreement

Read the following paragraph and find the five verbs that do not agree with their subjects. Decide what verbs are needed to make the sentences correct. Then write the paragraph using the correct verbs.

Has you ever seen a millipede? *Millipede* means "thousand-legged." This unusual insect, however, don't live up to its name. Though a few millipedes has two hundred legs, this number of legs make these millipedes record-breaking insects. Still, the average millipede's legs usually outnumber those of its closest rival. The centipede's legs, at most, adds up to no more than thirty.

Using Subject and Verb Agreement

Write five sentences that follow the directions below.

Write a sentence that...
1. includes the verb phrase *is sitting*.
2. includes the verb phrase *have listened*.
3. includes *doesn't* at the beginning.
4. includes *don't* at the beginning.
5. includes *my brother and sister* as the subjects.

Language and *Self-Expression*

Gerhard Marcks's print gives you a sense of what these highly independent cats are like. They certainly are not about to curl up in anyone's lap. What do you think these cats would say if they could think like humans?

Choose two cats like these or two other animals and imagine what they are talking about and how they spend their days. What do they do? Whom do they do it with? Write their conversation as dialogue for a play. Vary the verb tenses you use.

Prewriting Make a two-column chart with one column for each animal. Jot down your ideas about what each animal does. Number the activities to show the order in which they will be described. If necessary, look at a play to find out what format to use.

Drafting Write your dialogue. Remember that in conversation, one thought leads to another. Make sure that topics are introduced in a natural order and make sense. Your play should begin with greetings between the animals.

Revising Have one classmate listen while you and a partner read the dialogue aloud. Ask whether the listener can suggest any improvements that would make the dialogue seem more natural. Make sure that you have used the appropriate verb tenses.

Editing Check your dialogue for errors in punctuation and spelling. Check the endings on your verbs to make sure they agree with your subjects.

Publishing Record the dialogue from your final copy on an audiocassette. Have one classmate read the dialogue for one character while you read the dialogue for the other. Play the tape at home.

Another Look

Agreement of Subjects and Verbs

A verb must agree with its subject in number. *(pages L317–L319)*

> **A singular subject takes a singular verb.**

> **A plural subject takes a plural verb.**

A **verb phrase** is a main verb plus one or more helping verbs. *(page L320)*

The first helping verb in a verb phrase must agree in number with the subject. *(pages L324–L325)*

The agreement of a verb with its subject is not changed by any interrupting words. *(pages L329–L330)*

A sentence is in **natural order** when the subject comes before the verb. *(page L334)*

A sentence is in **inverted order** when the verb or part of a verb phrase comes before the subject. *(page L334)*

The subject and verb of a sentence in inverted order must agree in number. *(page L334)*

When the parts of a compound subject are joined by *and*, the verb is usually plural. *(pages L336–L337)*

When the parts of a compound subject are joined by *or, either/or,* or *neither/nor,* the verb agrees with the subject closer to it. *(page L337)*

A verb must agree in number with an indefinite pronoun used as a subject. *(pages L344–L345)*

Other Information About Subject and Verb Agreement

Recognizing the number of nouns and pronouns *(pages L317–L318)*

Using *doesn't* and *don't* *(pages L327–L328)*

Using prepositional phrases after subjects *(pages L329–L330)*

Recognizing agreement problems with the pronouns *you* and *I* as subjects *(page L342)*

Posttest

Directions

Read the passage and choose the word that belongs in each underlined space. Write the letter of the correct answer.

EXAMPLE   Scientists __(1)__ been exploring the sea floor.

        1 A has
           B have
           C is
           D are

ANSWER   **1 B**

    Hydrothermal vents __(1)__ through the sea floor. These __(2)__ like undersea volcanoes. Toxic metals and gases __(3)__ from the vents. The temperature near vents __(4)__ dramatically. The fluids from the vents often __(5)__ temperatures of 750°F. Yet the icy waters at this great depth __(6)__ likely to be 35°F. __(7)__ I mentioned that it is also pitch black there? Neither land plants nor sea plants __(8)__ without sunlight. To make things worse, thousands of feet of water __(9)__ tremendous pressure. __(10)__ you surprised to hear that animals live near the vents?

1	**A**	opens	6	**A**	was
	B	break		**B**	is
	C	lies		**C**	are
	D	is		**D**	drops
2	**A**	is	7	**A**	Has
	B	acts		**B**	Did
	C	behave		**C**	Have
	D	has		**D**	Aren't
3	**A**	erupt	8	**A**	survives
	B	pours		**B**	lives
	C	do		**C**	have
	D	does		**D**	grow
4	**A**	was	9	**A**	gives
	B	varies		**B**	create
	C	change		**C**	makes
	D	rise		**D**	does
5	**A**	go	10	**A**	Aren't
	B	rises		**B**	Isn't
	C	has		**C**	Wasn't
	D	reach		**D**	Doesn't

CHAPTER 11

Using Adjectives and Adverbs

 **Pretest**

Directions
Read the passage and choose the word or group of words that belongs in each underlined space. Write the letter of the correct answer.

EXAMPLE   The old house has been empty for __(1)__ than anyone can remember.

  1 A more long
     B more longer
     C longest
     D longer

ANSWER   **1 D**

There are few sights __(1)__ than an abandoned house. The house on the hill is the __(2)__ house in our neighborhood. It is also __(3)__ than its neighbors. The house has not been kept up __(4)__ for a long time. Its yard is the __(5)__ inviting yard that I have ever seen. Certainly the yard is __(6)__ than any other yard. The __(7)__ problem is the overgrown bramble bushes. It would be __(8)__ if someone bought the house and fixed it up. The house would be a __(9)__ sight than it is now. I walk past the house __(10)__ at night than in the daylight.

1	**A**	most sadder		**6**	**A**	weedy
	B	more sadder			**B**	weediest
	C	saddest			**C**	more weedier
	D	sadder			**D**	weedier
2	**A**	older		**7**	**A**	worst
	B	more older			**B**	worse
	C	oldest			**C**	more
	D	most oldest			**D**	most
3	**A**	more larger		**8**	**A**	well
	B	largest			**B**	more well
	C	large			**C**	good
	D	larger			**D**	more good
4	**A**	better		**9**	**A**	most cheerful
	B	well			**B**	more cheerful
	C	best			**C**	cheerfullest
	D	good			**D**	cheerfuller
5	**A**	lesser		**10**	**A**	hastily
	B	least			**B**	much hastily
	C	less			**C**	most hastily
	D	much less			**D**	more hastily

Zilker Gardens in Austin,
Texas, designed by
Isamu Taniguchi.

Describe   How would you describe this scene to help
a friend visualize it? What words and
phrases would you use?

Analyze   Think of this scene as a painting. What
elements in the landscape make it seem
gentle and serene rather than harsh or
stimulating?

Interpret   This garden did not just happen. A
landscape architect carefully designed it
to sit in the middle of a big city. What
experiences do you think Isamu Taniguchi
wanted visitors to the garden to have?

Judge   Imagine a descriptive paragraph written
about this garden. How might it be
different from what you see here? Would
you prefer one to the other? Why or why
not?

At the end of the chapter, you will use this artwork to
stimulate ideas for writing.

Comparison of Adjectives and Adverbs

When you write a description, you often use adjectives or adverbs to compare one person, place, thing, or action with another. Most adjectives and adverbs have three forms that you will need to know when you make such comparisons.

Most adjectives and adverbs have three degrees of comparison: the positive, the comparative, and the superlative.

The **positive degree** is used when a person, place, thing, or action is being described and no comparison is being made.

ADJECTIVE   The water in the neighborhood swimming pool is **cold.**

ADVERB   I swim **often.**

The **comparative degree** is used when two people, places, things, or actions are being compared.

ADJECTIVE   The water in the lake is **colder** than the pool water.

ADVERB   I swim **more often** than Leah.

The **superlative degree** is used when more than two people, places, things, or actions are being compared.

ADJECTIVE   The water in the river is the **coldest** water of all.

ADVERB   Of all my friends, I swim **most often.**

You can learn more about adjectives and adverbs in Chapter 4.

PRACTICE YOUR SKILLS

● Check Your Understanding
Determining the Degree of Comparison

Sports Topic **Label the underlined adjective or adverb *P* for positive, *C* for comparative, or *S* for superlative.**

1. Swimming is an <u>enjoyable</u> sport.

2. It is a <u>safer</u> workout than running.

3. Many people swim <u>faster</u> after only a few lessons.

4. The butterfly stroke is the <u>most difficult</u> stroke to perform correctly.

5. In the summer, swimming can be a <u>cooler</u> way to exercise than walking.

6. The crawl is an <u>easier</u> stroke to master than the backstroke.

7. That sport is <u>hard</u> work.

8. The <u>toughest</u> competitors swim for an hour each day.

9. Others swim even <u>longer</u> than that.

10. Many consider swimming the <u>greatest</u> way to exercise.

▶ Regular Comparisons

How an adjective or an adverb forms its comparative and superlative degrees usually depends on the number of syllables in the word.

Add *–er* to form the comparative degree and *–est* to form the superlative degree of one-syllable modifiers.

ONE-SYLLABLE MODIFIERS			
	POSITIVE	**COMPARATIVE**	**SUPERLATIVE**
ADJECTIVE	short	short**er**	short**est**
	big	big**ger**	big**gest**
ADVERB	soon	soon**er**	soon**est**

CONNECT TO WRITER'S CRAFT

When you are unsure of the spelling of a word form, do what professional writers do. Check a dictionary. You might find, for example, that when *–er* or *–est* is added to certain words such as *big,* a spelling change occurs.

Paul's dog is big, but Erin's dog is bi**gg**er.

Many two-syllable adjectives or adverbs are formed exactly the way one-syllable adjectives or adverbs are formed. You add *–er* or *–est* to the positive.

A two-syllable adjective such as *playful,* however, would be difficult to say with *–er* or *–est: playfuller* and *playfullest.* For such two-syllable adjectives and adverbs, you should add *more* or *most* to form the comparative and superlative forms—*more playful* and *most playful. More* and *most* should also be used with adverbs that end in *–ly.*

Use *–er* or *more* to form the comparative degree and *–est* or *most* to form the superlative degree of two-syllable modifiers.

TWO-SYLLABLE MODIFIERS			
	POSITIVE	**COMPARATIVE**	**SUPERLATIVE**
ADJECTIVE	narrow	narrow**er**	narrow**est**
	easy	easi**er**	easi**est**
	harmless	**more** harmless	**most** harmless

ADVERB	often	**more** often	**most** often
	early	earl**ier**	earl**iest**
	quickly	**more** quickly	**most** quickly
	bravely	**more** bravely	**most** bravely

Notice that a spelling change occurs in many modifiers that end in *y*, such as *easy* or *early*. The *y* changes to *i* before *–er* or *–est* is added.

The comparative and superlative degree of adjectives and adverbs with three or more syllables is formed by adding *more* and *most.*

Use *more* to form the comparative degree and *most* to form the superlative degree of modifiers with three or more syllables.

MODIFIERS WITH THREE OR MORE SYLLABLES			
	POSITIVE	COMPARATIVE	SUPERLATIVE
ADJECTIVE	serious	**more** serious	**most** serious
ADVERB	carefully	**more** carefully	**most** carefully

PRACTICE YOUR SKILLS

● Check Your Understanding
Forming the Comparison of Modifiers

Oral Practice **Say each modifier aloud, adding *–er* and *–est.* Then say the modifiers with *more* and *most.* Decide which form is correct, and then repeat your answer aloud.**

1. steep   **2.** frequently   **3.** steady

4. curious   **5.** tall

Forming the Comparison of Modifiers

Write each adjective or adverb. Then write its comparative and superlative forms.

6. slowly **11.** quick **16.** hot

7. little **12.** light **17.** near

8. happily **13.** smart **18.** rapidly

9. difficult **14.** cold **19.** neatly

10. long **15.** heavy **20.** delicious

● Check Your Understanding

Forming the Comparison of Modifiers

General Interest **Write the correct form of the adjective or adverb in parentheses.**

21. Which animal is the (fiercer, fiercest) in Africa?

22. Which moves (more quickly, most quickly), the chimpanzee or the gorilla?

23. Of all the animals in Africa, the hippopotamus looks (funnier, funniest).

24. Which is the (quicker, quickest) of your three favorite animals?

25. The cheetah is the (faster, fastest) animal on earth.

26. Which is (heavier, heaviest), the hippopotamus or the rhinoceros?

27. Which moves (more slowly, most slowly), a sloth or a tortoise?

28. Of all the animals in Africa, the giraffe is (taller, tallest).

29. Which is (friendlier, friendliest), an elephant or a lion?

30. I think Africa is the (more interesting, most interesting) continent on the earth.

⏺ Irregular Comparisons

A few adjectives and adverbs are compared in an irregular manner. The modifiers in the following list are very common. You will need to use them often.

IRREGULARLY COMPARED MODIFIERS		
POSITIVE	COMPARATIVE	SUPERLATIVE
bad	worse	worst
good *and* well	better	best
little	less	least
much *and* many	more	most

POSITIVE	I have too **much** homework for TV tonight.
COMPARATIVE	I have **more** homework than I did yesterday.
SUPERLATIVE	It is the **most** homework I've had all year.

PRACTICE YOUR SKILLS

⏺ Check Your Understanding
Supplying the Correct Form of Modifiers

Contemporary Life **Read the first sentence in each group. Then write the comparative and superlative forms of the underlined adjective or adverb.**

1. Lauren is a good actress.

She is a ▪ actress than I am.

In fact she is the ▪ actress in the sixth grade.

2. Jake watches too <u>much</u> TV to be a good actor.

Jake watches even ▨ TV than Aaron does.

He watches the ▨ TV of anyone I know.

3. I have <u>little</u> interest in acting.

I have even ▨ interest in TV.

I have the ▨ interest in movies.

4. The movie starring that popular actor is <u>bad</u>.

It is ▨ than his last movie.

In fact, it is the ▨ movie I've ever seen.

5. <u>Many</u> people have seen that movie.

▨ people saw his last movie.

▨ people saw his first movie.

● Connect to the Writing Process: Editing
Correcting Errors with Comparisons

Find and write each incorrect adjective or adverb. Then write the correct form. If the sentence is correct, write C.

6. I read the part worst today than yesterday.

7. Which do you like best, singing or dancing?

8. This is the better play I've ever seen.

9. Her acting is worst than his.

10. She has the few lines of anyone.

11. Today's practice is best than yesterday's.

12. I want to learn my lines in the least amount of time possible.

13. If I get some practice, I'll perform best tomorrow than I did today.

14. I should get more rest than usual.

15. I received most acting advice from the music teacher than from the drama teacher.

APPLY TO WRITING

Narrative: *Adjectives and Adverbs*

Write about a time when something embarrassing happened to you and tell what you learned from the experience. Use details and descriptions to allow your reader to feel your experience. Include the adjectives *worse, worst, better,* and *best* in your writing. Also underline at least two other comparative and one other superlative modifier you use in your narrative.

 **QuickCheck** Mixed Practice

Contemporary Life

If the underlined modifier is incorrect, write it correctly. If the modifier is correct, write C.

1. Which are <u>more fragrant</u>, violets, roses, or tulips?
2. Of those three flowers, I like tulips <u>better</u>.
3. Which are <u>easiest</u> to grow, pansies or daisies?
4. Which gardener works <u>hardest</u>, Blake or Rachel?
5. Which do you <u>more</u> like to grow, flowers, vegetables, or <u>fruit</u>?
6. The second watermelon on the table was <u>sweeter</u> than the first.
7. Which was <u>biggest</u>, the cantaloupe or the other melon?
8. This has been the <u>worse</u> year for pumpkins.
9. Of all vegetables, spinach is my <u>most favorite</u>.
10. When did the rain fall <u>heaviest</u> on your garden, at noon or at midnight?

The following section shows some special problems you should watch for when you are making comparisons.

● Double Comparisons

Use only one method of forming the comparative or the superlative form of an adjective or an adverb. Using both methods—for example, *-er* and *more* together—results in a **double comparison,** which is incorrect.

Do not use both *-er* and *more* to form the comparative degree, or both *-est* and *most* to form the superlative degree.

DOUBLE COMPARISON	No one played **more better** than Jackie Robinson.
CORRECT	No one played **better** than Jackie Robinson.
DOUBLE COMPARISON	He was the **most bravest** player.
CORRECT	He was the **bravest** player.
DOUBLE COMPARISON	Some people say baseball is **more easier** to play than soccer.
CORRECT	Some people say baseball is **easier** to play than soccer.
DOUBLE COMPARISON	Blake says soccer is **more interestinger** to watch than baseball.
CORRECT	Blake says soccer is **more interesting** to watch than baseball.

PRACTICE YOUR SKILLS

● Check Your Understanding
Identifying Double Comparisons

Sports Topic **Label the sentence I for incorrect if a double comparison is used. If the sentence is correct, write C.**

1. Who was the greatest player in baseball?

2. Well, Jackie Robinson is one of the most famousest baseball players ever.

3. He played more better than most other players on his team.

4. He was voted the most best new player in 1947.

5. Also in that year, he was voted the second-most popularest man in America.

6. Only the singer and movie star Bing Crosby was more popular with the American people.

7. In 1949, Jackie Robinson was the most valuablest player in baseball.

8. Jackie Robinson was one of the most courageous men of his time.

9. Above all, Jackie Robinson is most famous as the first African American in major league history.

10. In 1964, Jackie Robinson received the most highest honor of all as the first African American in the Baseball Hall of Fame.

● Connect to the Writing Process: Revising
Correcting Double Comparisons

11.–16. Rewrite the incorrect sentences from the preceding exercise, correcting the double comparisons.

Double Negatives

The following is a list of common negative words. Notice that all of these words begin with *n*.

COMMON NEGATIVES	
never	none
no	not (and its contraction, n't)
no one	nothing

Two negatives should not be used together to express the same idea. When they are, the result is a **double negative**, which is incorrect.

Avoid a double negative.

> DOUBLE NEGATIVE   We **don't never** bake cookies.
> CORRECT   We **don't** bake cookies.
> CORRECT   We **never** bake cookies.

PRACTICE YOUR SKILLS

● Check Your Understanding
Identifying Double Negatives

Contemporary Life   **Label the sentence *I* for incorrect if a double negative is used. If the sentence is correct, write C.**

1. We don't have no butter.

2. Sarah hasn't never baked cookies before.

3. The recipe doesn't call for no vanilla.

4. Kevin knows nothing about cooking.

5. There isn't no chocolate chips in the cabinet.

6. We haven't nothing to stir the batter with.

7. Ashley has never eaten fresh-baked cookies.

8. There isn't no milk to drink with these cookies.

9. There was no one to share our dessert.

10. We couldn't never eat them all by ourselves.

● Connect to the Writing Process: Revising
Correcting Double Negatives

11.–17. **Rewrite the incorrect sentences from the preceding exercise, correcting the double negatives.**

 *Good* or *Well?*

Good is always an adjective. Sometimes *good* comes before a noun, as most adjectives do. Other times *good* is used as a predicate adjective. A **predicate adjective** describes the subject and follows a linking verb such as *am, is, are, was, were, appear, feel, look, seem,* and *smell.*

Well is usually used as an adverb. When *well* means "in good health," however, it is an adjective.

ADJECTIVE	That old song is **good.**
	(*Good* is a predicate adjective that describes *song*.)
ADVERB	Sydney plays the piano **well.**
	(*Well* is an adverb that tells how Sydney plays.)
ADJECTIVE	Joey doesn't feel **well.**
	(*Well* means "in good health.")

You can learn more about predicate adjectives on pages L125–L126.

PRACTICE YOUR SKILLS

● Check Your Understanding
Using Good *and* Well *Correctly*

Contemporary Life   **Write *good* or *well* to complete each sentence correctly.**

1. They are a ▦ band.

2. He plays ▦.

3. This smooth drum feels ▦.

4. The band played ▦.

5. I feel quite ▦.

6. She speaks ▦.

7. His voice is ▦.

8. The concert is ▦.

9. That man plays guitar ▦.

10. She dances ▦.

11. That room looks ▦.

12. She plays the saxophone ▦.

13. He was ill, but now he's ▦.

14. The band's songs are ▦.

15. The band thanked the ▦ audience.

● Connect to the Writing Process: Revising
Correcting Errors in the Use of Good *and* Well

Rewrite the following sentences, correcting errors in the use of *good* and *well*. If a sentence is correct, write C.

16. The well child received a gold star from the teacher.

17. The little boy in the back of the class paints good.

18. The teacher had been sick, but today she felt quite good.

19. The class behaved well while she was out.

20. Does that little girl write good?

21. The class put on a good play.

22. Their teacher thought they did a well job.

23. She can teach very good.

24. That child's manners are good.

25. The class has a well time with the teacher.

Communicate Your Ideas

APPLY TO WRITING

Comparison and Contrast: *Adjectives and Adverbs*

Frida Kahlo. *Self-Portrait Dedicated to Leon Trotsky,* 1937.
Oil on masonite, 30 by 24 inches. The National Museum of Women in the Arts. Gift of the Honorable Clare Boothe Luce.

Mary Cassatt. *Self-Portrait,* c. 1880.
Watercolor on paper, 13 by 9⅝ inches (33 by 24.4 cm.). The National Portrait Gallery, Smithsonian Institution, Washington, D.C.

Artists often paint portraits of themselves. Look closely at the self-portraits of Frida Kahlo and Mary

Cassatt. These paintings are alike in some ways, but very different in others.

Imagine that your art teacher has asked you to write one paragraph comparing the two paintings, one paragraph contrasting them, and a final paragraph telling which painting you prefer and why. As you write, use comparative adjectives to make your point clear. Avoid using double comparisons and double negatives. Edit your work for errors.

Science Topic **Read the following paragraphs and find the errors in the use of modifiers. Then write the paragraphs correctly.**

If you went to a sea life park, would you see seals or sea lions? Some people can't never tell them apart. Both are mammals, and both have rounded, streamlined bodies. Both animals swim very good, and they are both awkward on land.

There are many differences, nevertheless, between seals and sea lions. A seal has the smallest head of the two. The seal also has a more shorter neck. If you saw these two animals on land, you would notice the most biggest difference. A seal moves by pulling its body forward with its front flippers only. A sea lion, on the other hand, moves by "walking" on all four flippers.

Using the Correct Form of Modifiers

Write the correct word.

1. Which do you like (better, best), deserts or forests?
2. There aren't (any, no) deserts in Oregon.
3. Which is the (bigger, biggest) desert in Utah?
4. Is Zion or Bryce Canyon National Park (nearer, nearest) to the Grand Canyon?
5. Riding down to the bottom of the canyon on a mule is the (scarier, scariest) thing I can imagine.
6. Mules are (steadier, more steady) animals than you would think.
7. Which rates are (cheaper, cheapest), those at the campground or those at the lodge?
8. The photographs of the campgrounds look (good, well)!
9. The lodge rooms were (warmer, more warmer) than the tents.
10. Our vacation trip went very (good, well).

Correcting Sentences with Modifiers

Write the following sentences, correcting each error. If the sentence is correct, write C.

1. I never saw a more lovelier place than the Ben Lomond Lake.
2. My family goes there more oftener than to any other park.
3. I like it when we are the earlier visitors to arrive.
4. The lake is most stillest then than at any other time of the day.

5. We can cross the lake most easily in the paddle boats than in the rowboats.

6. My oldest sister rows very good.

7. The shadiest picnic tables are in the redwood grove.

8. Do you think food tastes more better indoors or outdoors?

9. My favoritest picnic food is potato salad.

10. My mother's baked beans are the tastiest I have ever eaten.

Forming the Comparison of Modifiers

Write the correct form of each adjective or adverb written below. Then use each word in a sentence.

1. the comparative of *fast*
2. the superlative of *smart*
3. the superlative of *bravely*
4. the comparative of *good*
5. the superlative of *often*

Using Adjectives and Adverbs

Write ten sentences that follow the directions below.

Write a sentence that...

1. compares two pets.
2. compares three desserts.
3. uses a form of *bad* to compare chores.
4. uses a form of *slowly* to compare two actions.
5. uses a form of *good* to compare two kinds of friends.
6. uses a form of *little* to compare three places.
7. includes *never.*
8. includes *no one.*
9. includes the word *good.*
10. includes the word *well.*

Language and *Self-Expression*

Isamu Taniguchi's object was to create a landscape that would affect the emotions of its visitors.

You must have visited a place that affected your emotions. What did you see, hear, touch, and smell there? How did it affect you? Write a letter to a classmate, describing this place. Use a variety of adjectives and adverbs to describe sights, sounds, and movement. Find or draw a picture to go with your letter.

Prewriting Make a cluster diagram to help you record the details you remember. Create a separate cluster for the descriptive words and phrases that apply to each part of the scene. Decide in what order you will describe each part of the landscape.

Drafting Use your diagram and your list to help you draft your letter. Remember that when you describe a scene, you want to put the most striking details first and then add the less important details.

Revising Have a partner read your draft. Ask your partner: *Did I group related thoughts together? Did I make it easy for you to visualize the scene? Could my description have been clearer or my details more vivid?* As you revise, replace overused or dull adjectives with fresher ones.

Editing Check your letter for errors in punctuation and spelling. Be sure you have put commas where they are needed if you use adjectives in a series.

Publishing Give your letter to the classmate for whom you wrote it. Then read aloud the letter you received in return.

Another Look

Most adjectives and adverbs have three degrees of comparison: the positive, the comparative, and the superlative. *(page 359)*

The **positive degree** is used when a person, place, thing, or action is being described and no comparison is being made.

The **comparative degree** is used when two people, places, things, or actions are being compared.

The **superlative degree** is used when more than two people, places, things, or actions are being compared.

Add *-er* to form the comparative degree and *-est* to form the superlative degree of one-syllable modifiers. *(pages 360–361)*

Use *-er* or *more* to form the comparative degree and *-est* or *most* to form the superlative degree of two-syllable modifiers. *(pages 361–362)*

Use *more* to form the comparative degree and *most* to form the superlative degree of modifiers with three or more syllables. *(page 362)*

Do not use both *-er* and *more* to form the comparative degree, or both *-est* and *most* to form the superlative degree. *(page 367)*

Two negatives should not be used together to express the same idea. The result is an incorrect **double negative**. *(page 369)*

Placement of Adjectives and Adverbs

An adjective usually comes before the noun it modifies. *(page 370)*

A predicate adjective follows a linking verb and modifies the subject. *(page 370)*

An adverb can come before or after a verb. *(page 130)*

Other Information About Adjectives and Adverbs

Recognizing spelling changes in modifiers when *-er* or *est* is added *(pages 360–365)*

Recognizing irregular comparisons *(page 364)*

Posttest

Directions

Read the passage and choose the word or group of words that belongs in each underlined space. Write the letter of the correct answer.

EXAMPLE   In my opinion, November is the (1) appealing month of the year.

>   **1** **A** least
>   **B** less
>   **C** worst
>   **D** worse

ANSWER   **1** **A**

This is the (1) day we have had in a long time. The streets are (2) than they were a month ago. I can't ride my bike very (3) on icy streets. Riding a bike now is (4) than ever. The storms seem (5) in November than in December. Of the two months, December seems to have slightly (6) weather. It seems to me that this is the (7) November that I can remember. Today's winds seem to blow (8) than yesterday's. This is the (9) day I have seen all week. Do you think the sky has grown (10) since this morning?

1 **A** coldest
   B most coldest
   C colder
   D more colder

2 **A** more icier
   B icier
   C most icy
   D iciest

3 **A** best
   B better
   C good
   D well

4 **A** dangerouser
   B more dangerous
   C most dangerous
   D much dangerous

5 **A** less good
   B bad
   C worst
   D worse

6 **A** more better
   B good
   C better
   D best

7 **A** more chillier
   B chillier
   C most chilliest
   D chilliest

8 **A** most harshly
   B more harsher
   C more harshly
   D harshest

9 **A** drearier
   B dreariest
   C more dreary
   D more drearier

10 **A** so dark
   B more darker
   C darker
   D darkest

A Writer's Glossary of Usage

You have studied the fundamentals of usage in the last four chapters. Now you will study areas that give students special problems.

While studying these areas of difficulty, note that A Writer's Glossary of Usage refers to different levels of language. **Standard English** is the level that includes the rules and conventions most often used and accepted by English-speaking people throughout the world. **Nonstandard English** is the level that includes current slang and regional and dialectical differences. Even though nonstandard English is not wrong, it is not acceptable in certain situations. You should use standard English when you write or speak in formal situations, such as in school assignments.

Other special terms used in the glossary include formal and informal English. Because it maintains the conventional rules for grammar, usage, and mechanics, use **formal English** in your writing. The most common examples of formal English appear in business letters, technical reports, and well-written compositions. On the other hand, **informal English** follows the conventional rules, but it may use words and phrases that are not appropriate for formal writing situations. Informal English is often used in magazines, newspapers, and fiction.

Notice that the words in the glossary are listed alphabetically, which simplifies using the glossary as a reference guide.

a, an Use *a* before words beginning with consonant sounds and *an* before words beginning with vowel sounds.

> My best friend has **a** collection of seashells.
> She displays them in **an** antique curio cabinet.

CONNECT TO SPEAKING AND WRITING

Always keep in mind that this rule applies to sounds, not letters. For example, *an honor* is correct because the *h* is silent. On the other hand, *a hospital* is correct because the *h* is pronounced.

accept, except *Accept* is a verb that means "to receive with consent." *Except* is usually a preposition that means "but" or "other than."

> The agency for storm victims will **accept** any donations **except** perishable items.

affect, effect *Affect* is a verb that means "to influence" or "to act upon." *Effect* is usually a noun that means "a result" or "an influence." As a verb, *effect* means "to accomplish" or "to produce."

> Did the weather **affect** your vacation?

> It had a wonderful **effect** on our plans to ski.

> It **effected** a drop in temperature that resulted in snow.

all ready, already *All ready* means "completely ready." *Already* means "previously."

> When the members of the relay team are **all ready** to start the race, I'll give the signal.

> I have **already** instructed them to approach the starting line.

a lot People very often write these two words incorrectly as one. There is no such word as "alot." *A lot,* even as two words, should be avoided in formal writing.

INFORMAL	The shuttle lift-off created **a lot** of excitement.
FORMAL	The shuttle lift-off created **an enormous amount of** excitement.

among, between These words are both prepositions. *Among* is used when referring to three or more people or things. *Between* is used when referring to two people or things.

> **Among** the many tardy excuses I've heard, yours is the best.

> May I still sit in the front row **between** Robert and Chad?

amount, number *Amount* refers to a singular word. *Number* refers to a plural word.

> No **amount** of persuasion will cause me to reduce the **number** of assignments.

anywhere, everywhere, nowhere, somewhere Do not add *–s* to any of these words.

> **Nowhere** could I find a better friend than you.

> I looked **everywhere** for your letter.

at Do not use **at** after *where.*

NONSTANDARD	**Where** did you put my new sweater **at**?
STANDARD	**Where** did you put my new sweater?

PRACTICE YOUR SKILLS

● Check Your Understanding
Finding the Correct Word

Contemporary Life **Write the word in parentheses that correctly completes each sentence.**

1. Sixth grade usually involves (a lot of, many) changes.

2. For example, the (amount, number) of teachers often increases.

3. You will probably have a variety of classroom procedures to (accept, except).

4. Even the (amount, number) of homework assignments varies in each class.

5. Some schools provide lockers so that you don't have to carry all your books (everywhere, everywheres).

6. (Among, Between) classes, you might have to walk across campus.

7. You also have to choose (among, between) a list of electives.

8. For example, students (all ready, already) interested in farming might sign up for agriculture class.

9. Short exploratory courses often (affect, effect) your future courses of study.

10. I know that you are (all ready, already) for an eventful year in the sixth grade.

● Connect to the Writing Process: Editing
Recognizing Correct Usage

Write the underlined words. If the word is used correctly, write C beside the word. If the word is used incorrectly, write the correct form of the verb.

A important challenge students often face is peer pressure. You may all ready have had such an experience. Sometimes other students try to effect your decisions and actions. The effect on you depends on your ability to handle pressure. You could affect a change in their thinking through a positive example. When you cannot solve a problem alone, remember a great number of options are available. You can go to the guidance office, where the peer counseling is at. Except for unusual cases, a problem can usually be solved there. If you're all ready to help others, consider taking a peer counseling class. Learning to handle peer pressure prepares you to except leadership.

bad, badly *Bad* is an adjective and often follows a linking verb. *Badly* is used as an adverb. In the first two examples, *feel* is a linking verb.

NONSTANDARD	Don't feel **badly** about not being able to go.
STANDARD	Don't feel **bad** about not being able to go.
STANDARD	If you **badly** need me to go, I will change my plans.

You can learn more about using adjectives and adverbs in Chapter 4.

bring, take *Bring* indicates motion toward the speaker. *Take* indicates motion away from the speaker.

> **Bring** your permission slip to me and then **take** it to your homeroom teacher.

You can learn more about bring *and* take *on pages L246–L249.*

can, may *Can* expresses ability. *May* expresses possibility or permission.

> **Can** you program the VCR?
> Mother says that we **may** watch the TV special later.

doesn't, don't *Doesn't* is singular and must agree with a singular subject. *Don't* is plural and must agree with a plural subject.

> He **doesn't** have to be home early.
> They **don't** have to be home early.

double negative Words such as *but* (when it means "only"), *hardly, never, no, none, no one, nobody, not* (and its contraction *n't*), *nothing, nowhere, only, barely,* and *scarcely* are all negatives.

> NONSTANDARD   Do **not** give me **no** excuses.
> STANDARD   Do **not** give me any excuses.
> STANDARD   Give me **no** excuses.

You can learn more about double negatives on page L369.

fewer, less *Fewer* is plural and refers to things that can be counted. *Less* is singular and refers to quantities and qualities that cannot be counted.

> Why did you give me **fewer** pieces of candy this time?
> If you eat **less** candy, your teeth will be stronger.

good, well *Good* is an adjective and often follows a linking verb. *Well* is an adverb and often follows an action verb. However, when *well* means "in good health" or "satisfactory," it is used as an adjective.

Your voice sounds **good** on the CD.

(adjective)

You practiced **well** for your audition.

(adverb)

I hope I am **well** enough to attend the performance.

(adjective meaning "in good health")

You can learn more about good *and* well *on page L370.*

have, of Never substitute *of* for the verb *have*. When speaking, many people make a contraction of *have*. For example, they might say, "We should've gone." Because *'ve* sounds like *of, of* is often mistakenly substituted for *have* in writing.

NONSTANDARD	You should **of** watched the news program.
STANDARD	You should **have** watched the news program.

in, into Use *into* when you want to express motion from one place to another.

With our boat anchored **in** a cove, we dived **into** the lake.

CONNECT TO SPEAKING AND WRITING

Unlike the word *into*, the word *in* does not suggest that a motion is taking place.

We were **in** math class when the snow began.
Cathy and I met last year **in** El Paso.

PRACTICE YOUR SKILLS

● Check Your Understanding
Finding the Correct Word

Music
Topic
Write the word in parentheses that correctly completes each sentence.

1. A (good, well) variety of music courses is often available in sixth grade.

2. General music courses (doesn't, don't) usually require performances.

3. Many students, however, want (bad, badly) to perform in band, chorus, or orchestra.

4. Others prefer to enroll (in, into) courses such as keyboard or guitar.

5. Guitars fall (in, into) two basic categories— acoustic and electric.

6. The popularity of rock singers (could have, could of) influenced students to take a guitar course.

7. Guitars (can, may) be used in a variety of ways.

8. A guitar player (doesn't, don't) always perform solo.

9. (Fewer, Less) instruments are more popular than guitars.

10. Some schools (can, may) even use guitars in their bands.

● Connect to the Writing Process: Editing
Recognizing Correct Usage

Write the underlined words. If the word is used correctly, write *C* beside the word. If the word is used incorrectly, write the correct form of the word.

Music can be defined in many ways. One definition known <u>well</u> states that music is a "universal language" because it <u>don't</u> just speak to certain people. In fact, you <u>don't</u> even have to play music to enjoy it. It reaches <u>in</u> our emotions and feelings. Often it causes us to feel <u>well</u> even when we aren't <u>well</u>. For patients who <u>badly</u> need cheering up, music is therapy. It isn't <u>hardly</u> possible to remain unhappy when listening to soothing or lively music. <u>Less</u> things more positive than music affect our lives. Sometimes, however, music <u>takes</u> back memories that <u>take</u> us back <u>into</u> time. It <u>can</u> even make us feel <u>bad</u>, as it does the speaker in D. H. Lawrence's poem "Piano."

Communicate Your Ideas

APPLY TO WRITING

Personal Response: *Correct Usage*

Poets often express emotions through their poems. Read the second stanza of Lawrence's poem. Notice how the music saddens the speaker when it brings to mind a special moment from the past.

In spite of myself, the insidious mastery of song
Betrays me back, till the heart of me weeps to
belong To the old Sunday evenings at home, with
winter outside And hymns in the cosy parlour, the
tinkling piano our guide.

—*D. H. Lawrence*, "Piano"

You have been asked by your music teacher to record your personal response to a piece of music. You might recall a patriotic song featured at a Fourth of July celebration, a marching song played at a football game, or an upbeat song blaring at a concert. Did the music make you feel sad like the speaker in the poem, or did the music call up some other feeling?

Using any five of the glossary words from *a/an* through *in/into,* write an original paragraph in which you explain how the song made you feel. Be sure to use the correct form of the words.

its, it's *Its* is a possessive pronoun and means "belonging to it." *It's* is a contraction for *it is.*

> Even after reading the book, I didn't understand **its** message.
>
> **It's** important, of course, but there's nothing wrong with just enjoying its story.

lay, lie *Lay* is usually followed by a direct object. Its principal parts are *lay, laying, laid,* and *laid. Lie* means "to rest or recline." *Lie* is never followed by a direct object. Its principal parts are *lie, lying, lay,* and *lain. Lay* means "to put or set (something) down."

> LAY   Don't **lay** the damp paper on my antique table. (*Paper* is the direct object.)
>
>   Have you been **laying** anything else on the table?
>
>   You **laid** a magazine there yesterday.
>
>   When I have **laid** anything on that table, I have made sure it's dry.

LIE　　Whenever I **lie** down to rest, the phone rings.

I was **lying** on the lounge chair when the phone rang.

I **lay** for several rings before I went to answer it.

I wish I had **lain** there the entire time.

learn, teach *Learn* means "to gain knowledge." *Teach* means "to instruct or "to show how."

Learning is more enjoyable for students when **teaching** is performed with enthusiasm.

You can learn more about learn *and* teach *on page L248.*

leave, let *Leave* means "to depart" or "to go away from." *Let* means "to allow" or "to permit."

NONSTANDARD	Don't **leave** me forget to thank you.
STANDARD	Don't **let** me forget to thank you.
STANDARD	I won't **leave** without your gift.

You can learn more about leave *and* let *on page L250.*

passed, past *Passed* is the past tense of the verb *pass.* As a noun, *past* means "a time gone by." As an adjective, *past* means "just gone." As a preposition, *past* means "beyond."

In the **past,** the parade always **passed** by in the morning.

(*past* as an noun)

It is **past** my understanding why they held it in the evening this **past** week.

(*past* as a preposition and then as an adjective)

raise, rise *Raise* means "to lift (something) up," "to increase," or "to grow something." *Raise* is usually followed by a direct object. Its principal parts are *raise, raising, raised,* and *raised*. *Rise* means "to move upward" or "to get up." *Rise* is never followed by a direct object. Its principal parts are *rise, rising, rose,* and *risen*.

> The water in the river will **rise** during a heavy rainstorm.
> That's why they are **raising** money for flood control.

shall, will Formal English has always used *shall* with first-person pronouns and *will* with second- and third-person pronouns. Today *shall* and *will* are used interchangeably with *I* and *we,* except that *shall* is used with *I* and *we* for questions.

> **Shall** we march in the parade tomorrow?
> Yes, I think it **will** be great fun.

set, sit *Set* means "to put or place (something)." *Set* is usually followed by a direct object. Its principal parts are *set, setting, set,* and *set*. *Sit* means "to rest in an upright position." *Sit* is never followed by a direct object. Its principal parts are *sit, sitting, sat,* and *sat*.

> If you **set** your mind to it, I think you can **sit** through the entire performance. (*Mind* is the direct object.)

Practice Your Skills

● Check Your Understanding
Finding the Correct Word

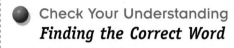

General Interest | **Write the word in parentheses that correctly completes each sentence.**

1. How will your little brother (learn, teach) about the care of a pet?

2. The family will (raise, rise) an animal from a baby to an adult.

3. When they are young, pets (shall, will) take up a great deal of time.

4. My brother and I will (raise, rise) early to care for the pet.

5. Perhaps we can (learn, teach) the pet some clever tricks.

6. I'll get advice from pet owners with (passed, past) experience.

7. (Lay, Lie) down clear rules at the start so your pet will not get confused.

8. You can't (leave, let) pets run your life.

9. Of course, many pet owners haven't (passed, past) that test!

10. (Shall, Will) we take a look at one of the more unusual pets?

● Connect to the Writing Process: Revising
Using the Correct Forms of Verbs

Rewrite the following sentences using the correct form of the verbs in parentheses.

11. Matt (learn) how to pick up the gerbil after Jennifer (teach) him.

12. The hermit crab was (lie) in the bowl when Kelly carefully (lay) the new shell beside it.

13. After Fred (raise) the iguana, he realized that his food bill had (rise).

14. George (sat) the new perch in the cage while the macaw (set) on the old one.

that there, this here Avoid using *here* or *there* in addition to *this* or *that*.

NONSTANDARD	Brett is buying **that there** surfboard.
STANDARD	Brett is buying **that** surfboard.

their, there, they're *Their* is a possessive pronoun. *There* is usually an adverb, but sometimes it begins an inverted sentence. *They're* is a contraction for *they are*.

Their science project looks very interesting.
There are others on display over **there** in the corner.
They're judging the projects now.

theirs, there's *Theirs* is a possessive pronoun. *There's* is a contraction for *there is*.

Our plane ride was smooth; **theirs** was bumpy.
They want to switch airlines if **there's** a chance.

them, those Never use *them* as a subject or a modifier.

NONSTANDARD	**Them** are the monarch butterflies. (subject)
STANDARD	**Those** are the monarch butterflies.
NONSTANDARD	**Them** butterflies are monarchs. (adjective)
STANDARD	**Those** butterflies are monarchs.

to, too, two *To* is a preposition. *To* also begins an infinitive. *Too* is an adverb that modifies a verb, an adjective, or another adverb. *Two* is a number.

If you go **to** the Florida Keys, be sure **to** go snorkeling.
The first **two** days, we'll probably be **too** busy.
Taste the lobster and conch chowder **too** while you're there.

use to, used to Be sure to add the *d* to *use*.

> NONSTANDARD   Are you **use to** having your own way?
> STANDARD   Are you **used to** having your own way?

who, whom *Who*, a pronoun in the nominative case, is used as either a subject or a predicate nominative. *Whom*, a pronoun in the objective case, is used as a direct object, an indirect object, or an object of a preposition.

> **Who** is coming to my recital? (subject)
>
> **Whom** did you invite? (direct object)

whose, who's *Whose* is a possessive pronoun. *Who's* is a contraction for *who is*.

> **Whose** are these boat keys?
> **Who's** waiting at the dock?

your, you're *Your* is a possessive pronoun. *You're* is a contraction for *you are*.

> When will we have **your** answer?
> If **you're** sure about the answer, I'll send it now.

PRACTICE YOUR SKILLS

● Check Your Understanding
Finding the Correct Word

Contemporary Life   **Write the word in parentheses that correctly completes each sentence.**

1. Many schools offer exploratory wheel courses (to, too, two) sixth grade students.

2. (Them, Those) courses allow students (to, too, two) explore (their, there, they're) interests.

3. (Their, There, They're) also designed to broaden (your, you're) interests.

4. (Theirs, There's) quite a wide range of courses (to, too, two).

5. While (your, you're) (their, there, they're), you will receive an introduction to the class.

6. (This, This here) approach is combined with special activities and projects.

7. One example is an introduction to technology course (whose, who's) activities might include computer graphics.

8. In shop, students find out (whose, who's) skilled in areas such as woodworking.

9. (To, Too, Two) classes on the exploratory wheel that encourage creativity are art and drama.

10. The exploratory wheel helps you get (use to, used to) a new subject.

● Connect to the Writing Process: Editing
Recognizing Correct Usage: Who and Whom

Write the underlined pronouns. If the pronoun is used correctly, write *C* beside the pronoun. If the pronoun is used incorrectly, write the correct form of the pronoun.

11. Whom taught drama in the exploratory wheel this year?

12. Who volunteered for the play?

13. To whom did Mrs. Lyndon finally assign a leading role?

14. Whom had supporting roles in the cast?

15. Whom likes to talk more, Matt or Louise?

Communicate Your Ideas

APPLY TO WRITING

Monologues: *Correct Usage*

Monologues in drama are uninterrupted lines spoken by a character. These lines often reveal insight about that particular character.

Imagine you have been asked by your drama teacher to write a paragraph that could be developed into a monologue. Using at least five of the glossary words from *its/it's* through *your/you're,* relate the story of an act of kindness, real or imagined, that demonstrates friendship or loyalty. Be sure to use the correct form of the words.

 **QuickCheck** Mixed Practice

Contemporary Life **Write the word in parentheses that correctly completes each sentence.**

1. In the (passed, past), family and consumer science courses were called home economics.

2. Today (theirs, there's) much (fewer, less) emphasis on cooking and sewing.

3. Many boys enroll (in, into) the family and consumer science classes.

4. Family relationships, interaction with peers, and self-esteem are (among, between) the (amount, number) of topics studied.

5. The instructor (learns, teaches) students about family relationships and (their, they're) roles in the family.

6. When students (learn, teach) about peer interaction, they understand the value of (good, well) friends.

7. Through setting goals, students often (raise, rise) self-esteem.

8. The (affects, effects) of proper nutrition on the body are introduced (to, too, two).

9. The food pyramid (affects, effects) almost everyone's grocery list.

10. (To, Too, Two) basics of food preparation are proper measurement and the correct utensils.

11. Interest (raises, rises) to (a, an) high level when actual cooking begins.

12. (Fewer, Less) activities are more fun than tasting (your, you're) own cooking.

13. (Who, Whom) will sample the goodies that students (bring, take) to the faculty lounge?

14. Fashion designing, interior decorating, child development, and sewing (can, may) also be offered in some schools.

15. Family and consumer science courses have (a, an) extraordinary range of topics compared to what they (use to, used to) have.

CHAPTER 12

Capital Letters

 **Pretest**

Directions
Write the letter of the group of words that corrects the capitalization error in one of the underlined parts. If a sentence contains no error, write *D*.

EXAMPLE

1. The city of Troy was located along today's Turkish coast.
   1 **A** The City of Troy
      B Turkish Coast
      C turkish coast
      D No error

ANSWER   1 **D**

1. Aunt Laura saw the great wall of China.
2. My brother attends yale university in New Haven.
3. The civil war began when Fort Sumter was attacked.
4. Suzuki is taking high school classes to get her american citizenship.
5. Ten moons orbit the planet Saturn.
6. My brother Reuben is rooting for the Chicago cubs.
7. The big dipper is in the Milky Way Galaxy.
8. During the middle ages, Italy traded with China.
9. Kate might be our next representative in the Nevada State Legislature.
10. *Mardi Gras* takes place before the celebration of easter.

1 **A** the Great Wall of China
   B aunt Laura
   C the great Wall of China
   D No error

2 **A** new Haven
   B Yale university
   C Yale University
   D No error

3 **A** fort Sumter
   B The Civil War
   C The civil War
   D No error

4 **A** American Citizenship
   B American citizenship
   C High School classes
   D No error

5 **A** the planet saturn
   B the Planet Saturn
   C Ten Moons
   D No error

6 **A** the Chicago Cubs
   B My Brother Reuben
   C The Chicago Cubs
   D No error

7 **A** Milky Way galaxy
   B The Big Dipper
   C The big Dipper
   D No error

8 **A** Italy traded with china
   B the Middle Ages
   C The Middle ages
   D No error

9 **A** the Nevada State legislature
   B our next Representative
   C the Nevada state Legislature
   D No error

10 **A** *Mardi gras*
   B the Celebration of Easter
   C the celebration of Easter
   D No error

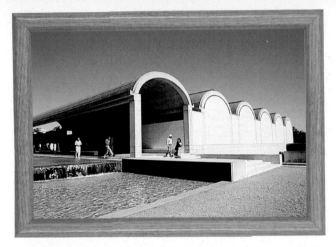

Louis Kahn, architect.
The Kimbell Art Museum, Fort Worth, Texas.

Describe What features of this building stand out for you? What makes it seem unusual?

Analyze What elements did the architect use to create unity and harmony in the structure?

Interpret The architect considered the use to which the building would be put when he designed it. Which elements of the design do you think reflect his ideas about what an art museum should be? What are these ideas?

Judge Would you rather see this photograph or listen to an informative speech in which the speaker explains the details and the architect's purpose? Explain your answer.

At the end of this chapter, you will use the artwork to stimulate ideas for writing.

Rules of Capital Letters

Imagine how difficult it would be to read a simple set of directions if the directions did not include any capital letters or end marks! It would be very confusing.

First Words and the Pronoun *I*

Without capital letters and end marks, one sentence would run into another. Capital letters clearly mark the beginning of new sentences.

Sentences

Capital letters at the beginning of sentences are necessary for clear understanding.

Capitalize the first word of a sentence.

> SENTENCES   **P**oetry is fun to read.
> **D**o you like the poems of Langston Hughes?

Lines of Poetry

Capital letters often mark the beginning of each new line of poetry.

Capitalize the first word in a line of poetry.

> LINES OF POETRY   **B**eautifully Janet slept
> **T**ill it was deeply morning. **S**he woke then
> **A**nd thought about her dainty-feathered hen,
> **T**o see how it had kept.
>
> *—John Crowe Ransom,* "Janet Waking"

Some modern poets deliberately misuse or eliminate capital letters in their poems. Notice the lack of capitalization at the beginnings of lines in this poem by William Carlos Williams.

> so much depends
> upon
>
> a red wheel
> barrow
>
> glazed with rain
> water
>
> beside the white
> chickens.
> —*William Carlos Williams,* "The Red Wheelbarrow"

When you are quoting lines of poetry, copy them exactly as the poet has written them, including any misused capitalization or punctuation.

Parts of Letters

Certain parts of a letter stand out because they begin with capital letters. A capital letter also marks the beginning of a letter and the end of a letter.

Capitalize the first word in the greeting of a letter and the first word in the closing of a letter.

GREETINGS AND CLOSINGS		
GREETINGS	Dear Aunt Sylvia, Dear Sir or Madam:	To whom it may concern: Dear fellow classmates,
CLOSINGS	Yours truly, Love,	Sincerely, Thank you,

Outlines

The most important points in an outline begin with capital letters. A capital letter also marks the beginning of a new item in an outline.

Capitalize the first word of each item in an outline and the letters that begin major subsections of the outline.

I. **P**rose
   A. Novel
   B. Short story
   C. Essay

II. **P**oetry
   A. Rhyming
      1. Sonnet
      2. Limerick
   B. Non-rhyming
      1. Haiku
      2. Blank verse

The Pronoun *I*

The pronoun *I* is always capitalized.

Capitalize the pronoun *I*, both alone and in contractions.

ALONE	Mom said **I** should read this book of poetry.
CONTRACTION	She thought **I**'d like it.

PRACTICE YOUR SKILLS

● Check Your Understanding
Capitalizing First Words and I

Write the letter of the correctly capitalized item.

1. a. dear Ms. Johnson,

   b. Dear Ms. Johnson,

2. a. I'm makin' a road

   for the cars to fly by on,

   Makin' a road

   through the palmetto thicket...

   Langston Hughes, "Florida Road Workers"

   b. I'm makin' a road

   For the cars to fly by on,

   Makin' a road

   Through the palmetto thicket...

   Langston Hughes, "Florida Road Workers"

3. a. I have read many poems, and i've liked most of them.

   b. I have read many poems, and I've liked most of them.

4. a. Sincerely yours,

   b. sincerely yours,

5. a. have you read any books by Amy Tan?

   b. Have you read any books by Amy Tan?

6. a. Modes of Writing

    I. Creative

        A. Short story

        B. Poetry

    II. Technical

        A. How-to

        B. Comparison

b. Modes of Writing

    I. Creative

        a. short story

        b. poetry

    II. Technical

        a. how-to

        b. comparison

7. a. Of all the kinds of poems, i like limericks best.

   b. Of all the kinds of poems, I like limericks best.

● Connect to the Writing Process: Editing
Correcting Errors in Capitalization

Rewrite the following letter, using capital letters correctly.

dear Grandma,

    next week my science project is due. for a while i couldn't think of anything. then i decided i'd make a wind vane and record the direction of the wind.

    Mom took me to the library, and i got a book about weather vanes. it wasn't very hard to make one.

    tomorrow i'll take the wind vane outside. with my

compass, i'll record the direction of the wind.

what have you been doing? write back soon.

your grandson,

Jeremy

Communicate Your Ideas

APPLY TO WRITING
Writer's Craft: *Analyzing the Use of Capitalization*

The African American poet Carl Wendell Hines was unconventional in his use of capitalization. Read the following poetry excerpt and then follow the directions.

> yeah here am i
> am standing
> at the crest of a tallest
> hill with a trumpet
> in my hand & dark
> glasses
> on.
> bearded & bereted i proudly stand!
> but there are no eyes to see me.
> i send down cool sounds!
> but there are no ears to hear me.
> —*Carl Wendell Hines, Jr.,* "Two Jazz Poems"

- How does the lack of capitalization in this poem affect you as a reader?

- Rewrite the lines of poetry capitalizing the words that, according to the rules, you should capitalize.
- Compare your new version with Hines's original. How does adding capitalization change the poem? Why do you think Hines chose to leave out capital letters?
- What other things did Hines do in this poem that are unusual?

Proper Nouns

A **common noun** is the name of any person, place, or thing. A **proper noun** begins with a capital letter because it is the name of a particular person, place, or thing.

COMMON AND PROPER NOUNS			
COMMON NOUN	girl	city	day
PROPER NOUN	Chelsea Green	Chicago	Friday (Fri.)

Capitalize proper nouns and their abbreviations.

Most proper nouns fit into one of the following groups. Use these groups to check the capitalization of proper nouns. Always do this when you edit your written work.

Names of persons and animals are capitalized. Also capitalize the initials that stand for people's names.

PERSONS AND ANIMALS	
PERSONS	Andrea, Chen Loo, Franklin **D.** Roosevelt, Avi
ANIMALS	Puff, Misty, Rover, Snowball

You can find out about the capitalization of people's titles on pages L426–L427.

PRACTICE YOUR SKILLS

● Check Your Understanding
Capitalizing Names of Persons and Animals

General Interest **Write correctly the words in the following sentences that should be capitalized.**

1. In movies, television, and cartoons, there have been many famous animals such as rin tin tin and mickey mouse.

2. roy rogers had a famous horse named trigger.

3. His wife, dale evans, had a horse named buttermilk.

4. In *The Wizard of Oz,* dorothy gale had a black dog named toto.

5. A cat named morris starred in cat food commercials.

6. A beautiful collie named lassie kept her owner timmy out of trouble.

7. bugs bunny and daffy duck are two funny cartoon characters.

8. the old movies about tarzan always featured a chimpanzee named cheetah.

9. In *The Lion King,* simba finds out the truth about his uncle's betrayal.

10. In the comics, dagwood and blondie bumstead have a dog named daisy.

11. My brother's favorite comic strip character is calvin.

12. calvin's best friend is a tiger named hobbes.

13. mom agrees that calvin and hobbes are funny characters.

14. The heroine of the movie *Beauty and the Beast* is a young girl named belle.

15. The movie *Beethoven* features a large saint bernard.

Geographical names, which include places and bodies of water, are capitalized.

GEOGRAPHICAL NAMES	
STREETS, HIGHWAYS	Lindsay Avenue (**Ave.**), Route 34 (**Rt.**), Ohio Turnpike (**Tpk.**), Highway 84 (**Hwy.**), Interstate 35, Fifty-third Street (**St.**) (The second part of a hyphenated numbered street is not capitalized.)
CITIES, STATES	Austin, Texas (**TX**); Helena, Montana (**MT**); St. Louis, Missouri (**MO**)
COUNTRIES	United States, Russia, Egypt, Zimbabwe
CONTINENTS	North America, Australia, Antarctica, Europe
WORLD REGIONS	Northern Hemisphere, South Pole, Scandinavia
ISLANDS	Maui, Vancouver, Philippines, Manhattan
MOUNTAINS	Andes Mountains, Mount Fuji (**Mt.**)
FORESTS AND PARKS	Kit Carson National Forest, Yellowstone National Park
BODIES OF WATER	Colorado River, Lake Michigan, Indian Ocean, Gulf of Mexico, Prince William Sound
SECTION OF THE COUNTRY	the Southwest, New England, the Great Divide (Simple compass directions are not capitalized. Go south on Spring Street.)

Words such as *street, mountain,* and *city* are capitalized only when they are part of a proper noun.

> You will come to a **s**treet named Golden **S**treet.

PRACTICE YOUR SKILLS

● Check Your Understanding
Capitalizing Geographical Names

Write the letter of the correctly capitalized item.

1. a. a green forest
   b. a green Forest

2. a. Sixty-Eighth St.
   b. Sixty-eighth St.

3. a. the north
   b. the North

4. a. Pacific Coast Highway
   b. Pacific coast highway

5. a. Houston, Tx
   b. Houston, TX

6. a. the Rocky mountains
   b. the Rocky Mountains

7. a. Baltic Sea
   b. baltic Sea

8. a. Cabo san lucas, Mexico
   b. Cabo San Lucas, Mexico

9. a. North pole
   b. North Pole

10. a. Indonesia
   b. indonesia

Writing Sentences with Proper Nouns

Write a sentence that mentions the name of each of the following places. Be sure to capitalize the beginning of each sentence and any proper nouns.

11. your hometown

12. the street on which your school is located

13. an ocean you've seen or would like to see

14. the place you'd most like to see

15. a foreign country in which you are interested

● Connect to the Writing Process: Editing
Correcting Errors in Capitalization

Rewrite the following sentences, using capital letters correctly.

16. The capital of the united states is washington, d.c.

17. phoenix, the capital of arizona, lies in the sonoran desert.

18. denver, colorado, is at the foot of the rocky mountains.

19. A beautiful feature of austin, texas, is town lake, which flows through the city.

20. augusta, maine, is located in the kennebec valley.

21. the capital of washington, olympia, is located on the shores of south puget sound.

22. pennsylvania's capital, harrisburg, was originally a ferry port on the susquehanna river.

23. Take interstate 64 from louisville to reach frankfort, the capital of kentucky.

24. The capital of massachusetts is boston.

25. Near the sangre de cristo mountains sits santa fe, the capital of new mexico.

APPLY TO WRITING

Directions: *Proper Nouns*

Your uncle is visiting from out of town. He is going to pick you up from school, but he does not know the way. Write directions to your school from your home. Be sure that they are accurate so that he doesn't get lost. As you write your directions, be sure to capitalize the proper nouns.

Nouns of historical importance, which include the names of historical events, periods, and documents, are capitalized.

HISTORIC NAMES	
EVENTS	Civil War, World War II (**WWII**), Battle of Little Bighorn
PERIODS	Industrial Revolution, Middle Ages, Ice Age
DOCUMENTS	Constitution, Treaty of Versailles

Prepositions, such as *of* in *Treaty of Versailles,* are not capitalized.

Specific time periods and events are capitalized. Capitalize the days of the week, the months of the year, civil and religious holidays, and special events. Also capitalize the following abbreviations: *A.D., B.C., A.M.,* and *P.M.*

TIME PERIODS AND EVENTS	
DAYS, MONTHS	Wednesday, Sunday, April, October
HOLIDAYS	New Year's Day, Fourth of July

SPECIAL EVENTS	Boston Marathon, Cotton Bowl Parade, the Olympics
TIME ABBREVIATIONS	By about 1100 B.C., Egypt had lost its great empire.

Do not capitalize the seasons of the year.

> I like spring better than summer.

PRACTICE YOUR SKILLS

● Check Your Understanding
Capitalizing Proper Nouns

Write the letter of the correctly capitalized item.

1. **a.** Thanksgiving Day Parade
   b. Thanksgiving day parade
2. **a.** June 12, 1977
   b. june 12, 1977
3. **a.** bronze Age
   b. Bronze Age
4. **a.** Declaration of Independence
   b. Declaration Of Independence
5. **a.** World war I
   b. World War I
6. **a.** Battle of San Juan Hill
   b. battle of San Juan hill
7. **a.** Winter
   b. winter
8. **a.** Super Bowl
   b. Super bowl

9. a. labor Day

   b. Labor Day

10. a. the Renaissance

   b. the renaissance

● Check Your Understanding
Using Capital Letters

History Topic **Write correctly the words in the following sentences that should be capitalized.**

11. The United States celebrates independence day on july 4.

12. On that date in 1776, fifty-six men signed the declaration of independence.

13. More than two hundred years later, we still celebrate the fourth of july as a national holiday.

14. The signing of this document led to the revolutionary war.

15. It was not until 1783 that the British and Americans signed the treaty of paris, officially ending the revolutionary war.

● Connect to the Writing Process: Drafting
Writing Sentences with Proper Nouns

Write one sentence about each of the following subjects. Be sure to capitalize the beginnings of your sentences and any proper nouns.

16. your favorite holiday

17. your favorite month

18. your favorite day of the week

19. a special event that interests you

20. your favorite season of the year

APPLY TO WRITING
News Story: *Proper Nouns*

Imagine that you are a reporter. You have been assigned to cover a sports event. Describe the event in the photograph or another sports event for the readers of the newspaper. Remember to answer the questions *Who? What? When? Where?* and *Why?* in your story. When you have finished your story, check that you have used capital letters for all proper nouns.

Names of nationalities and races begin with capital letters.

	NATIONALITIES AND RACES
NATIONALITIES	a **G**erman, a **N**avajo, a **C**anadian, a **J**apanese
RACES	**C**aucasian, **A**frican **A**merican, **M**aori, **L**atino

Names of religions, religious references, and religious holidays are capitalized.

RELIGIOUS NAMES	
RELIGIONS	**M**ethodism, **I**slam, **J**udaism, **B**uddhism
RELIGIOUS **H**OLIDAYS	**H**anukkah, **C**hristmas, **R**amadan, **E**piphany, **P**urim, **P**otlatch, **E**aster, **P**assover
RELIGIOUS **R**EFERENCES	**G**od, the **A**lmighty, the **O**ld **T**estament, the **T**almud, the **V**edas, the **K**oran, **A**llah

The word *god* is not capitalized when it refers to polytheistic gods. Their individual names, however, are capitalized.

The **g**od who was head of all others was **Z**eus.

PRACTICE YOUR SKILLS

● Check Your Understanding
Capitalizing Proper Nouns

Write the letter of the correctly capitalized item.

1. **a.** a Roman god
   b. a Roman God
2. **a.** Latino
   b. latino
3. **a.** Yom Kippur
   b. Yom kippur
4. **a.** native American
   b. Native American
5. **a.** Russians
   b. russians

6. a. Roman catholic

b. Roman Catholic

7. a. Greek Goddess

b. Greek goddess

8. a. the new Testament

b. the New Testament

9 a. The lord

b. the Lord

10. a. Good Friday

b. good friday

● Check Your Understanding
Using Capital Letters

General Interest **Write correctly each word that should be capitalized.**

11. An important holiday for christians around the world is christmas.

12. Many people across the globe go to church on christmas eve.

13. We americans celebrate the holiday with mistletoe and gifts.

14. The english began today's tradition of sending christmas cards.

15. The spanish dance and sing in the streets on christmas eve.

16. Some italians serve eels for dinner on the day before christmas.

17. The norwegians always ring bells at 5:00 P.M. on christmas eve.

18. The australians celebrate christmas with a six-week summer vacation.

19. The mexicans break piñatas, which contain candy or gifts.

20. The irish place a lighted candle in their windows on christmas eve.

● Connect to the Writing Process: Drafting
Writing Sentences with Proper Nouns

Use each of these proper nouns in a sentence. Be sure to capitalize the beginnings of your sentences and the proper nouns.

21. Brazilians

22. Americans

23. Mexicans

24. Chileans

25. Canadians

Names of groups and businesses begin with capital letters. Capitalize the names of organizations, businesses, institutions, teams, and government bodies and agencies.

NAMES OF GROUPS	
ORGANIZATIONS	United Nations (**UN**), Parent–Teacher Association (**PTA**), Boy Scouts of America (**BSA**)
BUSINESSES	National Bank, Alpha Hardware Store, Pete's Cafe
INSTITUTIONS	University of Texas (**U.T.**), Central High School, Mercy Hospital, Memorial Middle School
TEAMS	Dallas Cowboys, Boston Celtics, Detroit Redwings

GOVERNMENT BODIES AND AGENCIES	Federal Bureau of Investigation (**FBI**), the Senate, **F**ood and **D**rug **A**dministration (**FDA**), the Supreme Court

Names of planets, stars, constellations, and galaxies are capitalized. Do not capitalize *sun* and *moon*.

ASTRONOMICAL NAMES	
PLANETS	Jupiter, Mercury, Pluto
STARS	North Star, Sirius, Vega
CONSTELLATIONS	Taurus, Big Dipper
GALAXIES	Milky Way, Andromeda

Do not capitalize *earth* if the word *the* comes in front of it.

CAPITAL	The third planet from the sun is **E**arth.
NO CAPITAL	The moon rotates around *the* **e**arth.

Languages and specific school courses begin with capital letters. Capitalize the name of a school course when it is followed by a number.

LANGUAGES AND SCHOOL COURSES	
LANGUAGES	English, Spanish, Japanese, Russian
COMPUTER LANGUAGES	Java, Cobal, Visual Basic
NUMBERED COURSES	Art I, Chorus II, Astronomy 101

Course names such as *social studies, math, science,* and *physical education* are not capitalized.

Other proper nouns also begin with capital letters.

OTHER PROPER NOUNS	
AWARDS	Grammy, Oscar®, Nobel Peace Prize
BRAND NAMES	Fancy noodles, Deluxe oil, Crispy chips (The product itself—noodles, oil, chips—is not capitalized.)
BUILDINGS	Empire State Building, Johnson Space Center
MONUMENTS, MEMORIALS	Washington Monument, Mount Rushmore, Lincoln Memorial, Vietnam Memorial
TECHNOLOGICAL TERMS	Internet, Web, World Wide Web, Website, Web page
VEHICLES	Air Force One, Mariner 10, Metroliner (Also italicize or underline the names of vehicles.)

PRACTICE YOUR SKILLS

● Check Your Understanding
Capitalizing Proper Nouns

Write the letter of the correctly capitalized item.

1. **a.** library of congress
   b. Library of Congress
2. **a.** Central Intelligence Agency
   b. Central Intelligence agency
3. **a.** a yacht
   b. a Yacht

4. **a.** an Emmy

   b. an emmy

5. **a.** Biology 301

   b. biology 301

6. **a.** elementary school

   b. Elementary School

7. **a.** New Orleans Saints

   b. New Orleans saints

8. **a.** *mayflower*

   b. *Mayflower*

9. **a.** a bank

   b. a Bank

10. **a.** Marlin Junior High School

   b. Marlin Junior High school

● Check Your Understanding
Using Capital Letters

Geography Topic **Write correctly the words in the following sentences that should be capitalized.**

11. Washington, D.C., is filled with great places to visit, aside from the white house.

12. The capitol, seat of our government, was built on an elevated site.

13. The senate and the house of representatives make the laws of our land.

14. The pentagon houses the department of defense.

15. The smithsonian institution is a vast complex of museums and research centers.

16. You can see the *spirit of st. louis*, Charles Lindbergh's airplane, at the national air and space museum.

17. The holocaust memorial museum opened in 1995 to honor victims of the Holocaust during World War II.

18. The washington monument is a tall structure of white marble.

19. The vietnam memorial is almost five hundred feet long and made of black granite.

20. A college, georgetown university, is located in the nation's capital.

● Connect to the Writing Process: Drafting
Writing Sentences with Proper Nouns

Write a sentence about each of the following topics. Remember to capitalize proper nouns.

21. your favorite football team

22. your favorite soft drink

23. your favorite restaurant

24. a college you would like to attend

25. a high school in your area

● Connect to the Writing Process: Editing
Correcting Errors in Capitalization

Rewrite the following paragraph, correcting any errors in capitalization.

during different Seasons of the year, different Constellations are visible in the night sky. orion and columba can be seen best in the winter. the constellation leo, visible in april, includes the bright star regulus. *draco* means "dragon." this constellation can be seen best in july. the phoenix constellation is most visible in november.

APPLY TO WRITING
Advertisement: *Proper Nouns*

You have been hired by a rocket company to promote their tours of the galaxy. Write a radio announcement advertising their latest tour of the Milky Way. Tell people the following:

- what planets they will visit
- what activities they can participate in
- what luxuries will be offered to them

As you write your advertisement, be sure to capitalize any proper nouns that you use.

General Interest **Write correctly each word that should begin with a capital letter. Then write and underline the answer to the trivia question—if you know it.**

1. Who helped dorothy get back to kansas?

2. Who was the first woman to fly solo across the atlantic ocean?

3. who lives on paradise island and has super powers?

4. Who created mickey mouse and donald duck?

5. Who is buried at mount vernon, virginia?

6. Who lives at 1600 pennsylvania avenue in washington, dc?

7. Who was marie antoinette, a queen of france or a queen of england?

8. who won four gold medals at the 1936 olympics, jesse owens or arthur ashe?

9. Who had a horse named silver?

10. Who wrote the declaration of independence, thomas jefferson or john adams?

11. Who receives the cy young award, a baseball player or a football player?

12. who is on the five-dollar bill, george washington or abraham lincoln?

13. who is the cat in the sunday comics who eats too much, garfield or morris?

14. Who gave christopher columbus the money for his voyage to america, italians or spaniards?

15. Who played for the atlanta braves and broke the long-standing record set by babe ruth—hank aaron or sammy sosa?

Other Uses of Capital Letters

Most words you capitalize are proper nouns. There are, however, a few other uses for capital letters.

 Proper Adjectives

Proper adjectives are formed from proper nouns. Since proper nouns begin with capital letters, most proper adjectives also begin with capital letters.

PROPER NOUNS AND ADJECTIVES	
Proper Nouns	**Proper Adjectives**
Egypt	Egyptian pyramids
Russia	Russian music
South America	South American mountains

PRACTICE YOUR SKILLS

 Check Your Understanding
Capitalizing Proper Adjectives

Write the following items, adding capital letters only where needed.

1. british explorers
2. european nations
3. asian history
4. french perfume
5. roman leaders
6. danish farmers
7. japanese imports
8. african plains
9. chinese customs
10. north american rivers

Writing Sentences with Proper Adjectives

Use each of the proper adjectives in sentences.

11. Australian   **12.** English   **13.** Korean

14. American   **15.** Peruvian

Correcting Errors in Capitalization

Rewrite the following paragraph, correcting any errors in capitalization.

foods from around the world can be found in most american grocery stores. the shelves hold greek olives and french bread. in most produce sections, you'll find hawaiian pineapple, and on the spice aisle you'll find indian curries. mexican peppers and foods from south america are available in most stores.

▶ Titles

Certain titles are capitalized to show that they are the particular titles of people or things.

Capitalize the titles of people and works of art.

Titles Used with Names of People

Capitalize a title showing office, rank, or profession when it comes before a person's name. The same title is usually not capitalized when it follows a person's name.

BEFORE A NAME	Can **C**aptain Morris speak to us? (capital letter)
AFTER A NAME	James Morris is a **c**aptain in the Navy. (no capital letter)
BEFORE A NAME	Please welcome **G**overnor **R**eid. (capital letter)
AFTER A NAME	**M**arcus **R**eid was recently elected governor. (no capital letter)

Other titles or their abbreviations—such as Mrs., Rev., and Sgt.—should also be capitalized when they come before a person's name.

I have an appointment with **D**r. Simpson.
Are you **M**rs. O'Reilly?

Titles Used in Direct Address

A noun of **direct address** is used to call someone by name. Capitalize a title used alone, instead of a name, in direct address.

DIRECT ADDRESS	Do you know the governor, **D**octor? Please, **G**overnor, answer a few questions.

If the words *doctor* and *governor* were not being substituted for a name, they would not be capitalized.

NOT DIRECT ADDRESS	I asked the **d**octor if he knew the **g**overnor.
	The **g**overnor answered a few questions.

You can learn more about direct address on page L460.

PRACTICE YOUR SKILLS

● Check Your Understanding
Capitalizing Titles of People

Contemporary Life **Write correctly the words that should be capitalized.**

1. I met colonel Jackson today.

2. He is the brother of my teacher, ms. Smith.

3. Tell us, colonel, where are you stationed?

4. The governor requested that colonel Jackson and sergeant Little be stationed near the capital.

5. Yes, governor Jones and the colonel are old friends.

6. Excuse me, governor, do you know ms. Smith?

7. The governor and my teacher have already met sergeant Little.

8. The governor's wife, mrs. Jones, is a great hostess.

9. She made all the guests and governor jones very comfortable.

10. Thank you, governor and ms. Smith, for an enjoyable visit.

● Connect to the Writing Process: Editing
Correcting Errors in Capitalization

Read the following paragraphs and find the words that should begin with capital letters. Then write the paragraphs correctly.

in the early 1400s, prince henry of portugal wanted a better route to asia. the prince believed it was possible to reach india and china by sailing around africa. at the time no one knew whether he was right.

in 1419, one of the prince's ships reached madeira, a group of islands off the coast of morocco. for the next fifteen years, his sailors refused to go much farther south. they had heard that beyond cape bojador were man-eating monsters.

finally, fifty-four years later, bartholomeu dias, a portuguese sea captain, reached the cape of good hope, the southernmost tip of africa. prince henry's plan had worked.

Titles of Written Works and Other Works of Art

Capitalize the first word, the last word, and all important words in the titles of books, newspapers, magazines, short stories, poems, plays, musical compositions, and other works of art, such as the names of paintings and sculptures.

Do not capitalize a preposition, a coordinating conjunction, or an article (*a, an,* or *the*) unless it is the first or last word in a title.

BOOKS AND CHAPTER TITLES	This test will cover the chapter "**E**urope and the **M**iddle **A**ges" in your textbook *Our World from Past to Present.*
NEWSPAPERS, MAGAZINES	You can read more about that time period in that article from the *New York Daily News* or in the magazine *Discovering Archaeology.*
	(Generally, you do not capitalize *the* as the first word of a newspaper or magazine title.)

SHORT STORIES	Marcia read "**R**aymond's **R**un" by Toni Cade Bambara last week.
POEMS	My cousin Jessica's favorite poem now is "**T**he **S**ecret **H**eart."
MOVIES	Did you ever see the movie *The Sword in the Stone?*
MUSICAL COMPOSITIONS	I like the song "**I**f **E**ver **I** **W**ould **L**eave **Y**ou" from the musical *Camelot.*

You can learn out more about the punctuation of titles on pages L479–L481.

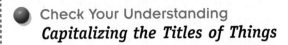

CONNECT TO WRITER'S CRAFT

An important part of your editing should be checking to see that you have included capital letters everywhere they are needed. You should also check to see whether you have used capital letters for some words, such as *moon* and *winter,* that do not need to be capitalized. As you edit your work, refer to the rules and the examples in this chapter, and correct errors when you find them.

PRACTICE YOUR SKILLS

● Check Your Understanding
Capitalizing the Titles of Things

Literature Topic **Write correctly each word that should begin with a capital letter.**

1. Many books, such as *kings and queens of early britain,* discuss the legend of king Arthur.

2. *the mists of avalon* by Marion Zimmer Bradley is a great book based on the same legends.

3. John Steinbeck wrote *the acts of king arthur and his noble knights.*

4. Works of art, such as Howard Pyle's *sir galahad of the grail,* have also been inspired by the legends of king Arthur and Camelot.

5. Movies such as *excalibur* and *first knight* have been based on the stories.

6. The musical *camelot* was a big hit.

7. The songs "how to handle a woman" and "camelot" are featured in the musical.

8. *the idylls of the king,* an epic poem by Alfred, Lord Tennyson, is about king Arthur.

9. Eleanor Fortescue-Brickdale painted a beautiful illustration called *merlin and vivien* for a 1910 edition of Tennyson's poem.

10. A black-and-white illustration called *the passing of arthur* by Florence Harrison depicts king Arthur's death.

● Connect to the Writing Process: Editing
Correcting Errors in Capitalization

Rewrite the following paragraphs, correcting the errors in capitalization.

for centuries the Moon has fascinated people. in 1865, jules verne, who wrote the book *twenty thousand leagues under the sea,* wrote a story about a man walking on the moon. his fantasy became a fact 104 years later.

it was president john f. kennedy who got the space program going in 1961. by 1968, american scientists felt they knew enough about the Moon to send Astronauts there. in december 1968, a spacecraft carried three astronauts ten times around the moon.

then, on july 16, 1969, a spacecraft took off from cape canaveral, florida. on july 20, neil armstrong and edwin aldrin landed on the sea of tranquillity on the moon. they spent over two and a half hours on the surface and collected forty-six pounds of stones and dust. their every move was watched on television by people across the united states and around the world. four days later they returned to Earth, splashing down in the pacific.

Communicate Your Ideas

APPLY TO WRITING

Friendly Letter: *Capital Letters*

The librarian at your school is buying new books for the library. She has asked students to let her know what books they really want. Write a letter to the librarian. Recommend two books that no library should be without. Be sure to write the titles and the author's names. Tell the librarian a little about each book. Be sure to use a friendly letter format and underline or italicize the titles of the books you recommend. After finishing your letter, edit it for any errors in capitalization.

General Interest **Write correctly each word that should begin with a capital letter. Then write and underline the answer to the trivia question—if you know it.**

1. in what movie would you hear the song "somewhere over the rainbow"?

2. what nation once ruled india, england or russia?

3. which planet is closer to Earth, mars or saturn?

4. What is the name of the largest state, california, texas, or alaska?

5. what kind of animal was thumper in the movie *bambi?*

6. what is the capital of ohio, cincinnati or columbus?

7. What was julius caesar's nationality, greek or roman?

8. on what continent would you find mount kilimanjaro, south america or africa?

9. what holiday is celebrated every year on july 4, independence day or labor day?

10. What occurs more often, an eclipse of the moon or an eclipse of the sun?

11. what is the largest country in south america, brazil or argentina?

12. What did general dwight d. eisenhower become in 1953, a senator or a president?

13. The missouri river is the second-longest river in the united states. what is the longest?

14. what language do the people in austria speak, english or german?

15. the congress is made up of the senate and what other legislative body?

Using Capital Letters

Write and capitalize each word that should begin with a capital letter.

1. martin luther king, jr., won the nobel peace prize.
2. can you tell us, professor, how old the sun is?
3. the world trade center in new york city is taller than the eiffel tower in paris, france.
4. in mexico i learned a few words of spanish.
5. the muslims first invaded spain in a.d. 711.
6. all the doctors at our local hospital belong to the american medical association.
7. on june 1, 1954, congress changed the name of armistice day to veterans day.
8. the story "the luck of pokey bloom" was good.
9. the jewish holiday yom kippur is celebrated at the end of september.
10. the giants and the yankees played the last game of that season in candlestick park in san francisco.

Editing for Proper Capitalization

Read the following paragraphs and find the 20 words that should begin with a capital letter. (Do not include words that are already capitalized.) Then write the paragraphs correctly.

In the early 1400s, prince henry of portugal wanted a better route to asia. He believed it was possible to reach india and china by sailing around africa. At the time no one knew whether he was right.

In 1419 one of his ships reached madeira, a group of islands off the coast of morocco. For the next fifteen years, his sailors refused to go much farther south. They had heard that beyond cape bojador were man-eating monsters.

Finally, fifty-four years later, bartholomeu dias, a portuguese sea captain, reached the cape of good hope, the southernmost tip of africa. prince henry's theory had been correct.

Using Capital Letters

Write ten sentences that answer the following questions.

1. On what date (day, month, and year) were you born? (*Put a comma between each item of the date.*)

2. In what town (or city) and state do you live? (*Put a comma between the city and the state.*)

3. What is the name of your favorite sports team or your family's favorite team?

4. What language would you like to learn?

5. What foreign countries would you like to visit some day?

6. What is the name of the most recent movie you have seen? (*Underline or italicize the name of the movie.*)

7. What is the name of a body of water, mountain, or park close to your home?

8. What is your favorite holiday?

9. What is the name of the biggest business in your neighborhood?

10. What is the name and author of a book you would recommend to your classmates? (*Underline or italicize the title of the book.*)

Language and *Self-Expression*

The architect who designed the Kimbell Art Museum intended his work to last for centuries. How do you think this museum will look to visitors one or two centuries from now?

Research a well-known art museum or other public building. Prepare an informative talk on it, giving facts about its history and appearance. Where is it? What is its name? Who built it? Is it associated with any historical events? If you can, display photographs of the building as you give your talk.

Prewriting Begin your research by listing the questions you want to find answers to, each on its own index card. As you find them, write the answers. Arrange the cards in chronological order or in another order that makes sense to you.

Drafting Write a draft of your talk. Begin with a general statement about the building and why it is significant. Then give the details. Begin a paragraph for each type of information.

Revising Have a classmate listen while you read your talk aloud. Find out whether any information needs to be made clearer. Your classmate can also give you feedback on how you deliver your speech.

Editing Make a final formal copy of your talk. Check for errors in punctuation and spelling. Be sure that you have correctly capitalized all proper nouns.

Publishing Use your script to give your talk to your classmates. Then keep a copy of everyone's speeches on file in a binder or file folder.

Another Look

Capitalize the first word of a sentence.

Capitalize the first word in a line of poetry.

Capitalize the first word in the greeting of a letter and the first word in the closing of a letter.

Capitalize the first word of each item in an outline and the letters that begin major subsections of the outline.

Capitalize proper nouns and their abbreviations.

Capitalize the pronoun *I*, both alone and in contractions

Names of persons and animals *(page L407)*
Geographical names *(pages L409-L410)*
Nouns of historical importance *(page L412)*
Specific time periods and events *(pages L412–L413)*
Names of nationalities and races *(page L415)*
Names of religions, religious references, and religious holidays *(page L416)*
Names of groups and businesses *(pages L418–L419)*
Names of planets, stars, constellations, and galaxies *(page L419)*
Languages and specific school courses *(page L419)*
Awards, brand names, buildings, monuments and memorials, technological terms, and vehicles *(page L420)*

Other Information About Capital Letters

Using abbreviations *(page L427)*
Using hyphenated numbers in street names *(page L409)*
Distinguishing between common nouns and proper nouns *(page L407)*
Capitalizing proper adjectives *(page L425)*
Capitalizing titles *(page L426–L430)*

Posttest

Directions
Write the letter of the word or group of words that corrects the error in capitalization in one of the underlined phrases. One or more sentences may not contain any errors.

EXAMPLE
1. Many <u>japanese people</u> immigrated to the <u>Hawaiian Islands</u>.

    1 A Japanese People
       B Japanese people
       C Hawaiian islands
       D No error

ANSWER
    1 B

1. In 1780 <u>the West Indies</u> was hit by a gale that went down in history as <u>"the great hurricane."</u>

2. The scientists took photographs of <u>the floor of the Atlantic Ocean</u> from inside <u>the *alvin*</u>.

3. <u>The buddha</u> was a great religious teacher in <u>eastern Asia</u>.

4. Please pass <u>the Christmas plum pudding</u> to <u>uncle Bob</u>.

5. We sat with <u>Eric's sister Kelsey</u> and watched <u>the Harlem globetrotters</u> play basketball.

6. The <u>battle of the Bulge</u> was a famous <u>World War II battle</u>.

7. Did you buy that <u>Irish fisherman's sweater</u> at <u>Bailey Brothers</u>?

8. Astronomers using the <u>Hubble Space Telescope</u> found evidence of oxygen on <u>Jupiter's Moon Europa</u>.

9. I have signed up for <u>Math I</u> and classes in <u>art and spanish</u>.

10. Five of the members of <u>our scout troop</u> have been to <u>the Kern Historical museum</u>.

1 A the west Indies
  B The Great Hurricane
  C the Great Hurricane
  D No error

2 A the Floor of the Atlantic Ocean
  B the *Alvin*
  C the floor of the Atlantic ocean
  D No error

3 A The Buddha
  B Eastern Asia
  C eastern asia
  D No error

4 A the christmas plum pudding
  B Uncle Bob
  C the Christmas Plum Pudding
  D No error

5 A Eric's Sister Kelsey
  B The Harlem Globetrotters
  C the Harlem Globetrotters
  D No error

6 A World War II Battle
  B world war II battle
  C Battle of the Bulge
  D No error

7 A Bailey brothers
  B Irish Fisherman's sweater
  C irish fisherman's sweater
  D No error

8 A Jupitor's moon Europa
  B Hubble space telescope
  C Jupiter's moon europa
  D No error

9 A Art and Spanish
  B art and Spanish
  C math I
  D No error

10 A our Scout Troop
  B the Kern historical museum
  C the Kern Historical Museum
  D No error

CHAPTER 13

End Marks and Commas

 **Pretest**

Directions
Write the letter of the group of words that shows how to correctly write the underlined words in each sentence.

EXAMPLE   <u>After dinner last night I wrote</u> to my
                                    (1)
friend Nick.

    1 A After dinner last night I wrote
      B After dinner, last night I wrote
      C After dinner last night, I wrote
      D After dinner, last night, I wrote

ANSWER   **1 C**

<u>Well I have just been much too busy</u> with school to
                        (1)
write sooner. Did I tell you about <u>my research paper</u>
                                                              (2)
<u>Nick</u> I chose <u>the Civil War period and hoped to find</u>
                                        (3)
someone unusual to write about. I found an <u>unusual</u>

<u>subject Mary Edwards Walker</u>. <u>At the Syracuse Medical</u>
          (4)   (5)
<u>College of New York she</u> studied medicine and got her

degree in 1855.

1
A Well, I have just been much, too busy
B Well, I have just been much too busy
C Well I have just been much, too busy
D Well I have just been much too busy

2
A my research paper, Nick.
B my research paper Nick.
C my research paper, Nick?
D my research paper Nick?

3
A the Civil War period and hoped to find
B the Civil War period, and hoped to find
C the Civil. War. period and hoped to find
D the Civil. War. period, and hoped to find

4
A unusual subject Mary Edwards Walker.
B unusual, subject, Mary Edwards Walker.
C unusual subject, Mary, Edwards Walker.
D unusual subject, Mary Edwards Walker.

5
A At the Syracuse Medical College of New York she
B At the Syracuse Medical College of New York, she
C At the Syracuse Medical College, of New York she
D At the Syracuse Medical College, of New York, she

Ynez Johnston. *Dark Jungle,* 1950.
Casein on cardboard, 23 ⅞ by 18 ½ inches. The Museum of Modern Art, New York.

Describe What objects does Ynez Johnston include in this painting? What colors does she use?

Analyze The picture contains many small details. How did the artist give the small details unity?

Interpret Why might the artist have named the picture *Dark Jungle?*

Judge Do you think a poet could paint a better picture with words? Why do you think as you do?

At the end of the chapter, you will use this artwork to stimulate ideas for writing.

End Marks

There are four different kinds of sentences. Each one has a different purpose. The purpose of a sentence determines its end mark.

Place a **period** after a statement, after an opinion, and after a command or request made in a normal tone of voice.

PERIODS

I am cooking dinner.

(statement)

I am a great cook.

(opinion)

Hand me that mixing bowl.

(command)

Place a **question mark** after a sentence that asks a question.

QUESTION MARK   Have you eaten meat loaf before?

Place an **exclamation point** after a sentence that states a strong feeling and after a command or request that expresses great excitement.

EXCLAMATION POINTS

Yikes, I just dropped the meatloaf on the floor!

(a sentence that expresses strong feeling)

Don't burn yourself!

(a command said with great excitement)

You can learn about end marks with direct quotations on pages L490–L491.

PRACTICE YOUR SKILLS

● Check Your Understanding
Using End Marks

Contemporary Life	**Write the correct end mark for each sentence.**

1. Tonight I'm cooking dinner for my family
2. Where's a baking pan, Mom
3. Peel the potatoes for me, Jon
4. Turn the oven on for me, Liz
5. I'm making meat loaf
6. The temperature is much too high
7. How long should the meat loaf cook
8. Dinner will be ready in thirty minutes
9. Dad, will you please cut the meat loaf
10. What a great meal this is

● Connect to the Writing Process: Editing
Correcting End Marks

Rewrite the sentences that have the wrong end mark, adding the correct one. If a sentence ends with the correct mark, write C.

11. Do you know how to spell that word!
12. Look it up in the dictionary?
13. That dictionary with the blue cover is the best.
14. Can you find the word.
15. Bring it to me.
16. Don't drop it?
17. Wow, it is a heavy book!
18. Did you know that you can find abbreviations in the dictionary.

19. Look at this?

20. I like this dictionary?

APPLY TO WRITING
Narrative Paragraph: *End Marks*

William Wegman. *Cinderella,* 1992.
Unique Polacolor ER photograph, 20 by 24
inches. ©William Wegman. From the book
Cinderella. Hyperion Books for Children,
New York, New York, 1993.

William Wegman is famous for his whimsical photographs of his dogs. He sometimes photographs the
Weimaraners without costumes, but he often dresses
them, as in this photograph. Imagine what this dog's
thoughts might be. For your teacher, write a narrative
paragraph from the dog's point of view. What are you,
as the dog, thinking? How do you feel? Use at least
one question mark and one exclamation point in your
paragraph. Be sure that all of the sentences in your
paragraph end with appropriate punctuation.

▶ Other Uses of Periods

Periods have other uses besides ending a sentence.

Periods with Abbreviations

Abbreviations are shortened forms of words. You can use abbreviations for notes and E-mail messages, but most abbreviations should not be used in formal writing, such as short stories or reports.

Use a period with most abbreviations.

The following list gives some common abbreviations. Notice that many abbreviations begin with capital letters. For the spelling and punctuation of other abbreviations, look in a dictionary. Most dictionaries have a special section that lists abbreviations.

COMMON ABBREVIATIONS	
DAYS	Sun., Mon., Tues., Wed., Thur., Fri., Sat.
MONTHS	Jan., Feb., Mar., Apr., Aug., Sept., Oct., Nov., Dec. (Other months are not abbreviated.)
ADDRESSES	Ave., Blvd., Dr., Hwy., Pl., Rd., Rt., Ln.
TITLES WITH NAMES	Mr., Mrs., Ms., Dr., Rev., Gov., Gen., Lt., Capt., Sgt., Jr., Sr.
INITIALS WITH NAMES	R. M. Jones, D. W. Griffith, Gerald R. Ford (Initials are also followed by periods.)
TIME WITH NUMBERS	55 B.C. (before Christ) A.D. 1066 (anno Domini—in the year of the Lord)

5:30 A.M. (*ante meridiem*—before noon)
9:45 P.M. (*post meridiem*—after noon)
(A colon [:] goes between the hours and the
minutes when time is written in numbers.)

COMPANIES   Assoc., Co., Corp., Dept., Inc.

Some organizations and companies are known by abbreviations that stand for their full names. The majority of these abbreviations do not use periods. A few other common abbreviations also do not include periods.

ABBREVIATIONS WITHOUT PERIODS

FBI = Federal Bureau of Investigation
UN = United Nations
E-mail = electronic mail
km = kilometer

Most people today use the post office's two-letter state abbreviations. These abbreviations do not include periods. A list of these abbreviations can be found in the front of most telephone books. The following are a few examples.

STATE ABBREVIATIONS

AK = Alaska	MI = Michigan	OR = Oregon
CA = California	NV = Nevada	TX = Texas
FL = Florida	NJ = New Jersey	VA = Virginia

If a sentence ends with an abbreviation that ends in a period, only one period is used. It serves as the period for the abbreviation and as the end mark for the sentence.

We will eat breakfast at 7:30 A.M.

Periods with Outlines

Periods are needed in outlines.

Use a period after each number or letter that shows a division in an outline.

I. Summer Foods
  A. Salads
    1. Caesar Salad
    2. Garden Salad
  B. Sandwiches

II. Winter Foods

PRACTICE YOUR SKILLS

● Check Your Understanding
Using End Marks with Abbreviations

Write the abbreviations that stand for the following items. Use a dictionary if you are not sure of an abbreviation.

1. Tuesday
2. Mister
3. before Christ
4. Street
5. Doctor
6. Captain
7. Avenue
8. after noon
9. December
10. Junior

● Connect to the Writing Process: Editing
Using End Marks

Rewrite the following outline, adding periods where needed.

I Language Arts
  A Reading
    1 Pocket dictionary
    2 Library book

B Writing
   1 Loose-leaf paper
   2 Writing utensils
     a Two pencils with erasers
     b Two pens with blue or black ink
     c One pen with red ink

II Math
  A Geometry
    1 Compass
    2 Protractor
  B Algebra
    1 Graph paper
    2 Calculator

III Science
  A Lab work
    1 Safety goggles
    2 Gloves
    3 Smock or apron
  B Seat work
    1 Loose-leaf paper
    2 Pen with blue or black ink

Communicate Your Ideas

APPLY TO WRITING

Invitation: *Periods with Abbreviations*

You are throwing a surprise birthday party for your favorite teacher. Make an invitation to send to your guests. Include all the important information on your invitation: where, when, why, and for whom the party is being given. You may wish to decorate your invitation with drawings. As you write the invitation, be certain to punctuate appropriately any abbreviations you use.

Commas That Separate

A comma (,) creates a slight pause in a sentence. Commas are often used to separate words and even some sentences from running together and causing confusion.

▶ Items in a Series

A series is three or more similar words or groups of words listed one after another. Commas are used to separate the items in a series.

Use commas to separate items in a series.

WORDS	We saw photographs of lions, giraffes, and zebras. (nouns)
	The elephants ran, stomped, and walked. (verbs)
	The zoo was fun, exciting, and educational. (adjectives)
GROUPS OF WORDS	We walked through the zoo, looked at the animals, and ate lunch. (complete predicates)
	Many animals live around swamps, on top of mountains, and in the deserts. (prepositional phrases)

CONNECT TO WRITER'S CRAFT

Commas work like caution lights. They slow readers down and prevent "accidents" of misunderstanding. Always edit your work for the correct use of commas. Make sure that you have included all necessary commas, but also eliminate any unnecessary commas.

PRACTICE YOUR SKILLS

● Check Your Understanding
Using Commas in a Series

General Interest | **If the sentence is punctuated correctly, write C. If the sentence is punctuated incorrectly, write I.**

1. You can learn much about animals birds, and sea life at the zoo.

2. Snow leopards, pumas, and lynxes, often live high in the mountains.

3. Wild cats and domestic cats share many traits.

4. Emus eat berries, and insects.

5. Emus are large, flightless, and feathery birds.

6. One of the most interesting beautiful and playful animals is the otter.

7. Otters live in the water on the shore, and in underground dens.

8. A giant otter in the wild will eat up to ten pounds of fish and, crabs a day.

9. The Eastern diamondback rattlesnake lives in Georgia, Florida, and Louisiana.

10. These snakes slither swim, and coil.

11. The aardvark is a strange, and intriguing animal.

12. You can find aardvarks in Africa's grassy plains, woodlands bush, or savanna.

13. Dolphins breathe air nurse their young and communicate vocally.

14. Large brains and, great intelligence, are characteristics of dolphins.

15. Dolphins use their flukes, dorsal fin, and pectoral fins to swim.

16.–25. **Rewrite the incorrect sentences from the preceding exercise, using commas correctly.**

● Connect to the Writing Process: Drafting
Writing Sentences with Items in a Series

Write five sentences that follow the directions. Use commas where necessary.

26. with a series of three nouns as the subject

27. with a series of three complete predicates

28. with a series of three adjectives

29. with a series of three verbs

30. with a series of three prepositional phrases

● Compound Sentences

A compound sentence is two or more simple sentences usually joined by the coordinating conjunction *and, but,* or *or.* A comma usually comes before the conjunction.

Use a comma before a coordinating conjunction that joins the parts of a compound sentence.

I like potatoes with my dinner, but she prefers rice with hers.

We can eat lunch at home, or I can buy our dinner at a café.

Do not confuse a compound sentence with a simple sentence that has a compound verb.

COMPOUND SENTENCE	Mom cooked the meal, and Dad washed the dishes.
	(A comma is needed.)
COMPOUND VERB	Mom cooked the meal and washed the dishes afterward.
	(A comma is not needed.)

One way to correct a run-on sentence is to use comma and a conjunction.

You can learn about run-on sentences and other ways to correct them on pages L215–L216.

CONNECT TO WRITER'S CRAFT

When you write, remember that two closely related simple sentences can be combined into a compound sentence. Variety in the length of sentences is a key ingredient to an interesting piece of writing.

Shawna peeled potatoes.

Dave cut up some celery.

Shawna peeled potatoes, and Dave cut up some celery.

You can learn more about compound sentences on pages L208–L209.

PRACTICE YOUR SKILLS

● Check Your Understanding
Using Commas with Compound Sentences

General Interest **If the sentence is punctuated correctly, write C. If it is incorrect, write I.**

1. Orange juice is the most popular fruit juice in the United States and, prune juice is the least popular.

2. Watermelon is considered one of America's favorite fruits but China is the world's top producer of watermelons.

3. Good quality cucumbers are dark green, and firm in texture.

4. People on vacation usually eat lots of fast food, but fruits, and vegetables are just as convenient.

5. Carrots keep well outside of the refrigerator, or they can be kept in a cooler.

6. Many people eat carrots and drink the juice of that vegetable.

7. Each American eats about 120 pounds of potatoes a year, and, potatoes are popular around the globe as well.

8. Potatoes are the most popular vegetable in the United States, and lettuce is the second.

9. People bake, and fry potatoes.

10. Red apples taste sweet but Granny Smith apples are firm and tart.

11. You can eat apples raw or, you can bake them with cinnamon and sugar.

12. The world's largest apple weighed over three pounds and was picked in Caro, Michigan.

13. Each day people should eat five different fruits, and vegetables and they will be healthier.

14. Tomatoes have lots of vitamin C and are related to peppers.

15. Tomatoes are not vegetables but they are fruits.

● Connect to the Writing Process: Editing
Correcting Comma Errors

16.–25. Rewrite the incorrect sentences from the preceding exercise, using commas correctly.

Combine each pair of simple sentences into a compound sentence. Remember to add a comma and a conjunction.

26. Strawberries are loaded with vitamin C Cherries are a good source of fiber.

27. Cherries and strawberries are members of the rose family But blueberries are members of the heath family.

28. Raspberries are extremely delicate You should take care when washing them.

29. Cranberries are harvested in the fall That is why we serve them at holiday meals.

30. Blackberries are very nutritious They are great in pies and cobblers.

▶ Introductory Words and Phrases

When certain words or certain prepositional phrases come at the beginning of a sentence, a comma is used to separate them from the rest of the sentence.

Use a comma after certain introductory elements.

Usually a comma follows words such as *no, oh, well,* and *yes* when they begin a sentence. When these words come at the beginning of a sentence, they are usually being used as interjections.

WORDS **Yes,** I know quite a lot about health.
Oh, it's all very interesting.

You can learn more about interjections on page L159.

A comma follows a prepositional phrase of four or more words when it comes at the beginning of a sentence. A comma also follows two or more prepositional phrases that come together at the beginning of a sentence.

PREPOSITIONAL PHRASES	**On the can's label**, you will find nutritional information.
	(one prepositional phrase with four words)
	At each meal of the day, you should eat a balance of foods.
	(two prepositional phrases)

You can learn more about prepositional phrases on pages L177–L185.

PRACTICE YOUR SKILLS

● Check Your Understanding
Using Commas with Introductory Words and Phrases

Science Topic **If the sentence is punctuated correctly, write C. If it is incorrect, write I.**

1. Well the heart pumps two thousand gallons of blood each day.

2. During the first six months of life, a baby's brain doubles in size.

3. With one normal breath you take in a pint of air.

4. In a lifetime, the average person will eat about six thousand pounds of food.

5. In the average adult human, there are ten pints of blood.

6. Yes blood travels from the heart to the lungs and throughout the body.

7. In the human body there are more than two hundred bones.

8. Wow, your blood circulates through your kidneys twenty times each hour!

9. With a total of eight bones, the cranium encloses and protects the brain.

10. Yes, the purpose of the nervous system is to control actions and thoughts.

11. Did you know, that 14 percent of your weight is bone?

12. In our skeletal system we produce blood cells and store certain minerals.

13. Oh the cartilage cushions long bones against shock.

14. During one week, you should exercise at least three times.

15. Well a healthy body requires sleep and regular exercise.

● Connect to the Writing Process: Editing
Correcting Comma Errors

16.–25. Rewrite the incorrect sentences from the preceding exercise, using commas correctly.

● Connect to the Writing Process: Drafting
Writing Sentences with Introductory Phrases

Write five sentences that follow the directions.

26. begin with *yes*

27. begin with *in an hour*

28. begin with *during last night's basketball game*

29. begin with *no*

30. begin with *before the beginning of the game*

APPLY TO WRITING

Explanatory Paragraph: *Commas*

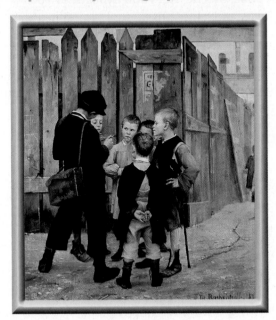

Marie Bashkirtseff. *The Meeting*, 1884. Oil on canvas, 74¹⁵/₁₆ by 68¹⁵/₁₆ inches. Musée d'Orsay, Paris, France.

Look closely at the details of Marie Bashkirtseff's painting *The Meeting*. Look at the setting, the way the boys are dressed, and the colors in the painting. Imagine that you are the tall boy whose back you see. Write a paragraph for your teacher in which you explain the following:

- What is happening in the painting?
- What has brought all of you together?
- What will happen after this scene?

In your narrative, use at least one introductory prepositional phrase, one compound sentence, and one series of words. Use commas as needed.

General Interest **Rewrite the following sentences, adding punctuation as needed.**

1. Well I'm going to tell you about contests

2. Who runs the fastest and who jumps the highest

3. Yes people have contests to answer these questions

4. Throughout history people have competed in contests of many kinds

5. People in ancient Greece held the Olympic Games and children in ancient Rome held tugs-of-war

6. Before the European discovery of America Native Americans competed in ball games and footraces

7. Today many contests are serious tests of athletic abilities but some are just for fun

8. People race their pet crabs worms and turkeys

9. Others race down a street and flip pancakes

10. Yes some even slide down ski slopes on inner tubes

11. Every year people in New Mexico hold the world's largest hot air balloon contest

12. Hundreds of balloonists compete

13. One silly race is held in Canada

14. Off Vancouver Island contestants cross the Strait of Georgia in power-driven bathtubs

15. This annual race began in 1925

16. No this is not a joke

17. The contestants mount fiberglass bathtubs on water skis and add motors

18. Since the race in 1981 safety has become an issue

19. In that year the waves were ten feet high

20. Well does that sound like fun to you

Other Uses of Commas

In the last section, you saw that commas eliminate confusion by separating different words or groups of words in a sentence. Commas also *enclose* some words and groups of words. When commas enclose a word, for example, one comma goes before it, and one comma goes after it. Commas usually enclose words or groups of words that interrupt the flow or meaning of a sentence.

Direct Address

When you talk or call to someone, you sometimes call that person by name. Such a name is called a noun of **direct address.** Nouns of direct address are a good example of a word or group of words that interrupts a sentence. Since they interrupt a sentence, they should be enclosed in commas. One comma should be placed before the noun of direct address, and one comma should be placed after it.

Use a comma or commas to separate a noun of direct address from the rest of a sentence.

Tonight, **Tiffany,** you will wash the dishes.

(Notice that the name *Tiffany* interrupts the sentence *Tonight you will wash the dishes.* A comma goes before and after *Tiffany.*)

In the following examples, only one comma is needed because the noun of direct address comes at the beginning or the end of the sentence.

Steve, take out the trash.
Are you going to cook dinner, **Dad**?

PRACTICE YOUR SKILLS

● Check Your Understanding
Using Commas with Direct Address

Contemporary Life **If the sentence is punctuated correctly, write C. If it is incorrectly punctuated, write I.**

1. Please Mom, let me help with dinner.

2. After dinner, Tiffany, Dr. Miller and his family are dropping by.

3. It's time to eat Steve.

4. Would you call Dad to the table?

5. That was a great dinner, Mom.

6. Dr. Miller, and his family are here.

7. Doctor please come in.

8. Tiffany you look like you've grown!

9. I'm in sixth grade now Dr. Miller.

10. May I take your coat, Mrs. Miller?

11. The truth is, Steve I feel rather chilly.

12. Could you build a fire in the fireplace Dad?

13. It's a perfect night, Dad, for a fire.

14. I'll get the coffee and dessert Mom.

15. Now Tiffany, be careful with that tray.

16. Steve would you please clear the table?

17. Later, Tiffany, I would like you to do the dishes.

18. Dad can I put another log on the fire?

● Connect to the Writing Process: Editing
Correcting Comma Errors

19.–30. Rewrite the incorrect sentences from the preceding exercise, using commas correctly.

Write sentences that follow the directions.

31.–32. Begin two sentences with nouns of direct address.

33.–34. Use a noun of direct address to interrupt two sentences.

35. End one sentence with a noun of direct address.

▶ Appositives

Like a noun of direct address, an appositive also interrupts a sentence. An **appositive** is a word or group of words that renames or explains a noun or a pronoun in a sentence. An appositive usually comes immediately after the word it renames or explains. Although appositives can be one word, they usually are written with modifiers. Since they interrupt a sentence, they also should be enclosed in commas.

Two Commas	Felipe**, a new student in my class,** is from Peru.
	(The appositive, *a new student in my class,* renames *Felipe.* Notice that one comma is placed before the appositive, and one comma is placed after it.)

In the following example, only one comma is needed because the appositive comes at the end of the sentence.

One Comma	Have you ever been to Lima**, the capital of Peru?**
	(*The capital of Peru* renames *Lima.*)

● Check Your Understanding

Using Commas with Appositives

Geography Topic | **If the sentence is punctuated correctly, write C. If it is incorrect, write I.**

1. Peru, a country in South America, has a population of over two million people.

2. Spanish, the main language is spoken throughout Peru.

3. Among the oldest, domesticated, animals is the llama.

4. The llama a member of the camelid family thrives in the Andes Mountains.

5. Llamas need to be sheared once a year or every other year.

6. The Andes Mountains stretch through Peru, and four other South American countries.

7. Copper a beautiful metal is abundant in the Andes.

8. The ancient, Inca, made their home in these mountains.

9. Francisco Pizarro, a Spanish conquistador, destroyed the Inca empire.

10. Machu Picchu an ancient Inca city, is high in the Andes Mountains.

11. Hiram Bingham, an American explorer discovered the ruins of Machu Picchu in 1911.

12. Natural disaster, a major earthquake, killed 50,000 people in Peru in 1970.

13. Peru's chief commercial crops sugar cane, and cotton, are sold to other countries.

14. Lima the largest city in Peru, is its cultural center.

15. The University of San Marcos in Lima is one of South America's best colleges.

● Connect to the Writing Process: Editing
Correcting Comma Errors

16.–25. Rewrite the incorrect sentences from the preceding exercise, using commas correctly.

Communicate Your Ideas

APPLY TO WRITING

Restaurant Review: *Appositives*

Your class is helping to put together a guide to local restaurants for newcomers to the community. You have been asked to write a review of your favorite restaurant. It can be any type of restaurant. In your review explain the types of food you can get there and why other people should try it. Use at least three of the following appositive phrases in your review.

- my favorite food
- a delicious dessert
- a perfect snack
- a tasty soft drink
- the best place to eat

▶ Commonly Used Commas

The examples on the following pages show the most common uses of commas.

Commas Used with Dates and Addresses

Commas between the parts of a date or an address are probably the most often used commas.

Use commas to separate elements in dates and addresses.

Notice in the following examples that when a date or an address comes within a sentence, another comma goes at the end to separate it from the rest of the sentence.

DATES
Born on Thursday, June 10, 1982, Tara Lipinski became in 1998 the youngest woman to win a gold medal for figure skating.

(No comma goes between the month and day, but a comma does go after the year to separate the date from the rest of the sentence.)

ADDRESSES
Write to the Colorado Springs Olympic Training Center, One Olympic Plaza, Colorado Springs, CO 80909, to find out about training for the Olympics.

(No comma goes between the state and the ZIP code, but a comma does go after the ZIP code to separate it from the rest of the sentence.)

The gymnast began her training in Baltimore, Maryland, but moved to a larger facility in Houston, Texas.

(Even without a ZIP code, the city and state are separated from the rest of the sentence with a comma.)

Commas Used in Letters

Use a comma after the salutation of a friendly letter and after the closing of all letters.

SALUTATIONS AND CLOSINGS	
SALUTATIONS	Dear Mom, Dear Mr. Jenkins,
CLOSINGS	Love, Your friend, Sincerely, Thank you,

You can learn about commas used with direct quotations on pages L488–L489.

PRACTICE YOUR SKILLS

● Check Your Understanding
Using Commas

General Interest

Note that none of the following sentences have commas. Write _C_ if a sentence is correct without commas. Write _I_ if it is incorrect without commas.

1. Many young people across the globe have accomplished great feats.

2. An eighteen-year-old boy set the world record for situps on December 19 1977.

3. An eleven-year-old boy became the organist at Leeds Cathedral in West Yorkshire England.

4. The youngest golfer to shoot a hole-in-one was five-year-old Cory Orr of Littleton Colorado.

5. Thirteen-year-old LeAnn Rimes recorded the hit *Blue* in Nashville.

6. Twelve-year-old Gertrude Ederle broke the women's 880-yard freestyle swimming world record in Indianapolis Indiana.

7. Gertrude was born on October 23 1906.

8. Ginetta La Bianca was born on May 12 1934.

9. She was born in Buffalo New York and became at age fifteen the youngest opera singer.

10. Tutankhamun ruled ancient Egypt as a teenager.

11. His tomb was discovered by Howard Carter in 1922.

12. A fifteen-year-old boy from Ontario Canada built a house of cards thirty-nine stories high!

13. On August 17 1974 a thirteen-year-old girl swam the English Channel.

14. An eight-year-old boy rode his bicycle from San Francisco California to Atlantic City New Jersey.

15. You can do amazing things when you set your mind to it!

● Connect to the Writing Process: Editing
Correcting Comma Errors

16.–25. Rewrite the incorrect sentences from the preceding exercise, adding commas where needed.

Communicate Your Ideas

APPLY TO WRITING

Friendly Letter: *Commas*

Your class is planning a special exhibition of all of the students' best work, regardless of the class subject. Write a letter to someone special, inviting him or her to attend the event. Include a time and date and the address of your school in the letter. After finishing, be sure to edit for proper comma use.

Contemporary Life

Rewrite the following letter, adding commas where necessary.

Dear Aunt Janet

On Sunday October 3 2000 at 8:00 P.M. Mom gave birth to a baby boy. You should see him Aunt Janet! He's so tiny and cute.

Of course I haven't seen him in person since I'm at summer camp with my best friend Melanie. Please write to me here. The address is Camp Sunrise 160 Linder Lane Collegeville Pennsylvania 19426.

Love

Kaitlyn

QuickCheck Mixed Practice

Science Topic

Rewrite the following paragraphs, correcting any punctuation errors.

Listen Ms Jackson to this interesting article The highest jumpers in the world are not people They are kangaroos One kangaroo jumped 10½ feet but the best human jumpers can only jump about 7 feet Can you believe that

Kangaroos are also very fast Some people in Sydney Australia once held a race On May 6 1927 a kangaroo raced against a horse The kangaroo won

In the wild in Australia kangaroos travel in groups called mobs Usually a mob of kangaroos includes one large male his mates and several younger animals Yes it's true With its front paws the leader of the mob boxes with other male kangaroos

Adult kangaroos are about $4\frac{1}{2}$ feet tall but their tails are $3\frac{1}{2}$ feet long They weigh about 155 pounds Kangaroos grow during their entire lives Oh the oldest kangaroos must be big ones

Kangaroos eat grasses small bushes and other green plants Here's one other interesting fact Ms. Jackson In at least one way kangaroos are like camels For long periods of time they can go without water

Did you know that the mother Kangaroo carries her baby around in a pouch The joey the name for the kangaroo baby completes its development in its mother's pouch After several months the joey will be able to live on its own.

Using Commas Correctly

Write each sentence, adding a comma or commas where needed. If a sentence is correct, write C.

1. Sheep elephants and camels snore loudly.
2. My sister and her family live in Wichita Kansas.
3. Oh we should wait for Rosa.
4. In the last 70 years the earth's population has tripled.
5. The tiger sprang to its feet and chased the antelope.
6. My grandparents immigrants from Poland settled here in 1936.
7. We could boil bake or mash the potatoes.
8. The library James is straight down the hall.
9. The Rose Bowl Game is held in Pasadena and the Sugar Bowl Game is held in New Orleans.
10. Columbus first sighted land on October 11 1492.

Using End Marks Correctly

Write each sentence, adding the necessary end mark. If a sentence is correct, write C.

1. On the day after tomorrow, our vacation begins
2. Well, don't you look nice today
3. Is it nine o'clock yet, Mom
4. The restaurant serves oysters and lobsters
5. In the park a mime was performing.
6. Santa Fe, New Mexico, receives an average of seventeen inches more snow each year than Fairbanks, Alaska
7. Pour soup into a pan and heat

8. On June 12, 1995, my older sister was married

9. The Death Cup, a mushroom found in Oregon, is poisonous

10. Is a baby kangaroo called a joey

Editing for the Correct Use of Commas

Find the 10 places where commas are missing. Then rewrite the paragraphs, adding the commas.

Bryan Allen of Bakersfield California did something that no one else had ever done. On June 12 1979 he pedaled across the English Channel. For nearly three hours he pumped the pedals that turned the propeller of a small aircraft the *Gossamer Albatross*. The aircraft had no engine and Allen's muscles were its only source of energy.

The *Gossamer Albatross* looked like a bicycle inside a thin shell. It had a propeller in the back a small control wing in the front and one very long wing overhead. Yes Allen's flight was the longest human-powered flight in history.

Using Commas

Write ten sentences that follow the directions below.

Write a sentence that...

1. includes a series of nouns.

2. has two sentences joined by a coordinating conjunction.

3. includes a prepositional phrase at the beginning.

4. includes a noun of direct address at the end.

5. includes a noun of direct address at the beginning.

6. includes a noun of direct address in the middle.

7. includes an appositive at the end.

8. includes an appositive in the middle.

9. includes the day, month, and year of your birth.

10. includes your street number and name, city, state, and ZIP code.

Language and *Self-Expression*

Ynez Johnston's artwork is very imaginative. In *Dark Jungle* she has painted in a style similar to that found in early African art. Her painting also has the look of a woven tapestry.

Think about the images the artist might have stored in her memory before bringing them together. What kind of poem might you write to describe this picture? What mood would you choose? Write a poem inspired by *Dark Jungle*. Your poem does not have to rhyme. Include a question, an appositive, and words or phrases in a series of three.

Prewriting On small cards write words and phrases that describe the features of *Dark Jungle*. Use your cards to make a sequence chart.

Drafting Use your notes and chart to write your poem. Your first lines should give a tantalizing overall view of your subject. If you need to, use a thesaurus to find just the right descriptive words.

Revising Read your poem aloud twice to a classmate. The first time ask your classmate to listen to how the poem sounds. Should you make changes to the rhythm? The second time ask your classmate to visualize the poem. Should your descriptions be clearer?

Editing Check your poem for errors in punctuation and spelling.

Publishing Read your poem aloud, or tape it and play the tape for classmates. Have your audience compare your poem and *Dark Jungle*.

Another Look

End Marks and Commas

Place a period after a statement, after an opinion, and after a command or request made in a normal tone of voice. *(page L443)*

Place a question mark after a sentence that asks a question. *(page L443)*

Place an exclamation point after a sentence that states a strong feeling and after a command or request that expresses great excitement. *(page L443)*

Use a period with most abbreviations. *(pages L446–L447)*

Use a period after each number or letter that shows a division in an outline. *(page L448)*

Use commas to separate items in a series. *(page L450)*

Use a comma before a coordinating conjunction that joins the parts of a compound sentence. *(pages L452–L453)*

Use a comma after certain introductory elements. *(pages L455–L456)*

Use a comma or commas to separate a noun of direct address from the rest of a sentence. *(page L460)*

Use a comma or commas to separate an appositive from the rest of the sentence. *(page L462)*

Use commas to separate the elements in dates and addresses. *(page L465)*

Use a comma after the salutation of a friendly letter and after the closing of all letters. *(page L466)*

Other Information About End Marks and Commas

Recognizing common abbreviations *(pages L446–L447)*

Abbreviations without periods *(page L447)*

State abbreviations *(page L447)*

Writing compound sentences with coordinating conjunctions *(pages L452–L453)*

Using commas with prepositional phrases *(pages L455–L456)*

Directions
Write the letter of the group of words that shows how to correctly write the underlined words in each sentence.

EXAMPLE   My cousin Hannah lives <u>in Indianapolis</u>
                                                            (1)
           <u>Indiana</u> on Park Avenue.
    1 A in Indianapolis Indiana.
       B in Indianapolis, Indiana,
       C in Indianapolis, Indiana
       D in Indianapolis Indiana

ANSWER   **1 B**

<u>Dear Cousin Hannah</u>
        (1)
    You are not going to believe <u>my amazing news and I can</u>
                                                        (2)
<u>hardly believe it myself</u> <u>July 8 2000 is definitely a day</u> that is
                                            (3)
going to go down in my personal history. I heard the phone

ring at about <u>7:30 PM and almost didn't answer it</u>. <u>Mom Dad</u>
                        (4)   (5)
<u>and Brian were out shopping</u> and I was busy with my

homework.

1 **A** Dear Cousin Hannah,
   B Dear Cousin Hannah:
   C Dear cousin Hannah
   D Dear cousin Hannah.

2 **A** my amazing news
         and I can hardly
         believe it myself.
   B my amazing news
         and, I can hardly
         believe it myself.
   C my amazing news,
         and I can hardly
         believe it myself.
   D my amazing news.
         and I can hardly
         believe it myself.

3 **A** July 8 2000 is
         definitely a day
   B July 8, 2000, is
         definitely a day
   C July 8 2000, is
         definitely a day
   D July 8, 2000 is
         definitely a day

4 **A** ring at about 7:30
         P.M., and almost
         didn't answer it.
   B ring at about 7:30
         P.M. and almost
         didn't answer it.
   C ring at about 7:30
         P.M, and almost
         didn't answer it.
   D ring at about 7:30
         PM, and almost
         didn't answer it.

5 **A** Mom Dad and Brian
         were out shopping,
   B Mom, Dad, and
         Brian were out
         shopping
   C Mom Dad, and Brian
         were out shopping,
   D Mom, Dad, and
         Brian were out
         shopping,

CHAPTER 14

Italics and Quotation Marks

Directions

Write the letter of the group of words that correctly rewrites the underlined portion of each sentence.

EXAMPLE

1. Have you read the book <u>A Tribe for Lexi</u>

1 A *A Tribe for Lexi.*
 B "A Tribe for Lexi"?
 C "A Tribe for Lexi."
 D *A Tribe for Lexi?*

ANSWER **1 D**

1. "This is a great <u>anthology exclaimed Dustin</u>.

2. O. Henry's short story <u>The Ransom of Red Chief</u> is hilarious.

3. We read the poem <u>The Indians Come Down from Mixco</u>.

4. Langston Hughes's poems were in a collection <u>called Shakespeare in Harlem</u>.

5. Courtney <u>said We enjoyed</u> our time in New York."

6. They liked George Segal's sculpture <u>Walk, Don't Walk</u>.

7. Did you read the article <u>Did Drake Land Here?</u>

8. Sir Francis Drake's ship was <u>The Golden Hind.</u>

9. <u>Actually, said Adam</u> "the article was very interesting."

10. Our paper is called <u>the Scotts Valley Times.</u>

1   **A**   anthology," exclaimed Dustin!

    B   anthology! exclaimed Dustin.

    C   *anthology*", exclaimed Dustin.

    D   anthology!" exclaimed Dustin.

2   **A**   The "Ransom of Red Chief"

    B   *The Ransom of Red Chief*

    C   "The Ransom of Red Chief"

    D   The *Ransom of Red Chief*

3   **A**   The "Indians Come Down from Mixco."

    B   *The Indians Come Down from Mixco.*

    C   "The Indians Come Down from Mixco."

    D   the *Indians Come Down from Mixco.*

4   **A**   called "Shakespeare in Harlem."

    B   called *Shakespeare in Harlem.*

    C   called "Shakespeare in Harlem".

    D   called, "*Shakespeare in Harlem.*"

5   **A**   said, "We enjoyed

    B   said ", We enjoyed

    C   said, We enjoyed

    D   said, "we enjoyed

6   **A**   "Walk, Don't Walk."

    B   *Walk, Don't Walk.*

    C   "Walk, don't Walk".

    D   "Walk, don't walk."

7   **A**   "Did Drake Land Here?"

    B   "Did Drake Land Here"

    C   *Did Drake Land Here?*

    D   "Did Drake Land Here?,"

8   **A**   "The Golden Hind."

    B   "The Golden Hind".

    C   The *Golden Hind.*

    D   *The Golden Hind.*

9   **A**   Actually, said Adam.

    B   "Actually, said Adam,

    C   "Actually," said Adam.

    D   "Actually," said Adam,

10   **A**   "the Scotts Valley Times."

    B   the "Scotts Valley Times."

    C   the *Scotts Valley Times.*

    D   the *Scotts Valley Times.*

Kenojuak Ashevak. *Young Owl Takes a Ride,* 1984.
Stonecut and stencil, 19 ½ by 25 ½ inches. © West Baffin Eskimo Cooperative, Cape Dorset, Nunavut.

Describe   What does the painting show? What colors does Kenojuak Ashevak use?

Analyze   In what way did the artist create unity in this print? How did she create variety?

Interpret   In what ways do you think the artist might be expressing her Eskimo heritage and experiences living in Canada's Baffin Region?

Judge   If you could have the print copied on an item for you to own, what item would you choose? Would you prefer to own the print or a story about the print? Why do you feel as you do?

At the end of the chapter, you will use this artwork to stimulate ideas for writing.

Writing Titles

When you write a report, sometimes you need to include the title of a book or a magazine that you used as one of your sources of information. However, not all titles are punctuated the same way.

● Titles with Italics (Underlining)

Titles of certain kinds of written works—books, magazines, newspapers, and movies—are printed in italics. Italic print is a special kind of printing that slants to the right. *It is the kind of print used in this sentence.* Since you cannot write in italics, you should underline any title that would be printed in italics.

When you use a computer, however, you can print in italics. To do this, first highlight the words you want to italicize. Then use the command for italics.

| ITALICS | Have you read *The Monument* by Gary Paulsen? |
| UNDERLINING | Have you read The Monument by Gary Paulsen? |

Italicize (underline) the titles of long written or musical works that are published as a single unit. Also italicize (underline) the titles of paintings and sculptures and the names of vehicles.

This rule applies to books, magazines, newspapers, full-length plays, movies, and very long poems. Long musical works include operas, symphonies, ballets, and albums. Vehicles include names of airplanes, ships, trains, and spacecraft.

BOOKS	I love the novel *The Voyage of the Frog* by Gary Paulsen.
MAGAZINES	The magazine National Geographic World is full of articles about adventure.
NEWSPAPERS	I read reviews of books in our newspaper, the *Sacramento Bee*.
PLAYS, MOVIES	That movie A Cry in the Wild was based on a book by Gary Paulsen.
WORKS OF ART	Winslow Homer's painting *A Summer Night* is a dark and beautiful work of art.
NAMES OF VEHICLES	One of Paulsen's novels is set on a sailboat called the Frog.

PRACTICE YOUR SKILLS

Check Your Understanding

Punctuating Titles

General Interest **Write the titles that should be italicized (underlined).**

1. A great adventure book is Hatchet by Gary Paulsen.

2. The River and Brian's Winter are two sequels to that book.

3. Have you read Downriver by Wil Hobbs?

4. I like real life adventures like the ones in the magazine Boy's Life.

5. You can read reviews of novels in most newspapers like the Chicago Tribune.

6. Merlyn's Pen, a great magazine, publishes the stories, poems, and artwork of adolescents.

7. Released in 1939, the movie The Wizard of Oz is still one of the greatest adventure films.

8. Another great fantasy movie is Willow.

9. Clara McDonald Williamson's painting The Old Chisholm Trail depicts the adventure of an Old West cattle drive.

10. Faith Ringgold's work of art Church Picnic Story Quilt shows the adventures at a church picnic.

● Titles with Quotation Marks

The titles of smaller parts of longer works are enclosed in quotation marks (" "). For example, a book, which is a longer work, is italicized or underlined. A smaller part of that book—such as a chapter title, a short story, or a poem—is enclosed in quotation marks. Remember that *enclosed* means that one pair of quotation marks is placed at the beginning of the title, and the other pair is placed at the end of the title.

Use quotation marks to enclose the titles of chapters, articles, short stories, poems, and songs.

CHAPTERS IN BOOKS	Have you read chapter 3, "The Last of the Apache Chiefs," in Dee Brown's book *Wounded Knee*?
ARTICLES IN MAGAZINES	I just finished the article "The Ancient Pueblo People" in *Cobblestone*.
SHORT STORIES IN BOOKS	"Spring Defeats Winter" is a Seneca story in the book *Native American Stories*.
POEMS IN BOOKS	"The Flower-Fed Buffalo" by Vachel Lindsay is in the book *Children's Verse in America*.
SONGS	"Indians" is a song by Native American singer Mitch Walking Elk.

● Check Your Understanding

Punctuating Titles

General Interest **Write the titles that should be enclosed in quotation marks.**

1. Two chapters in that book are Indian Writers 1900-1967 and Painting Tradition.

2. The article The Last Yahi tells the story of Oshi, the last surviving member of his tribe.

3. Sharon Burch, a Navajo woman, wrote the song All is Beautiful.

4. Blue Horses Rush In is a poem by Luci Tapahouse.

5. I just read a great article in that magazine called All Roads Lead to Canyon de Chelly.

6. The chapter Cheyenne Exodus discusses the lives of Dull Knife and Little Wolf.

7. Rain, written by Ofelia Zepeda, is a beautiful poem.

8. Have you read the short story The Siege of Courthouse Rock?

9. Shaman's Call is a song by flutist Carlos Nakai.

10. The Quillwork Girl and Her Seven Star Brothers is a Cheyenne tale.

● Connect to the Writing Process: Editing

Correcting Errors in the Punctuation of Titles

Rewrite the following sentences, correcting errors in the punctuation of titles. Remember that some titles are underlined and some are enclosed in quotation marks.

11. If you like humorous books, you should read either The Cat Ate My Gymsuit or The Pistachio Prescription by Paula Danziger.

12. Weird Al Yankovich is famous for his funny songs like Don't Wear Those Shoes and I Love Rocky Road.

13. My two favorite Shel Silverstein poems are in his book Where the Sidewalk Ends.

14. Ellen Conford's book If This Is Love is full of hilarious short stories like Loathe at First Sight and Double Date.

15. The movie Carry On, Jack is a great old comedy.

● **Connect to the Writing Process:** Prewriting
Writing Titles

Write a title that answers each of the following questions. Remember to punctuate each title correctly.

16. What is your favorite novel?

17. What magazine do you like to read?

18. What is your favorite song?

19. What is the title of a poem you like?

20. What is the best movie you have ever seen?

Communicate Your Ideas

APPLY TO WRITING
Friendly Letter: *Titles*

You have a new pen pal who lives across the country from you. Write a letter in which you introduce yourself to him or her. Tell your new pen pal about yourself and some of your likes and dislikes. Include at least three of the titles you wrote for the preceding exercise. After you finish your letter, read it again, correcting any errors in the punctuation of titles.

Writing Direct Quotations

The more you write, the more you will need to use quotation marks. When you write a report, for example, you should include the exact words from books to support what you are saying. To do this, you need to know how to use quotation marks correctly.

When you write a story, you should often include the conversations of the characters in your story. To be able to write dialogue, you need to know how to use quotation marks correctly.

▶ Quotation Marks with Direct Quotations

A **direct quotation** is the exact words of a person. Quotation marks go before and after a direct quotation.

Use quotation marks before and after a person's exact words.

DIRECT QUOTATIONS	Ms. Lister said, "Tropical fish is my hobby."
	She added, "I own many exotic fish."

If you are writing a one-sentence direct quotation, you can write it in three ways. You can place it before or after a speaker tag such as *she said* or *he asked*. You can also place a speaker tag in the middle of a direct quotation.

In all of these cases, place quotation marks only before and after the person's exact words. The words inside quotation marks should never include a speaker tag.

BEFORE	"For years I have been studying fish," she said.
AFTER	She said, "For years I have been studying fish."
MIDDLE	"For years," she said, "I have been studying fish."
	(Two sets of quotation marks are needed because the speaker tag interrupts the direct quotation.)

PRACTICE YOUR SKILLS

● Check Your Understanding
Quotation Marks with Direct Quotations

Science Topic

Write C if quotation marks are used correctly in the following sentences. Write I if the quotation marks are incorrect.

1. "Many fish simply fool their enemies," she explained.

2. "She added," Some fish live among bright coral, and they often have bright coloring.

3. You may be wondering," she said, "how this helps them.

4. "Their color," she said, "makes them look like corals."

5. She asked, Isn't that clever?

6. She added, Some fish can change their color."

7. "These fish have special color cells," she explained.

8. She said, They can match their backgrounds perfectly.

9. "Other fish swallow water, she stated, and puff up."

10. This is an especially funny trick, she laughed.

11. She explained, This action makes them look very big."

12. "Some fish," she added, "have a bad taste."

13. No fish wants to eat another fish that tastes bad! she exclaimed.

14. "Fish always avoid these bad-tasting meals, she said."

15. "This ends my lecture on the self-defense of fish," she concluded.

● Connect to the Writing Process: Editing
Correcting the Use of Quotation Marks

16.–25. Rewrite the incorrect sentences from the preceding exercise, placing quotation marks properly. Note: in this exercise, the comma or end mark goes *inside* the closing quotation marks.

▶ Capital Letters with Direct Quotations

Capitalize the first word of a direct quotation.

"**T**hese are the bones of a dinosaur," he said.

(*These* is capitalized because it is the first word of the sentence and the first word of the direct quotation.)

She said, "**T**hey look old."

(*She* is capitalized because it is the first word in the sentence. *They* is capitalized because it is the first word of the direct quotation.)

"**T**hese bones," he said, "are from a brontosaurus."

(*Are* is not capitalized because it is in the middle of a sentence.)

"**T**hey were discovered years ago," he said. "**O**nly a few bones were missing."

(*Only* is capitalized because it starts a new sentence of the direct quotation.)

PRACTICE YOUR SKILLS

● Check Your Understanding
Using Capital Letters with Direct Quotations

Science Topic | **Write *C* if capital letters are used correctly in the following sentences. Write *I* if capital letters are used incorrectly.**

1. "dinosaurs died out millions of years ago," Mr. Chin explained.

2. He added, "they haven't completely disappeared, however."

3. "In some places," he stated, "their bones remain."

4. He said, "one such place is Dinosaur Provincial Park in Alberta."

5. "Alberta is in Canada," he explained.

6. "there," he said, "people have found more dinosaur bones than in any other place on Earth."

7. "Three hundred skeletons have been found along a sixteen-mile stretch of the Red Deer River!" he exclaimed.

8. "Bones from many kinds of dinosaurs were found," he said. "in fact, bones from thirty different kinds were found."

9. "The remains," he continued, "Of other creatures like amphibians and fish have also been found."

10. "During the time of the dinosaurs," he said, "the climate on Earth was very different."

11. He explained, "the weather in Canada was like the weather is now in Florida."

12. "the climate was perfect for dinosaurs," he said.

13. He added, "that's why so many kinds lived there."

14. "The treasures found at the park," he informed us, "Are now housed at a museum."

15. "Who'd like to visit Dinosaur Provincial Park?" he asked.

● Connect to the Writing Process: Editing
Correcting the Use of Capital Letters

16.–25. Rewrite the the incorrect sentences from the preceding exercise, using proper capitalization.

▶ Commas with Direct Quotations

Commas are used to separate direct quotations from speaker tags.

Use a comma to separate a direct quotation from a speaker tag. Place the comma inside the closing quotation marks.

"The North Pole is a remarkable place," he said.

(The comma goes *inside* the closing quotation marks.)

He said, "The North Pole is a remarkable place."

(The comma follows the speaker tag.)

"The North Pole," he said, "is a remarkable place."

(Two commas are needed to separate the speaker tag from the direct quotation: one before and one after the speaker tag. The first comma goes *inside* the closing quotation marks.)

PRACTICE YOUR SKILLS

● Check Your Understanding
Using Commas with Direct Quotations

History Topic **Write *C* if commas are used correctly in the following sentences. Write *I* if commas are used incorrectly.**

1. "The North Pole is located in the middle of the Arctic Ocean" Ms. Winters began.

2. "It is a cold and unforgiving area," she said.

3. "The North Pole itself," she explained "is always moving."

4. "In 1981, the pole was miles away from where James Clark Ross located it in 1831," she said.

5. "In 1978, Naomi Uemura of Japan became the first person to reach the North Pole alone" Ms. Winters told us.

6. She said "His only companions were his sled dogs."

7. "They pulled his sled of supplies," she stated.

8. "He wore polar bear skins" she explained, "for protection from the Arctic cold."

9. "Once a polar bear raided his camp" Ms. Winters said.

10. "He often cut through huge ridges of ice" she said.

11. She stated, "Some ridges were three stories high."

12. "He walked over plates of shifting ice" she said.

13. "Sometimes" she said "the ice cracked open."

14. "In fifty-five days" she added "he crossed five hundred miles."

15. "This was truly a remarkable feat," she said.

● Connect to the Writing Process: Editing
Correcting the Use of Commas

16.–25. Rewrite the incorrect sentences from the preceding exercise, using commas correctly.

▶ End Marks with Direct Quotations

A period ends a regular sentence, and a period ends most direct quotations.

Place a period inside the closing quotation marks when the end of the quotation comes at the end of the sentence.

He said, "This is my favorite bat**.**"

(inside)

"My dad," he explained, "once used this bat**.**"

Usually, question marks and exclamation points also go *inside* the closing quotation marks.

He asked, "Would you like to use it**?**"

(inside)

She yelled, "Watch out for the ball**!**"

(inside)

When a question or an exclamation comes before a speaker tag, the question mark or the exclamation point is still placed *inside* the closing quotation marks—in place of the comma. Then a period ends the sentence.

"Did you hit the ball**?**" she asked.

(inside)

"That was a fantastic hit**!**" she exclaimed.

(inside)

PRACTICE YOUR SKILLS

● Check Your Understanding
Using End Marks with Direct Quotations

Sports Topic

**Write *C* if the end marks are used correctly.
Write *I* if the end marks are used incorrectly.**

1. "Have you heard of Ty Cobb" asked Coach Sandlin.

2. Coach Sandlin said, "He was known as the Georgia Peach."

3. "What a great player" he exclaimed.

4. Coach said, "Some people consider Ty Cobb to be the greatest player who ever lived."

5. "Do you know why" he asked.

6. He explained, "When Ty Cobb retired in 1928, he held ninety major league records"

7. "Ty Cobb was a tricky player" he exclaimed.

8. Coach shouted, "He batted left-handed, and he pitched right-handed"

9. "Do you know what else?" Coach asked.

10. He said, "Ty Cobb stole 892 bases in his career"

11. "Are you wondering if he could hit" Coach inquired.

12. Coach Sandlin said, "Ty Cobb won twelve batting championships in his career."

13. "He won that title nine years in a row—from 1907 to 1916" exclaimed the coach.

14. Coach Sandlin asked, "Do you know how much Ty Cobb memorabilia is worth today?"

15. "Ty Cobb's glove sold for over $18,000 at auction in 1993" said the coach with great excitement.

● Connect to the Writing Process: Editing
Correcting the Use of End Punctuation

16.–25. Rewrite the incorrect sentences from the preceding exercise, correcting the end punctuation.

● Connect to the Writing Process: Editing
Punctuating Direct Quotations

Correctly rewrite the following sentences, adding quotation marks, capital letters, commas, and end marks where they are needed.

26. do you wear glasses Mrs. Takai asked

27. well she continued people have been wearing glasses since the late 1200s

28. that's a long time Steve exclaimed

29. Cori asked who invented glasses

30. people in Venice, Italy Mrs. Takai replied

31. for the first four hundred years, glasses weren't worn she said they were held up to the eyes

32. Brittany exclaimed that must have made reading difficult

33. Mrs. Takai continued those people could never have imagined contact lenses

APPLY TO WRITING
Newspaper Article: *Direct Quotations*

You have been asked to write an article for your school newspaper. The title of the article is to be "The Best Pet." Interview two people about what animal they believe makes the best pet. As you listen to them talk, make note of two sentences that each of them says, exactly as they say them. Then write the article, using two direct quotes from the people you interviewed. After you finish your article, read it again. Fix any errors in punctuation and capitalization.

QuickCheck Mixed Practice

Literature
Topic

Correctly rewrite the following sentences, adding quotation marks, capital letters, commas, end marks, and italics or underlining where needed.

1. the book we're going to read is called Canyons by Gary Paulsen explained Mr. Garcia.

2. this book he said has two main characters and two plots that come together in the end

3. are you interested in stories about Native Americans he asked

4. then he exclaimed you'll love this book

5. it kept me on the edge of my seat he said we will all learn a lot about the history of the West

Writing Dialogue

The word **dialogue** means "a conversation between two or more people." Adding dialogue to a short story often makes the story more interesting. However, you have to write dialogue in a certain way to let readers know who is speaking.

When writing dialogue, begin a new paragraph each time the speaker changes.

In the following dialogue between Lily and Kevin, each sentence follows the rules for direct quotations you have just studied. Notice that a new paragraph begins each time Lily or Kevin speaks.

> "How was the social studies test today?" asked Lily.
>
> "Oh," answered Kevin, "I think I did really well. I studied for two days before the test."
>
> Lily inquired, "What did the test cover?"
>
> "We've been studying about the ancient Greeks," answered Kevin. "The test was about mythology."
>
> "I love reading about gods and goddesses!" exclaimed Lily.
>
> "Yeah," agreed Kevin, "it is pretty interesting."

CONNECT TO WRITER'S CRAFT

When authors write dialogue, they usually include information that is additional to what the characters are actually saying. They use the paragraphs containing dialogue to convey the characters' feelings and tell the reader what other actions are taking place. In the dialogue at the top of the next page, notice how the author gives additional information, both through the speaker tags and an extra sentence.

"Come on out, Ramona," said Howie. "Uncle Hobart helped me learn to ride my unicycle, so now you can ride my bicycle."

Ramona's wish had come true. "Hey, Beezus," she shouted, "I'm going out and ride Howie's bike."

"You're supposed to ask first," said Beezus. "You can't go out unless I say so."

Ramona felt that Beezus was showing off in front of Howie. "How come you're so bossy all of a sudden?" she demanded.

"Mom and Dad left me in charge, and you have to mind," answered Beezus.

—*Beverly Cleary*, Ramona Forever

PRACTICE YOUR SKILLS

● Check Your Understanding
Using Dialogue

 Read aloud the following dialogue between Dad and Lily. Point out each place where a new paragraph should begin.

"Dad, what do you remember about Greek mythology?" asked Lily. Dad replied, "There are so many great stories. I really remember the story of Icarus." "I don't think I know that story, Dad," she said. "Will you tell it to me?" "Well, Daedalus and his son Icarus had been imprisoned on an island by King Minos. Daedalus used feathers and wax to build wings for him and his son," explained Dad. "Wow!" exclaimed

Lily. "They just flew away! What a good plan!" "Yes," said Dad, "but Daedalus told Icarus not to fly too close to the sun. If he did, the wax would melt. He also told his son not to fly too low because the sea would make his wings wet." "Did Icarus follow his father's instructions?" asked Lily. "No," answered Dad. "Even though he was warned, Icarus flew too close to the sun." "Oh, no, the wax melted!" exclaimed Lily. "Yes," said Dad, "and Icarus fell into the sea."

● Connect to the Writing Process: Editing
Adding Proper Punctuation to Dialogue

Rewrite the following dialogue between Felicia and Greg. Add quotation marks, commas, end marks, and capital letters where needed. Also, begin new paragraphs as they are needed.

Look at this article about Moonlight Special Felicia said Greg replied what is a Moonlight Special It's a ten-inch robot mouse Felicia answered What did it do Greg asked It competed against other robot mice in the first Amazing Micro-Mouse Maze Contest Felicia answered Each mouse had three chances to run a maze How many mice were in the contest asked Greg There were sixteen mice in the race said Felicia Greg asked did Moonlight Special win Unfortunately Felicia said the article does not mention that

APPLY TO WRITING
Story: *Dialogue*

Beatrix Potter. *Jemima Puddle-duck and the foxy gentleman,* 1908.
Pen, ink and watercolor.© 1908, 1987, Frederick Warne & Co., London. Reproduced by permission of Frederick Warne & Co.

Look carefully at the illustration by Beatrix Potter. Think about what is happening. Imagine the conversation these two characters might be having. Write for first graders a short story that goes along with the picture. Include the dialogue between these two characters. After you have written your story, check to be sure that you began a new paragraph each time the speaker changed. Also, be sure you punctuated the quotations correctly.

Punctuating Direct Quotations

Write each direct quotation, adding quotation marks, commas, end marks, and capital letters where needed.

1. do you wear glasses Mrs. Yori asked

2. well she continued people have been wearing glasses since the late 1200s

3. that's a very long time Jacob exclaimed

4. Michelle asked who invented glasses

5. people in Venice, Italy Mrs. Yori replied

6. for the first 400 years, glasses weren't worn she said they were held up to the eyes

7. Megan exclaimed that must have made reading extremely difficult

8. Mrs. Yori continued finally in the 1720s, a London optician made glasses to be worn

9. were they like glasses today Michelle asked

10. not exactly said Mrs. Yori but they rested on the nose

Punctuating Titles

Write and punctuate each title correctly.

1. If I Were an Elephant is a funny poem.

2. Who wrote the book A Wrinkle in Time?

3. The short story How the Whale Got His Throat was written by Rudyard Kipling.

4. The magazine Your Big Backyard has wonderful pictures of animals in it.

5. Did you read the chapter The Start of Cities?
6. I like the comics in our newspaper the Grange Herald.
7. We watched the old movie Black Beauty on TV.
8. Healthy Bodies and Minds was an article in Time.
9. I read Eve Merriam's poem At the Edge of the World.
10. Our literature book, Reading About the World, contains a great short story called The Scribe.

Editing Dialogue

Rewrite the following dialogue between Mrs. Valdez and Emily. Add quotation marks, commas, end marks, italics, and capital letters where needed. Also begin new paragraphs as they are needed.

Mrs. Valdez clapped as the singers finished the song Getting to Know You. Her students were putting on the musical play The King and I. Your rehearsals are going great she told them. I really enjoy my part said Emily Did you know asked Ms. Valdez that this play is somewhat based on history Really exclaimed Emily. Yes her teacher answered Anna Leonowens was a real person. in 1862 she went to Siam Emily asked was she really a governess at court Yes replied Ms. Valdez afterwards she wrote a book called The English Governess at the Siamese Court.

Writing

Write an imaginary dialogue between you and someone famous in history. Write at least ten sentences, using end marks, commas, italics, quotation marks, and capital letters correctly throughout.

Language and *Self-Expression*

Baby owls don't really ride on their parents' backs, so perhaps there is a story behind Kenojuak Ashevak's print. She might have used a image from a folktale as an inspiration.

Folktales take root in our imaginations, especially if we hear them when we are young. What folktale has stayed in your imagination? From memory, write a scene from this tale, using dialogue as well as description. When you are finished, do research to find one or more books that contain this tale, and note their titles.

Prewriting When you have decided which scene to write about, make notes to remind you of details to include. Use a chart to put the details in chronological order.

Drafting Refer to your sequence-of-events chart to write your scene. After you have written your scene, add a sentence that tells readers how to find the complete story and read it for themselves.

Revising Work with a classmate to get feedback. Take turns reading your scenes aloud and asking whether the dialogue sounds natural. Make sure that it is clear who is saying what.

Editing Check your scene for errors in punctuation and spelling. Check whether you began a new paragraph for each speaker.

Publishing Have classmates help you tape your scene as a Readers' Theater performance. Play it to the class; then post a copy of your scene on a bulletin board or Website, along with the title or titles of books that contain the story.

Another Look

Italics and Quotation Marks

Italicize (underline) the titles of long written or musical works that are published as a single unit. Also italicize (underline) the titles of paintings and sculptures and the names of vehicles. *(pages L479–L480)*

Use quotation marks to enclose the titles of chapters, articles, short stories, poems, and songs. *(page L481)*

> A **direct quotation** is the exact words of a person. Quotation marks go before and after a person's exact words.

Capitalize the first word of a direct quotation. *(pages L486–L487)*

Use a comma to separate a direct quotation from a speaker tag. Place the comma inside the closing quotation marks. *(pages L488–L489)*

Place a period inside the quotation marks when the end of the quotation comes at the end of the sentence. *(pages L490–L491)*

> The word **dialogue** means "a conversation between two or more people."

When writing dialogue, begin a new paragraph each time the speaker changes. *(page L494)*

Other Information About Italics and Quotation Marks

Using end marks after a speaker's words *(pages L490–L491)*

Directions
Write the letter of the group of words that correctly rewrites the underlined portion of each sentence.

EXAMPLE **1.** Henry Moore's first famous sculpture was <u>Reclining Figure</u>.

    1 A "Reclining Figure".

    B "Reclining Figure."

    C *Reclining Figure.*

    D Reclining Figure.

ANSWER **1 C**

1. "I'm thinking of getting a paper <u>route Emily said.</u>

2. Brandon delivers <u>the Jefferson Tribune</u> in our neighborhood.

3. The first plane to fly around the world was <u>the Winnie Mae.</u>

4. <u>What I like to read Rachel said</u> "are stories about real people."

5. Gary Soto wrote about his childhood in his book <u>A Summer Life.</u>

6. In 1930, Grant Wood painted <u>American Gothic</u>.

7. Amanda exclaimed, <u>that's terrific</u>

8. The folktale <u>Maui Snares the Sun</u> begins on page 82.

9. "I just finished the <u>story said Kelsey It</u> is a Hawaiian myth."

10. The poem <u>Kentucky Belle</u> is about a cherished horse.

1 A route", Emily said.
  B route." Emily said.
  C route," Emily said.
  D route" Emily said.

2 A the *Jefferson Tribune*
  B the "Jefferson Tribune"
  C the *"Jefferson Tribune"*
  D the Jefferson Tribune

3 A the "Winnie Mae".
  B the *Winnie Mae.*
  C the "Winnie Mae."
  D the *"Winnie Mae."*

4 A "What I like to read", Rachel said
  B "What I like to read," Rachel said,
  C "What I like to read" Rachel said
  D "What I like to read," Rachel said

5 A a *Summer Life.*
  B "A Summer Life".
  C A "Summer Life."
  D *A Summer Life.*

6 A *American Gothic.*
  B "American Gothic."
  C "American Gothic".
  D American Gothic.

7 A "that's terrific"!
  B "that's terrific!"
  C "That's terrific!"
  D "That's terrific"!

8 A *"Maui Snares the Sun"*
  B *Maui Snares the Sun*
  C "Maui Snares the Sun"
  D Maui Snares the Sun

9 A story," said Kelsey, "it
  B story," said Kelsey. "It
  C story." said Kelsey "it
  D story." said Kelsey. "It

10 A Kentucky Belle
   B *"Kentucky Belle"*
   C "Kentucky Belle"
   D *Kentucky Belle*

Other Punctuation

Pretest

Directions

Write the letter of the word or punctuation mark that correctly completes each sentence.

EXAMPLE   My best friend and I have names that begin with __(1)__ .

    1 A *I*s
      B *I*'s
      C *I*'
      D *I*s'

ANSWER   **1 B**

__(1)__ names go in and out of fashion. My __(2)__ names, Jessica and Ashley, were the two most popular girls' names in the 1990s. In 1998, Hannah was the most popular girl's name in __(3)__ of the states in the U.S. Michael, my __(4)__ name, was the number-one name for boys in the 1990s. In the 1990s, Jessica was at the top of the list, but now Kaitlyn has taken __(5)__ place. My name, Courtney, was in __(6)__ place on the 1990s' list. I have a list of the 100 most popular names from 1998 __(7)__ now Courtney is in sixth place. Names like Susan, Jane, and Nora __(8)__ even on the list. Almost __(9)__ baby is given a name like Chester, Edgar, or Herbert anymore. In 1998, Madison was the most popular girl's name in the following states __(10)__ Idaho, Montana, Utah, Wyoming, and Kansas.

1 **A** Childrens'
   B Childrens
   C Children's
   D Childrens's

2 **A** sisters's
   B sister's
   C sisters
   D sisters'

3 **A** one-fifth
   B one fifth
   C onefifth
   D one:fifth

4 **A** brothers'
   B brother's
   C brothers
   D brothers's

5 **A** its
   B it's
   C its'
   D its's

6 **A** twenty second
   B twentysecond
   C 20–second
   D twenty-second

7 **A** ;
   B :
   C ,
   D .

8 **A** aren't
   B are'nt
   C arent
   D are n't

9 **A** no ones'
   B no ones
   C no one's
   D no-one's

10 **A** ;
   B :
   C ,
   D .

Janet Fish. *Yellow Pad*, 1997.
Oil on canvas, 36 by 50 inches. The Columbus Museum, Columbus, GA. ©Janet Fish/ Licensed by VAGA, New York, NY.

Describe There are a lot of details in this picture. How many items can you name?

Analyze A color seems more intense if it is put near its opposite on the color wheel. How did Janet Fish use that principle to bring out colors in her painting?

Interpret Why do you think the artist created this painting? Do you think she wanted to create a mood? If so, what mood and why do you think so?

Judge What is your reaction to this painting? Is it attractive to you? Do you like the choice of colors? Explain why you feel as you do.

At the end of this chapter, you will use this artwork to stimulate ideas for writing.

Apostrophes

Every time you write a contraction, you use an apostrophe (').
Apostrophes are also used to show ownership or possession.

Apostrophes to Show Possession

To show ownership, nouns have special forms that include
apostrophes. You use these special forms when *of* phrases
could be substituted for the nouns.

> Tyler's sneakers = the sneakers **of Tyler**
>
> the coaches' whistles = the whistles **of the coaches**
>
> the children's hats = the hats **of the children**

The Possessive Forms of Singular Nouns

To write the possessive form of any singular noun, write the
noun just as it is. Do not add or leave out any letters. Then
add an apostrophe and an *s*.

Add **'s** to form the possessive of a singular noun.

team + 's = team's	Jamie is the team's new mascot.
Jamie + 's = Jamie's	That is Jamie's costume.
Bess + 's = Bess's	Bess's costume looks very different.
band + 's = band's	She is the band's lead marcher.

PRACTICE YOUR SKILLS

● Check Your Understanding
Forming Possessive Singular Nouns

Rewrite each expression, using the possessive form.

1. tail of a fox
2. leaves of the tree
3. keys of Mr. Ryan
4. ride of an hour
5. silence of the forest
6. friend of David
7. farm of my grandmother
8. tent of a camper
9. howls of a wolf
10. vacation of a month

● Connect to the Writing Process: Drafting
Writing with Possessive Nouns

11.–15. Use five of the possessive phrases you formed in the preceding exercise to write five sentences.

The Possessive Forms of Plural Nouns

The plural of most nouns is formed by adding an *s: skates, hours,* and *horses,* for example. There are a few exceptions, such as *women* and *geese.* These plurals are formed by changing the words. If you are not sure how to form the plural of a noun, look it up in the dictionary.

How the possessive form of a plural noun is written depends on the ending of the noun.

Add only an apostrophe to form the possessive of a plural noun that ends in *s.*

boys + ' = boys'	The boys' pants were covered with mud.
trees + ' = trees'	The trees' limbs whipped in the wind.

Add an 's to form the possessive of a plural noun that does not end in s.

children + 's = children's   The children's swings were damaged.

mice + 's = mice's   The mice's nests did not survive the storm.

When you write the possessive of a plural noun, take the following steps. First, write the plural of the noun. Then, look at the ending of the word. If the word ends in *s,* add only an apostrophe. If the word does not end in *s,* add an apostrophe and an *s.*

FORMING THE PLURAL OF NOUNS			
Plural	**Ending**	**Add**	**Possessive**
books	*s*	' =	books' covers
boxes	*s*	' =	boxes' labels
men	no *s*	's =	men's wallets
geese	no *s*	's =	geese's nests

Never use an apostrophe when writing a regular plural noun. Apostrophes show possession or ownership, and misusing them will confuse your reader.

INCORRECT   Seven new boys' joined the club.
CORRECT   Seven new boys joined the club.

CONNECT TO WRITER'S CRAFT

Sometimes a phrase with a possessive plural noun may sound awkward. In that case, you may prefer to write or say, for example, "the names of the girls," rather than "the girls' names." Both expressions are correct.

PRACTICE YOUR SKILLS

● Check Your Understanding
Forming Possessive Plural Nouns

Rewrite each expression, using the possessive form.

1. coats of the men
2. labels of the boxes
3. soles of the shoes
4. home of the bees
5. tracks of two deer
6. saddles of the horses
7. formation of the geese
8. meeting of the scouts
9. clothes of the children
10. names of the women

● Check Your Understanding
Forming Possessive Nouns

 History Topic **Write each underlined word and add an apostrophe or an apostrophe and an *s* to make the noun possessive.**

11. The U.S. <u>presidents</u> backgrounds have all been very different.

12. These <u>men</u> legacies will be remembered through history.

13. <u>George Washington</u> career was as a surveyor before he became president.

14. One <u>president</u> son, John Quincy Adams, would also serve the nation as president.

15. <u>Grover Cleveland</u> wedding took place during his presidency.

16. After four <u>years</u> service, presidents are sometimes reelected.

17. <u>Franklin Roosevelt</u> popularity allowed him to be elected four times.

18. The first <u>ladies</u> roles in the White House have varied.

19. Few <u>presidents</u> elections have been as surprising as that of Harry Truman in 1948.

20. Our <u>leaders</u> assassinations have always shocked Americans.

● Connect to the Writing Process: Editing
Correcting Possessive Nouns

Rewrite each sentence, correcting the possessive form. If the possessive form is correct, write C.

21. Bird's hearts are similar to ours.

22. A humans' heart has four chambers.

23. These feathered creature's hearts do also.

24. This animals' young is hatched from eggs.

25. Chickens' eggs are a popular breakfast food.

26. They are also an important ingredient in bakers recipes.

27. Ducks feathers are waterproof, and their feet are webbed.

28. The toucan's home is the Amazon rain forest of South America.

29. Our nations' symbol is the bald eagle.

30. Unlike a bald eagle, a golden eagle's legs are feathered to the toes.

The Possessive Forms of Pronouns

To show ownership or possession, personal pronouns change form. They do not use an apostrophe as nouns do. The table at the top of the next page lists both singular and plural possessive pronouns.

POSSESSIVE PRONOUNS	
SINGULAR	my, mine, your, yours, his, her, hers, its
PLURAL	our, ours, your, yours, their, theirs

Do not add an apostrophe to form the possessive of a personal pronoun.

PERSONAL PRONOUNS	That poodle is **hers.** The poodle wagged **its** tail.

Indefinite pronouns, however, form the possessive by adding 's, the same way that singular nouns do.

COMMON INDEFINITE PRONOUNS	
SINGULAR	anybody, anyone, each, either, everybody, everyone, neither, nobody, no one, one, somebody, someone
PLURAL	both, few, many, several

Add 's to form the possessive of an indefinite pronoun.

INDEFINITE PRONOUNS	Someone**'s** dog barked all night long. Everyone**'s** windows were closed tightly.

PRACTICE YOUR SKILLS

● Check Your Understanding
Using Possessive Pronouns

Contemporary Life
Write the correct form of the pronoun in parentheses.

1. Is that beagle (your's, yours)?

2. (Nobody's, Nobodys) dog is allowed in here without supervision.

3. Are you (it's, its) master?

4. No, that beagle is (their's, theirs).

5. (Everyone's, Everyones) dog should take this obedience class.

6. Classes really helped (our's, ours).

7. (Anybody's, Anybodys) pet is welcomed in this class.

8. That German Shepherd with the beautiful coat is (her's, hers).

9. That dog is certainly bigger than (our's, ours).

10. (Someone's, Someones) dog chewed my shoe.

● Connect to the Writing Process: Drafting
Writing Sentences with Possessive Pronouns

Use the possessive form of each pronoun in a sentence.

11. somebody   13. everyone   15. no one

12. your   14. our

● Connect to the Writing Process: Editing
Correcting Errors with Possessive Pronouns

Rewrite each sentence, correcting the incorrect possessive forms of pronouns. If the pronoun is correct, write C.

16. The dog was searching for it's master.

17. That nice little poodle is our's.

18. Yours is the little black terrier.

19. Someones cat was chased by a big dog.

20. I know that dog was not our's.

21. No ones cat should go into that yard.

22. The dog that chases cats is their's.

23. Oh, I thought it was hers.

24. In this neighborhood almost everyones' pet is well-behaved.

25. Our neighbors will help train anyones dog.

Communicate Your Ideas

APPLY TO WRITING
Dialogue: *Possessive Nouns and Pronouns*

Lois Mailou Jones. *Mère du Senegal,* 1985.
Acrylic on canvas, 24 by 36 inches. From the collection of the artist.

Imagine that you are listening to the conversation taking place between this child and her mother braiding her hair. Who or what might these people be discussing? What are they saying? Write a brief dialogue using these characters as the speakers. In your dialogue, use at least three possessive pronouns and three possessive nouns. Underline them.

Contemporary Life

Find and correct the incorrect possessive form in each sentence. If a sentence is correct, write C.

1. I was invited to Jenni Salazars birthday party.
2. That last apartment is her's.
3. Her familys' home is very beautiful.
4. Jenni opened everyones present at the end of the party.
5. There is a swimming pool at her apartment complex.
6. Jennis mom was pleased that we all could swim.
7. The pool at her apartment is bigger than the one at our's.
8. Somebodys shoes fell into the pool.
9. The huge piñata brought a smile to everyones face.
10. Everyones attempt to break the piñata failed.
11. Finally, Brets' swing of the bat sent candy everywhere!
12. The piñata's candy and prizes even landed in the pool.
13. Then Jenni opened her gifts.
14. She liked everybodys present.
15. Her favorite gift was mine's.

Apostrophes with Contractions

A contraction usually combines two words into one. An apostrophe is added to replace one or more missing letters.

Use an apostrophe in a contraction to show where one or more letters have been omitted.

Some contractions combine a pronoun with a verb.

CONTRACTIONS	
I + am = I'm	I + would = I'd
you + are = you're	they + have = they've
she + will = she'll	that + is = that's
it + is = it's	there + is = there's

Some contractions combine a verb with the word *not*. In this kind of contraction, the apostrophe replaces the *o* in *not*.

CONTRACTIONS	
is + not = isn't	was + not = wasn't
are + not = aren't	do + not = don't
has + not = hasn't	could + not = couldn't
have + not = haven't	would + not = wouldn't

When you write a contraction, do not add or move around any letters. There is only one common exception to the way contractions are formed: *will + not = won't*.

PRACTICE YOUR SKILLS

● Check Your Understanding
Substituting Words for Contractions

Write the contraction for each pair of words.

1. I am   **4.** is not   **7.** could not   **10.** I would

2. are not   **5.** we are   **8.** she will   **11.** you are

3. it is   **6.** they have   **9.** have not   **12.** has not

13. I have **15.** she has **17.** will not **19.** did not
14. was not **16.** he is **18.** they are **20.** we have

● Connect to the Writing Process: Revising
Replacing Contractions

Rewrite each sentence, replacing the underlined contraction with the words it stands for.

21. That wasn't a very good movie.

22. We're all disappointed by it.

23. Those men aren't good actors.

24. She's a good actress.

25. I'm not going to recommend that movie to anyone.

26. Don't you think her last movie was better?

27. She'll still be nominated for an award.

28. The movie theater won't sell too many tickets.

29. You're going to leave now.

30. It's time for me to go home, too.

Contraction or Possessive Pronoun?

Do not confuse a contraction with a possessive pronoun.

CONTRACTIONS AND PRONOUNS			
CONTRACTIONS	it's	you're	they're	there's
PRONOUNS	its	your	their	theirs

To avoid any confusion when you write these words, always say to yourself the individual words of a contraction separately.

It's (It is) time for the TV special.
They're (They are) in the gym.

If you forget to add an apostrophe or if you misplace an apostrophe, a reader may completely misunderstand your meaning. If you forget to add an apostrophe to *we'll,* for example, a reader will read the word *well.* If you want to say that two girls each own one pony and you write *girl's ponies,* a reader will think that only one girl owns the ponies.

PRACTICE YOUR SKILLS

● **Check Your Understanding**

Distinguishing Between Contractions and Possessive Pronouns

Contemporary Life **Write the correct word in parentheses.**

1. (It's, Its) time to leave.

2. (They're, Their) apartment is somewhere near the park.

3. Did you find (you're, your) map of the city?

4. (There's, Theirs) a map in the car.

5. Folding the map back into (it's, its) original shape is almost impossible.

6. We will go in (they're, their) car.

7. (You're, Your) the best map reader in the car.

8. (There's, Theirs) is the apartment building on the corner of Pine and Valley Streets.

9. (It's, Its) a very tall building.

10. (You're, Your) going to like the view from their balcony.

Writing Sentences

Use each word in a sentence. Remember to determine first whether the word is a contraction or a possessive pronoun.

11. they're   **16.** you're

12. their   **17.** theirs

13. its   **18.** there's

14. it's   **19.** we'll

15. your   **20.** we're

Connect to the Writing Process: Editing

Correcting Errors with Apostrophes

Rewrite the following paragraphs, correcting the use of contractions and possessive pronouns.

Were going to visit Grandma at the Golden Years Retirement Home. Well all be very glad to see her. Its been awhile since Ive visited her. Grandma hasnt lived at Golden Years very long.

After Grandpa died Grandma wasnt happy living all alone, so my dad found her a place to live. At her new home, she wont be alone. She has people around her all the time. Its great to see Grandma playing dominoes and drinking tea with her new friends. Their all so happy to be with people they're own age.

Im glad Grandma is happy now. The best part is that her new home is even closer to our's than her old one.

⊙ Apostrophes with Certain Plurals

Apostrophes are used to show that some items are plural. To prevent confusion, certain items form their plural by adding 's.

> Add 's to form the plural of lowercase letters and some capital letters.

Notice that the letters in the following examples are italicized (underlined), but the apostrophe and the *s* are not.

LOWERCASE LETTERS When they learn to write, children often confuse *b*'**s** and *d*'**s**.

CAPITAL LETTERS Children usually have trouble writing cursive *I*'s.

(If the apostrophe were left out, the plural form might be confused with the word *Is*.)

The plurals of most numerals can be formed by adding *s*.

Many children write their 5**s** backwards.

In the 1960**s**, scientists learned much about child development.

PRACTICE YOUR SKILLS

● Check Your Understanding
Using Apostrophes

Write the plural form of each of the following items.

   1. *f*

   2. 1950

   3. *r*

4. *A*

5. *7*

● Connect to the Writing Process: Drafting
Writing Sentences

6.–10. Use your answers from the preceding exercise to write five sentences.

Communicate Your Ideas

APPLY TO WRITING

Writer's Craft: *Analyzing the Use of Apostrophes*

Writers use apostrophes in their writing for all the reasons that you have learned. Read this poem by Shel Silverstein. Then follow the directions at the top of the next page.

> Thanksgiving dinner's sad and thankless
> Christmas dinner's dark and blue
> When you stop and try to see it
> From the turkey's point of view.
>
> Sunday dinner isn't sunny
> Easter feasts are just bad luck
> When you see it from the viewpoint
> Of a chicken or a duck.
>
> Oh how I once loved tuna salad
> Pork and lobsters, lamb chops too
> Till I stopped and looked at dinner
> From the dinner's point of view.
>
> *—Shel Silverstein,* "Point of View"

- Write each word that contains an apostrophe. Beside each word, write the reason for the apostrophe.
- Write the words that each contraction stands for.
- Write the possessives as "*of* expressions." For instance, the last phrase *the dinner's point of view* would become *the point of view of the dinner.*
- Now read the poems with the new phrases in place. Which do you like better? Why?

QuickCheck Mixed Practice

Science Topic

Rewrite the paragraphs, correcting any errors in the use of possessives, contractions, or apostrophes.

Im writing my science report about ostriches, but I couldnt find any information. Then a librarian showed me that books about animals are located in the shelves of books with 800's on them. I found a wonderful book!

Ostriches are birds, but they dont fly. They're wings are too small to lift their heavy bodies off the ground. An ostrichs legs, however, move very fast. One ostrich was clocked at 50 miles per hour. It's two-toed feet are good for something else, too. An ostrich can kick very hard. Thats a good defense. One kick can break a lions back.

Semicolons

A semicolon (;) signals a longer pause than a comma. Most often a semicolon is used with a compound sentence. A **compound sentence** is made up of two simple sentences. These sentences can be joined by a comma and a conjunction or by a semicolon.

Use a semicolon between the two simple sentences of a compound sentence that are not joined by a coordinating conjunction.

COMMA AND CONJUNCTION	There are volcanoes all over the world, and many of them are active.
SEMICOLON	There are volcanoes all over the world; many of them are active.

Using a semicolon is one way to correct run-on sentences.

RUN-ON	Volcanoes exist in the state of Washington the most famous volcano is Mt. St. Helens.
CORRECT	Volcanoes exist in the state of Washington; the most famous volcano is Mt. St. Helens.

You can learn more about run-on sentences on pages L215–L216.

You can use semicolons to combine two closely related simple sentences. Using compound sentences makes your writing more mature and polished. Notice at the top of the following page that two closely related sentences have been joined by a semicolon.

SIMPLE SENTENCES	Some scientist study volcanoes. They are called volcanologists.
COMPOUND SENTENCES	Some scientist study volcanoes; they are called volcanologists.

You can learn more about compound sentences on pages L208–L210. For a list of coordinating conjunctions, see page L157.

PRACTICE YOUR SKILLS

● Check Your Understanding
Using Punctuation with Compound Sentences

Science Topic **Write C if the compound sentence is punctuated correctly. Write I if the sentence is incorrect.**

1. Mt. Vesuvius is a volcano in Italy; it is located near the Bay of Naples.

2. Mt. Vesuvius erupted in A.D. 79 its eruption buried the cities of Pompeii and Herculaneum.

3. Huge columns of smoke and ash filled the air; and earthquakes related to the eruption caused tsunamis.

4. Tsunamis are tidal waves they are usually caused by geological disturbances.

5. Volcanic ash and other material buried Pompeii, and Herculaneum suffered the same fate.

6. People were buried the city was destroyed.

7. Diggers discovered the remains of Pompeii in the late 1500s; archaeologists began to study the city in the 1800s.

8. Today many people live and work near Mt. Vesuvius the surrounding cities are threatened by the volcano.

9. People in the area are always on alert, no city wants to be the next Pompeii.

10. An active volcano caused major damage in the United States in 1980; it was Mount Saint Helens in Washington.

● Connect to the Writing Process: Editing
Punctuating Compound Sentences

11.–16. Rewrite the incorrect sentences from the preceding exercise, using proper punctuation.

● Connect to the Writing Process: Drafting
Writing Compound Sentences

Write a compound sentence about each topic. Use a semicolon to join the sentences.

17. sports   **18.** exercise   **19.** health   **20.** food

● Connect to the Writing Process: Revising
Combining Sentences with Semicolons

Rewrite the following paragraphs. Combine some of the simple sentences into compound sentences joined with a semicolon.

Fashions change constantly. What is stylish today will be outdated soon. In the 1700s, it was stylish for men to wear wigs. They wore kneepants with stockings. It's hard to imagine wearing an outfit like that to school. Your classmates would certainly laugh.

Prior to the 1920s, women rarely wore pants. They wore skirts with petticoats or bustles. Girls today would find these styles very uncomfortable. These fashions would certainly be a problem in tennis or soccer!

APPLY TO WRITING

Descriptive Paragraph: *Compound Sentences*

Styles do change from one generation to the next, and even from one year to the next. Imagine that you have been asked to participate in putting together objects for a time capsule that will be opened in ten years. Your assignment is to write a descriptive paragraph of the current style of clothing for young teens. Be sure to use some compound sentences joined by semicolons in your description. If you can, include a picture that shows the style you are describing.

QuickCheck Mixed Practice

Geography Topic **Correctly rewrite the following sentences. If the sentence is correct, write C. You may find errors in the use of apostrophes and semicolons.**

1. Antarcticas location has made it difficult to study the continent is not accessible in the winter.

2. Roald Amudsens party was the first to reach Antarctica in 1911.

3. Australia is the globes smallest continent it also is it's driest.

4. Much of Australia is desert; humid areas are found along the coast.

5. Its the only continent that is occupied by only one nation.

Colons

A colon (:) often comes before a list of items.

Use a colon before most lists of items, especially when the list comes after an expression like *the following*.

Notice that commas go between the items in each series.

I have three hobbies: reading, writing, and running.

The following kinds of books are my favorites: mystery, humor, adventure, and biography.

Never place a colon between a verb and a complement or directly after a preposition.

INCORRECT	My favorite authors are: Madeleine L'Engle, Scott O'Dell, and Roald Dahl.
	(*Are* is the verb, and the names in the series rename the subject *authors,* making them predicate adjectives.)
CORRECT	My favorite authors are the following writers: Madeleine L'Engle, Scott O'Dell, and Roald Dahl.
INCORRECT	These books are for: my teacher, my brother, and my best friend.
	(*For* is a preposition.)
CORRECT	These books are for the following people: my teacher, my brother, and my best friend.

You can find out more about commas in a series on page L450.

There are a few other special situations that also need a colon.

COLON USAGE	
HOURS AND MINUTES	5:30 A.M.
SALUTATIONS IN BUSINESS LETTERS	Dear Sir: Dear Madam:

PRACTICE YOUR SKILLS

● Check Your Understanding

Using Colons

Contemporary Life

Write C if the sentence is punctuated correctly. Write I if it is incorrect.

1. My three favorite books are: *A Wrinkle in Time, Island of the Blue Dolphins,* and *Matilda.*

2. I read before I go to bed at 930 P.M.

3. The following are my favorite characters from *A Wrinkle in Time:* Meg, Charles Wallace, and Calvin.

4. The children meet three very interesting women: Mrs. Whatsit, Mrs. Who, and Mrs. Which.

5. I learned the following new words while reading this book; *prodigious, dubiously,* and *decipher.*

6. Scott O'Dell's novels can be described in three words: *exciting, touching,* and *fascinating.*

7. Three other books by Scott O'Dell are *The Black Pearl, Zia,* and *Sing Down the Moon.*

8. In *Island of the Blue Dolphins,* Karana makes the following items: clothing, weapons, and tools.

9. Three great books by Roald Dahl are: *The BFG, The Witches,* and *Danny, Champion of the World.*

10. Three characters in *Matilda* are: Miss Honey, Miss Trunchbull, and Matilda.

11.–15. Rewrite the incorrect sentences from the preceding exercise using proper punctuation.

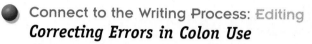

Communicate Your Ideas

APPLY TO WRITING

Writer's Craft: *Analyzing the Use of Colons*

Authors use colons in their writing, but they don't use them very often. Using the colon and many lists would become boring for a reader. Read the following excerpt and answer the questions that follow.

> Red Cloud led us north to the mouth of Prairie Dog Creek. It was the Moon of Ripening Cherries, July, the time when we hold our Sun Dance every year. It is then that the sun begins to go back from its highest place in the sky and the time of year when the sage covering the prairie is fully grown and the buffalo roll their great bodies in its fragrant leaves. Everything in nature rejoices: the birds, the animals, the trees and flowers and also the little things which crawl.
>
> —*Paul and Dorothy Goble,*
> **Brave Eagle's Account of the Fetterman Fight**

- Write the sentence that contains the colon. Why is a colon necessary?

- Try rewriting the sentence without the colon. Has the sentence become easier or harder to understand? Why?

- Do you ever use colons when you write? Explain your answer.

History Topic · **Rewrite the following sentences, correctly punctuating them. If the sentence is correct, write C.**

1. In the 1800's, thousands of settlers headed across our continent.

2. Some of these people left comfortable homes most were looking for a new life.

3. Some wanted to build farms and ranches for their childrens futures.

4. Crossing the country wasnt easy there werent buses, trains, or planes.

5. People traveled across the country in three ways: driving covered wagons, riding horses, or walking on their own two feet.

6. The trip was strenuous, many people died along the way.

7. These traveling pioneers began their day at 5;00 A.M.

8. By 900 P.M., they were in bed for the night.

9. Some families slept in tents; most slept right on the ground.

10. The pioneers progress was about fifteen miles per day.

11. They werent moving very quickly.

12. They're campfires used a great deal of fuel wood wasnt easy to find.

13. Horses werent used to pull covered wagons.

14. The wagons power was supplied by mules or oxen.

15. The pioneers faced: harsh weather, disease, and sometimes starvation.

Hyphens

If you ever have to divide a word, you will need to use a hyphen (-).

Hyphens with Divided Words

Dividing a word is the most common use of a hyphen.

Use a hyphen to divide a word at the end of a line.

You cannot divide a word just anywhere. The following guidelines will help you divide words at the end of a line. If you are not certain about where each syllable in a word ends, look up the word in a dictionary. Each entry word is divided into syllables.

GUIDELINES FOR DIVIDING WORDS

1. Divide words only between syllables. If you do not know where each syllable in a word ends, look up the word in a dictionary.

    syl•la•ble: syl-lable or sylla-ble

2. Never break a one-syllable word.

    DO NOT BREAK   send   know   love

3. Do not divide a word after the first letter.

    DO NOT BREAK   again   echo   over

PRACTICE YOUR SKILLS

● Check Your Understanding
Using Hyphens to Divide Words

Write the letter of the correctly divided word. Refer to the chart on page L531 to help decide whether a word should be divided.

1. a. un-roll
   b. unr-oll

2. a. o-mit
   b. omit

3. a. po-wer
   b. pow-er

4. a. di-saster
   b. disa-ster

5. a. sud-den
   b. su-dden

6. a. le-ave
   b. leave

7. a. cam-ping
   b. camp-ing

8. a. agree
   b. a-gree

9. a. gover-nor
   b. gove-rnor

10. a. oboe
   b. o-boe

● Connect to the Writing Process: Editing
Correcting Errors in Hyphen Use

If a word has been incorrectly divided, rewrite it, placing the hyphen in the proper place. If the word is correctly divided, write C.

11. dev-ote

12. Germ-an

13. ev-er

14. no-te

15. be-tray

16. gymn-asium

17. no-vel

18. a-gainst

19. des-troy

20. met-al

Other Uses of Hyphens

Although dividing words is the most common use of hyphens, there are a few other uses as well.

Hyphens with Certain Numbers

When you write numbers out in a story or report, you will use a hyphen to spell most numbers correctly.

Use a hyphen when writing out the numbers twenty-one through ninety-nine.

We baked thirty-one pies for the bake sale.

Fifty-five cookies were sold to the principal.

If a number is the first word of a sentence, it must always be written out.

Four students shared the cost of a cake.

One hundred twenty-two people attended the bake sale.

Hyphens with Certain Fractions

Fractions used as adjectives are hyphenated.

Use a hyphen when writing out a fraction used as an adjective.

HYPHEN	I need one-quarter teaspoon of vanilla for the cake batter. (*One-quarter* is an adjective that describes *teaspoon*.)
NO HYPHEN	One quarter of the profits will go to charity. (*One quarter* is a noun. It is the subject.)
HYPHEN	The recipe calls for one-half cup of butter. (*One-half* is an adjective that describes *cup*.)
NO HYPHEN	We sold one half of the pies right away. (*One half* is a noun. It is the direct object.)

You can learn more about adjectives on pages L113–L126.

Hyphens with Some Compound Words

A **compound noun** is a noun made up of two or more nouns. The words in a compound noun may be written in one of three ways: (1) together, as one word; (2) as two separate words; or (3) as two words joined with a hyphen.

Use a hyphen to separate the parts of some compound nouns.

COMPOUND NOUNS	
ONE WORD	trapdoor, crackerjack, catnap
TWO WORDS	tree house, tea cake, sea lion
HYPHENATED	crack-up, fast-forward, hocus-pocus

If you are unsure of the spelling of a compound noun, check it in a dictionary.

● Check Your Understanding
Using Hyphens

Choose the letter of the correctly written item.

1. **a.** two-thirds majority
   b. two thirds majority
2. **a.** two thirds of the country
   b. two-thirds of the country
3. **a.** sister-in-law
   b. sister in law
4. **a.** egg-beater
   b. egg beater
5. **a.** three fourths of my friends
   b. three-fourths of my friends
6. **a.** sea-shell
   b. seashell
7. **a.** stepmother
   b. step-mother
8. **a.** one-quarter teaspoon
   b. one quarter teaspoon
9. **a.** fancy-free
   b. fancy free
10. **a.** one-half cup
    b. one half cup

Writing Sentences with Hyphenated Words

Follow the directions to write five sentences.

11. Use *one-half* as an adjective.

12. Use *one half* as a noun.

13. Use *three quarters* as a noun.

14. Use *three-quarters* as an adjective.

15. Use *one tenth* as a noun.

● Connect to the Writing Process: Editing
Correcting Errors in Hyphenation

Rewrite the following sentences, correcting the use of hyphens. If the sentence is correct, write C.

16. My step-father is a great cook.

17. He makes the best spaghetti-sauce.

18. He puts two and one half tablespoons of garlic with some tomatoes in a pan.

19. He adds a pinch of salt and one half teaspoon of oregano.

20. He puts one and one-quarter cups of sliced mushrooms into this tasty sauce.

21. He adds about one half pound of Italian sausage to the mixture.

22. I can eat two-thirds of the sauce by myself!

23. We usually invite my sister and brother in law to dinner.

24. My sister always bakes home-made bread.

25. My step-brother puts a lot of Parmesan cheese on his spaghetti.

APPLY TO WRITING

Narrative Paragraph: *Hyphens*

Write for your teacher a narrative paragraph about a meal at your house. Use the order in which things happen as you tell about the meal. When you come to the end of a line of writing, use a hyphen to divide a word. If you aren't sure about where to divide a word, look it up in the dictionary.

QuickCheck Mixed Practice

Contemporary Life **Rewrite the following sentences, correctly punctuating them. If the sentence is correct, write C.**

1. That stew recipe calls for one and one half pound of beef.

2. Put in two thirds cup of carrots.

3. The recipe calls for one-half of an onion I always leave that out.

4. Instead of the fresh ones, I use canned-tomatoes.

5. This is everybody's favorite meal.

6. My sister in law always serves it in the winter.

7. This recipe is her's.

8. Its best with corn-bread.

9. My mom always makes a big Caesar salad, too.

10. My familys favorite dishes are: stew, chili, and spaghetti.

Using Apostrophes

Correctly write each word that needs an apostrophe. Some sentences may contain more than one error.

1. The camps name is Camp Evergreen.
2. Dylans tent mates are planning their day.
3. Hes looking at the activity schedule with his friends.
4. No ones name is on the list for arts and crafts class.
5. Hasnt anyone read this class description?
6. Look, its at the same time as Amandas swim class.
7. Im sure that its hours should be ten to eleven.
8. Thats probably just someones typing error.
9. Luis and Nathan are coming out of the mens showers.
10. Lets find out whether they've made a mistake.

Using Semicolons and Colons

Write each phrase or sentence, adding a semicolon or colon wherever necessary. If a sentence does not need punctuation, write C.

1. Dear Captain Salazar
2. The ship will leave the harbor at 420 P.M.
3. I have never been to Puerto Rico I am looking forward to my visit.
4. I have visited the following states Georgia, North Carolina, South Carolina, and Louisiana.
5. These are the towns we plan to visit Aguadilla, Arecibo, Dorado, and San Juan.

Using Hyphens with Divided Words

Write the letter of the word in each pair that is divided correctly.

1. a exit
   b e-xit

2. a but-terfly
   b butt-erfly

3. a ins-ect
   b in-sect

4. a ma-ximum
   b max-imum

5. a de-cide
   b dec-ide

6. a ac-tive
   b active

7. a stra-ight
   b straight

8. a aboard
   b a-board

9. a min-us
   b mi-nus

10. a chil-dren
    b child-ren

Writing Sentences

Write ten sentences that follow the directions below.
Write a sentence that . . .

1. includes the possessive form of the noun *sister*.

2. includes the possessive form of the noun *horse*.

3. includes the possessive form of the noun *men*.

4. includes the possessive form of the pronoun *anyone*.

5. includes the words *they're* and *their*.

6. includes the plural of *B*.

7. includes two simple sentences joined by a semicolon.

8. includes a colon with a list of items.

9. includes *two thirds* as an adjective.

10. includes a compound noun that is hyphenated.

Language and *Self-Expression*

Even though Janet Fish did not paint this picture in a realistic way, it is obvious that she paid close attention to details. What are some of the things in this picture that suggest that she was painting from life rather than from memory?

Writers must also notice details to give good descriptions. Pretend you are a detective. Examine one limited area of the classroom or of a room at home. Write a professional report describing exactly what you see. Try to use semicolons at least twice and a colon at least once. If you use numbers, spell them out. Then read your report aloud to your classmates or family.

Prewriting Examine the items, count them, and write a description of each one. Then group the items geographically as you review your notes.

Drafting Write your report. Begin with a sentence that tells your reader when and where you made your observations. Be as precise as possible in describing the color, shape, and size of each item.

Revising Give your report to a classmate to read, and ask for feedback. Discuss whether the descriptions are as clear as they might be and whether the items seem grouped in a way that makes sense.

Editing Check your report for errors in punctuation and spelling. Be sure that you used hyphens, semi-colons, and colons correctly.

Publishing Read your report aloud to a group of classmates. You may wish to leave out the opening sentence and have them guess what kind of place you are describing.

Another Look

Other Punctuation

Add **'s** to form the possessive of a singular noun. *(page L507)*

Add only an apostrophe to form the possessive of a plural noun that ends in *s*. *(page L508)*

Add an **'s** to form the possessive of a plural noun that does not end in s. *(page L509)*

Do not add an apostrophe to form the possessive of a personal pronoun. *(pages L511–L512)*

Add **'s** to form the possessive of an indefinite pronoun. *(page L512)*

Use an apostrophe in a contraction to show where one or more letters have been omitted. *(pages L515–L516)*

Add **'s** to form the plural of lowercase letters and some capital letters. *(page L520)*

Use a semicolon between the two simple sentences of a compound sentence that are not joined by a coordinating conjunction. *(pages L523–L524)*

Use a colon before most lists of items, especially when the list comes after an expression like *the following*. *(pages L527–L528)*

Use a colon between hours and minutes and after the salutation in a business letter. *(page L528)*

Use a hyphen to divide a word at the end of a line. *(page L531)*

Use a hyphen when writing out the numbers twenty-one through ninety-nine. *(page L533)*

Use a hyphen when writing out a fraction used as an adjective. *(pages L533–L534)*

Use a hyphen to separate the parts of some compound nouns. *(pages L534–L535)*

Other Information About Other Punctuation

Using contractions with verbs *(page L516)*

Writing contractions with *not* *(page L516)*

Recognizing contractions and possessive pronouns *(pages L517–L518)*

Writing plurals of numerals *(page L520)*

Breaking words into syllables *(page L531)*

Posttest

Directions

Write the letter of the word or punctuation mark that correctly completes each sentence.

EXAMPLE   Andy carried his __(1)__ camera to the car.

      1 A fathers
        B father's
        C fathers'
        D fathers's

ANSWER   **1 B**

  __(1)__ family was getting ready for a picnic at the lake. His parents packed the following items in the picnic basket __(2)__ pickles, sandwiches, cupcakes, potato salad, grapes, pears, and orange juice. They set out on the road at 9 __(3)__ 30 A.M. Andy counted only __(4)__ other cars on the winding road to the lake. They __(5)__ have any trouble finding a picnic table in a quiet place. The lake looked clear and inviting __(6)__ the children wanted to swim right away. Alexis was wearing a __(7)__ and cut-offs. She changed into her bathing suit in the __(8)__ restroom. The two __(9)__ plan was to rent a rowboat. The boat's name appeared to be *My Lice* because the __(10)__ were too faded to read.

1 **A** Andys'
   B Andys
   C Andy's
   D Andy

2 **A** ;
   B :
   C ,
   D .

3 **A** ;
   B :
   C ,
   D .

4 **A** twenty one
   B twentyone
   C twenty-one
   D twenty:one

5 **A** didn't
   B did'nt
   C didnt
   D did'not

6 **A** ;
   B :
   C ,
   D .

7 **A** Tshirt
   B T-shirt
   C T shirt
   D T'shirt

8 **A** womens's
   B womens'
   C womens
   D women's

9 **A** adult's
   B adults
   C adults's
   D adults'

10 **A** As's
    B As'
    C A's
    D As

A Writer's Guide to Citing Sources

When you write a report, you sometimes need to use other people's ideas to help you make your own point. You must give people credit whenever you use their words. Notes that credit the original source of a quotation are called **citations.**

A **parenthetical citation** is a brief note in parentheses that is placed right after the quotation you have used. It gives the reader enough information to find the source in a list of works cited at the end of your report. Use the following examples to help you write parenthetical citations correctly.

BOOK BY ONE AUTHOR	Give author's last name and page number(s): (Alexander 25).
BOOK BY MORE THAN ONE AUTHOR	Give all authors' last names and page number(s): (Hoffa and Morgan 89–90).
ARTICLE WITH AUTHOR NAMED	Give author's last name and page number(s): (Lyman and Mather 55).
ARTICLE WITH AUTHOR UNNAMED	Give a shortened form of the title of the article—unless full title is already short—and page number(s): ("Finding a Voice" 70).
ARTICLE IN A REFERENCE WORK; AUTHOR UNNAMED	Give title (full or shortened). No page number is necessary if the article is a single page from an encyclopedia arranged alphabetically: ("Disabled").

Keep a parenthetical citation as close as possible to the quotation. Place it at the end of the phrase or sentence so that you will not interrupt the flow of the sentence.

A **works-cited page** should be included at the end of your paper. This page is a complete list of all the sources you used to write your report. The sources are listed alphabetically by the author's last name or by the title if no author is listed. Use the following examples to help you create a works-cited page.

GENERAL REFERENCE WORKS	"Disabled." World Book Encyclopedia. 1998 ed.
BOOKS BY A SINGLE AUTHOR	Alexander, Sally Hobart. Taking Hold: My Journey into Blindness. New York: Simon & Schuster, 1995.
BOOKS BY MORE THAN ONE AUTHOR	Hoffa, Helynn and Gary Morgan. Yes You Can: A Helpbook for the Physically Disabled. New York: Pharos Books, 1990.
ARTICLES IN MAGAZINES	Lyman, Michael and Mary Anne Mather. "Equal Opportunity Learning: Assistive Technology for Students with Special Needs." Technology & Learning. Nov. 1998: 55.
ARTICLES IN NEWSPAPERS	Felton, Bruce. "Technologies That Enable the Disabled." The New York Times 14 Sept. 1997, sec. 3:1.
ARTICLE FROM A CD-ROM	Personal Communicator. CD-ROM. Lansing: MSU Communication Technology Lab, 1995.
ARTICLE FROM AN ONLINE DATABASE WITH A PRINT VERSION	Brightman, Alan. "Apple's Computer Passport: The Challenge of Designing for People with Disabilities." Ability: 9 pars. 6 Oct. 1999 <http://www.Abilitymagazine.com/smithAP.html>.
ONLINE MATERIAL WITH NO PRINT VERSION	"Superhawk Plus: New Communication Device." Closing the Gap: Computer Technology in Special Education and Rehabilitation: 6 pars. 6 Oct. 1999 <http://www.closingthegap.com/news/weeklynews/pr2.html>.

CHAPTER 16

Spelling Correctly

 **Pretest**

Directions
Write the letter of the choice that correctly respells each underlined word. If the underlined word contains no error, choose *D.*

EXAMPLE   Those who value nature often provide
<u>invalueable</u> services.
         (1)

1 A invaluable
   B invaluible
   C invaluabel
   D No error

ANSWER   **1 A**

Wildlife <u>sanctuaries</u> for birds provide <u>pertection</u> and
        (1)   (2)
care for those injured, hurt, or abandoned. <u>Awarenes</u> of
                                              (3)
the birds' needs assists in their <u>recoverey</u>. Understanding
                                    (4)
patterns of <u>behaveor</u> allows workers to enter the <u>cages</u>
             (5)   (6)
without danger. Through tours, <u>peopel</u> learn more about
                                (7)
the dangers these creatures face. Pelicans and herons

often <u>recieve</u> injuries from entanglement in fishing lines.
      (8)
Other birds are <u>victimes</u> of being struck by golf <u>balls</u>.
                  (9)   (10)

1 **A** sanctuarys
   B sanctuarees
   C santuaries
   D No error

2 **A** protectshun
   B portection
   C protection
   D No error

3 **A** Awarness
   B Awareness
   C Awearness
   D No error

4 **A** reecovery
   B recovery
   C recoverie
   D No error

5 **A** behavior
   B beehavior
   C beehaveor
   D No error

6 **A** cagess
   B cajes
   C kages
   D No error

7 **A** peeple
   B peepel
   C people
   D No error

8 **A** receive
   B receeve
   C reeceive
   D No error

9 **A** victems
   B victims
   C victemes
   D No error

10 **A** bals
   B bawls
   C balles
   D No error

Strategies for Learning to Spell

Learn to spell correctly by using hearing, sight, and touch.
Study this five-step strategy used successfully by many
people for spelling unfamiliar words.

1 Auditory

Say the word aloud. Answer these questions.
- Where have I heard or read the word before?
- What was the context in which I heard or read the
  word?

2 Visual

Look at the word. Answer these questions.
- Does the word divide into parts? Is it a compound word?
  Does it have a prefix or a suffix?
- Does the word look like any other word I know? Is it
  part of a word family I recognize?

3 Auditory

Spell the word to yourself. Answer these questions.
- How is each sound spelled?
- Are there any surprises? Does the word follow spelling
  rules I know, or does it break the rules?

4 Visual/Kinesthetic

Write the word as you look at it. Answer these questions.
- Have I written the word clearly?
- Are my letters formed correctly?

5 Visual/Kinesthetic

**Cover up the word. Visualize it. Write it. Answer the
question.**
- Did I write this word correctly?
- If the answer is no, return to step 1.

Spelling Strategies

Spelling errors distract your readers' attention from your ideas. Some spelling errors can cause readers to misunderstand you. This chapter will introduce you to strategies and generalizations to help you improve your spelling.

STRATEGY **Use a dictionary.** If you are not sure how to spell a word, or if a word does not "look right," check its spelling in a dictionary.

STRATEGY **Proofread your writing carefully.** You may find it easier to proofread your writing several times. Focus on finding misspellings in one reading.

PRACTICE YOUR SKILLS

 Check Your Understanding
Recognizing Misspelled Words

Write the letter of the misspelled word in each set. Then write the word correctly.

1. (a) favorite (b) creetures (c) principal
2. (a) against (b) headache (c) diffrent
3. (a) believe (b) intresting (c) poison
4. (a) height (b) humorous (c) wieghs
5. (a) eether (b) celebration (c) sugar
6. (a) wreath (b) remanes (c) hopefully
7. (a) except (b) minute (c) allways
8. (a) science (b) insted (c) tractor
9. (a) decorate (b) straight (c) calender
10. (a) truely (b) stubborn (c) invitation

Be sure you are pronouncing words correctly.
"Swallowing" syllables or adding extra syllables can cause you to misspell a word.

PRACTICE YOUR SKILLS

● Check Your Understanding
Pronouncing Words

Oral
Expression
Practice saying each syllable in the following words to help you spell the words correctly.

1. veg•e•ta•ble   **6.** res•tau•rant

2. qui•et•ly   **7.** ru•in

3. dif•fer•ent   **8.** re•spon•si•bil•i•ty

4. cru•el•ty   **9.** math•e•mat•ics

5. val•u•a•ble   **10.** in•tro•duce

STRATEGY **Make up mnemonic devices.** A sentence like "*Rare* books are in the lib*rar*y" can help you remember that the letters *r-a-r* are in *library*.

STRATEGY **Keep a spelling journal.** Use it to record the words you have had trouble spelling. Here are some suggestions for organizing your spelling journal.

- Write the word correctly.
- Write the word again, underlining or circling the part of the word that gave you trouble.
- Write a tip that will help you remember how to spell the word in the future.

arithmetic   arithmetic   A rat in the house might
*   eat the ice cream.*

You can spell hundreds of words correctly by learning a few helpful spelling generalizations. Write the generalizations in your spelling journal, along with examples to help you remember them. Also write down any exceptions. Adding new words as you come across them will help you keep these generalizations fresh in your mind.

 Spelling Patterns

Some spelling generalizations are based on the patterns of letters in words. One common pattern is spelled with *ie* or *ei*, and another common pattern sounds like the word *seed*.

Words with *ie* and *ei*

You probably know this rhyme for spelling words with *ie* and *ei*.

> Put *i* before *e*
> Except after *c*
> Or when the sound is long *a*
> As in *neighbor* and *weigh*.

When you spell words with *ie* or *ei*, *i* frequently comes before *e*, except when the letters follow *c* or when they stand for the sound long *a*.

IE AND *EI*			
I Before *E*	bel**ie**ve	misch**ie**f	n**ie**ce
	p**ie**ce	th**ie**f	br**ie**f

Except After **C**	ceiling	conceit	deceive
	perceive	receipt	receive
Sounds Like **A**	eight	freight	sleigh
	veil	weight	neighbor

These words do not follow the pattern.

EXCEPTIONS			
either	foreign	height	ancient
leisure	protein	their	seize
conscience	friendly	weird	species

Word Alert

Long lists of words with unusual spellings may be difficult to memorize. One mnemonic trick that can help you is to create a sentence using groups of words with the same spelling. For example, if you can remember how to spell *their,* you can spell every word in this sentence.

Either for**ei**gn army can s**ei**ze the sh**ei**kdom at th**ei**r l**ei**sure.

Words with *–cede, –ceed,* and *–sede*

Some other words that cause problems are those that end with a "seed" sound. This sound can be spelled *–cede, –ceed,* or *–sede.* Most words that end with this sound are spelled *–cede.*

In all but four words that end with the "seed" sound, this sound is spelled *–cede.*

–CEDE			
Examples	precede	recede	concede	intercede

You'll have no trouble spelling these words if you memorize the four exceptions.

EXCEPTIONS			
ex**ceed**	pro**ceed**	suc**ceed**	super**sede**

Of course, types of seeds are spelled with the *seed* ending: *birdseed, cottonseed,* and *hayseed.* This mnemonic might help you remember the exceptions.

As you can s**ee**, the exceptions don't *exceed* four. You'll *succeed* if you *proceed* to spell the first thr**ee** with *eed*. S**et** as**ide** all generalizations for *supersede.*

PRACTICE YOUR SKILLS

● Check Your Understanding
Using Spelling Patterns

Write each word, adding *ie* or *ei*.

1. f▢ld
2. misch▢f
3. rec▢ve
4. dec▢ve
5. v▢l
6. w▢gh
7. conc▢t

8. for▢gn
9. br▢f
10. n▢ce
11. n▢ther
12. sl▢gh
13. n▢ghbor
14. prot▢n

15. ▢ght
16. c▢ling
17. bel▢ve
18. rec▢pt
19. r▢gn
20. y▢ld

Write each word, adding *-sede, ceed,* or *-cede*.

21. pre▢
22. inter▢
23. ex▢

24. pro▢
25. re▢
26. suc▢

27. ac▢
28. con▢
29. super▢

30. se▢

Using Spelling Patterns

General Interest **Find and rewrite the ten words that have been spelled incorrectly.**

In 1911, my great-great-aunt came to America. She had the beleif that if she worked hard, she was sure to succede. A friendly nieghbor suggested she and her neice earn money by sewing. Aunt Magda proceeded to the factory to get the peicework to bring home. She signed a reciept for the materials and was told she would recieve eght cents for each one she finished. Although both women worked as quickly as they could, niether worked fewer than ten hours a day. Their expenses ate up all they earned. Aunt Magda's hopes of succeeding slowly receeded.

Plurals

The following generalizations will help you spell the plurals of nouns correctly. When you're in doubt about an exception, check a dictionary.

Regular Nouns

To form the plural of most nouns, simply add *s*.

MOST NOUNS				
SINGULAR	tree	rock	cage	house
PLURAL	trees	rocks	cages	houses

If a noun ends with *s, ch, sh, x,* or *z,* add *es* to form the plural.

	S, CH, SH, X, OR Z				
SINGULAR	grass	bran**ch**	bu**sh**	fo**x**	buz**z**
PLURAL	grass**es**	branch**es**	bush**es**	fox**es**	buzz**es**

Follow the same generalizations when you write the plural forms of proper nouns.

> the McClean family = the McClean**s**
> the Cruz family = the Cruz**es**
> the Pressley family = the Pressley**s**
> the Haas family = the Haas**es**

As you can see from the preceding examples, an apostrophe is not used to make the plural form of proper nouns. It is used only to show possession.

Nouns Ending in *y*

Add *s* to form the plural of a noun ending in a vowel and *y.*

	VOWELS AND Y			
SINGULAR	jay	monk**ey**	cowb**oy**	freew**ay**
PLURAL	jay**s**	monkey**s**	cowboy**s**	freeway**s**

Change the *y* to *i* and add *es* to a noun ending in a consonant and *y.*

CONSONANTS AND Y				
SINGULAR	coun**ty**	assemb**ly**	wor**ry**	batter**y**
PLURAL	coun**ties**	assemb**lies**	wor**ries**	batter**ies**

PRACTICE YOUR SKILLS

● Check Your Understanding
Forming Plurals

Write the plural form of each of these nouns.

1. donkey	**6.** Hearst	**11.** crash	**16.** birch
2. caddy	**7.** loss	**12.** bus	**17.** journey
3. match	**8.** decoy	**13.** ash	**18.** discovery
4. class	**9.** wax	**14.** fly	**19.** mist
5. guppy	**10.** spy	**15.** box	**20.** Valdez

● Connect to the Writing Process: Editing
Spelling Plural Nouns

Science Topic **Rewrite these sentences, changing the underlined singular nouns to plural nouns.**

21. The <u>baby</u> of some <u>creature</u> have special <u>name</u>.

22. Of course, <u>collie</u> and other <u>dog</u> have <u>puppy</u>.

23. Did you know that <u>fox</u> have <u>cub</u>?

24. <u>Bear</u> and <u>lioness</u> have <u>cub</u> as well.

25. <u>Donkey</u> as well as <u>filly</u> are the parents of <u>colt</u>.

26. Surprisingly, baby <u>bunny</u> are called <u>kit</u> or <u>kitten</u>!

27. In hidden <u>nest</u>, wild <u>turkey</u> raise their <u>chick</u>.

28. You can find young <u>shoat</u> in <u>pigsty</u>.

29. <u>Kangaroo</u> carry <u>joey</u> in their <u>pouch</u>.

30. <u>Cowboy</u> call young stray calves <u>dogie</u>.

Nouns Ending in *o*

Add *s* to form the plural of a noun ending in a vowel and *o.*

VOWELS AND *O*			
SINGULAR	ster**eo**	cam**eo**	kangar**oo**	tatt**oo**
PLURAL	stereo**s**	cameo**s**	kangaroo**s**	tattoo**s**

Add *s* to form the plural of musical terms ending in *o.*

MUSICAL TERMS ENDING WITH *O*			
SINGULAR	solo	alto	piano	banjo
PLURAL	solo**s**	alto**s**	piano**s**	banjo**s**

Add *s* to form the plural of words that are borrowed from the Spanish language.

SPANISH WORDS WITH *O*			
SINGULAR	patio	rodeo	taco	rancho
PLURAL	patio**s**	rodeo**s**	taco**s**	rancho**s**

The plurals of nouns ending in a consonant and *o* do not follow a regular pattern.

CONSONANTS AND *O*			
SINGULAR	kim**ono**	phot**o**	her**o**	pot**ato**
PLURAL	kimono**s**	photo**s**	hero**es**	potato**es**

When you are not sure how to form the plural of a word that ends in *o,* go to a dictionary. Sometimes you will find that either spelling is acceptable. In this case, use the first form given. If the dictionary does not give a plural form, the plural is usually formed by adding *s.*

Nouns Ending in *f* or *fe*

To form the plural of some nouns ending in *f* or *fe,* just add *s.*

F AND *FE*			
SINGULAR	roo**f**	cli**ff**	gira**ffe**	ca**fe**
PLURAL	roo**fs**	cli**ffs**	gira**ffes**	ca**fes**

For some nouns ending in *f* or *fe,* change the *f* to *v* and add *es* or *s.*

F AND *FE* TO *V*			
SINGULAR	lea**f**	kni**fe**	cal**f**	your**self**
PLURAL	lea**ves**	kni**ves**	cal**ves**	your**selves**

Because there is no sure way to tell which generalization applies, use a dictionary to check the plural form of a word that ends in *f* or *fe.*

 Word Alert Watch out! Misspelling some of these plurals can turn them into verbs and confuse your reader. For example, a person *loafs* around, *leafs* through a book, and *wolfs* down food.

PRACTICE YOUR SKILLS

● Check Your Understanding
Forming Plurals

Write the plural form of each of these nouns. Use a dictionary to check the spelling of the ones you do not know.

1. cuckoo   **6.** motto   **11.** earmuff   **16.** soprano

2. sheriff   **7.** proof   **12.** studio   **17.** thief

3. rodeo   **8.** safe   **13.** reef   **18.** curio

4. elf   **9.** igloo   **14.** silo   **19.** bluff

5. trio   **10.** shelf   **15.** burro   **20.** gulf

● Connect to the Writing Process: Editing
Spelling Plural Nouns

General Interest   **Rewrite this paragraph, correcting eight spelling errors.**

The clowns who work in rodeoes are nothing to laugh at. When riders are thrown, the clowns distract the wild broncoes. Otherwise, their sharp hoofs will trample the fallen riders. These skillful actors present themselfs as clowns. They also keep audiences entertained. They often dress in huge sombreroes and bright kerchieves. They may act like big oafs and pretend to fall off little burroes. Actually, the clowns are really unrecognized heros because they sometimes save lifes.

Numerals, Letters, Symbols, and Words as Words

To form the plurals of most numerals, letters, symbols, and words used as words, add an *s*.

> Your *2***s** look like *Z***s**.
> The 1920**s** were known as the Roaring Twenties.
> What do these *?***s** in the margin mean?
> The fireworks produced *oh***s** and *ah***s**.

To prevent confusion, it is best to use an apostrophe and *s* with the lowercase letters, some capital letters, and some words used as words. When you use this method to create the plural of an italicized letter or word, you do not italicize the apostrophe and *s*.

> How many *s'***s** are in *misspell?*
> The dark portholes looked like black *O'***s.**
> Beginning English-speakers may confuse *was'***s** and *were'***s**.

You can learn more about the use of italics on pages L479–L480.

Other Plural Forms

Irregular plurals are not formed by adding *s* or *es.*

IRREGULAR PLURALS				
SINGULAR	tooth	man	ox	woman	child
PLURAL	tee**th**	m**en**	ox**en**	wom**en**	child**ren**
SINGULAR	foot	goose	mouse	person
PLURAL	f**ee**t	g**ee**se	m**ice**	pe**ople**

Some nouns have the same form for singular and plural.

SAME SINGULAR AND PLURAL			
Chinese	sheep	scissors	Swiss
moose	headquarters	Sioux	deer
series	salmon	politics	pliers

PRACTICE YOUR SKILLS

● Check Your Understanding
Forming Plurals

Write the plural form of each noun.

1. Cheyenne
2. F
3. '60
4. fireman
5. pants
6. ?
7. *yes*
8. i
9. 7
10. species
11. *Hello*
12. t
13. sheep
14. 1700
15. Japanese
16. ABC
17. chairwoman
18. prey
19. snowman
20. up and down

● Connect to the Writing Process: Editing
Spelling Plural Nouns

General Interest **Decide whether the underlined plurals are formed correctly. If any are incorrect, write the correct form.**

21. Did you know that $s are composed of Us on top of Ss?

22. Some bamboo plants grow three foot per day.

23. Humans, dogs, and domestic cats have only two sets of <u>tooth</u> per lifetime.

24. There are three *C*s and two *X*s in the Roman numeral that stands for 320.

25. There were no *O*s in the original Roman number system.

26. The majority of <u>people</u> who live past 100 are <u>woman</u>.

27. There are two *o*s, two *k*s, and three *e*s in the word *bookkeeper*.

28. The number of <u>people</u> alive in the <u>1900s</u> was greater than the number of all the <u>people</u> who had ever lived.

29. The ~s in Web addresses are called *tildes*.

30. <u>Oxes</u> are actually cattle, not members of different <u>specieses</u>.

Communicate Your Ideas

APPLY TO WRITING

Friendly Letter: *Plurals*

Does television tell the truth about how people really live? Imagine that you are a visitor to the United States who has never seen American TV before. What conclusions would you draw about American life from what you see on the television screen? Would those conclusions be accurate? Pretend you are the visitor, and write a letter back home. Compare the impressions you get from television to the impressions you get from looking around you. Use at least ten plural nouns in your letter.

QuickCheck Mixed Practice

Write the plural form of each of these words. Use a dictionary whenever necessary.

1. alley	**8.** hoax	**15.** lasso
2. E	**9.** *hi*	**16.** echo
3. ditch	**10.** 7	**17.** dance
4. stuntwoman	**11.** 1860	**18.** brakeman
5. monkey	**12.** dormouse	**19.** sky
6. shelf	**13.** soprano	**20.** campus
7. drapery	**14.** chief	

 Prefixes and Suffixes

A **prefix** is one or more syllables placed in front of a base word to form a new word. When you add a prefix, the spelling of the base word does not change.

PREFIXES	
in + correct = **in**correct	**im** + polite = **im**polite
pre + view = **pre**view	**over** + paid = **over**paid
dis + agree = **dis**agree	**mis** + spell = **mis**spell
re + place = **re**place	**un** + nerve = **un**nerve
ir + rational = **ir**rational	**il** + legal = **il**legal

In a very few cases you must add a hyphen after a prefix to avoid confusing your reader. Check a dictionary if you're not sure of the spelling.

HYPHENATED PREFIXES		
re-cover	**semi**-independent	**anti**–social

It's easy to misspell *misspell*—but you won't if you keep it firmly in mind that the base word never changes when a prefix is added. **Mis***shapen,* **dis***satisfy,* **il***logical,* and **over***ripe* needn't give you any trouble either.

A **suffix** is one or more syllables placed after a base word to change its part of speech and possibly also its meaning. In many cases you simply add the suffix.

SUFFIXES WITH CONSONANTS	
kind + **ness** = kind**ness**	quiet + **ly** = quiet**ly**
ship + **ment** = ship**ment**	harm + **ful** = harm**ful**

In other cases, however, you must change the spelling of the base word before you add the suffix.

Words Ending in e

Drop the final *e* before a suffix that begins with a vowel.

SUFFIXES WITH VOWELS	
amaze + **ing** = amaz**ing**	cure + **able** = cur**able**
educate + **ion** = educat**ion**	nature + **al** = natur**al**

Keep the final *e* in words that end in *ce* or *ge* if the suffix begins with an *a* or *o*. The *e* keeps the sound of the *c* or *g* soft before these vowels.

CE AND GE	
manage + **able** = manage**able**	notice + **able** = notice**able**
courage + **ous** = courage**ous**	trace + **able** = trace**able**

Keep the final *e* when adding a suffix that begins with a consonant.

SUFFIXES WITH FINAL *E*	
EXAMPLES	peace + **ful** = peace**ful**
	amuse + **ment** = amuse**ment**
	hope + **less** = hope**less**
	wise + **ly** = wise**ly**
EXCEPTIONS	wise + **dom** = wis**dom**
	judge + **ment** = judg**ment**
	true + **ly** = tru**ly**

PRACTICE YOUR SKILLS

 Check Your Understanding
Adding Suffixes

Combine these base words and suffixes. Remember to make any necessary spelling changes.

1. waste + ful
2. assure + ance
3. active + ity
4. peace + able
5. graduate + ion
6. change + able
7. true + ly
8. globe + al
9. love + able
10. repay + ment
11. locate + ion
12. tattoo + ing
13. rude + ness
14. dance + er
15. outrage + ous
16. note + able
17. grade + ing
18. universe + al
19. use + ful
20. judge + ment

Spelling Words with Prefixes and Suffixes

General Interest **Write the underlined words in the paragraph, correctly spelling those that are misspelled.**

In 1953, a <u>couragous</u> French doctor wanted to prove that sailors should not die of thirst and <u>starveation</u>. To prove that deaths were <u>unecessary</u>, he <u>dareingly</u> set sail across the Atlantic in a fifteen-foot boat. For the sake of <u>making</u> his experiment <u>realstic</u>, he refused to take food or water. He <u>dissagreed</u> that seawater was <u>unsafe</u> to drink. He drank <u>nearly</u> two pints each day along with liquid from the fish he <u>skilfully</u> caught. He prevented scurvy by <u>resourcfully</u> scooping up plankton, a <u>natureal</u> source of vitamins. He reached his destination after fifty-six sometimes <u>nightmareish</u> days at sea. He proved it was not <u>impossible</u> to survive without provisions.

Words Ending in *y*

To add a suffix to most words ending in a vowel and *y*, keep the *y*.

VOWELS AND *Y*	
EXAMPLES	enjoy + **able** = enjoy**able** relay + **ing** = relay**ing** obey + **ed** = obey**ed** employ + **ment** = employ**ment**

| EXCEPTIONS | day + **ly** = da**ily** |
| | gay + **ly** = ga**ily** |

To add a suffix to most words ending in a consonant and *y*, change the *y* to *i* before adding the suffix.

	CONSONANTS AND *Y*
EXAMPLES	vary + **able** = var**iable**
	beauty + **ful** = beaut**iful**
	easy + **ly** = eas**ily**
	empty + **ness** = empt**iness**
EXCEPTIONS	shy + **ness** = shy**ness**
	study + **ing** = study**ing**

Doubling the Final Consonant

Sometimes the final consonant in a word is doubled before a suffix is added.

Double the final consonant in a word before adding a suffix if all of the following are true:
(1) the suffix begins with a vowel.
(2) the base word has only one syllable *or* is stressed on the last syllable.
(3) the base word ends in one consonant preceded by a vowel.

	DOUBLE CONSONANTS
ONE-SYLLABLE	skid + **ing** = ski**dding**
WORDS	stub + **ed** = stu**bbed**
	bat + **er** = ba**tter**
	red + **est** = re**ddest**

FINAL SYLLABLE STRESSED	prefer + **ing** = preferring
	commit + **ed** = committed
	begin + **er** = beginner

You do not double the final *r* in words that end in *fer* when you add the suffix *–ence* or *–able*. You can recognize these words because the pronunciation of the base word changes when the suffix is added.

FINAL *R*	
refer + ence = reference	defer + ence = deference
infer + ence = inference	transfer + able = transferable

Be sure not to double the final letter if it is preceded by two vowels.

TWO VOWELS	
head + **ing** = heading	seem + **ed** = seemed
wait + **er** = waiter	cool + **est** = coolest

PRACTICE YOUR SKILLS

● Check Your Understanding
Adding Suffixes

Combine these base words and suffixes. Remember to make any necessary spelling changes.

1. rely + ance

2. permit + ed

3. tidy + ness

4. slam + ed

5. sway + ed

6. hot + est

7. annoy + ing

8. zip + y

9. noisy + ly

10. pay + able

11. bud + ed   16. refer + ence

12. mercy + ful   17. raid + er

13. transfer + ing   18. study + ing

14. regret + ed   19. cheat + ed

15. day + ly   20. defy + ance

● **Connect to the Writing Process: Editing**
Spelling Words with Prefixes and Suffixes

General Interest **Write the underlined words in the paragraph, correctly spelling those that are misspelled.**

The sloppyest, sillyest summer festival you can imagine has been occuring in Buñol, Spain for five decades. It is hostted by the city at the end of every summer, when tomatoes are especially plentyful. More than a ton of tomatoes are lugged into the Calle San Luís at the begining of the morning. In the meantime, thousands of warriors have been rowdyly getting ready for battle. They have been outfiting themselves in safety goggles, masks, and helmets. Grabing their ammunition, they pelt one another with the soft fruit, skiding and sliping in the red slush underfoot. They continue lobing tomatoes without stoping, until no whole tomatoes remain. It's undenyably one of the wackyest celebrations anyone has dreammed up yet!

APPLY TO WRITING

Narrative Paragraph: *Prefixes and Suffixes*

Being extremely messy or silly can be fun sometimes. You must have at some time made a terrible mess or done something you knew was totally wacky. Write a narrative paragraph to share with your classmates. Explain what you did. Use five of the following words with prefixes or suffixes in your narrative:

- yucky + ness
- giddy + ly
- permit + ed
- horrify + ed *or* ing
- dirty + er *or* est
- sloppy + er *or* est

- outrage + ous *or* ously
- judge + ment
- muddy + er *or* ed
- sog + y
- grin + ed + ing
- un + forget + able

QuickCheck Mixed Practice

Add the prefix or suffix to each of these base words and write the new word.

1. spire + al

2. dim + est

3. dis + satisfied

4. omit + ing

5. un + natural

6. roam + ing

7. slug + ish

8. study + ed

9. true + ly

10. damage + able

11. sincere + ly

12. coward + ly + ness

13. begin + er

14. imagine + able

15. un + deny + able

Make it your goal to learn to spell these fifty words this year. Use them in your writing and practice writing them until spelling them correctly comes automatically.

achievement	height	preferred
admitted	heroes	prejudice
aisles	hoaxes	proceed
allegiance	immediately	scissors
alleys	jewelry	seize
athletics	judgment	sheriffs
calendar	lovable	similar
committed	manageable	species
conscience	mileage	succeed
courageous	mischievous	sufficient
echoes	misspell	surrounded
eighth	neighbor	tomatoes
embarrassment	ninety	truly
exceed	occurrence	unnecessary
excellent	perceive	vegetable
gaily	physical	weird
genuine	precede	

Applying Spelling Generalizations

Write the letter of the misspelled word in each group. Then write the word, spelling it correctly.

1. (A) breifs   (B) illegal   (C) beaches
2. (A) imature   (B) precede   (C) grateful
3. (A) niece   (B) analizes   (C) parties
4. (A) excede   (B) soprano   (C) carrying
5. (A) crashes   (B) releive   (C) calmness
6. (A) fiftieth   (B) beggar   (C) scenry
7. (A) coyly   (B) darknes   (C) courteous
8. (A) laziness   (B) slider   (C) disect
9. (A) chefes   (B) hoaxes   (C) finally
10. (A) delaying   (B) sieze   (C) tallest
11. (A) painfull   (B) intercom   (C) operate
12. (A) mismatch   (B) oxes   (C) duos
13. (A) chiefs   (B) receive   (C) hastyly
14. (A) sieve   (B) traceing   (C) marrying
15. (A) scarfs   (B) yesterdays   (C) bridesmaids
16. (A) stoping   (B) chilly   (C) valleys
17. (A) ceiling   (B) raised   (C) hideus
18. (A) ferrying   (B) jewelery   (C) aerobics
19. (A) loyal   (B) earrings   (C) imobile
20. (A) rodeos   (B) dissapoint   (C) tomatoes

Another Look

Spelling Patterns

In words with *ie* or *ei*, *i* often comes before *e* except when the letters
follow *c* or when they stand for the sound long *a*. *(pages L551–L552)*

The "seed" sound at the end of a word is spelled *cede* except for these
four words: *exceed, proceed, succeed, supersede*. *(pages L552–L553)*

Plurals

If a noun ends with *s, ch, sh, x,* or *z,* add *es* to form the plural. *(page L555)*

Add *s* to form the plural of a noun ending in a vowel and *y. (page L555)*

Change the *y* to *i* and add *es* to a noun ending in a consonant and *y.*
(pages L555–L556)

Add *s* to form the plural of a noun ending with a vowel and *o,* musical
terms ending in *o,* and words from Spanish ending in *o. (page L557)*

To form the plural of some nouns ending in *f* or *fe,* just add *s. (page L558)*

For some nouns ending in *f* or *fe,* change the *f* to *v* and add *es* or *s.*
(page L558)

To form the plurals of most numerals, letters, symbols, and words used as
words, add an *s. (page L560)*

Some nouns have the same form for singular and plural. *(page L561)*

Prefixes and Suffixes

The spelling of a base word does not change when you add a prefix.
(pages L563–L564)

When you place a suffix after a base word, especially when the base word
ends in a consonant, you simply add the suffix. *(page L564)*

Drop the final *e* before a suffix that begins with a vowel. *(page L564)*

Keep the final *e* when the suffix begins with a consonant or when the
base word ends in *ce* or *ge* if the suffix begins with an *a* or *o.*
(pages L564–L565)

Keep the *y* when adding a suffix to most words that end in a vowel and
y. Change *y* to *i* when adding a suffix to words that end in a
consonant and *y. (pages L566–L567)*

Other Information About Spelling

Doubling the final consonant. *(pages L567–L568)*

Directions

Write the letter of the choice that correctly respells the underlined word. If the underlined word contains no error, choose D.

EXAMPLE   The abillity to read provides you with
                    (1)
           lifelong skills.
              1 A   abilitee
                 B   abilitea
                 C   ability
                 D   No error

ANSWER   1 C

Reading opens the door to entertainment, imagenation,
                                                    (1)
and information. Many schools set aside a Reading Day to

stimulate interest and to emphasize the role reading plays in
                           (2)
learning. They use many methods to encurage students to
                                          (3)
take part. Students, teachers, and administrators sometimes
                                        (4)
dress up in clothing representing their faverite author.
                                         (5)
Everyone is asked to bring a book, magazine, or newspaper to
                                        (6)
read. The school librarie also makes reading material
                  (7)
availabel. For a certain portion of the day, the entire school
  (8)   (9)
celebrates the power of the writtin word.
                            (10)

1	**A**	imagineation	**6**	**A**	magazin
	B	emagination		**B**	magezine
	C	imagination		**C**	magazeen
	D	No error		**D**	No error
2	**A**	emfasize	**7**	**A**	libery
	B	emphasise		**B**	librery
	C	emphesize		**C**	library
	D	No error		**D**	No error
3	**A**	incourage	**8**	**A**	availabl
	B	encourage		**B**	available
	C	encouraje		**C**	availeble
	D	No error		**D**	No error
4	**A**	administrators	**9**	**A**	certin
	B	admenistrators		**B**	sertain
	C	adddministrators		**C**	sertine
	D	No error		**D**	No error
5	**A**	favorit	**10**	**A**	written
	B	faverit		**B**	ritten
	C	favorite		**C**	writen
	D	No error		**D**	No error

A Study Guide for Academic Success

Academic success depends a great deal on preparation. You must be familiar with the material presented in textbooks and in the classroom; you must also be aware of various test-taking strategies. In some ways, preparing for a test is like learning to play football. You can't simply grab the ball and run with it. You must first learn the rules of the game and strategies for offense and defense. If you learn the strategies and apply helpful pointers, for example, you can become both a better football player and a better test taker. Also, the more practice you have, the better prepared you are to play a difficult game or take an important test.

In the following chapter you will become familiar with the different kinds of questions asked on standardized tests. Pay close attention to the "rules" for each type of question and the strategies used to master them. These lessons and practice exercises will help you develop your test-taking muscles.

Keep in mind that the abilities you acquire in this chapter will carry over into homework and daily classroom assignments—and even into areas outside school. Learning how to read for various information and how to approach different kinds of questions and problems will sharpen the critical thinking skills you use when you participate in classroom discussions, play sports, and make important life decisions.

Learning Study Skills

Applying good study habits helps you in taking tests as well as in completing daily classroom assignments. Begin to improve your study habits by using the following strategies.

> **Strategies for Effective Studying**
>
> - Choose an area that is well lighted and quiet.
> - Equip your study area with everything you need for reading and writing, including a dictionary and a thesaurus.
> - Keep an assignment book for recording assignments and due dates.
> - Allow plenty of time for studying. Begin your reading and writing assignments early.
> - Adjust your reading rate to suit your purpose.

Adjusting Reading Rate to Purpose

Your reading rate is the speed with which you read. Depending on your purpose in reading, you may choose to read certain materials more quickly than others.

If your purpose is to get a quick impression of the contents of a newspaper, you should scan the headlines. If you want to learn the main ideas of a certain article, you should skim it. If your purpose is to learn new facts or understand details, you should read the article closely.

Whether you are reading a newspaper, an article in a periodical, or a textbook, you can read with greater effectiveness and efficiency if you adjust your reading rate to suit your purpose for reading the material.

Scanning

Scanning is reading to get a general impression and to prepare for learning about a subject. To scan, you should read the title, headings, subheadings, picture captions, words and phrases in boldface or italics, and any focus questions. Using this method, you can quickly determine what the passage is about and what questions to keep in mind. Scanning is also a way to familiarize yourself with everything a book has to offer. Scan the table of contents, appendix, glossary, and index of a book before reading.

Skimming

After scanning a chapter, section, or article, you should quickly read or skim the introduction, the topic sentence of each paragraph, and the conclusion. **Skimming** is reading quickly to identify the purpose, thesis, main ideas, and supporting ideas of a selection.

Close Reading

Close reading means reading to locate specific information, follow the logic of an argument, or comprehend the meaning or significance of information. After scanning the selection or chapter, read it more slowly, word for word.

Reading a Textbook—SQ3R

In studying a textbook, the techniques of scanning, skimming, and close reading are combined in the **SQ3R** study strategy. This method helps you to understand and remember what you read. The *S* in *SQ3R* stands for *Survey*, the *Q* for *Question*, and the *3R* for *Read, Recite,* and *Review*.

● Taking Notes

Taking notes when reading a textbook or listening to a lecture will help you identify and remember important points. Three methods of taking notes are the informal outline, the graphic organizer, and the summary.

In an **informal outline,** you use words and phrases to record main ideas and significant details. Notes in this form are helpful in studying for an objective test because they emphasize specific facts.

In a **graphic organizer,** words and phrases are arranged in a visual pattern to indicate the relationships between main ideas and supporting details. This is an excellent tool for studying information for an objective test, for an open-ended assessment, or for writing a composition. The visual organizer allows you instantly to see important information and its relationship to other ideas.

In a **summary** you use sentences to express important ideas in your own words. A summary should not simply restate the ideas presented in the textbook or lecture. Instead, a good summary should express relationships between ideas and draw conclusions. For this reason, summaries are useful in preparing for an essay test.

In the following passage from a textbook, the essential information for understanding the custom of shaking hands is underlined. Following the passage are examples of notes in an informal outline, in a graphic organizer, and in summary form.

> **MODEL: Taking Notes**

> Long ago it was common for men to carry a sword for protection. When two armed male strangers met by chance, their meeting could lead to trouble. To show that he was friendly, one of the two would stretch out his empty sword hand. The other would do the same, and the two

would clasp hands. While each was holding tightly to the other's hand, neither man could draw his sword. This is how the custom of shaking hands began.

The Custom of Shaking Hands

1. If two armed men met by chance, trouble might occur.

2. One man would offer his hand to show he was friendly.

3. The second man would clasp the first man's hand.

4. Neither man could draw his sword.

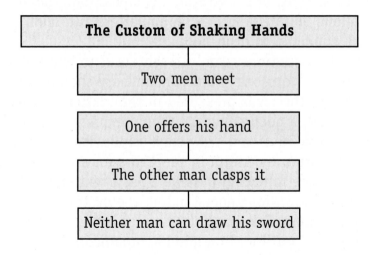

The Custom of Shaking Hands

Two men meet

One offers his hand

The other man clasps it

Neither man can draw his sword

The Custom of Shaking Hands

Long ago men carried swords. When two men would meet, one would offer his hand to show he was friendly. While the two men were clasping hands, neither could draw his sword.

Whichever note-taking method you use, the following strategies will help you make those notes clear and well organized.

Strategies for Taking Notes

- Label your notes with the title and page numbers of the chapter or the topic and date of the lecture.
- Record only the main ideas and important details.
- Use the titles, subtitles, and words in special type to help you select the most important information.
- Use your own words; do not copy word for word.
- Use as few words as possible.

Taking Standardized Tests

A standardized test measures your academic progress, skills, and achievement in such a way that results can be compared with those of other students who have taken the same test. Standardized tests that assess your ability to use language—or verbal—skills include vocabulary tests, analogy tests, sentence-completion tests, reading tests, and tests of standard written English.

The best way to do well on standardized tests is to work consistently on your school subjects throughout the year, to read widely, and to learn the strategies of test-taking.

Strategies for Taking Standardized Tests

- Read the test directions carefully. Answer the sample questions to be sure you understand what the test requires.
- Relax. Although you can expect to be a little nervous, concentrate on doing the best you can.
- Preview the whole test quickly by skimming to get an overview of the kinds of questions on the test.
- Plan your time carefully, allotting a certain amount of time to each part of the test.
- Answer first the questions you find easiest. Skip hard questions, coming back to them later if you have time.
- Read and reread all choices before you choose an answer. If you are not sure of the answer, try to eliminate choices that are obviously wrong. Educated guessing often helps.
- If you have time, check your answers. Be sure you have not made a mistake in marking your answer sheet.

Vocabulary Tests

One kind of vocabulary test asks you to find **antonyms**— words that are opposite in meaning. For instance, in the following test item, you must find the antonym for *cautious* among the five choices.

> CAUTIOUS: (A) guess   (B) careless   (C) imitation
>   (D) poor   (E) safe
>
> (The answer is *(B)* because *careless* is an antonym for *cautious*. The other choices are wrong because they have no relationship to the word *cautious*.

Synonym items have the same format as antonym items, but instead of choosing the answer that means the opposite, you choose the word that means the same.

> AMAZE: (A) astonish   (B) heavy   (C) fast
>   (D) bore   (E) weary
>
> (The answer is *(A) astonish,* which means the same as *amaze.*)

Always consider every choice carefully. You can often figure out the meaning of a word by using a prefix, a root, or a suffix as a clue.

Practice Your Skills

 Check Your Understanding
Recognizing Antonyms

Write the letter of the word that is opposite in meaning to the word in capital letters.

1. WEALTHY:
   (A) poor   (B) rich   (C) old
   (D) funny   (E) pricey

2. GRACEFUL:
   (A) slender   (B) careful   (C) curved
   (D) clumsy   (E) large

3. ABSENT:

    (A) tardy   (B) prepared   (C) without

    (D) present   (E) occupied

4. VICTORY:

    (A) win   (B) defeat   (C) tired

    (D) weak   (E) lazy

5. RAPID:

    (A) add   (B) more   (C) slow

    (D) less   (E) speedy

● Check Your Understanding

Recognizing Synonyms

Write the letter of the word that is similar in meaning to the word in capital letters.

6. VACANT:

    (A) warm   (B) better   (C) full

    (D) empty   (E) occupied

7. EXPENSIVE:

    (A) costly   (B) excellent   (C) shocking

    (D) huge   (E) discount

8. BRIEF:

    (A) long   (B) slide   (C) short

    (D) help   (E) case

9. GORGEOUS:

    (A) pleasant   (B) beautiful   (C) thin

    (D) distrustful (E) ugly

10. TREMENDOUS:

    (A) lovely   (B) average   (C) vacant

    (D) huge   (E) small

● Analogies

Analogy questions test your skill at figuring out relationships between words. Your first step is to decide how the given words—the first, capitalized pair of words—are related to each other. The next step is to decide which other pair has the same kind of relationship as the given pair.

The single colon in an analogy question stands for the words *is to,* and the double colon stands for the word *as.*

> HAT : HEAD : : shoe : foot

The above example reads, "Hat is to head as shoe is to foot." That is, a hat has the same relationship to a head as a shoe has to a foot. A hat and a shoe are items of clothing. Explaining an analogy to yourself in one sentence can help you to figure out the answer. In the following example, you might say, "One kind of flower is a tulip."

> FLOWER : TULIP : :
> (A) deer : buffalo   (B) fever : virus
> (C) automobile : station wagon   (D) plumber : wrench
> (E) garden : plant
>
> (The answer, *(C) automobile : station wagon,* expresses the same category-to-item relationship.)

Keep in mind that the word order in an analogy is very important. If the given pair of words in the analogy expresses a part-to-whole order, for example, the words in the correct answer should also be taken in the order of part to whole.

Some analogies are written in sentence form.

> *Car* is to *gas* as *people* is to ■.
> (A) clothes   (B) children   (C) food
> (D) houses   (E) world
>
> (In the first example, a car needs gas to keep going. The answer should show the same kind of relationship. Since people need food to keep going, the answer is *(C) food.*)

Knowing some of the common types of analogies, like those in the following chart, will help you figure out word relationships.

COMMON TYPES OF ANALOGIES	
Analogy	**Example**
word : synonym	slim : slender
word : antonym	exciting : dull
part : whole	wing : airplane
cause : effect	drought : famine
worker : tool	carpenter : hammer
worker : product	baker : bread
item : purpose	ruler : measure
item : category	robin : bird

PRACTICE YOUR SKILLS

● Check Your Understanding
Recognizing Analogies

Write the letter of the word pair that has the same relationship as the word pair in capital letters.

1. BOY : MAN : :
   (A) girl : woman   (B) mother : father
   (C) daughter : mother   (D) child : brother
   (E) dog : cat

2. WARM : HOT : :
   (A) summer : spring   (B) ice : cold
   (C) cool : cold   (D) cloud : storm
   (E) day : night

3. SNAKE : BITE : :
   (A) dog : eat   (B) bee : sting
   (C) chicken : egg   (D) puppy : ball
   (E) cat : mouse

4. ACTOR : THEATER : :
   (A) doctor : hospital   (B) patient : shot
   (C) athlete : football   (D) doctor : profession
   (E) teacher : student

5. FINGER : HAND : :
   (A) spine : hair   (B) leg : pants
   (C) toe : foot   (D) voice : read
   (E) hair : bow

● Check Your Understanding
Completing Analogies

Use the chart on page L586 to determine the relationship of the first pair of words. Then complete the analogy with the choice that correctly completes the second pair.

6. *Railway* is to *train* as *highway* is to ▦.
   (A) truck   (B) land   (C) bridge
   (D) pavement   (E) sign

7. *Assemble* is to *construct* as *brave* is to ▢.
    (A) cowardly   (B) scared   (C) courageous
    (D) run   (E) cower

8. *Photograph* is to *photographer* as *book* is to ▢.
    (A) author   (B) page   (C) cover
    (D) reader   (E) index

9. *Rudder* is to *airplane* as *bulb* is to ▢.
    (A) light   (B) electricity   (C) white
    (D) lamp   (E) chair

10. *Bacteria* is to *microscope* as *star* is to ▢.
    (A) sun   (B) telescope   (C) astronaut
    (D) moon   (E) night

▶ Sentence-Completion Tests

Sentence-completion tests measure your ability to comprehend what you read and to use context correctly. Each item consists of a sentence with one or more words missing. First read the entire sentence. Then read the answer choices and select the one that completes the sentence in a way that makes sense. For example, in the following item, read the sentence and then find the word that most appropriately completes the sentence.

After they ▢ the old school, they will start building a new one.
(A) rebuild   (B) attend   (C) demolish
(D) enlarge   (E) build

(The answer is *(C) demolish,* which means "tear down.")

Some sentence-completion questions have two blanks in the same sentence, with each answer choice including two words. Find the correct answer in the example on the following page.

We are having the ■ Fourth of July picnic at the park this ■.

(A) rainy . . . night   (B) short . . . house
(C) daily . . . exciting   (D) annual . . . year
(E) wonderful . . . yesterday

(The answer is (D) annual . . . year. The other choices do not make sense.)

PRACTICE YOUR SKILLS

● Check Your Understanding
Completing Sentences

Write the letter of the word that best completes each of the following sentences.

1. To avoid an accident, you should be extra ■ when you drive in bad weather.
   (A) cautious   (B) reckless   (C) speedy
   (D) long   (E) sleepy

2. You will get ■ if you go out in this storm without an umbrella.
   (A) parched   (B) cold   (C) drenched
   (D) warm   (E) dry

3. The ■ house was so small you could hold it in your hand.
   (A) tremendous   (B) miniature   (C) large
   (D) clumsy   (E) brick

4. Because we like carrots, we ■ eat them.
   (A) hardly   (B) sometimes   (C) frequently
   (D) rarely   (E) cannot

5. Even though all the tickets were sold, many seats in the auditorium were ■ during the concert.
   (A) filled   (B) large   (C) comfortable
   (D) vacant   (E) red

Completing Sentences with Two Blanks

Write the letter of the words that best complete each of the following sentences.

6. The ▮ shirt made my skin ▮ and turn red.
   (A) silky . . . soft   (B) coarse . . . itch
   (C) red . . . burn   (D) large . . . wrinkle
   (E) wool . . . crawl

7. Having a ▮ pulled can be very ▮.
   (A) hair . . . pleasant   (B) cavity . . . comfortable
   (C) tooth . . . painful   (D) shirt . . . expensive
   (E) party . . . fun

8. After ▮ in line for hours, I was able to ▮ tickets for the concert.
   (A) running . . . make   (B) listening . . . sell
   (C) singing. . . lose   (D) waiting . . . obtain

9. She wore a ▮ so no one would ▮ her.
   (A) hat . . . see   (B) disguise . . . recognize
   (C) coat. . . catch   (D) dish . . . know
   (E) hood. . . hug

10. A newspaper ▮ should know how to use ▮.
   (A) article . . . words   (B) advertisement . . . paper
   (C) editor. . . words   (D) reader . . . soap
   (E) deliverer . . . dishes

▶ Reading Comprehension Tests

Reading tests assess your ability to understand and to analyze written passages. The information you need to answer the test questions may be either directly stated or implied in the passage. You must study, analyze, and interpret a passage in order to answer the questions that follow it. The following strategies will help you answer questions on reading tests.

Strategies for Reading Comprehension Questions

- Begin by skimming the questions that follow the passage.
- Read the passage carefully and closely. Notice the main ideas, organization, style, and key words.
- Study all possible answers. Avoid choosing one answer the moment you think it is a reasonable choice.
- Use only the information in the passage when you answer the questions. Do not rely on your own knowledge or ideas on this kind of test.

Most reading questions will focus on one or more of the following characteristics of a written passage:

- **Main idea** At least one question will usually focus on the central idea of the passage. Remember that the main idea of a passage covers all sections of the passage—not just one section or paragraph.

- **Supporting details** Questions about supporting details test your ability to identify the statements in the passage that back up the main idea.

- **Implied meanings** In some passages not all information is directly stated. Some questions ask you to interpret information that the author has merely implied.

- **Purpose and Tone** Questions on purpose and tone require that you interpret or analyze the author's attitude toward his or her subject and the author's purpose for writing.

PRACTICE YOUR SKILLS

● Check Your Understanding
Reading for Comprehension

Read the following passage and write the letter of each correct answer.

Think about Hawaii and what it might be like. Most people think about golden beaches, warm sunshine, palm trees, and surfboarding. Hawaii has these beautiful features, but what is life like for ordinary families who live and work there? Most of them are involved in Hawaii's three main industries: tourism, the military, and agriculture.

Tourism is the business of travel. It includes all the money travelers spend when they visit a place. Many people who live in Hawaii work for hotels, restaurants, airlines, and bus and tour companies.

The military is the part of the government that defends the country and fights wars when necessary. The United States Army and the United States Navy keep large bases in Hawaii. Many soldiers and sailors are stationed there for a year or more. Also, many local people work for the military.

Last but not least, agriculture, or farming, is an important industry in Hawaii. Farming contributes a third of the state's income each year. Many people work on farms. The main Hawaiian crops are sugar cane, pineapple, and coffee. Many people work on cattle ranches, too.

1. The best title for this passage is
   (A) The Isolated Island of Hawaii.
   (B) The Beaches of Hawaii.
   (C) Surfing in Hawaii.
   (D) Working in Paradise.
   (E) The Pacific.

2. Farming in Hawaii
   (A) is a major source of income for the state.
   (B) is rarely successful.
   (C) does not include sugar crops.
   (D) creates environmental problems.
   (E) is limited to pineapple crops.

3. The passage indicates that the United States
   (A) does not have large military bases in Hawaii.
   (B) stations many troops in Hawaii.
   (C) cannot keep troops in Hawaii.
   (D) would like to take troops out of Hawaii.
   (E) does not approve of military force.

4. This passage would most likely appear in
   (A) a science textbook.
   (B) a fashion magazine.
   (C) an article on the state of Hawaii's Website.
   (D) a book about oceans.
   (E) a newspaper editorial.

The Double Passage

You may be asked to read two paired passages, called the **double passage,** and then answer questions about each passage individually and about how the two passages relate to each other. The two passages may present similar or opposing views, or they may complement each other in various ways. A brief introduction preceding the passages may help you anticipate the relationship between them.

All the questions follow the second passage. The first few questions relate to Passage 1, the next few questions relate to Passage 2, and the final questions relate to both passages. You may find it helpful to read Passage 1 first and then immediately find and answer those questions related only to Passage 1. Then read Passage 2 and answer the remaining questions.

PRACTICE YOUR SKILLS

● Check Your Understanding
Reading for Double Passage Comprehension

The following passages are about vending machines in public schools. Read each passage and answer the questions that follow.

Passage 1

In everyday life, most people are allowed to make choices. This right is not being extended to all schoolchildren. Children in public schools are not allowed to decide what they want to eat for lunch—they are given the same cafeteria lunch as everyone else. The solution to this problem is simple: install vending machines in schools. Children could then choose what they would like for lunch and, at the same time, begin to experience the sense of freedom they should have in their preteen years. Students need to learn how to make responsible choices, and that the learning process begins with making the everyday choices that most people are allowed to make.

Passage 2

Too many schoolchildren are being allowed to substitute unhealthy snacks from vending machines for their school lunch. The fact is that middle school children do not have the sense of responsibility to use vending machines wisely. Not only are they eating too many fatty foods, they are also spending too much money. Middle school children cannot control their spending, and schools should not provide an additional temptation to spend in the form of vending machines. If schoolchildren want to eat a lunch other than the cafeteria lunch, they can bring a lunch from home that their parents have approved. Eating healthily and controlling their personal finances will help children become healthy, responsible adults.

1. According to the author of Passage 1, which of the following best explains the reason why children should have vending machines in schools?
   (A) Students need to learn how to make responsible choices.
   (B) Students like to buy vending machine items.
   (C) Students need to eat healthier food.
   (D) Students will spend all their money on snack foods.
   (E) The cafeterias cannot serve all the children.

2. The purpose of Passage 1 is to
- (A) persuade people to keep vending machines out of schools.
- (B) persuade people to put vending machines in schools.
- (C) entertain readers with stories about vending machines.
- (D) inform readers about vending machines.
- (E) persuade students to spend money on snacks.

3. According to the author of Passage 2, which of the following will result from allowing vending machines in schools?
- (A) Students will eat unhealthy food.
- (B) Students will save their money.
- (C) Parents will pack more lunches.
- (D) The cafeteria will serve more food.
- (E) Students will make responsible choices.

4. The tone of Passage 2 is
- (A) lighthearted.
- (B) emphatic.
- (C) serious.
- (D) humorous.
- (E) cheerful.

5. Which of the following is not mentioned by either author?
- (A) Students will learn to make responsible choices.
- (B) Students will spend too much money on snacks from vending machines.
- (C) Students should eat the cafeteria lunch.
- (D) The cafeteria lunch is too expensive for most students.
- (E) Students cannot control their finances.

⏵ Tests of Standard Written English

Objective tests of standard written English assess your knowledge of the language skills used for writing. They contain sentences with underlined words, phrases, and punctuation. The underlined parts will contain errors in grammar, usage, mechanics, vocabulary, and spelling. You are asked to find the error in each sentence, or, on some tests, to identify the best way to revise a sentence or passage.

Finding Errors

The most familiar way to test a student's grasp of grammar, usage, capitalization, punctuation, word choice, and spelling is through finding errors in a sentence. A typical test item of this kind is a sentence with five underlined choices. Four of the choices suggest possible errors in the sentence. The fifth states that there is no error. Read the following sentence and identify the error, if there is one.

> The Empire State <u>building</u> is in the <u>city</u> of <u>Manhattan</u>
>   **A**   **B**   **C**
> in New <u>York</u>. <u>No error</u>
>   **D**   **E**
>
> (The answer is *A*. The word *building* should be capitalized as part of the proper name, the *Empire State Building*.)

The following list identifies some of the errors you should look for on a test of standard written English:

- lack of agreement between subject and verb
- lack of agreement between pronoun and antecedent
- incorrect spelling or use of a word
- missing, misplaced, or unnecessary punctuation

- missing or unnecessary capitalization
- misused or misplaced italics or quotation marks

Sometimes you will find a sentence that contains no error. Be careful, however, before you choose *E* as the answer. It is easy to overlook a mistake, since common errors are the kind generally included on this type of test.

Remember that the parts of a sentence that are not underlined are presumed to be correct. You can use clues in the correct parts of the sentence to help you search for errors in the underlined parts.

PRACTICE YOUR SKILLS

● Check Your Understanding
Recognizing Errors in Writing

Write the letter of the underlined word or punctuation mark that is incorrect. If the sentence contains no error, write E.

(1) For nearly 3,000 years, egypt was ruled by
                                    A   B
powerful pharoahs whom the people believed to be
                    C
both god and ruler. (2) part of every crop the people
         D   A   B
raised was given to the pharoah each year. (3) Each
              C   D
year slaves were forced to build huge stone temples to
                     A   B
the gods and pyramids, which were tombs for the
                        C
pharohs. (4) King tutankhamun, a minor pharoah, had
    D   A   B
a small burial chamber by comparison. (5) Cut into the
         C   D
rock of the Valley of Kings, they escaped robbery.
           A   B C   D
(6) When it was discovered in the 1920s, it reveals
              A   B   C

many priceless treasures. **(7)** It also showed the
<u>D</u>   <u>A</u>   <u>B</u>
splendor in which these god-kings lived?
          <u>C</u>   <u>D</u>

Sentence-Correction Questions

Sentence-correction questions assess your ability to recognize appropriate phrasing. Instead of locating an error in a sentence, you must select the most appropriate and effective way to write the sentence.

In this kind of question, a part of the sentence is underlined. The sentence is then followed by five different ways of writing the underlined part. The first way shown, *(A)*, simply repeats the original underlined portion. The other four give alternative ways of writing the underlined part. The choices may involve grammar, usage, capitalization, punctuation, or word choice. Be sure that the answer you choose does not change the meaning of the original sentence.

Look at the following example.

<u>Where was you last</u> Saturday night?
(A) Where was you last
(B) Where were you last
(C) Where did you last
(D) Where have you last
(E) Where, were you last

(The correct answer is *B;* subject and verb must agree.)

● Check Your Understanding
Correcting Sentences

Write the letter of the correct way, or the best way, of phrasing the underlined part of each sentence.

1. Ida, Sarah, and me will head the project.
   (A) Ida, Sarah, and me will head
   (B) Ida, Sarah, and I will head
   (C) Ida, Sarah and I, will head
   (D) Ida, Sarah, and I will heed
   (E) Me, Ida, and Sarah will head

2. Uncle Dan will arrive on the nine o'clock flight.
   (A) Uncle Dan will arrive
   (B) Uncle dan will arrive
   (C) Uncle Dan arriving
   (D) Uncle Dan will arrives
   (E) uncle dan arrives

3. Ms. Ramirez car didn't start this morning.
   (A) Ms. Ramirez car didn't
   (B) Ms. Ramirez's car didn't
   (C) Ms. Ramirez' car wasn't
   (D) Ms. Ramire'z car didn't
   (E) Ms Ramirez' car didn't

4. All of them forgot to bring they're books.
   (A) forgot to bring they're books.
   (B) forgot to bring their books.
   (C) forgots to bring their books.
   (D) forgetting to bring their books.
   (E) forgot to bring its books.

5. I told you, You will enjoy seeing the movie."
   (A) I told you, You will enjoy
   (B) I tell you, You will enjoyed
   (C) I told you, 'You will enjoy
   (D) I told you, "You will enjoy
   (E) I telling you, You will enjoy

Revision-in-Context

Another type of multiple-choice question that appears on some standardized tests is called revision-in-context. These questions are based on a short passage that is meant to represent an early draft of student writing. The questions following the passage ask you to choose the best revision of a sentence, a group of sentences, or the essay as a whole or to clearly identify the writer's intention. This type of test assesses your reading ability, your writing skills, and your understanding of standard written English.

MODEL: Correcting Sentences

> **(1)** In 1271, Marco Polo set off on an adventure. **(2)** It was an adventure of a lifetime. **(3)** With his trader father, the teenager was bound for Cathay an exciting land in the Far East. **(4)** A brilliant student, Marco made quite an impression on Kublai Khan. **(5)** The great Mongol leader made Polo an official. **(6)** Marco became the first European to travel through China. **(7)** Polo wrote about all he saw.

1. In relation to the rest of the passage, which of the following best describes the writer's intention in sentence 6?
   (A) to state the main idea of the passage
   (B) to interest the reader in the story
   (C) to entertain the reader with interesting details
   (D) to summarize the paragraph
   (E) to persuade people to travel to China

2. Which of the following is the best revision of sentence 3?
   (A) With his trader father, the teenager was bound for Cathay; an exciting land in the Far East.
   (B) With his trader father. The teenager was bound for Cathay, an exciting land in the Far East.
   (C) An exciting land in the Far East, Cathay, Polo was bound for with his trader father.

(D) With his trader father, the teenager was bound for Cathay, an exciting land in the Far East.

(E) With his trader father: the teenager was bound for Cathay, an exciting land in the Far East.

3. Which of the following is the best way to combine sentences 1 and 2?

(A) In 1271, Marco Polo set off on the adventure of a lifetime.

(B) Marco Polo set off on an adventure, an adventure of a lifetime, in 1271.

(C) In 1271, Marco Polo set off; it was an adventure of a lifetime.

(D) In 1271, the adventure of a lifetime occurred and Marco Polo set off.

(E) Marco Polo's adventure of a lifetime occurred in 1271 when he set off.

PRACTICE YOUR SKILLS

● Check Your Understanding
Correcting Sentences

Carefully read the following passage, which is an early draft of an essay about the Aztec people. Write the letter of the correct answer next to each number.

(1) The Aztecs were a fierce society. (2) They were a warrior society. (3) In time, their powerful army pushed outward. (4) They pushed outward from the Valley of Mexico. (5) They conquer the city states all around them. (6) The Aztecs took the wealth of the city states and built up a store of gold and silver and riches and treasures for their city.

1. What is the purpose of sentences 1 and 2?
   (A) to state the main idea of the essay
   (B) to entertain the reader with unusual facts
   (C) to persuade the reader to study the Aztecs
   (D) to inform the reader about war
   (E) to persuade the reader to travel to Mexico

2. The best revision of sentence 6 is
   (A) The Aztecs took the wealth of the city states: built up a store of gold, silver, riches, treasures for their city.
   (B) The Aztecs took the wealth of the city states and built up a store of gold, silver, riches, and treasures for their city.
   (C) The Aztecs take the wealth of the city states and build up a store of gold, silver, riches, and treasures for their city.
   (D) The Aztecs take the wealth of the city states and built up a store of gold, silver, riches, and treasures for their city.

3. The best way to combine sentences 1 and 2 is
   (A) The Aztecs were a fierce society; they were a warrior society.
   (B) The Aztecs were a fierce warrior society.
   (C) The Aztecs were a fierce society that was filled with warriors in the society.
   (D) The Aztecs were a fierce society, warrior society.
   (E) The Aztecs were fierce and warriors in their society.

4. What is the best way to combine sentences 3 and 4?
   (A) In time: their powerful army pushed outward from the Valley of Mexico.
   (B) In time, their powerful army pushing outward from the Valley of Mexico.

(C) In time, their powerful army pushed outward from the Valley of Mexico.

(D) In time, their powerful army, pushing outward from the Valley, of Mexico.

(E) Their powerful army, pushed out in time, from the Valley of Mexico.

5. What is the purpose of sentence 6?
   (A) to persuade people to save money
   (B) to inform people about the treasures available in Mexico
   (C) to create sympathy for the Aztecs
   (D) to provide support for the main idea
   (E) to state the thesis of the passage

Taking Essay Tests

Essay tests are designed to assess both your understanding of important ideas and your ability to see connections, or relationships, between these ideas. To do well, you must be able to organize your thoughts quickly and to express them logically and clearly.

 ## Kinds of Essay Questions

Always begin an essay test by carefully reading the instructions for all the questions on the test. Then, as you reread the instructions for your first question, look for key words, such as those listed in the following box. Such key words will tell you precisely what kind of question you are being asked to answer.

KINDS OF ESSAY QUESTIONS	
ANALYZE	Separate into parts and examine each part.
COMPARE	Point out similarities.
CONTRAST	Point out differences.
DEFINE	Clarify meaning.
DISCUSS	Examine in detail.
EVALUATE	Give your opinion.
EXPLAIN	Tell how, what, or why.
ILLUSTRATE	Give examples.
SUMMARIZE	Briefly review main points.
TRACE	Show development or progress.

As you read the instructions, jot down everything that is required in your answer, or circle key words and underline key phrases in the instructions, as in the following example:

(Explain) the origin of passive resistance and the history behind the Ghandi's rise in leadership. Write three paragraphs, giving (specific examples) or illustrations.

PRACTICE YOUR SKILLS

● Check Your Understanding
Interpreting Essay Test Items

Write the key direction word in each item. Then write one sentence explaining what the question asks you to do.

EXAMPLE   Trace the life cycle of a frog.

POSSIBLE ANSWER Trace—Show the development, in order, of the stages in the life of a frog.

1. In your own words, define *photosynthesis*.

2. How does the appearance of a toad compare with that of a frog?

3. Briefly summarize the lead story in today's paper.

4. John F. Kennedy said, "Ask not what your country can do for you. Ask what you can do for your country." Discuss his meaning.

5. Evaluate one of Sandra Cisneros's short stories.

▶ Writing an Effective Essay Answer

The steps in writing a well-constructed essay are the same for an essay test as they are for a written assignment. The only difference is that in a test situation you have a strict time limit for writing. As a result, you need to plan how much time you will spend writing each answer and how much time you will devote to each step in the writing process. As a rule of thumb, for every five minutes of writing, allow two minutes for planning and organizing and one minute for revising and editing.

Prewriting — Writing Process

Begin planning your answer by brainstorming for main ideas and supporting details. Then organize your main ideas into a simple informal outline. Your outline will help you to present your ideas in a logical order, to cover all your main points, and to avoid omitting important details.

INFORMAL
OUTLINE:

Ghandi and the Origin of Passive Resistance

1. explanation of passive resistance

2. reasons for the rise of passive resistence

3. history of Ghandi's rise in leadership

GRAPHIC
ORGANIZER:

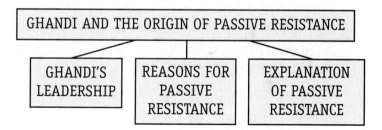

Your next step is to write a statement that states your main idea and covers all of your supporting ideas. Often you can write a suitable main idea statement by rewording the test question.

ESSAY QUESTION:	Explain the origin of passive resistance and the history behind Ghandi's rise in leadership. Write three paragraphs, giving specific examples or illustrations.
MAIN IDEA STATEMENT:	A small, quiet man named Mohandas Ghandi spoke out and led the fight for independence.

Drafting Writing Process

As you write your essay answer, keep the following strategies in mind.

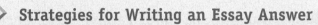

> ### Strategies for Writing an Essay Answer
> - Write an introduction that includes the main idea statement.
> - Follow the order of your outline. Write one paragraph for each main point, beginning with a topic sentence.
> - Be specific. Support each main point by using supporting details, such as facts and examples.
> - Use transitions to connect your ideas and examples.
> - End with a strong concluding statement that summarizes your main idea statement.
> - Write clearly and legibly because you will not have time to copy your work.

MODEL: Essay Test Answer

The year was 1919. The native people of India longed for independence. After nearly two and a half centuries of British rule, they were ready to fight to live as free people on their own land. The British who ruled India sensed a change in the air. Soon they passed tougher laws. They censored newspapers and banned freedom of assembly. In

MAIN IDEA STATEMENT:

particular, the laws said it was a crime to organize opposition to the government. A small, quiet man named Mohandas Ghandi spoke out and led the fight for independence. Soon people were listening. There is a better way, he said, than choosing violence or terrorism. He taught his fellow Indians the principles of nonviolent protest.

Soon Ghandi was the leader of freedom seekers. He led demonstrations and protests. And always the actions were nonviolent. If marchers and protesters were clubbed by British police, they endured it and did not strike back. Ghandi called this technique passive resistance.

The world began to notice and be impressed by this man's courage and principles. For the next thirty years, he would be a great spiritual leader. **CONCLUDING STATEMENT:** This man who originated passive resistance would be called Mahatma, or "Great Soul," by the millions who followed and loved him.

Revising ◄ Writing Process

Leave time to revise and edit your essay answer. To keep your paper as neat as possible, mark any corrections or revisions clearly and write additional material in the margins. As you revise, ask yourself the following questions.

- Did you follow the instructions completely?

- Did you interpret the question accurately?

- Did you begin with a main idea statement?

- Did you include facts, examples, or other supporting details?

- Did you sequence your ideas and examples logically in paragraphs, according to your informal outline?

- Did you use transitions to connect ideas and examples?
- Did you end with a strong concluding statement that summarizes your main idea?

After you have made any necessary revisions, quickly read your essay to check for mistakes in spelling, usage, or punctuation. As you edit, check your work for accuracy in the following areas:

- agreement between subjects and verbs *(Chapter 10)*
- forms of comparative and superlative adjectives and adverbs *(Chapter 11)*
- capitalization of proper nouns and proper adjectives *(Chapter 12)*
- use of commas *(Chapter 13)*
- use of apostrophes *(Chapter 15)*
- division of words at the end of a line *(Chapter 15)*

Communicate Your Ideas

APPLY TO WRITING
Prewriting: *Essay Test Question*

Conferencing

Select any subject area such as English, science, or social studies. With your teacher's permission, form a small group with other students who are interested in the same subject. Brainstorm together a list of essay test questions related to a topic you are currently studying in the course.

EXAMPLE: Computer technology and the Internet have changed the way of life for many Americans. Many people can now accomplish tasks faster than ever before. The growth of the Internet has also created a global population with people around the world working together for different purposes. What do you think about the growth of the Internet? How is it beneficial? What are the negative aspects of the Internet? Use the organizer below to think about both sides of the argument.

GRAPHIC ORGANIZER:

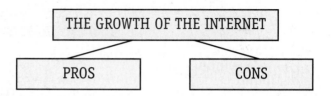

Timed Writing

Throughout your school years, you will be tested on your ability to organize your thoughts quickly and to express them in a limited time. Your teacher may ask you to write a twenty-minute, two-hundred-word essay that will then be judged on how thoroughly you covered the topic and organized your essay. To complete such an assignment, you should consider organizing your time in the following way.

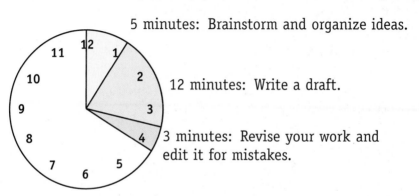

5 minutes: Brainstorm and organize ideas.

12 minutes: Write a draft.

3 minutes: Revise your work and edit it for mistakes.

The more you practice writing under time constraints, the better you will be able to apply these effective writing strategies during timed tests.

 Strategies for Timed Tests

- Listen carefully to instructions. Find out if you may write notes or an outline on your paper or in the examination book.
- Find out if you should erase mistakes or cross them out by neatly drawing a line through them.
- Plan your time, keeping in mind your time limit.

Communicate Your Ideas

APPLY TO WRITING

Prewriting, Drafting, Revising, Editing: *Timed Writing*

Choose one side of the Internet argument. Then give yourself twenty minutes to write a response. Begin by writing a list of important points and a main idea statement. As you draft your essay, follow the Strategies for Writing an Essay Answer on page L608. Be sure to revise and edit your essay answer.

A **Abbreviation** shortened form of a word that generally begins with a capital letter and ends with a period.

Action verb word that tells what action a subject is performing.

Adjective word that modifies, or describes, a noun or a pronoun.

Adverb word that modifies, or describes, a verb, an adjective, or another adverb.

Antecedent word, or group of words, that a pronoun refers to or replaces.

Antonym word that means the opposite of another word.

Audience the person or persons who will read your work or hear your speech.

B **Body** one or more paragraphs comprised of details, facts, and examples that support the main idea.

Brainstorming prewriting technique of writing down ideas that come to mind about a given subject.

Business letter writing form that uses formal language and includes six parts: the heading, inside address, greeting, body, closing, and signature.

C **Chronological order** the time order in which events occur.

Clarity the quality of being clear.

Collective noun word that names a group of people or things.

Complete predicate all the words that tell what a subject is doing or that tell something about the subject.

Complete subject all the words used to identify the person, place, thing, or idea the sentence is about.

Compound noun two or more nouns in one sentence written separately or as one word.

Compound sentence two simple sentences, usually joined by a comma and a coordinating conjunction.

Compound subject two or more subjects in one sentence that have the same verb and are joined by a conjunction.

Compound verb two or more verbs in one sentence that have the same subject and are joined by a conjunction.

Concluding sentence a strong ending added to a paragraph that summarizes the major points, refers to the main idea, or adds an insight.

Conclusion paragraph that completes a composition and reinforces its main idea.

Conjunction a word that connects words or groups of words.

Contraction word that combines two words into one. It uses an apostrophe to replace one or more missing letters.

D | **Declarative sentence** a statement or expression of opinion. It ends with a period.

Descriptive writing writing that creates a vivid picture of a person, an object, or a scene by stimulating the reader's senses.

Dialogue conversation between two or more people in a story or play.

Direct object noun or pronoun that answers the question *What?* or *Whom?*

Direct quotation passage, sentence, or words stated exactly as the person wrote or said them.

Double negative use of two negative words to express an idea when only one is needed.

Drafting stage of the writing process in which the writer expresses ideas in sentences, forming a beginning, a middle, and an ending in a composition.

E | **Editing** stage of the writing process in which writers polish their work by correcting all errors.

Elaboration addition of details, facts, and examples that improve the quality of written work by giving greater support to a composition.

Electronic Publishing use of technology to create documents, audio and video recordings, and online publishing such as Websites.

E-mail electronic mail that can be sent from one computer to another.

Exclamatory sentence expression of strong feeling. It ends with an exclamation point.

F | **Fable** story in which animal characters act like people to teach a lesson or moral.

Fact a statement that can be proven.

Fiction stories about imaginary people and events.

Folktale story that was told aloud long before it was written.

Fragment group of words that does not express a complete thought.

Freewriting prewriting technique of writing freely without concern for mistakes made.

Friendly letter writing form that may use informal language and includes a heading, greeting, body, closing, and signature.

G | **Generalization** a conclusion based on facts, examples, or instances.

Glittering generality word or phrase that most people associate with virtue and goodness that is used to trick people into feeling positively about a subject.

H **Helping verb** auxiliary verb that helps to make up a verb phrase.

Homographs words that are spelled alike but have different meanings and pronunciations.

Homophones words that sound alike but have different meanings and spellings.

I **Imperative sentence** a request or command that ends with either a period or an exclamation point.

Indirect object noun or a pronoun that answers the question *To or from whom?* or *To or for what?* after an action word.

Informative writing writing form that provides information or explains a process.

Interjection word that expresses strong feeling.

Internet worldwide network of computers. (See also *Basic Internet Terminology* in *A Writer's Guide to the Internet.*)

Interrogative sentence a question. It ends with a question mark.

Introduction paragraph in a composition that introduces a subject, states or implies a purpose, and presents a main idea.

Irregular verb verb that does not form its past and past participle by adding *–ed* to the present tense.

L **Linking verb** verb that links the subject with another word that renames or describes the subject.

M **Modifier** word that makes the meaning of another word more precise.

N **Narrative writing** writing that tells a real or an imaginary story with a clear beginning, middle, and end.

Nonfiction prose writing that contains facts about real people and real events.

Noun a word that names a person, place, thing, or idea. A common noun gives general information. A proper noun names a specific person, place, or thing and always begins with a capital letter.

O **Object pronoun** type of pronoun used for direct objects, indirect objects, and objects of prepositions.

Occasion motivation for composing; the fact that prompts communication.

Opinion judgment or belief that cannot be absolutely proven.

Order of importance a way of organizing information by arranging details in the order of most to least (or least to most) pertinent.

Outline information about a subject organized into main topics and subtopics.

P **Paragraph** group of related sentences that present and develop one main idea.

Personal pronoun type of pronoun that can be categorized into one of three groups, dependent on the speaker's position: first person (*I*), second person (*you*), and third person (*she/he*).

Persuasive writing writing that expresses an opinion and uses facts, examples, and reasons to convince the reader.

Plot sequence of events leading to the outcome or point of the story. The plot contains the climax, or high point, the resolution of the conflict, and the outcome, or ending.

Possessive pronoun pronoun used to show ownership or possession.

Predicate adjective adjective that follows a linking verb and modifies, or describes, the subject.

Predicate nominative noun or pronoun that follows a linking verb and identifies, renames, or explains the subject.

Prefix one or more syllables placed in front of a base word to form a new word.

Preposition word that shows the relationship between a noun or a pronoun and another word in the sentence.

Prepositional phrase group of words made up of a preposition, its object, and any words that describe the object.

Prewriting invention stage of the writing process in which the writer plans for drafting based on the subject, occasion, audience, and purpose for writing.

Principal parts of a verb the *present*, the *past*, and the *past participle*. The principal parts help form the tenses of verbs.

Pronoun word that takes the place of one or more nouns.

Proofreading carefully rereading and making corrections in grammar, usage, spelling, and mechanics in a piece of writing.

Publishing stage of the writing process in which the writer may choose to share the work with an audience.

Purpose reason for writing or speaking on a given subject.

R **Reflexive pronoun** pronoun formed by adding the suffix *–self* or *–selves* to a personal pronoun.

Regular verb verb that forms its past and past participle by adding *–ed* or *–d* to the present tense.

Report composition of three or more paragraphs that uses specific information from books, magazines, and other sources.

Revising stage of the writing process in which the writer rethinks what is written and reworks it to increase its clarity, smoothness, and power.

Root part of a word that carries the basic meaning.

Run-on sentence two or more sentences that are written as one sentence. They are separated by a comma or have no mark of punctuation.

S **Sensory details** details that appeal to one of the five senses: seeing, hearing, touching, tasting, and smelling.

Sentence group of words that express a complete thought.

Sentence fragment group of words that do not express a complete thought.

Setting the place and time of a story.

Simple predicate main word or phrase in the complete predicate.

Simple subject main word in a complete subject.

Spatial order order in which details are arranged according to their location.

Standard English proper form of the language that follows a set pattern of rules and conventions.

Style visual or verbal expression that is distinctive to an artist or writer.

Subject word or group of words that names the person, place, thing, or idea that the sentence is about; topic of a composition.

Subordinating conjunction single connecting word used in a sentence to introduce an idea of less importance than the main idea.

Suffix one or more syllables placed after a base word to change its part of speech and possibly its meaning.

Supporting sentence specific details that explain or prove a topic sentence.

Synonym word that has nearly the same meaning as another word.

T **Tense** form a verb takes to show time. The six tenses are the *present, past, future, present perfect, past perfect,* and *future perfect.*

Thesaurus online or print dictionary of synonyms.

Topic sentence statement of the main idea of the paragraph.

Transitions words and phrases that show how ideas are related.

U **Unity** combination or ordering of parts in a composition so that all the sentences or paragraphs work together as a whole to support one main idea.

V | **Verb** word used to express an action or state of being.

Verb phrase a main idea plus one or more helping verbs.

Voice particular sound and rhythm of language that the writer uses (closely related to *tone*).

W | **World Wide Web** network of computers within the Internet capable of delivering multimedia content and text over communication lines into personal computers all over the world.

Writing process recursive stages that a writer proceeds through in his or her own way when developing ideas and discovering the best way to express them.

INDEX

Note: Italic page numbers indicate skill sets.

Note: Italic page numbers indicate skill sets.

INDEX

Note: Italic page numbers indicate skill sets.

Note: Italic page numbers indicate skill sets.

INDEX

Note: Italic page numbers indicate skill sets.

INDEX

Note: Italic page numbers indicate skill sets.

Note: Italic page numbers indicate skill sets.

INDEX

Every effort has been made to trace the ownership of all copyrighted selections in this book and to make full acknowledgment of their use. Grateful acknowledgment is made to the following authors, publishers, agents, and individuals for their permission to reprint copyrighted material.

L26: From *Collected Poems* by Langston Hughes. Copyright © 1994 by the Estate of Langston Hughes. Reprinted by permission of Alfred A. Knopf, Inc. **L36:** © Christine Hemp. **L155:** Excerpt from "Masses" in *Chicago Poems* by Carl Sandburg, copyright 1916 by Holt, Rinehart and Winston and renewed 1944 by Carl Sandburg, reprinted by permission of Harcourt, Inc. **L334:** Excerpt from "The Shovel Man" in *Chicago Poems* by Carl Sandburg, copyright 1916 by Holt, Rinehart and Winston and renewed 1944 by Carl Sandburg, reprinted by permission of Harcourt, Inc. **L388:** "Piano", from *The Complete Poems of D.H. Lawrence* by D.H. Lawrence, edited by V. de Sola Pinto and F.W. Roberts, copyright © 1964, 1971 by Angelo Ravagli and C.M. Weekley, Executors of the Estate of Frieda Lawrence Ravagli. Used by permission of Viking Penguin, a division of Penguin Putnam Inc. **L401:** From *Selected Poems* by John Crowe Ransom. Copyright 1927 by Alfred A. Knopf, Inc. and renewed 1955 by John Crowe Ransom. Reprinted by permission of Alfred A. Knopf, a Division of Random House, Inc. **L402:** By William Carlos Williams, from *Collected Poems: 1909-1939*, Volume I. Copyright © 1938 by New Directions Publishing Corp. Reprinted by permission of New Directions Publishing Corp. **L404:** From *Collected Poems* by Langston Hughes. Copyright © 1994 by the Estate of Langston Hughes. Reprinted by permission of Alfred A. Knopf, a Division of Random House, Inc. **L406:** Carl Wendell Hines, Jr. for "Two Jazz Poems" by Carl Wendell Hines, Jr. from *American Negro Poetry*, © 1963 by Carl Wendell Hines, Jr. Published by Hill and Wang, Inc. **L521:** "Point of View" from *Where the Sidewalk Ends: the poems and drawings of Shel Silverstein*. © 1974 by Snake Eye Music, Inc. Published by Harper and Row, Publishers, Inc.

PHOTO CREDITS

Key: (t) top, (c) center, (b) bottom, (l) left, (r) right.

L4, L44: Gift of the Container Corporation of America, National Museum of American Art, Smithsonian Institution, Washington, D.C./Art Resource, New York. Courtesy of the artist and Francine Seders Gallery, Seattle, Washington. **L50, L70:** Spencer Collection, The New York Public Library. Astor, Lenox and Tilden Foundations. **L56:** © Telegraph Colour Library/FPG International. **L76, L106:** The Metropolitan Museum of Art, Rogers Fund, 1927 (27.152.2). Photograph © 1992 The Metropolitan Museum of Art. **L80:** SPIDER-MAN:TM & © 1999 Marvel Characters, Inc. Used with permission. **L101:** From the Girard Foundation Collection in the Museum of International Folk Art, a unit of the Museum of New Mexico, Santa Fe, NM. Photograph by Michel Monteaux. **L112, L142:** The Metropolitan Museum of Art, Gift of Cornelius Vanderbilt, 1887. (87.25). Photograph copyright © 1997 The Metropolitan Museum of Art. **L135:** National Museum of American Art, Washington, D.C./Art Resource, NY. © Luis Jiménez. **L148, L170:** The Art Institute of Chicago. Mr. and Mrs. Frank G. Logan Prize Fund. Photograph © The Art Institute of Chicago. All rights reserved. 1935.313. **L161:** Reprinted with permission from the publisher, Children's Book Press, San Francisco, California. Copyright © 1990 by Carmen Lomas Garza. **L181:** Billy R. Allen Folk Art Collection. African American Museum, Dallas, Texas. Gift of Mr. and Mrs. Robert Decherd. **L187:** SuperStock. **L192:** © Bettmann/Corbis. **L213:** BL Productions/SuperStock. **L219:** © 2001 Estate of Pablo Picasso/Artists Rights Society (ARS), New York. **L252:** From *Why Mosquitoes Buzz in People's Ears* by Verna Aardema, pictures by Leo and Diane Dillon, copyright © 1975 by Leo and Diane Dillon, pictures. Used by permission of Dial Books for Young Readers, a division of Penguin Putnam Inc. **L261:** © 2001 Red Grooms/Artists Rights Society (ARS), New York. Photograph courtesy Marlborough Gallery, New York. **L274, L310:** Courtesy of Lyons Matrix Gallery, Austin, Texas. **L283:** Wadsworth Atheneum, Hartford. The Ella Gallup Sumner and Mary Catlin Sumner Collection Fund. 1948.116. **L316, L352:** Philadelphia Museum of Art: Print Club Permanent Collection. Photograph by Laura Voight, 1996. **L332:** AFP/Corbis. **L358, L376:** © Reagan Bradshaw. **L372: (l)** © Fiduciario en el Fideicomiso relativo a los Museos Diego Rivera y Frida Kahlo. Reproduction authorized by the Bank of Mexico, Mexico City. Av. 5 de Mayo No. 2, Col. Centro 06059, Mexico, D.F.; **(r)** The National Portrait Gallery, Smithsonian Institution. Art Resource, New York. **L400, L436:** Texas Department of Commerce/Tourism. **L415:** David Madison/SuperStock. **L423:** Ron Chapple/FPG International. **L442, L472:** The Museum of Modern Art, New York. Katherine Cornell Fund. Photograph © 1996 The Museum of Modern Art, New York. **L458:** Musée d'Orsay, Paris, France. Giraudon/Art Resource, New York. **L497:** Illustration from *The Tale of Jemima Puddle-Duck* by Beatrix Potter. Copyright © Frederick Warne & Co., 1908, 1987. Reproduced by kind permission of Frederick Warne & Co. **L506, L540:** Photo by Beth Phillips, courtesy DC Moore Gallery, NY.